D1017078

DIGITAL CODE OF LIFE

How Bioinformatics is Revolutionizing
Science, Medicine, and Business

Glyn Moody

John Wiley & Sons, Inc.

Published by John Wiley & Sons, Inc., Hoboken, New Jersey
Published simultaneously in Canada

For general information on our other products and services, or technical support, please contact our Customer Care Department within the United States at 800-762-2974, outside the United States at 317-572-3993 or fax 317-572-4002.

Wiley also publishes its books in a variety of electronic formats. Some content that appears in print may not be available in electronic books.

For more information about Wiley products, visit our Web site at www.wiley.com.

Library of Congress Cataloging-in-Publication Data

Moody, Glyn.
  Digital code of life : how bioinformatics is revolutionizing science, medicine, and business / Glyn Moody.
    p. cm.
Includes bibliographical references and index.
  ISBN 0-471-32788-3
  1. Genetics—Data processing. 2. Genomics—Data processing. 3. Bioinformatics. 4. Genetic code. I. Title.
QH441.2 .M664 2004
572.8—dc22

2003022631

Printed in the United States of America

10 9 8 7 6 5 4 3 2 1

To our parents and children

Contents

Preface

Digital and analogue seem worlds apart. Digital is about a circumscribed set of options and jumps between them, like the consecutive display of numbers on a bedside alarm clock. Analogue, by contrast, is infinitely divisible, as smooth as the movement of the hands on a traditional timepiece. Analogue stands for the authentic, the natural, the vital; digital for the negation of these: the artificial, the mechanistic, the dead. And yet, over the last 50 years, a revolution in science has seen biology shift from an analogue approach, built squarely on chemicals and their interactions, to an underpinning that is thoroughly digital—one based on the information content of the genome, the immense program stored in the cell's DNA.

This book is about that transition, one of the most profound in history, and about its implications for biology, medicine, healthcare, and everyday life. Although the Human Genome Project—the international endeavor to list completely the digital instructions stored in our DNA—played an important part in this shift, what follows is not a retelling of that story. Instead, it is a history of how life became digital, and the rise of the discipline called bioinformatics that helped make this happen, told largely through the words of the scientists who had the original insights, created the new tools, and conducted the key experiments.

Acknowledgments

One of the aims of this book is to introduce to a wider audience some of the most exciting and important scientific literature to have been published during the last decade, by decoding it for the nonspecialist.

The vast majority of the papers discussed in this book are available online. Some, like those describing the sequence of the human genome, are free; others require a subscription to the journal in question. The preponderance of papers from *Nature* and *Science* is explained by the fact that for some time these titles have been the undisputed leaders in the field of scientific publishing. As a result, most of the key moments in genomics can be found in their pages. This is fortunate, in a way, since both journals take considerable pains to make their contents accessible to as wide an audience as possible. In the hope that readers might be tempted to investigate the original sources and to give credit for the passages that I have quoted, there are notes at the end of each chapter. The book also contains suggestions for further reading, one or two relevant Web sites, a glossary, and an index.

The unreferenced material is based on interviews conducted between October 2002 and June 2003 with many of the leading figures in the world of genomics, and my thanks go to them for their thoughts and time. I am also grateful to Alan Moody for his technical advice and to those who have read parts or the entire book in draft, particularly Anna O'Donovan and Sean Geer. Naturally, all errors remain my responsibility alone. I would be happy to receive corrections as well as general comments on the text at glynmoody@rebelcode.net.

My editor, Jeanne Glasser, played a key role in making this book happen, and my thanks go to her for invaluable help and advice, and to her assistant, Melissa Scuereb. I am also grateful to Todd Tedesco for steering the book through production so efficiently, and to Matthew J. Kushinka for his sensitive copyediting. As ever, I owe my greatest debt of gratitude to my wife and family, without whose constant support this book would not have been possible.

GLYN MOODY
London 2003

CHAPTER 1

The Code of Life

The digital era of life commenced with the most famous understatement in the history of science:

We wish to suggest a structure for the salt of deoxyribose nucleic acid (D.N.A.). This structure has novel features which are of considerable biological interest.

Thus began a paper that appeared in the journal *Nature* on April 25, 1953, in which its authors, James Watson and Francis Crick, suggested the now-famous double helix form of DNA. The paper was extraordinary in several ways: first, because Watson and Crick, both relatively young and unknown researchers, had succeeded in beating many more famous rivals in the race to explain the structure of DNA. Second, their proposal managed to meld supreme elegance with great explanatory power—a combination that scientists prize highly. Most of all, the paper was remarkable because it ended once and for all decades of debate and uncertainty about the mechanism of inheritance. In doing so, it marked the starting point for a new era in genetics, biology, and medicine—an era whose first phase would close exactly 50 years after Watson and Crick's paper with the announcement of the complete elucidation of human DNA. The contrast of that half-century's dizzying rate of progress with the preceding centuries' slow groping towards an understanding of inheritance could hardly be greater.

Oﬀne hundred and fifty years ago, Gregor Mendel, an Augustinian monk working in what is now the city of Brno in Moravia, carried out the first scientific investigations of heredity. Prior to his meticulous work on crossbreeding sweet peas, knowledge about heredity had existed only as a kind of folk wisdom among those rearing animals or propagating plants.

Mendel crossed sweet peas with pairs of traits—two different seed shapes or flower colors—in an attempt to find laws that governed the inheritance of these characteristics in subsequent generations. After thousands of such experiments, painstakingly recorded and compared, he deduced that these traits were passed from parent to offspring in what he called *factors*. Mendel realized that these factors came in pairs, one from each parent, and that when the two factors clashed, they did not mix to produce an intermediate result. Rather, one factor would dominate the other in the offspring. The subjugated factor would still persist in a latent form, however, and might reappear in subsequent generations in a remarkably predictable way.

Although it offered key insights into the mechanism of inheritance, Mendel's work was ignored for nearly half a century. This may have been partly due to the fact that his work was not widely read. But even if it had been, his factors may have been too abstract to excite much attention, even though they turned out to be completely correct when recast as the modern idea of genes, the basic units of heredity. In any case, work on heredity shifted to an alternative approach, one based on studying something much more tangible: cells, the basic units of life.

Hermann Muller used just such an approach in 1927 when he showed that bombarding the fruit fly with X-rays could produce *mutations*—variant forms of the organism. This was important because it indicated that genes were something physical that could be damaged like any other molecule. A chance discovery by Fred Griffith in 1928 that an extract from disease-causing bacteria could pass on virulence to a strain that was normally harmless finally gave researchers the first opportunity to seek out something chemical: the molecule responsible for transmitting the virulence. It was not until 1944, however, that Oswald Avery and his coworkers demonstrated that this substance was deoxyribonucleic acid—DNA.

In many ways, this contrasted sharply with the accepted views on the biochemical basis for heredity. Although DNA had been known for three quarters of a century—Johann Friedrich Miescher discovered it in pus-filled bandages discarded by a hospital—it was regarded as a rather dull chemical consisting of a long, repetitive chain made up of four ingredients called nucleotides. These nucleotides consist of a base—adenine, cytosine, guanine or thymine—each linked to the sugar deoxyribose at one end and a phosphate group at the other. Chemical bonds between the sugar and phosphate group allow very long strings of nucleotides to be built up.

The conventional wisdom of the time was that genetics needed a suitably complex molecule to hold the amazing richness of heredity. The most complex molecules then known were proteins. They not only form the basic building blocks of all cells, but also take on all the other key roles there such as chemical signaling or the breakdown of food. It was this supposition about protein as the chosen carrier for heredity that made Watson and Crick's alternative proposal so daring. They not only provided a structure for DNA, they offered a framework for how "boring" DNA could store inherited traits.

This framework could not have been more different from the kind most researchers were using at the time. The key properties of a protein are its physical and chemical properties; to use a modern concept, its essence is analogue. Watson and Crick's proposal was that DNA stored heredity not physically (through its shape or chemical properties), but through the information encoded by the sequence of four nucleotides. In other words, the secret of DNA—and of life itself—was digital.

Because it is the information they represent rather than the chemical or physical properties they possess that matters, the four nucleotides can, for the purposes of inheritance and genetics, be collapsed from the four bases (adenine, cytosine, guanine, and thymine) to four letters. The bases are traditionally represented as A, C, G, and T. This makes explicit the fact that the digital code employed by Nature is not binary—0 and 1—as in today's computers, but quaternary, with four symbols. But the two codes are completely equivalent. To see this, simply replace the quaternary digit A with the binary digits 00, C with 01, G with 10 and T with 11. Then any DNA sequence—for example AGGTCTGAT—can be converted into an equivalent binary sequence—in this case, 00 10 10 11 01 11 10 00 11. Even though the representation is different, the information content is identical.

With the benefit of hindsight, it is easy to see why a digital mechanism for heredity was not just possible but almost necessary. As anyone knows who has made an analogue copy of an audio or video cassette from another copy, the quality of the signal degrades each time. By contrast, a digital copy of a digital music file is always perfect, which is why the music and film industries have switched from a semi-official tolerance of analogue copying to a rabid hatred of the digital kind. Had Nature adopted an analogue storage method for inheritance, it would have been impossible to make the huge number of copies required for the construction of a typical organism. For example, from the fertilized human egg roughly a hundred thousand billion cells are created, each one of which contains a copy of the original DNA. Digital copying ensures that errors are few and can be corrected; analogue copying, however, would have led to a kind of genetic "fuzziness" that would have ruled out all but the simplest organisms.

In 1953, computers were so new that the idea of DNA as not just a huge digital store but a fully-fledged digital program of instructions was not immediately obvious. But this was one of the many profound implications of Watson and Crick's work. For if DNA was a digital store of genetic information that guided the construction of an entire organism from the fertilized egg, then it followed that it did indeed contain a preprogrammed sequence of events that created that organism—a program that ran in the fertilized cell, albeit one that might be affected by external signals. Moreover, since a copy of DNA existed within practically every cell in the body, this meant that the program was not only running in the original cell but in all cells, determining their unique characteristics.

Watson and Crick's paper had identified DNA as the digital code at the heart of life, but there remained the problem of how this was converted into the analogue stuff of organisms. In fact, the problem was more specific: because the analogue aspect of life was manifest in the proteins, what was needed was a way of translating the digital DNA code into analogue protein code. This endeavor came to be known as "cracking the DNA code." The metaphor was wrong, though—perhaps it was a side effect of the Cold War mentality that prevailed at that time. DNA is not a cryptic code that needs to be broken, because this implies that it has an underlying message that is revealed once its code is "cracked." There is no secret message, however.

D NA is another type of code—computer code. DNA is the message itself—the lines of programming that need to be run for the operations they encode to be carried out. What was conventionally viewed as cracking the code of life was in fact a matter of understanding *how* the cell ran the DNA digital code.

One step along the way to this understanding came with the idea of *messenger RNA* (mRNA). As its name suggests, ribonucleic acid (RNA) is closely related to DNA, but comes as a single strand rather than the double helix. It, too, employs a digital code, with four nucleotides. Thymine is replaced by uracil and the deoxyribose sugar by ribose, but for information purposes, they are the same.

It was discovered that mRNA is transcribed (copied) from sections of the DNA sequence. In fact, it is copied from sections that correspond to Mendel's classical *factors*—the genes. Surrounding these genes are sections of DNA text that are not transcribed, just as a computer program may contain comments that are ignored when the program is run. And just as a computer copies parts of a program held on a disc and sends them down wires to other components of the system, so the cell, it seemed, could copy selected portions of DNA and send them down virtual wires as mRNA.

These virtual wires end up at special parts of the cell known as *ribosomes*. Here the mRNA is used to direct the synthesis of proteins by joining together chemical units called amino acids into chains, which are often of great length. There are twenty of these amino acids, and the particular sequence in the chain determines a protein's specific properties, notably its shape. The complicated ensemble of attractions and repulsions among the constituent atoms of the amino acids causes the chain of them to fold up in a unique form that gives the protein its properties. The exact details of this protein are determined by the sequence of amino acids, which are in turn specified by the mRNA, transcribed from the DNA. Here, then, was the device for converting the digital data into an analogue output. But this still left the question of how different mRNA messages were converted to varying amino acids.

A clever series of experiments by Marshall Nirenberg in the early 1960s answered this question. He employed a technique still used to this day by computer hackers (where *hacker* means someone who is interested in understanding computers and their software, as opposed to malevolent *crackers*, who try to break into computer systems). In order to learn more about how an unknown computer system or program is working, it is often helpful not only to measure the signals passing through the circuits naturally, but also to send carefully crafted signals and observe the response.

This is precisely what Nirenberg did with the cell. By constructing artificial mRNA he was able to observe which amino acids were output by the cell's machinery for a given input. In this way he discovered, for example, that the three DNA letters AAA, when passed to a ribosome by the mRNA, always resulted in the synthesis of the amino acid lysine, while CAG led to the production of glutamine. By working through all the three-letter combinations, he established a table of correspondences between three-letter sequences—known as codons—and amino acids.

This whole process of converting one kind of code into another is very similar to the process of running a computer program: the program lines are sent to the central processing unit (CPU) where each group of symbols causes certain actions that result in a particular output. For example, this might be a representation on a monitor. In the same way, the ribosome acts as a kind of processing unit, with the important difference being that its output consists of proteins, which are "displayed" not on a screen but in real, three-dimensional space within the cell.

Viewed in this way, it is easy to understand how practically every cell in the body can contain the same DNA code and yet be radically different in its form and properties—brain, liver, or muscle cells, for example. The DNA can be thought of as a kind of software suite containing the code for every kind of program that the body will ever need. Among this is operating system software, basic housekeeping routines which keep cells ticking over by providing energy or repairing damaged tissue. There are also more specialized programs that are only run in a particular tissue—brain code in brain cells or liver code in liver cells, for example. These correspond to more specialized kinds of programs like word processors or spreadsheets: very often they are present on a computer system, but they are only used for particular applications. The operating system, however, is running constantly, ensuring that input is received from the keyboard and output is displayed on the screen. The details of the analogy are not important; what is crucial is that DNA's information is digital. From this has flowed a series of dramatic developments that are revolutionizing not just biology but medicine, too. All of these developments have come about from using powerful computers to search the digital code of life for the structures hidden within.

It may not be immediately apparent why computing power is important or even necessary. After all, on one level, the totality of information contained within an organism's DNA—termed its genome—is not complex. It can be represented as a series of letters, turning chemicals into text. As such, it can be read directly. This is true, but even leaving aside the problem of interpretation (what these letters in a particular order mean), there is another fundamental issue that genome researchers must address first: the sheer quantity of the data they are dealing with.

So far, the digital content of the genome has been discussed in the abstract. To understand why computers are indispensable, though, it is helpful to consider some specific facts. For example, the DNA within a typical human cell is twisted into a double helix; this helix is wound up again into an even more convoluted structure called a chromosome. Chromosomes were first noted within the nucleus of certain cells over one hundred years ago, but decades were to pass before it was shown that they contained DNA. Normal human cells have 46 chromosomes—22 similar pairs, called autosomes, and the two sex chromosomes. Women have two X chromosomes, while men possess one

X chromosome and one Y chromosome. The number is not significant; chromosomes are simply a form of packaging, the biological equivalent of CD-ROMs.

Even though these 46 chromosomes (23 from each parent) fit within the nucleus, which itself is only a small fraction of the microscopic cell's total volume, the amount of DNA they contain collectively is astonishing. If the DNA content of the 23 chromosomes from just one cell were unwound, it would measure around 1 meter in length, or 2 meters for all 46 chromosomes. Since there are approximately one hundred thousand billion cells in the human body, this means that laid end-to-end, all the DNA in a single person would stretch from the earth to the sun 1,200 times.

Things are just as dramatic when viewed from an informational rather than physical point of view. Each of the two sets of 23 chromosomes—found in practically every human cell—makes up a genome that contains some 3 billion chemical digits (the As, Cs, Gs and Ts). Printed as ordinary letters in an average-sized typeface, a bare listing representing these letters would require roughly 3,000 books each of 330 pages—a pile about 60 meters high. And for any pair of human beings (except twins deriving from the same fertilized egg), every one of the million pages in these books would have several letters that are different, which is why some people have brown eyes and others blue.

Now imagine trying to find among these 3,000 volumes the subprograms (the genes) that create the particular proteins which determine the color of the iris, say, and the letter changes in them that lead to brown rather than blue eyes. Because genes have about 12,000 chemical letters on average—ranging from a few hundred to a couple of million—they spread over several pages, and thus might seem easy enough to spot. But the task of locating these pages is made more difficult by the fact that protein-producing code represents only a few percent of the human genome. Between the genes—and inside them, too, shattering them into many smaller fragments—are stretches of what has been traditionally and rather dismissively termed "junk DNA." It is now clear, however, that there are many other important structures there (control sequences, for example, that regulate when and how proteins are produced). Unfortunately, when looking at DNA letters, no simple set of rules can be applied for distinguishing between pages that code for proteins and those that represent the so-called junk. In any case, even speed-reading through the pile of books at one page a second would require around 300 hours, or nearly two days, of nonstop page flicking. There would be little time left for noting any subtle signs that might be present.

The statistics may be simplistic, but they indicate why computers have become the single most important tool in *genomics*, a word coined only in 1986 to describe the study of genomes. Even though the data are simple almost to the point of triviality—just four letters—the incomprehensible scale makes manipulating these data beyond the reach of humans. Only computers (and fast ones at that) are able to perform the conceptually straight-forward but genuinely challenging operations of searching and comparing that lie at the heart of genomics.

The results of marrying computers with molecular biology have been stunning. Just fifty years after Watson and Crick's general idea for DNA's structure, we now have a complete listing of the human genome's dig-ital code—all 3 billion chemical letters of it. Contained within them are the programs for constructing every protein in our bodies. There are instructions that tell the fertilized egg how to grow; there are specialized programs that create muscles, skin, and bone. As we begin to understand how this happens, we can also appreciate how things go wrong. Like all software, the DNA code has bugs, or errors, in it. Most of these are of no consequence, occurring in noncritical places of the program. They are the equivalent of misspelled words in the comments section of programming code. However, some errors can be devasting. Consider the following two listings:

```
AGTAATTTCTCACTTCTTGGTACTCCTGTCCTGAAAGATAT
TAATTTCAAGATAGAAAGAGGACAGTTGTTGGCGGTTGCTG
GATCCACTGGAGCAGGCAAGACTTCACTTCTAATGATGATTA
TGGGAGAACTGGAGCCTTCAGAGGGTAAAATTAAGCACAGT
GGAAGAATTTCATTCTGTTCTCAGTTTTCCTGGATTATGC
CTGGCACCATTAAAGAAAATATCATCTTTGGTGTTTCCTA
TGATGAATATAGATACAGAAGCGTCATCAAAGCATGCCAA

AGTAATTTCTCACTTCTTGGTACTCCTGTCCTGAAAGATAT
TAATTTCAAGATAGAAAGAGGACAGTTGTTGGCGGTTGCTG
GATCCACTGGAGCAGGCAAGACTTCACTTCTAATGATGAT
TATGGGAGAACTGGAGCCTTCAGAGGGTAAAATTAAG
CACAGTGGAAGAATTTCATTCTGTTCTCAGTTTTCCTGGAT
TATGCCTGGCACCATTAAAGAAAATATCATTGGTGTTTCCTA
TGATGAATATAGATACAGAAGCGTCATCAAAGCATGCCAA
```

The two listings show only a tiny fraction of the 250,000 DNA letters that code for an important human protein. The difference between the two por-tions of code is just three chemical letters—CTT is missing in the second list-ing. The absence of these three letters, however, is enough to result in cystic fibrosis for many people who have this apparently trivial software glitch. Similarly, just one wrong letter in another region can lead to sickle cell ane-mia, while the addition of a few extra letters in the wrong place elsewhere causes Huntington's disease. Even more serious errors can mean embryos fail to develop at all—a fatal flaw in the operating system that causes the human system to crash as it boots up.

With the cell's digital code in hand, scientists can begin to understand these problems and even treat them. Often a DNA software bug causes the wrong protein to be produced by the ribosomes. Drugs may be able to block its production or operation in some way. Similarly, knowledge about the genomes of viruses and bacteria can aid pharmaceutical companies in their search for effective drugs and vaccines to combat them.

Driving these developments is bioinformatics: the use of computers to store, search through, and analyze billions of DNA letters. It was bioinformatics that turned the dream of sequencing the human genome into reality. It is bioinformatics that will allow humanity to decode its deepest secrets and to reveal the extraordinary scientific riches contained in the digital core of life.

NOTES

1. p. 7   *it would measure around 1 meter in length*   20 facts about the human genome. Online at *http://www.sanger.ac.uk/HGP/draft2000/facts.shtml.*

2. p. 7   *one hundred thousand billion cells in the human body*   20 facts about the human genome. Online at *http://www.sanger.ac.uk/HGP/draft2000/facts.shtml.*

3. p. 7   *genes have about 12,000 chemical letters*   Tom Strachan and Andrew P. Read, *Human Molecular Genetics* 2 (1999): 150.

4. p. 7   *a word coined only in 1986*   P. Hieter and M. Boguskis, "Functional genomics: it's all how you read it," *Science* 278 (1997): 601–602.

CHAPTER 2

Blast from the Past

Unlike DNA, with its neatly paired double helix, the history of bio-informatics involves many strands, often woven together in complex ways. If the field has a point of departure, it can perhaps be traced to a moment right on the cusp of computing history, and even before Watson and Crick's momentous paper. It was back in 1947 that a remarkable scientist called Margaret Dayhoff used punched-card business machines to calculate molecular energies of organic molecules. The scale of these computations made the use of traditional hand-operated calculators infeasible. Dayhoff's conceptual leap to employing protocomputers as an aid showed daring and doggedness—a calculation typically took four months of shuffling punched cards around—that was to prove a hallmark of her later career in the world of DNA and proteins.

One of her main spiritual heirs and a key figure in the bioinformatics world, David Lipman, has no doubts about her importance, telling me that: "she was the mother and father of bioinformatics." He bases this view on the fact that "she established the three major components of what a bioinformaticist does: a mixture of their own basic discoveries with the data, which are biological discoveries; tool development, where they share those tools with other people; and resource development. She did all three, and she did incredibly important things in all three."

As the long list of her publications indicates, her main interest was in the origin of life. It was the research into the evolution of biological molecules that led her in 1961 to begin a lifelong study of the amino acid sequences that make up proteins.

Since proteins form the building blocks of life, their amino acid sequences have changed only slowly with time. The reason is clear: any major difference in sequence is likely to cause a correspondingly major change in a key biological function, or the loss of it altogether. Such an alteration would often prove fatal for the newly evolved organism, so it would rarely be propagated to later generations. By contrast, very small changes, individually without great implications for biological function, could gradually build up over time to create entirely new functions. As a result, when taken together, the slowly evolving proteins provide a rich but subtle kind of molecular fossil record, preserving vestiges of the very earliest chemical structures found in cells. By establishing which proteins are related and comparing their differences, it is often possible to guess how they evolved and to deduce what their common ancestor was hundreds of millions of years ago.

To make these comparisons, it was first necessary to collect and organize the proteins systematically: these data formed the basis of Dayhoff's famous *Atlas of Protein Sequence and Structure*, a book first published in 1965. Once the data were gathered in this form, Dayhoff could then move on to the next stage, writing software to compare their characteristics—another innovative approach that was a first for the period. Thanks to this resource and tool development, Dayhoff was able to make many important discoveries about conserved patterns and similarities among proteins.

The first edition of the *Atlas* contained 65 protein sequences; by the time the fourth edition appeared in 1969, there were over 300 proteins. But the first DNA sequence—just 12 chemical letters long—was only obtained in 1971. The disproportion of these figures was due to the fact that at the time, and for some years after, sequencing DNA was even harder than elucidating the amino acids of proteins. This finally changed in 1977, when two methods were devised: one by Allan Marshall Maxam and Walter Gilbert in the United States, at Harvard; the other by Frederick Sanger in the United Kingdom, at Cambridge. Gilbert and Sanger would share the 1980 Nobel Prize in chemistry for these discoveries. Remarkably, it was Sanger's second Nobel prize. His first, in chemistry, awarded in 1958, was for his work elucidating the structure of proteins, especially that of insulin, which helps the body to break down sugars.

As Sanger wrote in a 1988 autobiographical memoir aptly titled *Sequences, sequences, sequences*: "I cannot pretend that I was altogether overjoyed by the appearance of a competitive method. However, this did not generate any sort of 'rat race'." Maybe not, but Sanger's *dideoxy* method, as it was called, did win in the sense that his rather than Gilbert's turned out to be the key sequencing technology for genomics, because it later proved highly amenable to large-scale automation. It involved taking an unknown sequence of DNA and using some clever biochemistry—the dideoxy part—to create from it four sets of shorter subsequences, each of which ended with a known chemical letter (A, C, G or T). One group of subsequences consisted of a complete set of progressively longer sections of the unknown sequence, each of which ended in the letter A. Another group of partial sequences, all of which had slightly different lengths from the first group (because for a given length there was only one ending), ended in G, and so on.

For example, from the initial unknown sequence ATTGCATGGCTAC, the dideoxy method would create three subsequences ending in A (A, ATTGCA, ATTGCATGGCTA), three in G (ATTG, ATTGCATG, ATTGCATGG), three in C (ATTGC, ATTGCATGGC, ATTGCATGGCTAC) and four ending in T (AT, ATT, ATTGCAT, and ATTGCATGGCT).

Sanger ran these groups side by side through a gel slab (a special kind of porous material) using an electric field placed across it. The field exerted a force on the fragments, all of which carried a tiny electric charge. The various fragments moved through the gel at different speeds according to their length. The shorter fragments were able to move more quickly through the tiny gaps in the gel and ended up further down the slab. Longer ones had a harder time squeezing through and were left behind by their smaller, nimbler fellows, causing a series of distinct bands to appear across four lanes in the gel.

By comparing all four lanes together—one for each of the groups—it was possible to work out the order of the chemical letters. In the previous example, the lane with all the fragments ending in A would show the band that was farthest away from the starting point, so the first chemical letter was an A. Similarly, the lane with the band slightly behind was in the T group, which meant that the next letter in the original sequence was a T, and so on. The overall result can be represented diagrammatically as follows, where the bands are shown as asterisks (*):

```
Gel lanes:        A     C     G     T     sequence reading

Start points:     .     .     .     .

                        *                       C
                  *                             A
                              *           T
                        *                       C
                              *                 G
                              *                 G
                                    *           T
                  *                             A
                        *                       C
                              *                 G
                                    *           T
                                    *           T
                  *                             A
```

In this way, the complete sequence could be determined by reading off the bands in order across the lanes in the gel, shown in the right-hand column.

For the fastest-moving fragments (the shortest), this technique worked well. At the other end, however, the distance between slower-moving large fragments became progressively smaller, so it was difficult to tell them apart. This placed an upper limit on the length of DNA that could be sequenced using this method—typically around 500 chemical letters. But the ever-inventive Sanger came up with a way around this problem. He simply broke larger pieces of DNA into smaller ones at random until they were below the size that caused problems for resolving the slower bands. The smaller fragments were separated and then sequenced. Rather dramatically, this approach was called the *shotgun technique*, since it was conceptually like blasting the DNA into small pieces with a shotgun.

In fact, several copies of the unknown sequence were broken up in this way. Since the breaks would often occur in different places, the resulting overall collection of fragments would overlap at various points. By sequencing all of these shorter fragments using Sanger's dideoxy technique, and then aligning all the overlaps, it was possible to reconstruct the original sequence.

For example, from the (unrealistically short) sequence AATCTGTGAGA initially unknown, the fragments

```
AAT CTG TGAGA
```

might be obtained from one copy, and

```
A ATCT GTGA GA
```

from another, to give the following group of fragments:

```
A ATCT GTGA GA AAT CTG TGAGA
```

These could then be separated, sequenced, and aligned as follows:

```
AAT
 ATCT
   CTG
    GTGA
     TGAGA
```

which allows the original sequence

```
AATCTGTGAGA
```

to be reconstructed.

A few such fragments can easily be matched by eye, but as the length of the original unknown fragment increases, so does the scale of the alignment process. In fact, things are even worse than they might seem: if the sequence length doubles, the number of shorter fragments also doubles, but the number of possible comparisons required to find all the overlaps goes up by a factor of four. This means that the sequence lengths routinely encountered in genomes—millions or even billions of nucleotides—are incomparably more difficult to reassemble than the simplified sequence in the previous example.

Fortunately, this is precisely the kind of task for which computers were made—one that is conceptually simple but involves repetition on a large scale. Computers were employed from the very earliest days of the shotgun method. The first two shotgun assembly programs were written in 1979, one of them by Rodger Staden. He worked in Sanger's Cambridge lab and has made a wide range of important contributions to bioinformatics.

One of Staden's early innovations was to carry out the computational assembly of sequences directly in the laboratory. The earliest programs used by Sanger were submitted on paper tape or even punched cards to a central IBM mainframe that formed part of Cambridge University's computing services. This meant that there was a delay in obtaining the results of experiments. As Staden told me: "Personally, I found that very frustrating—I wanted immediate gratification, or at least to know I had a bug in line 1" of his programs. More subtly, it formed a conceptual barrier between the biology and the computing, one that Staden helped break down. "I felt it important that those doing the sequencing experiments were able to run the software and take responsibility for their own data and its editing," he says, "So the programs were written to run interactively on PDP-11s in the lab."

The PDP-11 was a popular minicomputer of the time. Staden's decision to write his software for this departmental machine rather than the more powerful but physically remote mainframe was an important step towards making computers a standard part of the molecular biologist's equipment. Even Sanger used the PDP-11. Staden recalls: "He entered and edited his data just like everyone else. He started work very early in the morning, and he seemed to like to get his computing done before anyone else was around. If I came in early to do some programming I'd often find him at the keyboard."

Staden published a series of papers describing successive improvements to the shotgun assembly software he had developed and wrote many other early tools. As he notes with characteristic modesty: "It never occurred to me to name the collection of programs I was distributing, but other people started to refer to it as the 'Staden Package'." He also made another important, if rather different, contribution to the new field of bioinformatics. As he explains: "When I was designing my first useful shotgun sequencing programs it was clear that the data consisted of gel readings"—the sequences of the DNA fragments—"and sets of overlapping gel readings"—generated by finding the overlaps between the DNA fragments—"and that many operations would be on these overlapping sets. I got tired of writing phrases like 'sets of contiguous sequences' and started abbreviating it to contig." The word *contig* first appeared in print in 1980, and soon became one of the most characteristic neologisms in genomics as researchers started piecing together gel readings to reconstruct progressively longer DNA sequences.

Around the time that Staden was laying the computational foundations for sequencing, a pioneer across the Atlantic was beginning important work on what was to prove another enduring thread of the bioinformatics story: online databases. Doug Brutlag, a professor of biochemistry at Stanford University, explained to me how this came about: "We were studying sequences as far back as 1975–1976, that was when I first became aware of the informatics problems of analyzing the data we were getting from sequencing." One of the central issues that he and his colleagues grappled with was "to try to find out how was best to serve the scientific community by making the sequences and the applications that worked on the sequences available to the scientific community at large. At that time there was no Internet, and most people were exchanging sequences on floppy discs and tapes. We proposed distributing the sequences over what was then called the ARPANET." The ARPANET was created in 1969 and was the precursor to the Internet.

Brutlag and his colleagues achieved this in part through the MOLGEN (for Molecular Genetics) project, which was started in 1975 at Stanford University. One aim of MOLGEN was to act as a kind of intelligent assistant to scientists working in that field. An important part of the system was a series of programs that was designed to aid molecular biologists in their study of DNA by helping them carry out key tasks using a computer, but without the need to program.

For example, Brutlag and his colleagues described the SEQ analysis system, based on earlier software, as "an interactive environment for the analysis of data obtained from nucleotide sequencing and for the simulation of recombinant DNA experiments. The interactive environment and self-documenting nature of the program make it easy for the non-programmer to use."

The recombinant DNA experiments refer to an important breakthrough in 1973, when a portion of the DNA from one organism was inserted into the sequence of another to produce something new that was a combination of both—the *recombinant DNA*, also known as genetic engineering. That this was possible was a direct consequence of not just the digital nature of DNA —had an analogue storage process been involved, it is not clear how such a simple addition would have been possible—but also of the fact that the system for storing the digital information through the sequence of As, Cs, Gs, and Ts was generally identical, too. Put another way, the biological software that runs in one organism is compatible with the computing machinery—the cells—in every other. While mankind uses messy and inefficient heterogeneous computer standards, Nature, it seems, has sensibly adopted a universal standard.

The practical consequence of this single platform was the biotechnology revolution of the 1980s. Biotech pioneers like Genentech (for Genetic Engineering Technology) were able to use one organism—typically a simple bacterium—as a biological computer to run the DNA code from another species—humans, for example. By splicing a stretch of human DNA that coded for a particular protein—say, insulin—into bacteria, and then running this recombinant DNA by letting the modified bacteria grow and reproduce, Genentech was able to manufacture insulin artificially as a by-product that could be recovered and sold. Similarly, thanks to recombination, researchers could use bacteria as a kind of biological copying system. Adding a DNA sequence to a bacterium's genome and then letting the organism multiply many times generates millions of copies of the added sequence.

In 1983, Kary Mullis devised an even more powerful copying technique called the *polymerase chain reaction* (PCR). This employs the same mechanism as that used by living organisms to make an error-free copy of the genome during cell division, but carries it out in a test tube. A special protein called DNA polymerase moves along the DNA sequence to produce a copy letter by letter. Using what are called *primers*—short sequences of nucleotides from the beginning and end of a particular stretch of DNA—it is possible to make copies of just that section of the genome flanked by the primers. PCR soon became one of the most important experimental techniques in genomics. It provides a way of carrying out two key digital operations on the analogue DNA: searching through huge lists of chemical letters for a particular sequence defined by its beginning and end, and copying that sequence perfectly billions of times. In 1993, Mullis was awarded the Nobel Prize in chemistry.

MOLGEN's SEQ software included a kind of software emulator, allowing scientists to investigate simple properties of various combinations of DNA code before implementing it in live organisms. In many ways, the most important part of SEQ was the DNA sequence analysis suite. There was a complementary program for analyzing proteins, called PEP, similar to Margaret Dayhoff's early software. Similarities in DNA produce protein similarities, though protein similarities may exist even in the absence of obvious DNA matches. Different DNA can produce the same proteins. The reason is that several different codons can correspond to the same amino acid. For example, alongside AAA, the codon AAG also adds lysine, while CAA has the same effect as CAG, coding for glutamine. If one sequence has AAA while the other has AAG, the DNA is different, but the amino acid that results is not. When Dayhoff began her work, there were so few defined nucleotide sequences that most similarity searches were conducted on the relatively more abundant proteins. By the time SEQ was written, however, there were many more known DNA sequences, and the new techniques of Sanger and Gilbert were beginning to generate a flood of them.

MOLGEN was made available to researchers on the Stanford University Medical Experimental computer for Artificial Intelligence in Medicine (SUMEX-AIM). As Brutlag explains: "That computer was intended specifically for artificial intelligence research and medicine. In order to make it available to many of their collaborators they had that computer available on what was then the ARPANET, which let other collaborators that had access to the ARPANET access it." Brutlag and his colleagues were able to take advantage of this existing infrastructure to create the first online molecular databases and bioinformatics tools: "so we made use of that and we got permission from the developers of SUMEX-AIM to make our programs and databases available to the molecular biology community." But they wanted to go further.

"We had tried to get a central resource funded before from NSF"—the National Science Foundation, the main government funding body for science in the United States. "We proposed to take programs from many individuals around the world that were written in different [computer] languages and to put them onto one kind of computer." These programs would then be made available over the ARPANET. But the NSF was not interested. "They said well, this is the sort of thing that should really be done in the commercial sphere, and they didn't fund us," Brutlag recalls.

Unable to find a suitable business partner, Brutlag and his colleagues in 1979 decided to found IntelliGenetics, the first bioinformatics company. Brutlag says that he and his fellow founders were undeterred by the fact that no one else was offering similar services. "We thought that since we couldn't find any company that supported it, there would be lots of opportunities," Brutlag says. "What we didn't realize is that a lot of the pharmaceutical firms saw this as a strategic problem, and didn't want to license logistics from a third party, but instead wanted to develop the programs in-house. They thought they could do better themselves than licensing from other places." Nonetheless, IntelliGenetics prospered. "We had lots of good companies" as subscribers, Brutlag notes.

In 1982, a division of the National Institutes of Health announced that it had "funds for a national resource that would distribute the data, but using novel methods, and they were requesting people to put in grants," he says. "We put in a proposal saying that here we have a company IntelliGenetics that already supports these databases" including DNA, RNA, and protein sequences, and that it could offer a similar service to academic researchers. IntelliGenetics won the contract. The NIH picked up the fixed costs for what was to be called Bionet, and users paid $400 per year per research group to cover the cost of communications.

Bionet arrived just in time. A molecular biology service called GENET was offered to researchers on SUMEX-AIM; it included MOLGEN along with DNA sequences and many other tools. GENET was soon swamped by the demand. Because GENET had only two ports into which users could dial with their computers, it meant that gaining access could be problematic. It was decided to exclude commercial users in August 1982 so that academic use could expand. IntelliGenetics received around $5.6 million over five years for the Bionet contract, which finally started on March 1, 1984. The company was doubtless disappointed, however, that it had just recently missed out on an even more prestigious bioinformatics contract: to set up a national DNA database for the United States.

Alongside Margaret Dayhoff's pioneering efforts, there were several other groups working on consolidated sequence databases throughout the late 1970s and early 1980s. But this piecemeal approach vitiated much of the benefit of using a centralized database, since it meant that researchers needed to check sequences they were investigating against several stores of information. What was needed was the establishment of a single repository where all DNA sequences were entered as a matter of course. After much discussion and many workshops, the NIH announced in August 1980 that it would fund such a center, and the competition among the existing databases began to increase. When proposals were officially requested at the end of 1981, there were three: one from Margaret Dayhoff's group, one from IntelliGenetics, and one from a company called Bolt Beranek and Newman, Inc.

More deliberation ensued, however, during which time the European DNA database was set up in April 1982 at the European Molecular Biology Labs in Heidelberg, Germany. On June 30, 1982, the contract for the U.S. DNA sequence databank, to be known as GenBank (short for Genetic Sequence Data Bank), was finally awarded to Bolt, Beranek and Newman (BBN). Perhaps BBN was chosen because it was well established—the company had been set up in 1948—and had worked on numerous important U.S. government contracts before. Brutlag says of IntelliGenetics' bid: "I'm not sure that we were competitive. IntelliGenetics had only been in existence for two years, whereas BBN was an ongoing company. And so we were a big risk in a way." And yet, as things turned out, there was a certain irony in the award to the older company.

BBN is probably best known today as the company that built the original four-site ARPANET in 1969 and helped develop its successor, the Internet. Yet neither the old ARPANET nor the emerging Internet formed part of BBN's GenBank work. As Brutlag explains: "Acquisition was done exclusively by hiring students to read the literature, keypunchers to punch it in, and then distributing it on floppy discs and tapes," with network access of secondary importance. IntelliGenetics, by contrast, was showing with its Bionet just how powerful and popular an online database system could be.

Both BBN and IntelliGenetics submitted their bids in conjunction with a DNA database group working under Walter Goad at Los Alamos, the famous and previously top-secret weapons development center located in New Mexico. What might be called "the Los Alamos connection" is perhaps the strangest thread in the complex tapestry that makes up bioinformatics' early history.

It begins with the Polish mathematician Stanislaw Ulam. He came to the United States as a Harvard Fellow just before the outbreak of the Second World War. After some time in Madison, Wisconsin, he went to New Mexico to work on the Manhattan Project, the aim of which was the development of the first atomic bomb. The project's contributors were an outstanding group of the world's top engineers, physicists, and mathematicians. Ulam made his biggest contribution working on the next Los Alamos project, code-named "Super"—a project designed to produce the hydrogen bomb. He not only showed that the original proposed method would not work, but also went on to devise a system that was used in the real thing. It is curious that one of the people responsible for the most profound study of life—bioinformatics and the genomics that it made possible—was also the theoretician behind the greatest death device yet invented.

Ulam devised a new technique that later came to be called the Monte Carlo method, named after the famous casino there. The idea for the technique came to him one day while he was playing the solitaire card game. As he wrote in his autobiography: "I noticed that it may be much more practical to get an idea of the probability of the successful outcome of a solitaire game . . . by laying down the cards . . . and merely noticing what proportion comes out successfully, rather than to try to compute all the combinatorial possibilities which are an exponentially increasing number so great that . . . there is no way to estimate it." Similarly, when studying complex equations like those governing the thermonuclear fusion at the heart of the H-bomb,

Ulam's idea was to "lay down the cards"—use random input conditions—to see what outputs they produced. He realized that if enough of these random inputs were used (if enough games of solitaire were played) the outputs could be aggregated to provide a good approximation of the final result.

Independently of its use at Los Alamos, the Monte Carlo technique has become one of the most important ways of studying complex equations, particularly through the use of computers. It is noteworthy that because of his work at Los Alamos, Ulam had access to some of the first electronic computers built.

Although fully aware of the implications of his work, Ulam also seems to have been an archetypal pure mathematician, so involved—obsessed, even—with the underlying theory, its challenges and beauties, that he could remain distant from its practical consequences. The same could be said of his pioneering studies in biological mathematics, which followed his work on "Super" and became the foundation of much later research in bioinformatics. In his autobiography, Ulam explained: "After reading about the new discoveries in molecular biology which were coming fast"—this was in the wake of the papers of Watson, Crick, and others—"I became curious about a conceptual role which mathematical ideas could play in biology." He then went on to emphasize: "If I may paraphrase one of President Kennedy's famous statements, I was interested in 'not what mathematics can do for biology but what biology can do for mathematics'." In other words, it was not so much a desire to use mathematics to make discoveries in molecular biology that attracted him as the possibility that the underlying operations there might open up completely new theoretical vistas in mathematics—the dream of every pure mathematician.

Whatever the motivation, he was one of the first to study rigorously the mathematics of sequence comparison. In a letter to the top U.S. journal *Science*, William Beyer, one of Ulam's earliest collaborators at Los Alamos, recalled: "S. M. Ulam in the late 1960's often gave talks at Los Alamos on the mathematics of sequence comparison," which is matching up different DNA fragments. By then he had retired from Los Alamos and had become a professor at the University of Colorado in Boulder. The work in this area culminated in an article called "Some ideas and prospects in biomathematics." It appeared in the first volume of a new journal called the *Annual Review of Biophysics and Bioengineering* in 1972, an interesting indication that the marriage of biology with mathematics, physics, and even engineering was definitely in vogue at the time.

Ulam's comments on this paper in his autobiography are characteristic: "It concerns ways of comparing DNA codes for various proteins by considering distances between them. This leads to some interesting mathematics that, *inter alia*, may be used to outline possible shapes of the evolutionary tree of organisms." That is, facts about evolution came as something of an incidental bonus to the real attraction of "interesting mathematics." Despite this rather detached manner of regarding the subject matter, Ulam's influence was important in two ways.

First, it was he who devised a precise measure for the degree of similarity between two sequences. His idea was to use a mathematical concept called a *metric*—a generalized kind of distance. Ulam's metric depended on calculating the least number of changes of bases required to transform one DNA sequence into another. Underlying this approach was a profound logic. It implicitly built on the fact that the interesting reason two sequences are similar to each other is that they have both evolved from a common ancestor through the substitution, omission, or addition of elements in the original sequence. In this case, the sequences are said to be homologous. Because all life is ultimately related, the search for homology permeates much of bioinformatics. Moreover, thanks to these roots in evolutionary theory, it turns out that the apparently cold and abstract world of mathematical equations and their computer implementations have at their core the same connection with the origin of life that powered Dayhoff's investigations.

Ulam is also of note for passing on his interest in the application of rigorous mathematical techniques to other researchers who later made key contributions to the bioinformatics field. Among these was Temple Smith, who in 1974 published a paper with Ulam and two other colleagues from Los Alamos entitled "A molecular sequence metric and evolutionary trees." He had met Ulam around 1970, a year that saw another important contribution to the nascent bioinformatics area. It was an algorithm—a mathematical technique —from Saul Needleman and Christian Wunsch for comparing the similarity of two sequences. The authors described their work as follows: "A computer adaptable method for finding similarities in the amino acid sequences of two proteins has been developed. From these findings it is possible to determine whether significant homology exists between the proteins. This information is used to trace their possible evolutionary development."

What is striking here is the fact that computers are explicitly mentioned; these words were written in 1969, however, when computers were still relatively rare, low-powered and expensive. Equally striking is that the main use of the algorithm is given as the study of evolutionary development. In addition to demonstrating this general prescience, the Needleman-Wunsch algorithm also offered a useful starting point for later work, notably a paper co-written by Smith and Michael Waterman in 1981. This paper has become one of the most cited in the field.

Waterman had been invited to join a project at Los Alamos studying molecular biology and evolution. He described his meeting with

Smith as follows: "I was an innocent mathematician until the summer of 1974. It was then that I met Temple Ferris Smith and for two months was cooped up with him in an office at Los Alamos National Laboratories. That experience transformed my research, my life and perhaps my sanity." Smith and Waterman used a similar approach to the previous work, but made it more general by allowing incomplete alignments between sequences; the original Needleman-Wunsch algorithm tried to find the best overall fit, which sometimes meant that even better local ones were overlooked. The Smith-Waterman algorithm was clearly more powerful in that it found likely similarities between sections of the sequence. As sequences grew longer, the overall fit might not be of much significance, but local homologies—particularly if there were several of them—might point to important relationships.

It was Smith who had alerted fellow researchers at Los Alamos to the need for a DNA database in the first place. He later formed with Goad and Waterman part of the successful partnership that won the contract for the U.S. national DNA sequence database, GenBank, which finally started up in October 1982. As if on cue, a paper by Russell Doolittle that appeared just a few months later demonstrated the enormous potential for a resource like GenBank when combined with sequence comparison software.

In 1981, Doolittle had published a paper whose title summed up the doubts of many at that time: "Similar amino acid sequences: chance or common ancestry?" In it, he mentioned that he had created his own database of recently published sequences, called NEWAT (NEW ATlas), to complement Margaret Dayhoff's *Atlas of Protein Sequence and Structure*. His overall message in the paper was one of caution: "The systematic comparison of every newly determined amino acid sequence with all other known sequences may allow a complete reconstruction of the evolutionary events leading to contemporary proteins. But sometimes the surviving similarities are so vague that even computer-based sequence comparison procedures are unable to validate relationships."

Undaunted, Doolittle himself regularly checked new protein structures as they were published against his growing database and that of Dayhoff in the hope that there might be some interesting homologies. On Saturday morning, May 28, 1983, he typed in two more sequences, both believed to be part of a protein involved in normal human cell growth. To Doolittle's amazement, he not only found a match—he found something extraordinary. His sequence comparison program showed that the growth factor appeared closely related to parts of a gene found in a cancer-causing virus in monkeys. The implication was clear: that this cancer was a kind of malign form of normal cell growth. The discovery caused something of a sensation, for Doolittle was not the only one to notice this similarity.

A team led by Michael Waterfield at the Imperial Cancer Research Fund in London had been studying the same growth factor. Once his team had determined the protein sequence, Waterfield decided that it would be worth comparing it with existing protein databases to search for homologies. He got in touch with David Lipman, at that time a researcher at the National Institute of Diabetes and Digestive and Kidney Diseases (NIDDK), part of the U.S. National Institutes of Health. Lipman was working on molecular evolution and, together with John Wilbur, had come up with an early program for carrying out sequence comparisons against databases.

The Wilbur-Lipman approach was important because it jettisoned the exact but computationally slow methods used by the Needleman-Wunsch and Smith-Waterman algorithm. It adopted instead what is known as a *heuristic* method—one that was not completely exact but much faster as a result. Hence it was ideal for carrying out searches against computerized databases. Lipman recalled for this book: "Waterfield's people contacted us and we sent them the existing protein sequence database which people at Georgetown had been doing, and sent them our program for doing database comparisons." The Georgetown database was the one started by Margaret Dayhoff, who had died shortly before in February 1983.

Waterfield found the homology with the previously sequenced simian cancer virus gene, but as a true experimentalist decided to dig a little deeper. "They started to do the next level of experiments before publishing because they felt that this was very exciting," Lipman explains. Then Waterfield's team heard through the academic grapevine that Doolittle had also discovered the sequence similarities and was about to publish his findings. As ill luck would have it, "Waterfield was on some island on vacation," Lipman says, "but they contacted him and they rushed things through and they got their paper out a week earlier."

Such was the excitement of this race to publish that *The New York Times* ran a story about it. "It was the first sequence similarity case I know that made the newspapers," recalls Lipman. But he believes it also possessed a deeper significance. "It was the first example I knew of where the scientists used computational tools themselves as opposed to having some expert do it." In this respect, it followed in the tradition of Rodger Staden's PDP-11 programs. It also presaged the coming era when a key piece of laboratory equipment would be a computer and when molecular biologists would regard familiarity with bioinformatic tools as a core part of their professional skills.

The other paper, though denied the honor of prior publication—Lipman recalls that Doolittle was "really angry about this"—was also emblematic in its way. Doolittle had arrived at this important and unlooked-for result not through years of traditional "wet lab" research involving hypotheses and experiments, but simply by sitting down one Saturday at his computer, typing in a string of letters representing the newly sequenced growth factor, and running some software to compare it against his protein database. This, too, foreshadowed a time when such *in silico* biology—literally, biology conducted in silicon, in the chips of a computer—would replace much of the traditional *in vivo* work with animals, and the *in vitro* experiments carried out in test tubes.

The episode also proved to be something of a turning point for Lipman: "I was thinking that because people were sequencing DNA primarily at this point, and not proteins, that the important thing would be DNA sequence comparisons. But in fact the most important early find there, was this protein finding. And so I started looking at other examples where unexpected but important protein matches had been found and that brought me to some papers by Doolittle, but especially some papers by Dayhoff. And I took our tool, which had aspects which were quite sophisticated, and tried to find things that Dayhoff had found which were important earlier, but which didn't make as big a splash as the [cancer gene and growth factor] case, and our tool didn't work well for those."

This set him wondering how he could improve the tool that he and Wilbur had created, taking into account the particular requirements of protein comparisons. The result was a program called FASTP (pronounced *fast pea*), written with William Pearson. It improved on the performance of the earlier program of Wilbur and Lipman when carrying out protein comparisons because it incorporated the relative probability of amino acid substitutions occurring by chance. That is, because some changes take place more often in Nature—as became evident as increasing numbers of protein sequences were determined and compared—so matches may be better or worse than a simple calculation based purely on finding exact correspondences would suggest. In a sense, the FASTP program's matching was fuzzier, but still in accordance with the body of statistics on amino acid substitutions accumulated through the ages.

By taking into account how evolution has proceeded—and building once more on work originally carried out by Dayhoff—Lipman and Pearson's new program was both more sensitive to matches and much faster. The increased speed had an important consequence: it was now feasible to carry out large-scale protein comparisons on a personal computer. By a happy coincidence, the IBM PC had appeared just a few years before FASTP was published. It seems likely that FASTP, and particularly its improved successor FASTA, played an important part in augmenting the use of computers within laboratories. As Lipman and Pearson wrote in their 1985 paper describing FASTP (FASTA followed in 1988): "Because of the algorithm's efficiency on many microcomputers, sensitive protein database searches may now become a routine procedure for molecular biologists."

If the algorithmic side of bioinformatics was making steady progress, the same cannot be said for the databases. Barely four years after GenBank was founded, *Science* ran the dramatic headline: "DNA databases are swamped." In 1982, when GenBank was founded, the Los Alamos database had around

680,000 base pairs, about two-thirds of all those available. By 1986, the database had grown to 9,600,000, and the increasing rate of production of DNA sequences meant that GenBank was unable to cope. As a result, only 19 percent of sequences published in 1985 had been entered, and the backlog included some that were two years old. Although faring better, the database at the European Molecular Biology Laboratory (EMBL) was also struggling to keep up with the flood of data coming in.

Clearly, much of the benefit of a centralized database, where researchers could routinely turn in order to run homology searches against more or less all known sequences, was negated in these circumstances. Worryingly, things promised to get worse as the flow of sequences continued to accelerate (in fact, by the 20th anniversary of GenBank, its holdings had swelled to over 22 billion base pairs). Fortunately, more funding was secured and various actions were taken over the next few years to speed up input and deal with the backlog. The original idea was to annotate all the DNA sequences that were entered. This important task involves adding indications of structure within the raw DNA sequence (where genes begin and end, for example, and other structures of interest). Annotation was extremely time-consuming and could not be easily automated. Dropping it speeded things up but considerably reduced the inherent value of the database for researchers. Another measure was equally controversial at the time, but it turned out to be an unequivocal blessing in due course.

Unlikely as it may sound, the raw sequence data were generally entered by hand, letter by letter. This was mind-numbingly boring for those carrying out the work; it was also prone to errors. GenBank tried to get sequences submitted on a floppy disc, but the response from the researchers providing the data was poor. To overcome this reluctance, efforts were made to ease the submission of sequences and annotation data electronically. This move was aided when IntelliGenetics won the second round of bidding to run GenBank in 1987. IntelliGenetics had already created a program called GenPub, "a forms-oriented display editor that allows individuals to fill in a template based on the GenBank submission form . . . giving all the requisite data about a sequence." Although this was only available to Bionet users, it proved extremely popular: "about 15 percent of all the GenBank entries in the last year came from Bionet users using this GenPub program," Brutlag told me.

When IntelliGenetics won the contract to run GenBank, it rewrote GenPub and called it AuthorIn. "It was quite a different program," Brutlag says, "because GenPub only worked on the Internet or the ARPANET." But for GenBank, "one of the requirements was there were people that weren't connected to the network then, and they wanted to have a program that was forms oriented"—allowing users to fill in a simple series of boxes on the computer screen—"something where they could record the output to a floppy disc and send it to us" physically. AuthorIn added this facility to GenPub, and the result was a huge success. When IntelliGenetics took over the GenBank contract, Brutlag says, "there was a two-year backlog in '87, and by the time we finished in '92, the backlog was about 24 hours."

This had two important consequences. As Brutlag explains: "We increased our productivity tenfold in five years by making most of the work [done] by the sequencers and not by the resource itself, which meant that it would scale —it could grow another tenfold or a hundredfold, it would still work. And I think we've proven the point now because the databases have continued to grow and most of the work is being done by the people who do the sequencing." The fast turnaround had another important side effect. "We told all the publishers [of sequence information] that we have this program, which allows people to contribute and annotate their sequence prior to publication. Could you please require that in order to publish a sequence that people first deposit their sequences [into GenBank or EMBL]? We will give them an accession number within 24 hours of the time they send their sequence to us, and they agreed"—but not immediately. As Temple Smith wrote with evident weariness in 1990: "One can hardly overemphasize the time and political effort this arrangement required."

In the early days of genomics, printing sequences as part of journal publication was not a problem. In 1972, for example, the longest sequence consisted of just 20 bases. In 1978, though, a paper describing the DNA sequence of the simian virus 40 was published. Fully three and half pages of text, each with 26 lines and 50 bases per line, were devoted to displaying the 5,000 or so nucleotides in the full genome. By the late 1980s, a full listing was impossibly onerous not just for the publisher, but also for the reader. Even if a complete sequence were published, it would be difficult to take in any but its most salient features and nearly impossible to copy it error-free by hand. As a result, such information became useless. The alternative employed at the time was to publish partial data (for example, the complete DNA listing of a gene). This was unsatisfactory in a different way, because it meant that GenBank never saw the bulk of the sequenced information while it relied on the printed page as its primary source of data. However, researchers clearly needed the full data. Science was based on the principle that the results of experiments had to be verifiable by others; without the entire DNA sequence there was no way of knowing whether the deductions from it were justified or whether even more important insights had been missed.

Requiring researchers to submit their complete sequences to public online databases as a matter of course was the obvious solution. It spared editors the need to agonize over how many pages should be allotted to an unappetizing printout of the same four letters repeated many times over. It allowed others to check the results and enabled scientists to download the data for experiments that built on the earlier work. Most importantly of all, perhaps, this new procedure would allow databases like GenBank and EMBL to fulfill their promise by bringing together most DNA data in a single, searchable resource. This was made possible when the relationship between GenBank, EMBL, and the equivalent Japanese institution, the DNA Database of Japan (DDBJ), was formalized. Adopting common formats for sequences allowed information to be pooled among these organizations. By sharing the inputting and annotating of DNA information according to spheres of influence, the work of each body was reduced. The regular exchange of data ensured that all databases were kept up to date and synchronized.

Some editors were reluctant to embrace the use of electronic databases in this way, which may seem curious considering the practical difficulties it solved almost at a stroke. It surely reflected, though, a deeper intuition on their part that this was in fact indicative of a much more profound change. Until that time, the distinction between data and results was clear: data were something scientists used as a stepping stone to the greater achievement of the overall result. The result was generally something that was abstracted from the mass of the data, and that could be stated succinctly. The rise of techniques like Sanger's brought with them increasingly long sequences. While it was still possible to use these data as the basis of results that could be stated concisely—as with the famous similarity between the monkey virus gene and the human growth factor—something new was happening to the data themselves: they had acquired a value of their own independent of the results derived from them by the original researcher.

The reason for this goes back to Watson and Crick's pivotal paper and the inherently digital nature of DNA. The common digital code meant that regarded purely as information, all DNA is similar in kind: it consists of a sequence of As, Cs, Gs, and Ts. As a result, comparisons were not only possible but, as the short history of bioinformatics convincingly demonstrated, often revelatory. In other words, the more DNA sequences one could bring together in a database, the more chance there was that further relationships and discoveries could be made from them. They had an inherent richness that was not exhausted by the results derived from them initially. As a result, the meaning of sequence publication changed. It was no longer just a matter of announcing a result to your peers in a respected journal; it also entailed placing the raw materials of your work in the public domain for others to study. This clearly diminished the role of the traditional journals, which had been created to serve the old model of science, though they still served an important function.

By 1988, the head of GenBank was David Lipman. The way he ended up in this key position was somewhat unusual: "The [NIH's] National

Library of Medicine had a long-range planning committee that suggested that it should get involved in factual databases, and especially molecular biological databases," he explained to me. "The Library went to Congress and got money to set up the National Center for Biotechnology Information [NCBI]. I had looked at the possibility of moving over to be part of the research branch of what was going to be NCBI. But I was concerned that they didn't have anybody in mind to head that I felt was knowledgeable, and I was concerned about coming over and having a boss that didn't know about the area. So I gave them some suggestions of names of people that I thought would be good to have as my boss, and they either didn't try or they didn't succeed with them. And so I said 'Well, either I'm not going to go, or you make me the head'—not that I was so eager to be the head, but I was reluctant to see this opportunity to go by. And somehow they decided to make me the head."

Doug Brutlag offers some inside information on that long-range planning committee, and the longer-term ramifications. "I was on a National Library of Medicine [NLM] planning council in 1985 to plan the future directions of NLM," he says. "NLM wanted a 20-year vision of where the library was going. And there were many biotechnologists that were on this panel. We mentioned that biotechnology was an area that would help medicine enormously, and that there were databases that would be critical for diagnosing disease and for understanding molecular biology. And so we made a proposal that NLM should be heavily involved in these databases as well. And Don Lindberg, the director of NLM, really took this recommendation to heart. So he decided politically to move the biotechnology infrastructure into the National Library of Medicine. Within NIH he held a series of seminars for these scientists at NLM, and he invited something like 12 people to come to speak, including myself."

"What I don't think we realized at the time is that several of the people who were asked to speak were being considered for the director of what's now the NCBI. And it must have been pretty close, because Don Lindberg called me asking me for my opinion of a resource like this, trying to convince me to leave California and to come there"—Bethesda, Maryland, where the NLM was based—"which I didn't want to do. I held a faculty position at Stanford, and I wanted to stay at Stanford. I politely said 'no.' Don also asked me for my opinion of David Lipman, for whom I had the highest regard."

"Don Lindberg chose him, and they made the decision then to not only move the GenBank and the Bionet resource into NLM, but also not to contract it out. So in 1992, they decided to keep it in-house, which of course upset me. I didn't imagine when I had suggested NLM be involved in these databases that they wouldn't continue the outsourcing" and that Brutlag's company IntelliGenetics would lose an important contract as a result. This was doubly unfortunate, since IntelliGenetics had earlier lost the contract for Bionet in 1989. Despite these setbacks, the first bioinformatics company kept going for a couple of more years with considerable success in various niche markets, before disappearing completely in 1994 through its acquisition by Oxford Molecular. In 2001, Oxford Molecular merged with three other companies, including another bioinformatics pioneer, Genetics Computer Group (GCG), to form Accelrys.

IntelliGenetics' rough ride should serve as a warning to all those with thoughts about making money from providing online access to sequence data. The basic problem is that the raw stuff of its business—digital data—is so easy to move around and to repackage that it is almost impossible for any one company or organization to maintain any kind of control over it. As a result, bioinformatics has always been a contest of who could produce data for the lowest costs. Unfortunately for the companies involved, this could only lead to one result: giving away the data for nothing or next to nothing. Even if there were no money to be made in doing so, some public-spirited individual or group—or even company—was prepared to offer something comparable, destroying the market for everyone else.

This very situation cropped up almost immediately after Lipman took over the reins at GenBank. An early manifestation of Lipman's growing ambitions for the NLM's National Center for Biotechnology Information was the Entrez CD-ROM, which first appeared in September 1992. This provided an integrated view of the public DNA and protein databases, as well as related bibliographic references. Entrez was available as a CD-ROM subscription, issued six times a year, for an annual fee of $57. In the years prior to this, a number of bioinformatics companies had sprung up that offered similar services, but for considerably more money. One was DNAStar, set up Fred Blattner, who was a geneticist at the University of Wisconsin. Because of Lipman's business moves, he told *Science*, "Believe me, my product is dead." Letters were sent to powerful members of Congress while accusations and counteraccusations flew in the heated atmosphere that ensued. Everything finally quieted down without any firm conclusions being reached.

This is not to suggest that Lipman ever had problems with the commercialization of his database holdings. "We actually encouraged it," he says. "The real important notion about GenBank, which preceded NCBI's involvement, was the notion that this data was the community's data, and that it should be accessible and disseminated and broadly used in as many different ways as possible. One argument we made over and over again is that scientists can get the data from us, they can get it from the group in Europe, which was the EMBL, they can get it from the group in Japan, but furthermore we provide it to a whole bunch of different companies and academic groups and they can get the data from them."

The idea of providing a service to a community that powers the service through its data submissions is another reflection of the novel status that data enjoy in this world of digital DNA. These data are no longer something ephemeral and disposable, there to serve an immediate purpose. Rather, they comprise a kind of communal resource that through responsible nurturing by the appointed custodian not only becomes richer but encourages the community to add to and enrich them further—a kind of virtuous circle that is quite new.

Lipman, described in the *Science* story as being "known for his brightness and brashness," was probably willing to risk stirring up trouble by extending the range of the NCBI's activities at this time because his own position had become so strong within the bioinformatics community. The reorganized GenBank had turned into a community repository and a real information powerhouse; Lipman had recently complemented and enhanced it by helping to create the most powerful sequence comparison tool so far, one that remains to this day perhaps the single most important bioinformatics program: the Basic Local Alignment Search Tool (BLAST).

Like that of bioinformatics itself, the genesis of BLAST involved the union of a number of elements. Lipman gives some background. "There was an ongoing problem that there were methods like FASTP and FASTA but not good statistics to tell you how significant a match would be." What Lipman wanted to add was some indication of just how good the match was. Once again, the issue of metric was central: "I felt that it would have been helpful if there was a different measure of similarity, one that would still work pretty well in terms of finding distant relationships, but one that would be more amenable to mathematical analysis. I read a paper where people were coming up with a way to align three sequences at once and find something, and the main idea that I took from that paper was what measure of similarity would be a little bit simpler than the one we were using for the FASTP which was like a Waterman-Smith, Needleman-Wunsch type thing, and one that would still work well."

The basic work on coming up with a new kind of measure was done by a mathematician at Stanford named Sam Karlin. Meanwhile, Stephen Altschul, who also worked at the NCBI, had some interesting insights into some of Dayhoff's work on the various rates of amino acid substitution, the extra ingredient that Lipman added to his earlier work with Wilbur to create FASTP. The final element in the birth of BLAST came "out of the blue," as Lipman puts it. "Gene Myers was a computer scientist down in Arizona, who I knew," he explains, "and he said he had an idea for an algorithm that will be faster and it would be good to develop it and I invited him to spend a week or two here" at the NCBI. Although nothing came of this work directly, "it seemed to me it would have some potential for DNA sequence comparisons but not for protein comparisons, but it was an interesting idea, it was a fun idea." It seems to have been added to the cauldron of ideas that was simmering in Lipman's mind.

The cauldron finally came to a boil in Lipman's kitchen: "One day I was doing the dishes, and some ideas just kept grinding through my mind about combining some of the stuff that Stephen Altschul had talked about. And I realized, aha, really what you could do is a very powerful gambling game." This gambling game allowed "trade-offs between speed and sensitivity, if we don't mind missing it with a certain probability." That is, using this approach one could find matches between proteins to a given level of similarity much faster, but with the small chance of missing a match.

First published in 1990, BLAST soon became the preeminent sequence similarity search tool. Lipman explains some of its advantages. "One, it is sensitive enough and fast enough that it dealt with a wide range of problems people would have. Sometimes people really are only looking for such close similarities that they don't need anything that's that sensitive; rarely there are cases where they want something that's so subtle that maybe this would miss it." In other words, BLAST was just good enough for the vast majority of practical uses, and didn't waste time—especially computational time—searching for the last few matches that probably didn't really matter anyway. "The other aspect of it, and this was an insight of Warren Gish who worked on the project here at the time, was that we should put this up as a server online so that people could very easily do searches against the database, and do it in a way where they don't have to know too much to stick their sequence in and off they go."

BLAST was the culmination of a process that began when researchers like Michael Waterfield were able to employ Wilbur and Lipman's early sequence comparison tool directly, rather than having a dedicated technician carry out the work. BLAST went even further, making searches so easy that scientists could use it as a matter of course. It also helped that the BLAST server was located in the organization running GenBank. "Since it was connected to the place that was actually producing the data, the databases, somebody could search this and feel that, well, it's most likely the latest stuff is in here and I've done my deal, I'm confident that I got my results," Lipman explains. "And so it's the comprehensiveness and the timeliness of the database, coupled with sufficient speed and sensitivity was good enough."

But even more critical was the availability of the Internet. "One of the things that's so interesting," Lipman notes, "is that there was really a feedback between high-throughput sequencing, the increasing sequencing in general, and the ubiquity of access to the Internet." This was recognized very early on. A 1991 paper entitled "Electronic Data Publishing and GenBank," written by a group of researchers at Los Alamos, noted: "In recent years, many people in the scientific community have become accustomed to participating in global 'conversations' as they unfold on various electronic bulletin boards around the Internet. Perhaps more than any other advance in computer science, computer networks have the potential to radically alter the way in which people access information."

Just as FASTP benefited from the appearance of relatively low-cost PCs, so BLAST was fortunate that in 1991 Tim Berners-Lee made freely available the ultimate tool for 'global conversations,' the World Wide Web. A couple of years later, in 1993, the Mosaic program appeared; it provided the first widely used graphical Web browser. The benefits were many. "From that browser most biologists could answer most of their questions," Lipman explains. The fusion between bioinformatics and the Internet, as represented by the Web-based BLAST, was so seamless that it was probably hard for many users to tell where one ended and the other began.

In a sense, BLAST represents the coming-together of all the main strands in the bioinformatics story. Through the Internet, it provided a window into the core DNA and protein databases, as well as a powerful engine for analyzing them. The roots of its mathematics could be traced back to the dynamic programming algorithms of Needleman-Wunsch and Waterman-Smith, as well as the faster heuristic methods of Wilbur-Lipman and FASTP. At its heart lay key ideas from Dayhoff's work on protein substitutions and Ulam's probabilistic simulations of complex processes.

Although it would clearly be an exaggeration to claim that BLAST on its own drove the imminent genomics revolution, its appearance in 1990 was certainly emblematic of the new power and maturity of bioinformatics. It is also clear that without bioinformatics programs, the powerful computers used to run them, and particularly the new way of studying molecular biology that they together implied, the ever-quickening pace of scientific work in the following ten years would not have been possible. Without this giddying acceleration, it is highly unlikely that molecular biology's first crowning glory—the sequencing of the entire human genome—would have been achieved just in time for the 50th anniversary of Watson and Crick's paper in *Nature* that made it possible in the first place.

NOTES

Interviews included in this chapter were conducted by the author between October and November 2002 with the following individuals: D. Lipman, R. Staden, and D. Brutlag.

1. p. 12 *by the time the fourth edition* T.F. Smith, "The history of the genetic sequence databases," *Genomics* 6 (1990): 701–707.

2. p. 12 *But the first DNA sequence* F. Sanger, "Sequences, sequences, sequences," *Ann. Rev. Biochem* 57 (1988): 1–28.

3. p. 12 *I cannot pretend that I was altogether* F. Sanger, "Sequences, sequences, sequences," *Ann. Rev. Biochem* 57 (1988): 1–28.

4. p. 16 *One aim of MOLGEN* T. Lenoir, "Science and the Academy of the 21st Century: Does Their Past Have Future in an Age Computer-Mediated Networks?" Online at *http://www.stanford.edu/dept/HPS/TimLenoir/IdealAcademy.htm.*

5. p. 16 *an interactive environment for the analysis* D.L. Brutlag, et al., "SEQ: a nucleotide sequence analysis and recombination system," *Nucleic Acids Res* 10 (1982): 279–294.

6. p. 19 *It was decided to exclude commercial users* T. Lenoir, "Science and the Academy of the 21st Century: Does Their Past Have Future in an Age Computer-Mediated Networks?" Online at *http://www.stanford.edu/dept/HPS/TimLenoir/IdealAcademy.htm.*

7. p. 19 *IntelliGenetics received around $5.6 million* T. Lenoir, "Science and the Academy of the 21st Century: Does Their Past Have Future in an Age Computer-Mediated Networks?" Online at *http://www.stanford.edu/dept/HPS/TimLenoir/IdealAcademy.htm.*

8. p. 19 *the NIH announced in August 1980* T.F. Smith, "The History of genetic sequence databases," *Genomics* 6 (1990): 701–707.

9. p. 19 *When proposals were officially requested* T.F. Smith, "The History of genetic sequence databases," *Genomics* 6 (1990): 701–707.

10. p. 19 *On June 30, 1982, the contract* T.F. Smith, "The History of genetic sequence databases," *Genomics* 6 (1990): 701–707.

11. p. 20 *I noticed that* S.M. Ulam, *Adventures of a Mathematician* (Berkeley/Los Angeles/London: University of California Press, 1991), 196–197.

12. p. 21 *After reading about* S.M. Ulam, *Adventures of a Mathematician* (Berkeley/Los Angeles/London: University of California Press, 1991), 258–289.

13. p. 21 *S. M. Ulam in the late 1960's* W.A. Beyer, Letters, *Science* 218 (1982): 108.

14. p. 21 *It concerns ways of comparing* S.M. Ulam, *Adventures of a Mathematician* (Berkeley/Los Angeles/London: University of California Press, 1991), xxiv–xxv.

15. p. 22 *A computer adaptable method* S.B. Needleman and C.D. Wunsch, "A general method applicable to the search for similarities in the amino acid sequence of two proteins," *J. Mol. Biol* 48 (1970): 443–453.

16. p. 23 *I was an innocent mathematician* M. Waterman, *Skiing the sun*, 13. Online at *http://www-hto.usc.edu/people/msw/newmex.pdf.*

17. p. 23 *The systematic comparison of every newly* R. Doolittle, "Similar amino acid sequences: chance or common ancestry?" *Science* 214 (1981): 149–159.

18. p. 23 *On Saturday morning* J.L. Marx, "*onc* gene related to growth factor gene," *Science* 221 (1983): 248.

19. p. 25 *Because of the algorithm's efficiency* D.J. Lipman and W.R. Pearson, "Rapid and sensitive protein similarity searches," *Science* 227 (1985): 1435–1441.

20. p. 26 *about two-thirds of all those available* R. Lewin, "Long-awaited decision on DNA database," *Science* 217 (1982): 817–818.

21. p. 26 *As a result, only 19 percent* R. Lewin, "DNA databases are swamped," *Science* 232 (1986): 1599.

22. p. 26 *a forms-oriented display editor* D.L. Brutlag and D. Kristofferson, BIONET: An NIH computer resource for molecular biology. *Biomolecular data: a resource in transition* (Oxford University Press, 1988), 287–294.

23. p. 27 *One can hardly overemphasize* T.F. Smith, "The History of genetic sequence databases," *Genomics* 6 (1990): 701–707.

24. p. 27 *In 1972, for example, the longest sequence* T.R. Gingeras and R.J. Roberts, "Steps toward computer analysis of nucleotide sequences," *Science* 209 (1980): 1322–1328.

25. p. 30 *before disappearing completely in 1994* A.B. Richon, "A short history of bioinformatics." Online at *http://www.netsci.org/Science/Bioinform/feature06.html.*

26. p. 30 *for an annual fee of $57* L. Roberts, "The perils of involving Congress in a 'catfight'," *Science* 257 (1992): 156–157.

27. p. 30 *Believe me, my product is dead* L. Roberts, "The perils of involving Congress in a 'catfight'," *Science* 257 (1992): 156–157.

28. p. 33 *In recent years, many people in the scientific* M.J. Cinkosky, et al., "Electronic Data Publishing and GenBank," *Science* 252 (1991): 1273–1277.

CHAPTER 3

Genome Delight

“The possibility of knowing our complete set of genetic instructions seemed an undreamable scientific objective in 1953 when Francis Crick and I found the double helical structure of DNA.” So wrote James Watson in *Science* in 1990. It is hard to believe, however, that the idea had not at least crossed the minds of two such bold thinkers once they understood how DNA was structured. For the broader implications of their work on the structure of DNA were quite clear. Only a few weeks after the first, they published the second of their classic DNA papers, which concluded as follows:

> *“We feel that our proposed structure for deoxyribonucleic acid may help solve one of the fundamental biological problems—the molecular basis of the template needed for genetic replication. The hypothesis we are suggesting is that the template is the pattern of bases formed by one chain of the deoxyribonucleic acid.”*

If heredity, or “genetic replication” as they called it, was simply a matter of a “pattern of bases”—a string of chemical letters—it was clear that spelling out that pattern by sequencing the complete human genome must stand as a key goal of molecular biology until fully achieved. Doing so would also allow some of the practical implications of digital DNA—understanding human biology, promoting health, and fighting disease—to be explored in a way that was not possible with genomes of other organisms, however interesting they might be.

The fact that human DNA consisted of around 3 billion such bases was, of course, something of a problem when there was no way to sequence even short DNA strands. It was not until nearly a quarter of a century after Watson and Crick's hypothesis, in 1976, that Gilbert and Sanger developed their respective sequencing methods. Soon afterwards, people started dreaming the undreamable. For example, in 1981, the European Molecular Biology Laboratory (EMBL) was contemplating sequencing one of the human chromosomes. Though still far less than the full 3 billion bases, tackling tens of millions of DNA letters was a brave idea for the time. Nothing came of this, but it is indicative of how quickly things were moving.

The first serious proposal for a concerted assault on the entire human genome was discussed in May 1985, in Santa Cruz, California, at a meeting organized by Robert Sinsheimer. A biologist by training, Sinsheimer was at the time chancellor of the University of California at Santa Cruz. He was looking for a major project that would "put Santa Cruz on the map," as he said. The original plan was to build the world's biggest telescope at Santa Cruz, but when this fell through, Sinsheimer had the novel idea of setting up an institute to sequence the human genome. At the meeting, he sought the views of 12 leading researchers on whether such a project was feasible.

The meeting concluded that sequencing the human genome was technically possible, but the participants were evenly split on whether it would be worth doing or not. Although Sinsheimer's grand vision of a sequencing institute went no further, there were other, more immediate ripple effects from the meeting, particularly for two participants who were to become key players in the human genome story.

One was Walter Gilbert, who came away convinced that sequencing the human genome could—and should—be attempted straightaway. He tried to set up his own Human Genome Institute that would devote itself to sequencing, though concentrating perhaps on known genes and other regions of importance. When this came to nothing, Gilbert took a step in 1987 that sent shock waves through the world of molecular biology. He proposed forming a new company, called, rather provocatively, Genome Corporation, that would create a database containing all human genes, and allow customers to interrogate it.

For example, customers might ask where a particular protein-coding sequence was located on the human genome. "The company will say, for a price, that the gene is on chromosome 21, 1,300,000 bases from the left," Gilbert explained. Equally, "a user can call up any part of it and read it. Or a pharmaceutical company might like a copy of the whole sequence; we would license it." The only thing a user could not do was download the database and then sell it. Gilbert noted: "You can buy a book but you can't sell it. It is exactly that distinction."

Gilbert's inarguable scientific prowess made an otherwise preposterous idea look at least possible. The fact that he had already been involved with a start-up before—the biotech company Biogen, founded in 1978—made it seem downright plausible. The ramifications were wide-ranging.

Although Gilbert accepted that there was always the risk that someone else might emulate the company, he also noted that "once someone has done it, it is in no one else's interest to do it again. It would be cheaper to pay for it." As a result, if Genome Corporation succeeded, it would probably end up with a monopoly on the digital code underlying life. Clearly, privatizing this unique resource would have a huge impact on pharmaceutical companies and the healthcare industry. But the effects of such a monopoly would be just as profound on the biological sciences community. Jealously guarding the knowledge that it would spend so much to gain—$300 million was the expected price tag—it seemed inevitable that Genome Corporation would effectively become the gatekeeper of all genomic research.

Gilbert nearly pulled it off. In July 1987, *Science* reported he was "still shy of the $10 million in venture capital he says he needs, but he expects to be in business by mid-summer," and hoped to finish the sequence in about a decade. His confidence proved misplaced. Monday, October 19, 1987—which came to be known as "Black Monday"—saw the largest single percentage drop in the history of Wall Street. Approximately $1 trillion was wiped off the value of stocks. It was hardly the right atmosphere for brilliant but risky ideas like Genome Corporation. As Gilbert recalled later: "Venture capitalists weren't interested." In particular, they wondered how a genome company of the kind Gilbert proposed "could make commercial sense." Although this was the first time this question was posed, it would certainly not be the last.

Commercializing genomics was not the only area in which Gilbert was ahead of his time. His other innovative idea—the central role of computers in molecular biology—proved far less controversial. With each passing year, as the databases of GenBank steadily filled with sequences, it became clearer to everyone involved that the only way of dealing with this rising digital tide was through fast algorithms running on high-speed computers.

Gilbert himself played a part in starting the flood of DNA data when he developed a sequencing technique that could be applied systematically; in practice, however, Sanger's method proved more important in the long term. If one person can claim the credit for setting the pace at which the tide was rising, it was another of the participants in the Sinsheimer gathering who came away profoundly influenced by it: Leroy Hood. "The meeting totally clarified my thinking about these things, and I went out a passionate minister of the genome," Hood told me.

Hood was born in 1937 and was something of a polymath. Besides his main studies, he excelled in sports, acting, music, debating and journalism. He initially worked on proteins rather than DNA. In 1977, while working at Caltech, Hood created a protein sequencer that allowed even small quantities of material to be analyzed. He and his team then went on to create two machines that synthesized materials rather than analyze them— one for proteins, the other for DNA. Using these, it was possible to convert the information strings of amino acids or DNA bases into the corresponding chemicals; they became a kind of digital-to-analogue converter. But Hood's main claim to fame was his last machine: the automated DNA sequencer.

Hood used Sanger's sequencing technique as the basis for his system, but changed it in two crucial ways. Sanger had originally marked the DNA frag- ments using radioactive chemicals. To view the bands produced by his method, a photographic film was placed on the gel; the radioactive decay of the chem- ical labels produced a band on the film. Hood replaced the radioactive mark- ers with fluorescent dyes. Moreover, he used a different color dye for each of the four bases. This allowed him to combine the four lanes generated by the Sanger method into a single gel lane. A laser was used to excite the dyes, and a fluorescence detector recorded which of the four colors appeared.

The first change meant that problems of aligning the four gel lanes were minimized. Less space was occupied, so several combined lanes could be run in one gel, allowing multiple sequences to be read at once. The use of fluo- rescence and the fact that all four bases were read in the same lane allowed Hood to make his second important refinement of Sanger's approach: the use of a computer to record and analyze the fluorescent signals as they were read by the detector. In doing so, Hood opened up the possibility of magnifying the scale of sequencing way beyond what was possible with human operators. When Hood first made public the capability of his machines—called initi- ally "DNA sequenators"—in the early summer of 1986, he claimed that they would be able to sequence around 8,000 DNA bases a day, ten times higher than manual levels of the time.

The system was sold as the ABI 373 by Applied Biosystems, Inc. (ABI), a company that Hood had helped found in 1981. Like Gilbert, Hood had no problems mixing science with business. Despite a price tag of $110,000, ABI sold nearly 3,000 of the systems in less than 10 years, a testament to Hood's vision and to the machine's power.

In Hood's view, the turning point in the debate about whether to start a publicly-funded human genome project came at the end of 1986, when the U.S. National Academy of Sciences appointed a committee under Bruce Alberts to look into the issue. It took over a year to arrive at a decision. As *Science* wrote at the time of the publication of the group's report, in February 1988: "A sticking point in the debate over the project, for both the commit- tee and the biological community, has been whether the entire genome should be sequenced, with the cost and labor that implies, or whether the effort should be focused on known regions of interest, say the five percent of sequences thought to code for genes." The widely held belief was that most of the other 95 percent was without biological significance—junk DNA—and hence not worth sequencing. Nonetheless, the group eventually recommended sequencing all 3 billion bases. The committee boldly took the view that the "junk" might in fact contain important structures. Moreover, its members believed that it would probably be cheaper in the long-run to sequence everything rather than to spend time and money picking out particular sections.

Although the committee "came out resoundingly in favor of the project," as *Science* reported, it left open the question of who should run it. After some wrangling between the U.S. National Institutes of Health (NIH) and the Department of Energy (DOE), the Human Genome Project finally came into being on October 1, 1990, under the aegis of the former, with the stated goal of completing the sequence in 15 years, for a total cost of about $3 billion. The overall head was James Watson.

Watson later wrote: "I argued that one person had to be visibly in charge and that only a prominent scientist would simultaneously reassure Congress, the general public, and the scientific community that scientific reasoning, not the pork barrel, would be the dominant theme in allocating the soon-to-be-large genome monies." And he added, not entirely convincingly: "I did not realize that I could be perceived as arguing for my own subsequent appointment." Whatever Watson's real thoughts or motives, it was a good move for the Human Genome Project (HGP), and Watson's forceful if sometimes abrasive advocacy and defense of the undertaking in its early years were extremely important.

Despite Hood's advances in automating the basic technology, there was no intention to sequence the human genome immediately. Instead, it was agreed that a number of pilot projects would be run first on so-called "model organisms." These were representatives of various types of life that had already been used extensively for investigating a wide range of biological problems.

One of the earliest and most eloquent proponents of the model organism approach, and a key member of the Alberts committee, was Maynard Olson, professor of genome sciences and of medicine at the University of Washington. "The argument in favor of starting with model organisms was truly overwhelming," he says. "In a sense, it was just the old Sanger kind of strategy. [During the early days of sequencing,] Sanger would pick projects that were difficult but not impossible . . . choosing stepping-stones where as much as possible was already known. My idea was to keep that sensible approach to technology development and project development alive." By sequencing progressively more complex model organisms, researchers ensured that their goals at every stage were achievable. They were also constantly extending the technology as new challenges were met and overcome.

Model organisms turned out to be even more useful than simply as a preparatory series before tackling the real goal, the human genome. "If anything," Olson continues, "I think that people like me underestimated the information richness of genomic sequence in model organisms and would have made an even more pressing case if we had realized that you would be able to learn so much so quickly." It became clear that key elements of model organism sequences were closely related. Researchers thus saw that this made the results of decades of work conducted on animals like fruit flies even more relevant to studies of humans.

The philosopher's stone that turned model organisms' genomes into veritable goldmines for researchers in other fields was homology, the instance of two or more sequences deriving from a common ancestor. "You have to remember that the existence of so much homology between gene sequences is a recent discovery," Olson notes. "It was in the mid-80s that it started to become clear, but even then there was a tendency to think, well, that's an odd case"—an interesting but exceptional result. Olson says that it was not until the late 1980s that the pervasiveness of homology started to become apparent.

"If the richness with which homology can be mined bioinformatically had been clear earlier," Olson says, "then the wisdom of launching genomics would have been obvious much earlier. In the defense of a lot of the critics of the genome project in the early days, I think there was a lot of head in the sand resistance to change, but there was also a well-taken concern that data would just be too hard to analyze in any useful biological manner"—a fear that the quantities of digital information would be so vast that it would be simply impossible to understand it. "And it is homology and comparison that made that prediction wrong."

This is a key point. Had every genome been radically different, the extent of homology would have been limited, the power of bioinformatics greatly diminished, and the field of genomics would have been extremely shallow. What gradually emerged as a rich, highly structured web of relationships among different genomes, their genes, and the proteins for which they coded would instead have been reduced to a vast, formless (and therefore incomprehensible) assortment of unrelated DNA sequences.

The few who were chosen for admittance to the exclusive "model organisms club" were the bacterium E. (Escherichia) coli; baker's yeast (Saccharomyces cerevisiae); the tiny nematode worm (Caenorhabditis elegans); and the fruit fly (Drosophila melanogaster). Each has progressively more complex biology, with correspondingly larger genomes: that of E. coli has about 5 million letters of DNA, baker's yeast around 12 million, the nematode worm 100 million, and the fruit fly nearly 200 million. They therefore formed a series of "stepping stones," as Olson put it—practical exercises on the way to the full 3 billion bases found in the human genome.

E. coli is often referred to as the "white rat of microbiology," so widely has it been used in laboratory experiments. It is also notable for a wide range of diseases that it causes in its variant forms, some of them life-threatening. This double interest made it a natural choice to be included in the first round of "practice" sequencing.

It was back in 1983 that Frederick Blattner—who ten years later would lock horns with GenBank's David Lipman over the latter's Entrez service—had noted that the total quantity of sequenced DNA at that point amounted to almost exactly half that of the *E. coli* genome. This suggested that a concerted effort to obtain it was not out of the question, even then. But it was not until 1990 that Blattner obtained funding from the Human Genome Project for a full-scale project. Blattner and his team chose to sequence all of *E. coli* themselves. Even though it would have saved time to add in preexisting sequences from other researchers, this would have meant a loss of quality control. It would also have produced a mosaic of different *E. coli* genomes, since not all researchers used exactly the same varieties of the bacteria, and each had genetic variations. This would complicate the creation and analysis of an overall genome sequence.

This otherwise laudable rigor made things more difficult than they might have been. More serious, in many respects, was the fact that because he began earlier than most, Blattner had older sequencing technology. In particular, he was unable to take full advantage of ABI's latest machines until 1995. Thereafter, the rate of sequencing throughput increased dramatically, and was finally finished in 1997—well after other projects that had been started later by teams who had the advantage of buying newer and faster equipment.

Despite the high quality of the sequence data and the handicaps under which Blattner operated, many pessimists saw the *E. coli* project and its problems as a warning of what might happen with the Human Genome Project. But the real lesson to be learned from *E. coli* was that, when throughput is a critical issue, it is always worth upgrading to the best available technology.

Unlike *E. coli*, which is famous for its experimental utility even to many who are not scientists, *Saccharomyces cerevisiae*—commonly known as baker's or budding yeast and used for making bread and brewing beer and wine—may not seem an obvious choice for entrance to the select club of model organisms. But as Maynard Olson, one of the pioneers in yeast genomics, explains: "It's as though yeast were designed by a geneticist. If you asked a geneticist what properties would you like an organism to have if you were going to do really serious genetics on it, you would end with a list much like those that apply to yeast."

A 1988 paper in *Science* spelled out some of the advantages that the single-celled yeast has over *E. coli* and other available systems. For example, it is what is known as a *eukaryotic* organism, just as all other plants and animals are, including mankind. Whereas prokaryotes like *E. coli* are a kind of microscopic bag full of biochemicals, eukaryotes have a far more complex cell structure, including a separate nucleus. It is here where the DNA is held in the form of chromosomes. Thanks to homology, many of *E. coli*'s proteins are quite similar to equivalent chemicals found in animals. However, there are clearly many others that are missing (for example, those to do with cell structures that are completely absent in prokaryotes).

What was needed was at least one intermediate step between bacteria and animals like worms and flies—an organism that was eukaryotic but without the full complexity of an animal. Yeast seemed to fit the bill nicely. It grew relatively fast (roughly half as fast as *E. coli*). This was important, because it meant that many generations of yeast could be studied to follow longer-term effects of heredity.

Even more important, perhaps, was the fact that it was relatively straightforward to apply recombinant DNA technology to investigate the relationship between genes, the proteins they specified, and the biological function of those proteins. In fact, Maynard Olson notes, "You can change any base pair in the yeast genome at will." Put in digital terms, yeast was a great system for hacking around with the code—adding a new software module here, deleting another there, and then running the modified program to see what happened. By studying variant forms of baker's yeast, it was also possible to work out which gene was changed where.

Another advantage cited by the authors of the 1988 *Science* paper was the attitude of those working on yeast: "An important ingredient in the success of yeast studies as a scientific field is the attractiveness of the yeast community itself. Newcomers find themselves in an atmosphere that encourages co-operation." This view was borne out just a few years later. In contrast to *E. coli*, where the sequencing was completed by one laboratory under Blattner in a dramatic last-minute spurt ahead of a rival Japanese effort, the 12 million or so bases of the yeast sequence were elucidated by a carefully orchestrated effort involving some 600 scientists.

It began in 1989 as a smaller-scale project to sequence the third of the 16 yeast chromosomes. It was organized by the European Union (EU) and included 37 laboratories. The experiment was a great success; as well as delivering the sequence data in 1992, it showed that international collaboration on a complex project could work well even on a large scale. As a result, the EU decided to go ahead with the rest of the genome, and to expand the consortium to encompass 100 European laboratories, later joined by other yeast researchers around the world.

The yeast genome was obviously highly useful. The fact that collaboration on a global scale had been so successful was an important lesson, too. The teams working on another model organism, the nematode worm, certainly shared this view. It was in part thanks to the worm sequencers and their advocacy of an even closer collaboration that the yeast project had realized its full potential. But the influence of the worm genome went far beyond this. It was not only the closest thing to a dry run for all the technologies that would be employed on a larger scale for the human genome; it established a number of principles that were applied there which turned out to be absolutely vital to its success.

The nematode belongs to a family of worms that includes both parasitic and free-living members. The species that became the third model organism is *Caenorhabditis elegans*, a tiny creature barely a millimeter long, which lives in the soil, eating bacteria. It had been plucked from its lowly obscurity to become one of the undisputed genomic stars thanks to Sydney Brenner, one of the Grand Old Men of the molecular biology world. He had earlier played a crucial role in understanding how the digital information of genes was converted into the analogue proteins via messenger RNA.

Brenner picked the nematode because it was extremely simple, and yet a complete animal in miniature. It has skin, muscles, gut, a reproductive system, and nerve cells. Better still, it is transparent, which meant that every cell in its body can be studied individually. Brenner's plan was to trace the development of all the cells in the nematode's body from the egg to their final form in the adult. The person who realized this vision was one of the researchers working under Brenner, John Sulston. Born in 1942, Sulston joined Brenner at the UK Medical Research Council's Laboratory of Molecular Biology as a staff scientist in 1969.

Another reason Sydney Brenner chose the nematode worm as a subject of research was the remarkable fact that all normal specimens have exactly the same total number of cells, 959. Moreover, the larva—the immature form of the organism, intermediate between egg and adult—is born with the same number, which means that as the worm matures, the cells simply increase in size without multiplying. At least, that was what all the textbooks said. John Sulston noticed, however, that the larva begins with 15 neurons in the ventral cord (the worm's main nerve pathway), while the adult has 57. The textbooks, it seemed, were wrong.

Sulston decided to investigate just how those cells grew and multiplied. He did this in the simplest way imaginable: by using a special kind of microscope to watch every single neuron in the ventral cord as it changed. After sorting out just where the extra neurons came from—and laying the foundations for the 2002 Nobel Prize in Medicine or Physiology in the process—Sulston moved on to map out the entire development from larva to adult, known as the *postembryonic lineage*. He published the results in 1977 in a paper with Bob Horvitz, who later shared the Nobel Prize with Sulston and Brenner. Following the cell divisions for the larva were hard enough, but Sulston's next project—the embryonic lineage from egg to larva—was even more ambitious. "With the postembryonic lineage you could afford to leave the microscope for ten minutes or so in the course of watching a cell, but not with the embryo—things happened too fast," Sulston later wrote. "I worked out that if I was to finish the job, it would take a year and a half of looking down a microscope every day, twice a day, for four hours each time."

Sulston's work on the embryonic and postembryonic lineages was at the limits of analogue molecular biology—sorting out what every cell in an animal's body did at every moment. And just as it had been a logical move to progress from the postembryonic to the embryonic, so it was obvious that once he knew how the worm's cells grew and divided from egg to adult, the thing to explore next was the digital code that made it happen.

The worm's genome has 100 million DNA letters, and Sanger's dideoxy technique is limited in practice to sequences around 500 bases long. This would imply dealing with over 200,000 fragments if the shotgun approach were employed. Aside from the technical difficulty of producing a set covering the whole sequence, there was no hope of piecing them together at that time—or for many years afterwards—because of the huge computational requirements for such an analysis.

Instead, a kind of intermediate strategy was developed, whereby the genome was split up into relatively large overlapping fragments to allow special copies of these, called clones, to be produced. Each clone could be sequenced in turn using the shotgun approach, allowing the complete genome to be put together from the subsequences that were obtained. In order to sequence a large genome, then, one needed to create an overlapping set of fragments and then their clones. Together with a set of identifiable landmarks along their length, these formed what was known as a physical map.

Mapping the worm genome started in earnest in 1983, when Alan Coulson, previously Sanger's research officer, came to work with Sulston. Coulson describes Sanger as "unassuming, focused, relatively quiet, very oriented toward bench work," and Sulston as "advanced, forthright, significant." One manifestation of being "advanced" was the fact that Sulston employed computers even at this very early date—the IBM PC was still a novelty—to help with the creation of the physical map. He used computers to compare clones to create a series of overlaps that together would generate a complete physical map.

Another key figure in the mapping of the worm and of the sequencing of both the worm and the human genome was Bob Waterston. He, too, had been one of Brenner's postdoctoral students, before returning to the United States to set up his own lab at Washington University in St. Louis. Waterston explains just why he and so many other brilliant researchers got hooked on the worm. It was due in part to Brenner himself. "Sydney's a charismatic person," Waterston explains. "He could have made a career on the stage if he didn't do so well in science. So I'm sure I was not unaffected by that." But even more, it was "the vision that Sydney presented—the idea that you could get to the heart of what made an organism a whole. And not a bacterium: this was an animal, with muscles and nerves and gut and sex and even some primitive behavior."

Waterston played an important role in closing some of the final gaps in the worm's physical map. But even before this stage, Sulston and Waterston did something quite new: they made information on their physical map available electronically so that the worm geneticists could use it to locate genes. These genes would in turn become important landmarks on the emerging genomic landscape. "There wasn't really such a thing as online—we had to struggle with it to make it happen even," recalled Waterston for this book.

A tradition of sharing information at an early stage had already been established in the nematode research community. A newsletter whimsically called *Worm Breeders' Gazette* had appeared several times a year since the end of 1975; in it, scientists presented early prepublication results from their work. As Waterston explains, "To do so required a certain amount of societal contract that people would be interested in what you were doing but they wouldn't try to do what you were doing. There was an implicit understanding that if people were going to share things prior to them getting publications out of it, you would respect their right to work on it."

This was a critical issue: had anyone breached this societal contract of not using others' work directly in a publication, the whole system of collaboration would have been endangered. In the analogue world of genetics it worked well, but as later history would show, the move to working with digital DNA—the information rather than the chemical—presented difficult issues in this area.

The first paper on the physical map of the worm's genome was published in 1986. The year before, at the Sinsheimer meeting in Santa Cruz, which Sulston and Waterston both attended, the worm map was held up as evidence

that something similar might be achieved for the human genome in a reasonable amount of time. The map was more or less complete by 1989, and it
was around this time that Sulston and Waterston's plans to move from mapping to sequencing found an echo in the thoughts of James Watson. Watson
was the newly-appointed head of the Human Genome Project, which
received its first grant that year; the formal launch, however, was not until
1990. As Sulston noted later: "[Watson] saw very clearly that the way to convince people of the value of the project, as well as to drive the technology, was
to start small. . . . A successful model organism sequencing project would not
only act as a trial run for the human, it would perhaps persuade the wider biological community that the genome project was a good idea and not of benefit only to human geneticists."

A deal was struck: Sulston and Waterston's labs would sequence the first
3 million bases out of the worm's 100 million. In return, Watson would fund
them to the tune of $4.5 million during three years; since Sulston was work-
ing in the UK, he would have to seek further funding from the UK Medical
Research Council. The Council provided £1 million ($1.5 million), and Sulston
and Waterston found themselves in the sequencing business.

O ne of the key early appointments to the new sequencing team in
    Cambridge was Richard Durbin. He had helped Sulston write soft-
ware for the worm mapping, and in 1989 set to work on a new database
program called AceDB (A *C. elegans* Data Base), together with Jean Thierry-
Meg. A database is generally regarded as a fairly dull thing—a kind of electronic filing cabinet. But as the GenBank experience had shown, bringing
information together is extremely fruitful in the world of digital DNA. The
sheer quantity of data involved makes visualization hard, and computers can
play a vital role as aids to understanding. AceDB was designed in part to allow
various kinds of data to be viewed in a user-friendly way.

James Watson was soon reaping the benefits of his gamble on the sequencing skills of Sulston and Waterston. The DNA started to flow from the two
laboratories; the costs went down as the skills went up. As a result, there was
a gradual sea change in the views of the biological community, many of whom
had been skeptical of both the feasibility and the wisdom of large-scale sequencing projects.

For example, just a little while after the Human Genome Project had been
agreed upon, *The New York Times* ran a story entitled "Great 15-Year Project
to Decipher Genes Stirs Opposition." The *Times* went even further in its
opening paragraph: "As the human genome project drives steadily forward,
the vast new effort to delineate all three billion chemical building blocks of
humanity's genetic makeup is arousing alarm, derision and outright fury
among an increasingly activist segment of the biomedical community."

The worry expressed by some scientists interviewed for the article was one that had also been voiced in the earliest meetings to discuss the feasibility of sequencing the human genome: it would "drain talent, money, and life from smaller, worthier biomedical efforts." Although these fears proved unfounded, there was cause for some concern in that the Human Genome Project was the first example of a very large-scale biological project that was radically different from the traditional laboratory work practiced by most researchers up to that point.

However, barely two years later, the editorial of a special issue of *Science* focusing on the Human Genome Project was entitled "Genome Delight." The editorialist wrote: "Increasingly, researchers sense that many of the project's goals, which seemed grandiose when they were first proposed, are now realistic." The same issue reported that detailed physical maps had been produced for the male chromosome Y and chromosome 21, the latter being particularly rich in important genes such as those involved in Down's syndrome and Alzheimer's disease.

Science was not alone in noticing recent achievements in this area; entrepreneurs, too, were beginning to experience genome delight. The first to feel the effects of this newfound interest were Sulston and Waterston. At the end of 1991, Sulston received a phone call from Leroy Hood, who was looking to set up another company. "I have a proposition for you," Sulston recalled him saying. "I want to start a sequencing organization, and I want you and Bob [Waterston] to come and lead it." The idea was remarkably similar to that of Walter Gilbert five years earlier: to sequence the human genome and sell access to the data. This time, however, the money was available (from the investor Frederick Bourke). The technology had also moved on enormously, and in Sulston and Waterston the world had its first high-throughput sequencers.

Hood was fortunate in his timing: Sulston and Waterston were coming to the end of the three-year funding that Watson and the UK Medical Research Council had granted, and it was by no means clear that the money they needed to complete the worm genome would be forthcoming. Hood, through Bourke, offered a solution: Sulston and Waterston could finish their worm project as they began work on the human genome. Waterston says they had no illusions about the terms of the offer: "The worm was purely to placate us," he says. "To get us interested. We understood that, but at that point it wasn't clear that we were going to get government support for a scale-up." For the sake of the worm, they were prepared to consider working on the human genome, but agreeing to a data release policy proved more difficult. Waterston says that he and Sulston were "willing to tolerate maybe a three-month delay," but that Bourke wanted to keep the data out of the public domain for longer: "they were thinking of a more serious tie-up." This, of course, was anathema to Sulston and Waterston. Ready access had formed the cornerstone of their mapping and then sequencing of the worm. So they turned Bourke down.

What is remarkable about this episode is not that Bourke was prepared to realize Gilbert's vision, nor that Sulston and Waterston were at least prepared to contemplate the creation of a commercial sequencing operation. What is most striking is that as far back as 1992, Sulston and Waterston were fairly confident that they could sequence the whole human genome on their own. "We wouldn't do it in a year," Waterston hastens to add, "but we were convinced that from our experience, where we'd already quadrupled the efficiency of the [sequencing] operation, we knew we were just beginning to scratch the surface. And we knew that there was ongoing technology development all over the place. We weren't contemplating doing it the way we were doing it in '92, we just knew that by starting with that, by pushing the technology, it would continue to get better, and with investment we could build the capacity."

The Bourke incident generated several of the great "what ifs" in genomics. What if some kind of compromise had been found? What if Sulston and Waterston had been lost to public science? What if the human genome had been sequenced in the mid-1990s—and privatized? "It's pretty hard to figure because it just would have been a different world," muses Waterston. Even though these tantalizing possibilities never came to pass, the consequences of Bourke's approach were profound. They changed the course of genomics history in several important ways.

The first to feel the repercussions of the abortive attempt to set up a sequencing business was James Watson. He had become involved when he learned of Bourke's moves. According to a story that appeared in *Science* in April 1992, "Watson and Bourke had gotten into a shouting match a couple of months earlier when Watson learned that Bourke was trying to snare two stars of the genome project . . . for a sequencing company he was planning to start in Seattle." As Watson later explained, he was not against the idea in general of such a company, just the way that Bourke was going about it: "I worried that the NIH might lose its most successful genome-sequencing effort, and the UK government might abandon large-scale genome research. The Genome Project would then lose the great intellectual resources nurtured by the MRC [UK Medical Research Council]."

As a result of their clash, Bourke wrote a letter to Watson's immediate boss, Bernadine Healy, in which, according to *Science*, "Bourke blasted Watson for interfering with his legitimate business activities," and also raised "ethical concerns" about alleged conflicts of interests because of Watson's investments in biotech companies. The same item reported that Watson, his friends, and his lawyer maintained that "Healy alleged conflict of interest to force Watson out because of his vehement criticism of her policies." Certainly, Watson could not have been the easiest person to have as a nominal subordinate.

Watson felt that he had no choice but to resign; he officially left the Human Genome Project on April 10, 1992. His was a great loss, but the fact that *Science* could still speak of "genome delight" six months later bears eloquent testimony to the strength of the organization he had created. It took nearly a year before his successor was appointed, on April 4, 1993. Francis Collins was a shrewd choice: a well-respected scientist whose team in 1989 had located one of the most sought-after genes—the one responsible for cystic fibrosis. He had made many other major contributions in the field of genetics. He was also skilled at working within the system, unlike his more brilliant but less politic predecessor.

W atson left another enduring legacy that stands as the other major ripple effect of the Bourke episode, this one on the other side of the Atlantic. "I knew that John Sulston would prefer to stay in Cambridge but he was dependent on procuring committed funding from a UK source," Watson later recalled. "While the MRC had joined forces with the NIH to fund worm sequencing for three years, it wasn't clear that the MRC could find the much greater sums of money to join the USA as a major force in the Human Genome Project. Potentially the key UK role would be played by the Wellcome Trust, whose annual income had greatly risen as a result of the sale of a large proportion of its shares in its pharmaceutical company." Watson started talking to key people in the UK, and the idea took root.

The Wellcome Trust had been set up by Sir Henry Wellcome on his death in 1936. He and a fellow American, Silas Burroughs, had established the Burroughs Wellcome Company to promote a new form of compress pills in the United Kingdom, widely used in the United States. The Trust was the sole shareholder of the company and used the income from Burroughs Wellcome to fund medical and academic research. Starting in 1986, however, the trustees gradually sold off shares in order to diversify their assets. This culminated in the 1995 merger of Burroughs Wellcome with Glaxo plc, another major UK pharmaceutical company, to form Glaxo Wellcome.

As a result of these moves, the Wellcome Trust saw its assets increase from £3.8 billion ($5.7 billion) in 1988 to £15 billion ($22.5 billion) in 2000, becoming the richest medical research charity in the world. This was good timing for Sulston. Just when he needed major funding to finish the worm genome and join the U.S. Human Genome Project as an equal partner, the

Wellcome Trust found itself increasingly flush with money and keen to expand its programs. It did so in July 1992 with an unprecedented £48 million ($72 million) grant to set up a major new sequencing center, to be called the Sanger Centre in honor of the man who had done as much as anyone to make genomics possible. The site chosen was Hinxton Hall, about ten miles south of Cambridge. This ancient university town had laboratories, colleges, and an enviable tradition of molecular biology.

The creation of the Sanger Centre under John Sulston was to have profound implications for every aspect of the Human Genome Project. One immediate effect involved the European DNA databank, until then held at the European Molecular Biology Laboratory in Heidelberg, Germany. As a result of the continuing growth in importance of DNA sequences and the tools for manipulating them, a decision was taken not only to extend the database facilities, but to create a new European Bioinformatics Institute (EBI). The imminent creation of the Sanger Centre, which would be the largest sequencing facility in Europe, made the UK's bid to host the database and new EBI nearby irresistible, and in due course the EBI took up residence at Hinxton, too. Placing sequencing and bioinformatics side by side in this way offered a symbol for the shifts that were underway in molecular biology at this time.

When Gilbert failed in his attempt to set up Genome Corporation, there were no followers willing to pick up the baton that he dropped. By the time Bourke tried to do the same—and also failed—things were different. As Gilbert himself noted at the beginning of 1993: "The role of genetic information is ten-fold more obvious to everyone." Genomics was hot, and this time there was plenty of money floating around the venture capital world. The result was a spate of genomics start-ups. Walter Gilbert finally started a company, which was called Myriad Genetics. Its business plan was based on the development of therapeutic drugs drawing on insights gained from sequencing particular sections of the human digital code, rather than all of it. Leroy Hood was also involved in a new start-up, Darwin Molecular Technologies, which had similar intentions—"using a lot of different genomic tools to go after drug discovery," as he explains.

Yet it was neither of these genomic giants who emerged as the pivotal figure in this strange new hybrid world of science and business that would soon shake the edifice of molecular biology to its foundations. Instead, it was an obscure researcher working on brain receptors who was about to turn the genome delight of the early 1990s into something closer to genome delirium for the rest of the decade.

NOTES

Interviews included in this chapter were conducted by the author between November 2002 and May 2003 with the following individuals: L. Hood, M. Olson, A. Coulson, and R. Waterston.

1. p. 37 *The possibility of knowing* J.D. Watson, "The Human Genome Project: past, present and future," *Science* 248 (1990): 44–49.

2. p. 37 *We feel that our proposed structure* J.D. Watson and F.H.C. Crick, "Genetical implications of the structure of deoxyribonucleic acid," *Nature* 171 (1953): 964–967.

3. p. 38 *put Santa Cruz on the map* R. Cook-Deegan, *The Gene War*s (Norton, New York/London: 1995), 79.

4. p. 38 *he tried to set up his own Human Genome Institute* R. Lewin, "Proposal to sequence the human genome stirs debate," *Science* 232 (1986): 1598–1600.

5. p. 38 *The company will say* L. Roberts, "Who owns the human genome?" *Science* 237 (1987): 358–361.

6. p. 38 *You can buy a book* L. Roberts, "Who owns the human genome?" *Science* 237 (1987): 358–361.

7. p. 39 *once someone has done it* L. Roberts, "Who owns the human genome?" *Science* 237 (1987): 358–361.

8. p. 39 *$300 million was the expected price tag* L. Roberts, "Human genome: questions of cost," *Science* 237 (1987): 1411–1412.

9. p. 39 *still shy of $10 million* L. Roberts, "Who owns the human genome?" *Science* 237 (1987): 358–361.

10. p. 39 *Venture capitalists weren't interested* C. Anderson, "Genome project goes commercial," *Science* 259 (1993): 300–302.

11. p. 39 *he excelled in sports, acting, music, debating and journalism* E. Regis, "Hacking the mother code," *Wired* 3.09 (1995).

12. p. 40 *he claimed that they would* R. Lewin, DNA sequencing goes automatic, *Science* 233 (1986): 24.

13. p. 40 *Despite a price of tag of $110,000* E. Regis, "Hacking the mother code," *Wired* 3.09 (1995).

14. p. 40 *A sticking point in the debate over the project* L. Roberts "Academy backs genome project," *Science* 239 (1988): 725–726.

15. p. 41 *came out resoundingly in favor of the project* L. Roberts, "Academy backs genome project," *Science* 239 (1988): 725–726.

16. p. 41 *I argued that one person* J.D. Watson, "The Human Genome Project: past, present and future," *Science* 248 (1990): 44–49.

17. p. 44 *An important ingredient in the success* D. Botstein and G. Fink, "Yeast: an experimental organism for modern biology," *Science* 240 (1988): 1439–1442.

18. p. 44 *It began in 1989* N. Williams, "Genome projects: yeast genome sequence ferments new research," *Science* 272 (1996): 481.

19. p. 45 *John Sulston noticed*   J. Sulston and G. Ferry, *The Common Thread* (London/New York: Bantam Press, 2002), 26.

20. p. 46 *With the postembryonic lineage*   J. Sulston and G. Ferry, *The Common Thread* (London/New York: Bantam Press, 2002), 34.

21. p. 47 *The first paper on the physical map*   J. Sulston and G. Ferry, *The Common Thread* (London/New York: Bantam Press, 2002), 56.

22. p. 47 *the worm map was held up as*   J. Sulston and G. Ferry, *The Common Thread* (London/New York: Bantam Press, 2002), 59.

23. p. 48 *The map was more or less complete*   J. Sulston and G. Ferry, *The Common Thread* (London/New York: Bantam Press, 2002), 65.

24. p. 48 *saw very clearly that the way*   J. Sulston and G. Ferry, *The Common Thread* (London/New York: Bantam Press, 2002), 66.

25. p. 48 *Great 15-Year Project*   N. Angier, "Great 15-year project to decipher genes stirs opposition." *The New York Times*, June 5, 1990.

26. p. 49 *drain talent, money and life from smaller*   N. Angier, "Great 15-year project to decipher genes stirs opposition." *The New York Times*, June 5, 1990.

27. p. 49 *Increasingly, researchers sense that many*   B.R. Jasny, "Genome delight," *Science* 258, (1992): 11.

28. p. 49 *I have a proposition for you*   J. Sulston and G. Ferry, *The Common Thread* (London/New York: Bantam Press, 2002), 83.

29. p. 50 *Watson and Bourke had gotten into a shouting match*   L. Roberts, "Why Watson quit as project head," *Science* 256 (1992): 301–302.

30. p. 50 *he was not against the idea in general of such a company*   C. Anderson, "Genome project goes commercial," *Science* 259 (1993): 300–302.

31. p. 50 *I worried that the NIH might lose*   Hinxton Hall History. Online at *http://www.hinxton.wellcome.ac.uk/history/Research_History.htm*.

32. p. 50 *Bourke blasted Watson*   L. Roberts, "Why Watson quit as project head," *Science* 256 (1992): 301–302.

33. p. 50 *ethical concerns*   L. Roberts, "Why Watson quit as project head," *Science* 256 (1992): 301–302.

34. p. 51 *I knew that John Sulston*   Hinxton Hall History. Online at *http://www.hinxton.wellcome.ac.uk/history/Research_History.htm*.

35. p. 51 *The Wellcome Trust had been set up by*   "The history of the Wellcome pharmaceutical company and of the Wellcome Trust." Online at *http://www.wellcome.ac.uk/en/1/awtvishisbus.html*.

36. p. 52 *with an unprecedented £48 million*   M. Morgan, "Human genome project—new fields of research in global cooperation." Online at *http://www.mpiwg-berlin.mpg.de/ringberg/Talks/morgan/morgan.html*.

37. p. 52 *The role of genetic information is ten-fold more obvious*   C. Anderson, "Genome project goes commercial," *Science* 259 (1993): 300–302.

CHAPTER 4

Speed Matters

For a man who more than anyone came to symbolize the new genomics and to dominate its headlines, John Craig Venter's career had fairly inauspicious beginnings. Born in 1946, he did not excel at school; he later referred to his "lackluster academic record." Instead, he preferred to spend his time surfing. Then, as he put it: "I was drafted off my surfboard in 1965 and ended up in the [US] Navy Medical Corps."

He trained in emergency medicine and tropical diseases, and volunteered to go to Vietnam—"even though I thought the war in Vietnam was wrong." It proved to be the making of him. Speaking of the medical experiences with his fellow soldiers in Vietnam, Venter later explained: "Some died as a result of trauma, some of disease. The capacity of medicine while great was nowhere near great enough. . . . These life-altering experiences piqued my interest in learning how the cells in our bodies work and interact, and thus how life is created and sustained."

As well as this new interest in understanding health and sickness, Venter came back from Vietnam with something even more precious: "I also learned that I could no longer afford to waste one precious moment of life. I came back from the war with a burning sense of urgency to get an education and to somehow change the world."

Originally he had planned to go to medical school, but became fascinated by research. "I just so enjoyed the discovery process where, by doing experiments, I could uncover new knowledge." From the University of California at San Diego he earned a B.A. in biochemistry and a Ph.D. in physiology and pharmacology. In 1976, he moved to the State University of New York at

Buffalo as professor of pharmacology and physiology. There he met his future wife and close collaborator, Claire Fraser, whom he married in 1981. "We went to a meeting for our honeymoon, and wrote a grant proposal there," she recalled.

In 1984, they both moved to the National Institutes of Health in Bethesda, working at the National Institute of Neurological Disorders and Stroke (NINDS). Venter and his wife were trying to discover genes associated with neurological function and disease. In particular, they were looking for the gene for a receptor—a special kind of protein—in the brain that was triggered by adrenaline. In an article written in 1999, Venter and Fraser called these early attempts "tedious." It took them "an entire decade and considerable effort in two separate research institutions to determine the sequence of a single gene."

For a man who had come back from Vietnam determined not to "waste one precious moment of life," things were moving excruciatingly slowly. Along the way, however, there was a glimmer of hope. "In 1986 there was a key paper published, at least to us," Venter later recalled. "It was the paper that Lee Hood's group published describing how they were going to change DNA sequencing by attaching four fluorescent dyes to the DNA instead of the radioactivity and reading the X-ray films."

Venter seized the opportunity. "It was in February 1987, when my NIH lab and the Neurology Institute was the first test site for the first automated sequencer." Hood's new machine, the ABI Model 373, held out the hope of faster and automated sequencing, something that might allow the impatient Venter to cut out at least some of the tedium from his project. In fact, this work with Hood's technology turned out to be a striking foretaste of much of Venter's later career, foreshadowing both his early adoption of new technology and his continual search for faster, easier ways of doing things.

Even though Hood's machine would be a key element of Venter's first break-throughs, it did not provide an immediate solution to his needs. As Venter recalled: "We ran into problems, not with sequencing the DNA, but in the interpretation of it once we had the first sequences from human chromosomes, and we found that we could not interpret the human genetic code. The algorithms were inadequate, the computers were inadequate." In the end, Venter and his team managed to find eight genes in the 200,000 DNA letters that they had obtained. This was better, but still not good enough for someone in a hurry.

The problem arose from having to sift through these hundreds of thousands of letters to find the genes—the instructions that coded for proteins. This difficulty stemmed from the fact that less than three percent of the human digital code was involved. The rest consisted of control sequences or was the legacy of billions of years of evolution, molecular fossils that served no obvious purpose but which offered tantalizing glimpses of how the genome had evolved.

"The insight that occurred then was one of those ideas that, once you hear it, you go, 'Well, gee, I could've thought of that.' I think that's why it upsets so many scientists," Venter later reflected. "It was simply realizing that every cell in our body knows how to process this information. The heart cell knows how to go through the whole genetic code and find not just which are the genes, but which are the genes that are strictly specific for the heart. Our brain cells know how to do that for the brain. And maybe because I come from a physiology background, the idea seemed more obvious to me: why not use the cells as our supercomputer?"

In practical terms, the way that the heart cell uses the DNA is to convert the genes that are relevant to its function at that time into messenger RNA (mRNA). The mRNA is then sent to one of the heart cell's ribosomes, where it is converted into the corresponding protein. Venter's plan was to eavesdrop on this process, catching the mRNA as it was passed to a ribosome. Since this corresponded only to the genes in the DNA that were relevant to each tissue, he could then convert the mRNA back into DNA—known as *complementary DNA*, or cDNA—which would yield the parts of the genome that interested him. The results exceeded Venter's expectations: "We were stunned at how simple it was and how well it worked. In only a few months we doubled the number of human genes that were in the public database."

As Venter said in 1994: "I wasn't the first to see the value of the cDNA approach." Researchers had employed it in 1983 to investigate rabbit muscle and rat brain genes, and Sydney Brenner had suggested its use as a first step toward sequencing the human genome. Venter had two crucial advantages, though. One was the availability of the new high-speed sequencers from ABI. This made the actual sequencing of the cDNA much simpler, particularly because Venter realized that he did not need to sequence all of it. Instead, he sequenced several hundred bases of the cDNA, something that could be accomplished in a single pass with the ABI sequencers. He called these partial cDNA sequences *expressed sequence tags* (ESTs).

The other key element that made Venter's approach so successful was the growth of GenBank. In 1983, when cDNA had first been used to find genes, there were a couple of million bases in the sequence database but limited options for searching through them. When Venter revived the idea, there were 50 million DNA letters. Moreover, powerful new bioinformatics tools like BLAST, which had appeared around the same time (1990), made it straightforward for Venter to compare thousands of ESTs against the entire holdings of GenBank. If the corresponding gene was already there, there would be a near-perfect match. Even if it was not, there might be sequences from other organisms that coded for proteins that were homologous—descendants of a common ancestral gene.

Venter's EST strategy was a stunning success, and it propelled him into the scientific limelight. On June 21, 1991, *Science* magazine published the paper "Complementary DNA sequencing: expressed sequence tags and the human genome project," written by Venter and his team. The results included 337 new genes from the human brain, of which 48 had significant similarities to genes from other organisms. What is particularly striking is the fact that Venter used the article—particularly its title, which was thrown down like a gauntlet to the rest of the sequencing community—to stake his claim to a much bigger prize: the human genome.

These growing ambitions, however, provoked tensions with his employer, the National Institute of Neurological Disorders and Stroke (NINDS). As Venter later explained: "I had good funding for my program. I had a budget of somewhere, including salaries and staff, between $1 to $2 million a year, with no absolute requirements on what I did. They were very nervous in NINDS about me going into the field of genomics. . . . They were happy as long as I restricted my work to the human brain or to the nervous system." But for Venter, this was no longer enough: "I wanted to take the global overview of all of human-gene expression." This "global view" became the first step toward what turned out to be his ultimate goal: sequencing the entire human genome.

As a result of this new ambition and his increased visibility, Venter found himself embroiled in scientific politics. "Bernadine Healy, then NIH direc-tor, was one of the few early on, at least in the administrative structure, who really saw the promise of my work," he said. "She became an instant fan and supporter, and all that got mixed up in the problems she was having with Jim Watson." The situation was made worse by one of Healy's recent decisions. "Jim Watson viewed me as competition because Bernadine appointed me head of the ad hoc committee to have an intramural [internal] genome pro-gram at NIH," as well as funding those at other, "extramural" labs.

Although Watson left the Human Genome Project in April 1992, he would remain one of Venter's most vocal critics. Even with Watson gone, though, Venter felt unable to stay at the NIH, much as he would have liked to. "I was eager to scale up our research program at NIH in order to imple-ment a successful, large-scale genome sequencing and gene discovery pro-gram. However, the extramural genome community did not want genome funding being used on intramural programs. . . . I was frustrated that I would be unable to participate in the revolution in biology that we had helped start. I did not want to leave NIH, but after much soul-searching I felt it was the most appropriate option." Venter was not about to pass up what was likely to be his biggest opportunity to "somehow change the world." Not for the last time, luck was with him.

As Sulston and Waterston had found out at the beginning of 1992, the world of finance was beginning to discover the potential of genomics as an investment opportunity. Venter's EST publication in *Science* in June 1991, followed by another in *Nature* a year later, in which he added a further 2,375 genes expressed in the brain, made him an ideal candidate to join the exclusive club of scientists-turned-entrepreneurs that included leading figures like Walter Gilbert and Leroy Hood.

Venter's desirability from this point of view doubtless gave him a certain leeway in choosing his commercial partner. However, the unusual setup he insisted upon surely bears witness to the fact that he would much rather have remained within a publicly-funded research institute, and that he did his utmost to simulate the conditions he would have worked under there. Instead of simply bringing his technical know-how and reputation to a start-up, Venter got to create and run a new outfit called The Institute for Genomic Research (TIGR—pronounced *tiger*). As Venter later explained: "I formed TIGR as an independent, not-for-profit research institute to implement the programs that I had envisioned for my lab at NIH."

Paired with TIGR in a curious marriage of science and business was the new company Human Genome Sciences (HGS), which had exclusive rights to TIGR's work. It was designed to allow HGS's backer, Wallace Steinberg, to recoup the $70 million, 10-year grant he was giving to TIGR through HGS. A measure of the esteem in which Venter was already held by at least some in the scientific community was the fact that Steinberg managed to persuade William Haseltine to become chairman and chief executive officer of HGS. Haseltine was a highly successful Harvard professor who had received many awards for his achievements in cancer and AIDS research.

HGS's business plan was not simply a repeat of Bourke's attempted sequencing venture. Instead, like several of the other new start-ups of the time, it aimed to discover new drugs using the latest genomic techniques. In HGS's case, this meant Venter's ESTs, which allowed large numbers of tissue-specific genes to be isolated quickly, and then compared against GenBank to establish their likely roles and potential as sources of drugs or as drug targets.

Producing a new drug is a long and slow process involving numerous trials that must be conducted before a drug is deemed safe and finally approved. Partly as a result, it is also very expensive: according to figures from the Pharmaceutical Research and Manufacturers of America (PhRMA), the average cost of developing a new drug in 2000 was around $800 million. Generating sales, not to mention a profit, may take years, which can be a big problem for a start-up company that has no sources of income from existing products. Haseltine came up with a solution to this problem that was not only extremely clever but also became the benchmark for other genomic companies. It also probably played an important part in triggering the increasingly stratospheric valuations that were placed on these companies in the years to come.

"We chose an exclusive arrangement with SmithKline Beecham that gave us $125 million up front, plus 10 percent of royalties from drug sales, and the right to co-develop a product in 20 percent of the market," he later explained. Aside from the sum involved—a $125 million first payment to a company that had existed for barely a year and which was employing leading-edge technologies whose ultimate applicability in the clinical context was completely unproven—there are two other notable elements.

First, although the deal was exclusive—only SmithKline Beecham would be able to exploit whatever leads came out of Venter's work for the term of the deal—HGS retained the right to develop possible drug candidates in a fifth of the overall market. Second, for any drugs that SmithKline Beecham brought to market, HGS would receive a percentage of the royalties. It was a brilliant solution, because it provided immediate funds to tide the company over while it ramped up its development efforts and guaranteed that it would share in any long-term successes that resulted from its research.

Soon Venter and Haseltine had 80 sequencing machines working on cDNAs in 248 different kinds of tissues taken from 120 human bodies in emergency rooms and pathology labs. By 1994, Haseltine claimed that they had produced 35,000 ESTs, and would be able to identify 80 percent of all major human genes. The financial side seemed to be flourishing, too: in November 1993, when HGS stock began trading, Venter's 766,612 shares were worth $9.2 million, and had gone up another 50 percent a few months later.

Whatever their apparent scientific and financial successes were, however, the relationship between Venter and Haseltine—dubbed the "Gene Kings" by *Business Week* in 1995, but the "Genomics' Odd Couple" by *Science* in 1997—had begun to sour almost immediately. The sticking point, as would so often be the case in the world of digital genomics, was data access. Venter, who clearly regarded himself as a scientist first and foremost, intended to publish his EST results just as he had done in the past. Haseltine, as head of a fledgling start-up whose only assets were the ones that Venter's sequencing machines were churning out, wanted them kept out of the public domain. After all, why would SmithKline Beecham pay $125 million for information that was freely available? Haseltine's solution was surprising. As early as 1993, just a few months after the twin-headed venture first got off the ground, HGS launched its own internal EST program. These results could then be kept proprietary and delivered to SmithKline Beecham in accordance with the agreement.

In fact, all the data were later made publicly available, but with conditions attached. HGS would have first option on the commercial rights to any genes that were discovered through using the ESTs, and it would be notified up to 60 days in advance before any data derived from them were published. Many scientists found themselves in something of a quandary: HGS's database clearly contained a wealth of information that would help drive forward their research, but the conditions imposed were unacceptable for many who saw science and commerce as distinct domains.

Nonetheless, it was commerce that helped scientists resolve this dilemma. On September 28, 1994, the pharmaceutical giant Merck announced that it would be funding an EST project known as the Merck Gene Index, which would produce 300,000 human gene sequences over a two-year period. The driving force behind the idea, Merck's vice president for research strategy worldwide, Alan Williamson, explained the official thinking behind this unexpected generosity. "Merck's approach is the most efficient way to encourage progress in genomics research and its commercial applications: by giving all research workers unrestricted access to the resources of the Merck Gene Index, the probability of discovery will increase."

The person charged with carrying out the EST sequencing was Bob Waterston at the Washington University School of Medicine. He explains why Merck chose to put it in the public domain, rather than simply duplicating the work themselves, and keeping it proprietary: "Basically what they said is that Human Genome Sciences is doing this, we could do it too, but if we do it, then everybody else was going to do it, and so let's put it in the public domain. We are convinced that if it's in the public domain Merck has the research base to outcompete everybody. Make all this information pre-competitive, and we'll take everybody on. And they were very confident on that."

Of course, the Gene Index undercut HGS's agreement with SmithKline Beecham, but by now that was hardly a problem. HGS had not sold Smith-Kline Beecham exclusive access to genomic information forever. This was impossible, since other companies and researchers would, sooner or later, obtain the same EST sequences. What it really provided was access before anyone else could—temporary exclusivity. Moreover, HGS had plenty of potential drugs that it could work on as it evolved into a full-fledged (if novel) drug company.

Venter benefited from the Merck Gene Index, too. Because the Index was in the public domain, Venter was at liberty to take all of the ESTs there and to combine them with his own sequences to produce a consolidated database of even greater power. He was able to do this in part because DNA sequences are inherently digital: since they all consist of strings of four chemical letters, they can easily be combined together in a way that analogue entities from different sources cannot. By this stage, Venter's cDNA approach had yielded some 174,000 ESTs, each of which represented a few hundred nucleotides from a gene, sometimes from different positions in the same gene. By combining them with the 118,000 that became available in the Merck Gene Index, Venter was able to assemble these fragments into 30,000 combined sequences, plus another 58,000 nonoverlapping ESTs. Of these 88,000 distinct sequences, 10,000 showed significant similarities to previously known genes in the public databases.

The results were published in a special supplement to *Nature* in 1995, called simply and significantly "The Genome Directory." That is, not just a directory of genes, but a guide to that tantalizing endpoint Venter seemed to have had in the back of his mind from an early stage: the human genome. As with earlier publications of sequences, paper was not the ideal medium for conveying large amounts of essentially digital information, so Venter also made the data available over the Internet. As Venter explained at the time: "To make this information available to the international scientific community, we're now in the midst of [testing] the TIGR database via e-mail interactions. This testing includes over 50 academic institutions worldwide," he said, "without intellectual property agreements. In conjunction with the publication of our *Nature* paper, we will be providing World Wide Web access to the TIGR database covering 45,000 of those genes. The remaining 5,000 will be available via the e-mail server." That this took place only a few months after Netscape launched its first Web browser demonstrates again a willingness to embrace the very latest technology that has been a hallmark of Venter's career.

Despite the early criticisms of Venter's EST approach—that it was not original, that it would never find all human genes—the sheer scale of his output is noteworthy. Even the fact that the climax of his EST work, The Genome Directory, used significant amounts of data from other projects, misses the point: that it was Venter who prodded others into responding by emulating him. Indeed, even a decade after his groundbreaking EST paper in *Science*, ESTs formed the majority of all DNA sequences in GenBank, a reflection both of their utility and of the relative ease of acquisition.

Although The Genome Directory stands as a kind of monument to the first phase of Venter's rise, it also marked the definitive end of his interest in this area. And just as had happened with the appearance of a wealthy entrepreneur when he needed funds for his work, so at a time when he was beginning to cast about for a new challenge—one that would move him further along in his quest for the ultimate prize, the human genome—Venter was fortunate enough to meet precisely the person to show him the way. In the autumn of 1993, he traveled to a conference in Bilbao, Spain, to describe yet again the EST sequencing techniques that had made him famous. Also attending was Hamilton Smith. Part of an older generation of molecular biologists, Smith had played a key role in bridging the old analogue world with the new digital one.

Smith's great discovery was that bacteria like *E. coli* produce a special protein, called a *site-specific restriction enzyme*, as a defense against attacks by viruses. Viruses are simpler than bacteria and are unable to exist alone. Instead, they use independent organisms, including bacteria, as hosts, hijacking some of their genetic machinery to reproduce. Because viruses consist largely of DNA or RNA, with very little external "packaging," they are remarkably similar to the computer viruses that borrow their name: compact code whose only function is to reproduce by subverting its host. By inserting themselves into the organism, they are able to use the cell's "hardware" to run the parasitic program to produce new copies of the virus, which can then spread to other bacteria in the vicinity.

Smith found that some bacteria have developed an interesting defense against this digital attack. Since the problem was that parasitic DNA was running on their hardware, the optimal solution would be for the bacteria to render the viral digital code defective so that it would not run. Just as dividing up a computer program arbitrarily into two or more pieces is generally sufficient to render it useless (because key structural elements are missing in each part), so literally cutting up the viral DNA would stop it from subverting the bacterium's genetic processes. This is precisely what site-specific restriction enzymes do—they *restrict* the operation of the virus in the bacterium. They work on viral DNA by carrying out the equivalent of a text search: each restriction enzyme is able to recognize a unique string of chemical letters that might be found in the virus but is not part of the bacterium's own DNA sequence. When the enzyme locates such a string—the specific site—it cuts the DNA in a particular way, thus rendering the programming code around it useless. Because the search string is not found in the bacterium, its own DNA is left unharmed.

Smith's discovery opened the door to the whole field of recombinant molecular biology. Using restriction enzymes that cut the twin strands of the DNA in a jagged way, it was possible to splice together two similarly jagged pieces. The universality of the underlying digital code meant that these two pieces could come from totally different organisms, allowing the human insulin gene to be spliced into a bacterium, for example.

In 1978, Smith won the Nobel Prize in physiology or medicine for his work. Unfortunately, for many years it seemed to be more of a curse than blessing. Coupled with a feeling that he had just been lucky to describe what came to be a key tool in molecular biology was the burden of trying to live up to the high standards the prize implied. This does not seem to have impaired his sense of humor, though. When Smith spotted Venter in the bar during the Bilbao conference, he said: "You're Craig Venter, aren't you?" When Venter replied in the affirmative, Smith asked: "Where are your horns?" This was at a time when many within the genomics community believed that Venter had indeed sold his soul when teaming up with HGS. They soon hit it off, and Venter invited Smith to become an advisor to TIGR.

It was at a meeting to discuss research proposals that Smith asked: "Would you be interested in doing an actual genome sequence?" Venter replied: "Yeah. I'm very interested." But not so interested in Smith's initial idea as to which organism. "At first he suggested we sequence the *E. coli* genome, but the *E. coli* genome project was in its ninth year of federal funding, and it was about halfway done. We figured we would just antagonize the community even more if we sequenced that genome quickly," Venter recalled. "So Ham [Smith] suggested his laboratory pet *Haemophilus* that he isolated the first restriction endonuclease [enzyme] from, and led to his sharing of the Nobel Prize and led to some of the key tools all of us use."

This was a far better choice than *E. coli* in many ways. Smith knew more about *Haemophilus influenzae* than anyone, and so could offer invaluable advice and practical help when it came to sequencing. Moreover, as well as a scientific payoff, there would also be a practical one: *H. influenzae* was responsible for millions of cases of ear and respiratory infections in children (not the flu, as its name implies). It was also responsible for the rarer but more serious meningitis, an inflammation of the membrane lining the brain. Obtaining its sequence would give researchers unique insights into exactly how the bacterium caused these infections and suggest new avenues for preventing and curing them. It would be the first practical application of large-scale genomics to medicine.

It was the perfect solution: if Venter succeeded, not only would he gain plaudits and that longed-for respect, but he would also be doing good in the world. How could he turn the opportunity down? It would be an immense challenge, though. At that time, no free-living organism had ever been fully sequenced. Fred Sanger had led the way by tackling viruses, but he dealt with DNA which was much smaller since it did not contain all the code necessary for life: some of it came from the host organism that the virus infected. Venter and his team, by contrast, would have to deal with 1.8 million base pairs, ten times the size of any virus that had been sequenced.

The traditional method was the one currently being employed for the model organism sequencing projects then underway—*E. coli*, yeast, and the nematode worm. First, a physical map of the relevant genome was produced. Next, the overlapping clones that went to make up the physical map were sequenced individually using Sanger's shotgun method. This was a tried and tested method but a slow one, as the progress on the model organisms showed. Moreover, there were no maps for *H. influenzae* on which to build. What Venter needed was an altogether bolder—and speedier—approach.

In fact, the seeds of this approach were already present in his EST work. "In the early 90s it was a big problem to assemble more than 1,000 sequences and we had hundreds of thousands of EST sequences. We knew that there were not that many genes, so we knew that we had multiple sequences per gene. We had to develop a new algorithm to put those together and then new computer programs to track this information," Venter later explained. "So we hired some mathematicians at TIGR. The lead one was Granger Sutton who designed a new algorithm that is now known as the TIGR Assembler." The TIGR Assembler took the EST sequences and compared them with each other, trying to find which ones were actually fragments of the same gene. From any overlaps it might be possible to reconstruct what the larger gene looked like.

Even though it worked on quite different starting material, this is conceptually very similar to the shotgun method. Venter, his wife Claire Fraser, and Hamilton Smith had a hunch that this was the way forward. As Venter later recalled: "Claire and I were sitting around with our good friend and colleague Ham Smith and said, 'we have this wonderful tool [TIGR Assembler], let's think of how we can go back and approach genomes with it'." It was Smith who seems to have come up with the solution.

One of the things with which Smith had occupied himself during the lean years after winning the Nobel Prize was computer programming. As a result, he was in a good position to assess the feasibility of using computer-based assembly programs along the lines of the TIGR Assembler to tackle "an actual genome sequence" as he had put it to Venter. This would not be matching up ESTs, but the fragments of an entire bacterial genome. Of course, this was precisely what Sanger had done back in 1982. Where that had involved thousands of comparisons, though, this would require millions. The main problem with the shotgun approach was that it left gaps. This problem could be reduced by carrying out the shotgun process several times; the random nature of the fragmentation meant that any given gap might be covered by another fragment. Smith was able to model on a computer the likely number of gaps to see if they represented an insuperable problem or whether they were at a level that could be addressed by additional work.

When Smith presented his idea to Venter and his team at a meeting in December 1993, they were taken aback for a moment. As someone who was there later recalled: "This was radical in its approach. It wasn't that this had never been done before. But never on this scale." Venter displayed those qualities of boldness and decisiveness that would mark him out in the future, too. "Let's do it," he said. This willingness to gamble seems to go back once more to his time in Vietnam. As he once put it, "Feeling that I survived that year when a lot people around me did not, I felt that I had nothing to lose by taking risks."

Venter contemplated applying for an NIH grant, but decided that since he was likely to get turned down yet again (as he had for his EST work), it was hardly worth it. Surprisingly, Smith encouraged him to submit the application anyway. Smith, too, had been rebuffed earlier by the NIH. Confident that they were going to succeed this time, he wanted the inevitable rejection letter to brandish as future proof that the NIH had been wrong all along: "I want to frame it on the wall," he declared. With this shared animus toward the scientific establishment, no wonder Smith and Venter got on so well.

Venter went along with the idea. "We were somewhat skeptical that we would get funded so we dug into the TIGR endowment to fund the project, while we waited to hear from NIH," he later recalled. "We had the genome almost completely assembled and the paper was being written when we got our pink sheet from NIH telling us what we were doing was impossible and it couldn't possibly work. I called Francis Collins"—James Watson's successor as head of the Human Genome Project—"and explained that it was working extremely well and that we were close to finishing the project and publishing a paper and he said, 'No, the experts on the committee said it

absolutely won't work,' and he didn't think we could do it so he wasn't going
to fund it. A short while later we published this paper in *Science*."

Venter broke the news on May 24, 1995; it was at a session of the 95th
General Meeting of the American Society of Microbiology, held in
Washington D.C. It was a classic performance, particularly in two respects.
First, not content with amazing his scientific peers even more than he had when
he published his EST paper, "he also took obvious pleasure in noting that NIH
had refused to provide federal funds for the effort," as a *Science* report pointed
out. Despite this, Francis Collins had enough practice in the sound bite game
to summon up a couple of variants on a theme, calling Venter's work "a remarkable milestone" when interviewed by *Science* and "a significant milestone" when
interviewed by *The New York Times*. The second notable feature of Venter's
speech was his parting comment that his method, which he dubbed the "whole-
genome shotgun" approach, had worked so well and was so fast that his team
had actually sequenced not just one bacterium in a year, but two. The second
bacterium was *Mycoplasma genitalium*, one of the simplest bacteria; it is associated with reproductive tract infections. Venter later revealed that "TIGR had a
T-shirt that says 'I ❤ my genitalium'," an indication of the playful atmosphere
that reigned during those heady early days.

The 1995 paper in *Science*, entitled "Whole-genome random sequencing
and assembly of *Haemophilus influenzae* Rd" was, as Francis Collins had indicated, truly a milestone. It represented the first complete genome of a free-
living organism. With *H. influenzae*, scientists could for the first time
investigate the complete range of digital code—and hence analogue machinery in the form of the corresponding proteins—that was required for life.
This was important not only for the promise of future, detailed knowledge
about how cells function, but also for demonstrating that it was possible—at
least on a bacterium—to obtain the complete digital code that ran an organism. Until TIGR's paper, the possibility remained that there would be some
final, unsuspected obstacle to elucidating the detailed chemical text of the
program. In a sense, Venter's work also validated the entire concept of
genomics (the study of entire genomes) beyond that of traditional genetics
(the study of individual genes). It implicitly marked the start of a new phase
in molecular biology, one that was based on complete digital knowledge of an
organism. The long-term effects of this shift will be so profound that future
generations will probably struggle to imagine how it was possible to conduct
biological sciences and medicine without genomes.

The paper from Venter and his team provided some details of how the work
was carried out. First, it noted the continuity with his earlier EST work: "The
computational methods developed to create assemblies from hundreds of thousands of 300- to 500-bp [base pairs] complementary DNA (cDNA) sequences

led us to test the hypothesis that segments of DNA several megabases [millions of bases] in size could be sequenced rapidly, accurately and cost-effectively by applying a shotgun sequencing strategy to whole genomes." As with the EST work, the key to Venter's success was the use of plenty of powerful technology. The paper states that it took 14 ABI sequencing machines, run by eight technicians for three months, to produce 23,304 sequence fragments. These were put together using the TIGR Assembler program, running on a SPARCenter 2000 with 512 megabytes of RAM—a huge amount for 1995. Even so, the assembly took 30 hours of central processing unit time to produce 210 *contigs*— unbroken sequences formed from the overlapping shotgun fragments. The gaps between these contigs were closed using a variety of methods to complete the sequence. The lead writer of the *Science* paper, Robert Fleischmann, recalled the moment when everything came together: "Lo and behold, the two ends joined. I was as stunned as anyone." Unlike human chromosomes, bacterial DNA is generally in a closed, circular form.

The final result was a genome that was 1,830,137 base pairs long, obtained at an average cost of 48 cents each. This was another breakthrough for Venter. As he himself remarked at the time: "People thought [that bacterial genomes] were multiyear, multimillion-dollar projects. We've shown that it can be done in less than a year and for less than 50 cents per base." The consequence, he noted, was that "it's opened the floodgates." TIGR itself went on to sequence dozens more bacteria—discussed in chapter 14—and others soon followed in its footsteps. But Venter was keenly aware of even broader implications. The *Science* paper's peroration suggested various areas where the whole-genome shotgun approach could be usefully applied. And as usual, Venter saved his most provocative thought for the last, throwaway line: "Finally, this strategy has potential to facilitate the sequencing of the human genome."

I t was not Venter, however, who made the daring conceptual leap from applying the whole-genome shotgun method to bacteria to using it for the human genome. This honor belongs to two other leading researchers, James Weber and Gene Myers (one of the people behind BLAST). Weber and Myers published a paper expounding the idea in the journal *Genome Research* in 1997. As Myers later wrote: "The whole-genome shotgun sequencing of *H. influenzae* in 1995 showed that direct shotgun sequencing could handle a much larger source sequence segment than biologists had commonly thought. . . . This achievement inspired Jim Weber and me to propose the use of a shotgun approach to sequence the human genome."

Aside from the central idea of applying the whole-genome shotgun method to the human genome, the article's main contribution was to discuss ways of tackling the issue of gaps in the sequence. This was always the chief drawback of the shotgun method—Fred Sanger experienced it even with the first major application of the technique to a virus. And the bigger the genome, the greater the problem it represented. Moreover, the problem was exacerbated by the issue of repeated sections of DNA. For viruses, this is hardly an issue. As minimalist entities, their genomes are necessarily as compact as possible—practically the minimum required to enter and subvert the host organism. Bacteria have more complex genomes, and some sequences are repeated. In the human genome, though, vast stretches consist of nothing but different varieties of repeats. These make assembling the shotgun fragments much harder, leading to even more gaps that needed to be filled using alternative, and often expensive, approaches. For these reasons, much of Weber and Myers' paper was devoted to outlining a variety of clever techniques. These techniques were designed to minimize the number of gaps that would be left at the end of the highly-automated assembly process, before the final stage of meticulous and generally hand-crafted work known as finishing was done.

Weber had earlier presented the proposal at a major gathering of genome researchers held in Bermuda in 1996. The reception was hostile, but as Bob Waterston, who was there, recalls, this was only partly because of doubts about its technical feasibility. "There was this sense that he was being glib and he was presenting things from a self-interested perspective," he says. Weber had written with Myers in their paper: "Most research laboratories, both public and private, want discrete genomic sequence information, and they want it as early as possible." This presumably included Weber, too. But Waterston believed that there were "larger issues" at stake.

"The fundamental thing that genomes present to you is this ability to capture the full finite information that's behind living things, the genetic component," he explains. "And if you only get 98 percent, if you leave out the hard bits, you may think you've only left out the hard bits, but you don't know until you do it. And if you pass up this chance in biology to get an absolutely firm foundation, you've passed up something special." Weber and Myers, by contrast, had asserted that the "true motivation for sequencing the human genome" lay not in "the accomplishment of some arbitrary, mythical goal of 99.99 percent accuracy," but in achieving practical goals like sequencing all genes, determining regulatory sequences, and developing a methodology for other genomes.

The issue of sequence accuracy began, therefore, to take its place alongside data access, as one of the key themes of the digital world of genomics. The absolutist position, espoused by Waterston, was based in part on a deep sense of "the full finite information"—the digital nature of the genome. This meant that in contrast to traditional biology as it had been practiced for centuries, which had been analogue, with necessarily approximate answers, it was possible to strive for 100 percent accuracy in sequencing. There was such a thing as a "right" answer, perhaps for the first time. Moreover, due to the nature of the matter being studied—the digital code that is run in cells—missing a few chemical letters here and there is simply not "good enough," just as missing the odd character here and there in a computer program results in substandard function.

The other wing, represented by Weber and Myers, thought that the level of accuracy needed was dependent on what one was trying to achieve. For example, for the stretches of DNA encoding proteins or other important regulatory regions, it was obviously vital to have the highest accuracy; for many of the repeats, however, lower standards might be advantageous. It would allow one to spend more time on the real areas of interest, for example. This, in turn, would lead to more useful results, including clinical therapies, more quickly. As Weber and Myers said in conclusion: "We should sequence the human and other eukaryotic genomes using the most rapid, cost effective and productive strategy."

In a paper written some time after this proposal was made—which still stands as one of the best introductions to the whole-genome shotgun approach—Myers wrote: "We requested funding for a pilot project from the U.S. National Institutes of Health. The establishment community rejected our controversial proposal." Then, with one of those deft touches that academics possess, Myers added a helpful reference to one paper in particular, the implication being that this was one of the staunchest detractors. The paper, which appeared directly after Weber and Myers' initial 1997 proposal, was called with admirable frankness "Against a whole-genome shotgun." It was written by Philip Green of the University of Washington in Seattle.

In it, Green expressed the view that "Weber's and Myers' argument that the approach is feasible relies primarily on a greatly oversimplified computer simulation of the process of sequence reconstruction." He was equally dismissive of Venter's recent whole-genome sequencing of the *H. influenzae* as supporting evidence for the idea: "nor does success of a whole-genome shotgun approach with bacterial genomes . . . provide any confidence whatsoever that the same approach would work with the human genome." Finally, after magisterially pointing out in detail what he saw as the major drawbacks of the whole-genome shotgun approach compared to the traditional method of splitting a genome up into clones and then using the shotgun method to sequence those—difficulties that the scale of the human genome would only amplify—he concluded with crushing finality: "There is no reason to switch."

Green's words carried particular weight in the bioinformatics community. Trained originally as a mathematician, he had worked on many different aspects of the newly-emerging field of genomics, but it was a series of programs that he wrote in the middle of the 1990s that propelled him to the very forefront of his field—and which put in place the missing piece of the automated sequencing puzzle.

Sanger's dideoxy process allowed any small piece of DNA to be sequenced; his shotgun method provided a way of handling much longer stretches using computers for assembly. The limiting factor then became the speed at which the shorter shotgun fragments could be sequenced. Hood's work in

automating the sequencing process—notably in adopting four different fluorescent dyes for each of DNA's four chemical letters—meant that the raw
sequence data could be produced in great quantities. This shifted the rate-
limiting step to what was known as *base-calling*: deciding which of the four
bases—A, C, G or T—was indicated by the fluorescent bands. As Green noted
in 1996: "Editing (correction of base calls and assembly errors) is at present
one of the most skill-intensive aspects of genome sequencing, and as such is a
bottleneck to increased throughput, a potential source of uneven sequence
quality, and an obstacle to more widespread participation in genomic sequencing by the community. We are working toward the long term goal of completely removing the need for human intervention at this stage, with
short-term goals of improving the accuracy of assembly and base-calling, and
of more precisely delineating sequence regions requiring human review."

Green's solution was a pair of programs, called *Phred* (for *Ph*il's *read* *edi-*
tor) and *Phrap* (*Ph*il's *r*evised *a*ssembly *p*rogram). Phred takes the raw fluorescent output and then decides which bases are represented, assigning each
one a measure of how likely it is to be wrong. This is already useful, since it
flags up the least reliable sections, allowing human intervention to be concentrated where it is most needed. Phred's output can be fed into Phrap, an
assembly program like the TIGR Assembler. It is an intelligent one, though,
that can take into account the differing quality of base calls, rather than simply assuming that they are all correct. As a result, Phrap can make judgments
about which of several possible overlaps is more likely to be correct, leading
to higher-quality assembly and fewer errors.

Green's software allowed human intervention in the sequencing process to
be minimized. This meant that it was possible to run more machines faster,
and for longer, without the need to scale up the human personnel involved—
a critical requirement of the Human Genome Project, since sequencing three
billion base-pairs was necessary. When the possibility of sequencing the
human genome was first discussed back in the 1980s, it was generally
assumed that new sequencing technologies would need to be developed to
address the issue. As it turned out, the old technologies—dating right back
to the use of gels to separate biological molecules in 1954—proved adequate;
the trick was scaling the whole process up to unimagined levels. Hood's
machines together with Green's programs—and ones written by Rodger
Staden, a pioneer in the study of base call quality and in many other areas of
bioinformatics—helped make this possible.

Even before these tools were available, the public project was beginning to
gear up for the final stage of sequencing the human genome. In particular, the
two most experienced sequencers—John Sulston at the Sanger Centre, and
Bob Waterston at the Washington University School of Medicine—were
starting to push for an acceleration of the public genome project.

In his autobiography, Sulston wrote that toward the end of 1994
Waterston did some calculations on what might be possible, and sent what

Sulston called "an indecent proposal." It was a strategy for completing the human genome in even less time than the 15-year period laid down in the timetable at the start of the U.S. public project in 1990. That this was at all conceivable, as Sulston pointed out, was due to the fact that the suggestion "departed from our previous practice in proposing that we should churn out sequence as fast as possible and use automatic assembly and editing procedures to string it together to a reasonable but not absolute standard of accuracy—99.9 per cent rather than 99.99." This was by no means, however, a turning away from the absolutist principles that had hitherto guided them. It was merely a stepping stone toward the final destination. "We could continue the slower process of hand finishing," Sulston explained, but as a separate track alongside the faster sequencing. In this way, they would have the best of both worlds: obtaining the rough sequence more quickly but leading to the full 'gold standard' in due course.

Waterston presented this idea for the first time at a meeting in Reston, Virginia, on December 16, 1994. He explained how the experience gained in sequencing the nematode worm led him and Sulston to believe that it was time to move on to the final phase of the human genome project. He said that his own lab was producing 15,000 runs per week of 400–500 bases each on the automated sequencing machines. He projected that he could scale this up to 84,000 runs, and noted that if three laboratories managed this kind of output it would take just five years to sequence 99 percent of the human genome with 99.9 percent accuracy. Sulston and Waterston made more presentations in early 1995, and in June 1995, *Science* was reporting that "no pistol shot marked the start, but the race to sequence the human genome began in earnest this spring." In October of that year, one of the most respected voices in the genomic community, Maynard Olson, wrote an article entitled simply "A time to sequence" in which he looked back at the progress of the Human Genome Project so far, considering the way forward to the ultimate goal.

As Olson noted: "Many participants in the Human Genome Project, including this author, envisioned the project as a vehicle for developing powerful new sequencing tools that would displace the techniques of the 1980s through a combination of fundamental advances and automation. What has happened instead is arguably a better development for experimental biology. Sequencing methodology has improved incrementally in a way that is leading to convergence, rather than divergence, between the methods employed in 'genome centers' and those used in more typical molecular biology laboratories." Olson concluded grandly, with a striking observation: "While huge, the central task of the Human Genome Project is bounded by one of the most remarkable facts in all of science: The development of a human being is guided by just 750 megabytes of digital information. In vivo, this information is stored as DNA molecules in an egg or sperm cell. In a biologist's personal computer, it could be stored on a single CD-ROM. The Human Genome Project should get on with producing this disk, on time and under budget."

Although Olson called the technological convergence between genomic centers and traditional laboratories "a better development," it contained within it the seed of a change that was to prove unwelcome to many in the field. The genome centers achieved their increasingly impressive sequencing rates by scaling up the whole process. To gain the greatest advantage from this approach, though, it would be necessary to create a few high-throughput centers rather than to support many smaller laboratories where economies of scale would not be so great. These larger centers could push scaling to the limit. This meant that for the Human Genome Project to succeed under this regime, more and more resources would have to be concentrated at fewer centers. The move toward what has been called an "industrialization" of biology was a painful transition for the community in which many fine institutions found their grants becoming static or even being reduced. They also looked on with envy as more money was piled into a few select institutions that were being groomed as sequencing powerhouses.

The first signs of this major shift in policy came in April 1996. The National Human Genome Research Institute (NHGRI), the arm of the NIH responsible for organizing the U.S. project, announced "an unprecedented pilot study to explore the feasibility of large-scale sequencing of human DNA." As well as marking "the transition to the third and most technologically challenging phase of the HGP," the pilot also clearly signaled the appearance of the new elite among the U.S. sequencing labs. The six centers were those under Mark Adams at TIGR; Bob Waterston at Washington University; Maynard Olson at the University of Washington; a team at Stanford University under Richard Myers; one at Baylor College of Medicine under Richard Gibbs; and the Whitehead Institute of Biomedical Research under Eric Lander. In many ways, the most interesting member of this select group is Eric Lander and his team. His appearance here signals the arrival of a deeply gifted and hugely ambitious researcher who had gradually been moving ever closer to the center of the genomic world.

Lander first made many people sit up and take notice when, in December 1992, his group at the Whitehead Institute and MIT won a $24 million grant over five years from the NIH to map both the human and mouse genomes, in collaboration with other laboratories. His first historic contribution to the HGP was in December 1995, when he was one of the lead scientists to put together a physical map of the human genome.

The map had evolved from its original conception as a physical series of overlapping clones—as employed for the nematode worm, for example—to a well-spaced, ordered series of unique genomic landmarks called Sequence-Tagged Sites (STSs), devised a few years before. These landmarks could be used to determine the position of any physical clone, and hence to construct a minimally overlapping set of them, an essential prerequisite for large-scale sequencing projects. Because STSs typically consist of a few hundred base pairs—that is, a string of chemical letters of this length—they are inherently digital. The older kind of physical map, which consisted of clones, was purely analogue. To use the analogue physical map meant shipping pieces of DNA—in test tubes kept fresh on dry ice, for example. But as Maynard Olson, one of the originators of the STS idea, pointed out at the time Lander's work appeared: "This whole map, because it is STS-based, can be put up on the World Wide Web." An accompanying press release from the Whitehead Institute noted that it had already received 53,000 accesses to its STS Web site in just one week.

Equally significant, and certainly indicative of Lander's overall approach, was the fact that the physical map had been achieved using a specially constructed automated robotic system dubbed the Genomatron. Because the NHGRI pilot, for which Lander's team received $26 million over three years, was all about exploring automation and scaling up, it was hardly a surprise that Lander went on to create another robot, this time for sequencing, called the Sequatron. The Whitehead press release on the grant pointed out: "As a result of this robot, Whitehead's 25-member sequencing team is undertaking tasks that compete with 100-member teams at other sequencing centers."

The NHGRI pilot schemes were to run three years, until April 1999. But less than two years into the project, in May 1998, *Science* ran a sobering article entitled "DNA sequencers' trial by fire." In it, the chiefs of the six sequencing centers essentially hung their heads in shame and admitted that it was harder than they thought to scale up to the kinds of speeds and costs that the NHGRI—and the HGP itself—needed. Lander, described as previously being convinced that robots could bring tremendous savings in labor costs, was now quoted as admitting this was "hopelessly optimistic." At least he was not alone. "Our stated goal is 100 megabases [a year] by 1999 or 2000," Mark Adams, Venter's right-hand man at TIGR, told *Science*, adding: "I don't know how we're going to do that." Perhaps not, but he knew someone who did.

The day after the *Science* article appeared, on May 8, 1998, Craig Venter sprung another of his little surprises. This time, though, it was the surprise to end all surprises. He announced that he was not only going to sequence all human DNA using the whole-genome shotgun strategy within three years, and for just a few hundred million dollars, but that he would do it through a new start-up that would make money selling genomic information. Although the new company was initially without a name, the one eventually chosen for it could hardly have been more appropriate. As a press release explained: "The name Celera, [is] derived from the word 'celerity' which means swiftness of motion "—an idea that must have appealed to Venter, a keen and highly competitive yachtsman. The real swiftness lay elsewhere, however. Just in case people failed to grasp the real import of the name, the new company adopted for its motto "Speed matters— discovery can't wait." A distillation, almost, of Venter's entire post-Vietnam life.

NOTES

The author conducted interviews included in this chapter in October 2003 with the following individual: R. Waterston.

1. p. 55   *lackluster academic record*   J.C. Venter, "Forever remembering those on the wall," speech given at the Vietnam Veterans Memorial, November 11, 2000. Originally online at *http://www.thevirtualwall.org/community/ guest_column/column_venter.asp*. Available from *http://www.archive.org*.

2. p. 55   *I was drafted off my surfboard in 1965*   J.C. Venter, "Forever remembering those on the wall," speech given at the Vietnam Veterans Memorial, November 11, 2000. Originally online at *http://www.thevirtualwall.org/ community/guest_column/column_venter.asp*. Available from *http://www. archive.org*.

3. p. 55   *even though I thought the war in Vietnam was wrong*   J.C. Venter, "Forever remembering those on the wall," speech given at the Vietnam Veterans Memorial, November 11, 2000. Originally online at *http://www.thevir tualwall.org/community/guest_column/column_venter.asp*. Available from *http://www.archive.org*.

4. p. 55   *I also learned that I could*   J.C. Venter, "Forever remembering those on the wall," speech given at the Vietnam Veterans Memorial, November 11, 2000. Originally online at *http://www.thevirtualwall.org/community/ guest_column/column_venter.asp*. Available from *http://www.archive.org*.

5. p. 55   *I just so enjoyed the discovery process*   J.C. Venter, Pre-lecture interview at Marine Biological Laboratory. Online at *http://www.mbl.edu/videofiles/ lecture5/transcript-interview.html*.

6. p. 55   *he earned a B.A. in biochemistry*   Smithsonian Institution Archives, "Smallpox virus sequencing." Online at *http://www.si.edu/archives/ihd/ videocatalog/9564.htm*.

7. p. 56   *We went to a meeting for our honeymoon*   R. Lewis, "Exploring the very depths of life," *Rensselaer Mag* (March 2001).

8. p. 56   *An entire decade and considerable*   J.C. Venter, H.O. Smith, and C.M. Fraser, "Microbial Genomics: in the beginning," *ASM News* (May 1999): 65.

9. p. 56   *In 1986 there was a key paper published*   J.C. Venter, Lecture at Marine Biological Laboratory. Online at *http://www.mbl.edu/videofiles/lecture5/ transcript-print.html*.

10. p. 56   *It was in February 1987*   J.C. Venter, Lecture at Marine Biological Laboratory. Online at *http://www.mbl.edu/videofiles/lecture5/transcript- print.html*.

11. p. 56   *We ran into problems*   J.C. Venter, Lecture at Marine Biological Laboratory. Online at *http://www.mbl.edu/videofiles/lecture5/transcript- print.html*.

12. p. 56   *The insight that occurred then*   G. Taubes, "TIGR's J. Craig Venter takes aim at big questions," *ScienceWatch* (September/October 1997).

13. p. 57   *We were stunned at how simple*   G. Taubes, "TIGR's J. Craig Venter takes aim at big questions," *ScienceWatch* (September/October 1997).

14. p. 57 *I wasn't the first* E. Marshall, "The company that genome researchers love to hate," *Science* 266 (1994): 1800–1802.

15. p. 58 *I had good funding for my program* K.Y. Kreeger, "Genome investigator Craig Venter reflects on turbulent past and future ambitions," *The Scientist* 9 (15) (July 24, 1995): 1.

16. p. 58 *Bernadine Healy, then NIH director* K.Y. Kreeger, "Genome investigator Craig Venter reflects on turbulent past and future ambitions," *The Scientist* 9 (15) (July 24, 1995): 1.

17. p. 58 *I was eager to scale up our research program* J.C. Venter, Statement before the subcommittee on energy and environment, U.S. House of Representatives Committee on Science, June 17, 1998. Online at *http://www.house.gov/science/venter_06-17.htm.*

18. p. 59 *I formed TIGR as an independent* J.C. Venter, Statement before the subcommittee on energy and environment, U.S. House of Representatives Committee on Science, June 17, 1998. Online at *http://www.house.gov/science/venter_06-17.htm.*

19. p. 59 *the $70 million, 10-year grant* D. Hamilton, "Venter to leave NIH for greener pastures," *Science* 257 (1992): 151.

20. p. 60 *We chose an exclusive arrangement* E. Licking, "Interview with William Haseltine," *Business Week OnLine*, June 12, 2000. Online at *http://www.businessweek.com/2000/00_24/b3685010.htm.*

21. p. 60 *80 sequencing machines* E. Marshall, "A showdown over gene fragments," *Science* 266 (1994): 208–210.

22. p. 60 *248 different kinds of tissues* E. Marshall, "The company that genome researchers love to hate," *Science* 266 (1994): 1800–1802.

23. p. 60 *By 1994, Haseltine claimed* E. Marshall, "A showdown over gene fragments," *Science* 266 (1994): 208–210.

24. p. 60 *in November 1993* L.M. Fisher, "Profits and ethics clash in research on genetic coding," *The New York Times*, January 30, 1994.

25. p. 60 *As early as 1993* E. Marshall, "Genomics' odd couple," *Science* 275 (1997): 778.

26. p. 60 *with conditions attached* E. Marshall, "A showdown over gene fragments," *Science* 266 (1994): 208–210.

27. p. 61 *300,000 human gene sequences* Merck press release, February 10, 1995.

28. p. 61 *Merck's approach is the most efficient way* Merck press release, February 10, 1995.

29. p. 61 *By this stage* M.D. Adams, et al., "Initial assessment of human gene diversity and expression patterns based upon 52 million basepairs of cDNA sequence," *Nature* 377 supplement (1995): 3–174 .

30. p. 62 *To make this information available* K.Y. Kreeger, "Genome investigator Craig Venter reflects on turbulent past and future ambitions," *The Scientist* 9 (15) (July 24, 1995): 1.

31. p. 63 *You're Craig Venter* D. Birch, "The seduction of a scientist," *The Baltimore Sun*, April 12, 1999.

32. p. 63   *Would you be interested*   D. Birch, "The seduction of a scientist," *The Baltimore Sun*, April, 12 1999.

33. p. 63   *Yeah. I'm very interested*   D. Birch, "The seduction of a scientist," *The Baltimore Sun*, April 12, 1999.

34. p. 63   *At first he suggested that we sequence*   J.C. Venter, Lecture at Marine Biological Laboratory. Online at *http://www.mbl.edu/videofiles/lecture5/transcript-print.html*.

35. p. 64   *In the early 90s*   J.C. Venter, "Whole genome shotgun sequencing." Talk at Conference of the Max Planck Society, Ringberg Castle, October 4–7, 2000. Online at *http://www.mpiwg-berlin.mpg.de/ringberg/Talks/venter/venter.html*.

36. p. 64   *So we hired some mathematicians*   J.C. Venter, Lecture at Marine Biological Laboratory. Online at *http://www.mbl.edu/videofiles/lecture5/transcript-print.html*.

37. p. 65   *Claire and I were sitting around*   J.C. Venter, Lecture at Marine Biological Laboratory. Online at *http://www.mbl.edu/videofiles/lecture5/transcript-print.html*.

38. p. 65   *This was radical in its approach*   D. Birch, "The seduction of a scientist," *The Baltimore Sun*, April 12, 1999.

39. p. 65   *Let's do it*   D. Birch, "The seduction of a scientist," *The Baltimore Sun*, April 12, 1999.

40. p. 65   *Feeling that I survived that year*   K.Y. Kreeger, "Genome investigator Craig Venter reflects on turbulent past and future ambitions," *The Scientist* 9 (15) (July 24, 1995): 1.

41. p. 65   *I want to frame it on the wall*   D. Birch, "The seduction of a scientist," *The Baltimore Sun*, April 12, 1999.

42. p. 65   *We were somewhat skeptical*   J.C. Venter, Lecture at Marine Biological Laboratory. Online at *http://www.mbl.edu/videofiles/lecture5/transcript-print.html*.

43. p. 66   *he also took obvious pleasure*   R. Nowak, "Venter wins sequencing race—twice," *Science* 268 (1995): 1273.

44. p. 66   *a remarkable milestone*   R. Nowak, "Venter wins sequencing race—twice," *Science* 268 (1995): 1273.

45. p. 66   *a significant milestone*   N. Wade, "Bacterium's full gene makeup is decoded," *The New York Times*, May 26, 1995.

46. p. 66   *TIGR had a T-shirt*   J.C. Venter, Lecture at Marine Biological Laboratory. Online at *http://www.mbl.edu/videofiles/lecture5/transcript-print.html*.

47. p. 66   *The computational methods developed*   R.D. Fleischmann, et al., "Whole-genome random sequencing and assembly of *Haemophilus influenzae* Rd," *Science* 269 (1995): 496–512.

48. p. 67   *Lo and behold*   R. Nowak, "Bacterial genome sequence bagged," *Science* 269 (1995): 468–470.

49. p. 67   *People thought*   R. Nowak, "Bacterial genome sequence bagged," *Science* 269 (1995): 468–470.

50. p. 67 *The whole-genome shotgun sequencing* G. Myers, "Whole-genome DNA sequencing," *Computing in Science & Engineering* (May–June 1999): 33–43.

51. p. 68 *Most research laboratories* J.L. Weber and E.W. Myers, "Human whole-genome shotgun sequencing," *Genome Research* 7 (1997): 401–409.

52. p. 68 *true motivation for sequencing* J.L. Weber and E.W. Myers, "Human whole-genome shotgun sequencing," *Genome Research* 7 (1997): 401–409.

53. p. 69 *We requested funding for a pilot project* G. Myers, "Whole-genome DNA sequencing," *Computing in Science & Engineering* (May–June 1999): 33–43

54. p. 69 *Weber's and Myers' argument* P. Green, "Against a whole-genome shotgun," *Genome Research* 7 (1997): 410–417.

55. p. 70 *Editing (correction of base calls and assembly errors)* P. Green, "Toward completely automated sequence assembly," Santa Fe Meeting, 1996. Online at *http://www.ornl.gov/hgmis/publicat/96santa/informat/green.html*

56. p. 71 *an indecent proposal* J. Sulston and G. Ferry, *The Common Thread* (Bantam Press London/New York 2002), 115.

57. p. 71 *departed from our previous practice* J. Sulston and G. Ferry, *The Common Thread* (Bantam Press London/New York 2002), 116.

58. p. 71 *He said that his own lab* E. Marshall, "A strategy for sequencing the genome 5 years early," *Science* 267 (1995): 783–784.

59. p. 71 *no pistol shot marked the start* E. Marshall, "Emphasis turns from mapping to large-scale sequencing," *Science* 268 (1995): 1270–1271.

60. p. 71 *Many participants in the Human Genome Project* M.V. Olson, "A time to sequence," *Science* 270 (1995): 394–396.

61. p. 71 *While huge, the central task* M.V. Olson, "A time to sequence," *Science* 270 (1995): 394–396.

62. p. 72 *an unprecedented pilot study* National Human Genome Research Institute press release, dated April 1996.

63. p. 72 *won a $24 million grant over five years* L. Roberts, "NIH takes new tack on gene mapping," *Science* 258 (1992): 1573.

64. p. 73 *this whole map, because it is STS-based* J. Marx, "A new guide to the human genome," *Science* 270 (1995): 1919–1920.

65. p. 73 *it had already received 53,000* Whitehead Institute press release, December 1995.

66. p. 73 *As a result of this robot* Whitehead Institute press release, April 11, 1996.

67. p. 73 *hopelessly optimistic* E. Pennisi, "DNA sequencers' trial by fire," *Science* 280 (1998): 814–817.

68. p. 73 *The name Celera* Celera Genomics press release, August 5, 1998.

CHAPTER 5

Science versus Business

At the beginning of 1998, Craig Venter was doubtless tiring of sequencing yet another bacterial genome; he and his team had done seven of them by now. In some ways, his pioneering work sequencing *H. influenzae* had already been superseded: in 1996, the yeast consortium published its paper describing the full genome for that organism. Although Venter's bacterium had offered the first glimpse of the software of life, it was rather basic code. Yeast, despite its appearance, is a rich and complex organism. It is a eukaryote, like animals—like humans. The paper emphasized the gulf that separated yeast from mere prokaryotes even in its title: "Life with 6000 genes." *H. influenzae* had less than 2,000 of them.

Venter, however, found himself in no position to compete by taking on some project even more complex than yeast. On June 24, 1997, he had opened up the databases at TIGR, allowing anyone to access all of the data freely. This marked the definitive end of the deal between Venter's science institute and Haseltine's business unit, which meant that Venter would forgo the $38 million that Human Genome Sciences (HGS) was to pay to TIGR over the next five and a half years. Although this freed him from the onerous conditions that he obviously felt cramped him as a scientist, it left him considerably less well off than he might have been otherwise. As he put it: "I just walked away from more money than most scientists have in their whole careers to do research." Venter always loved the grand gesture.

Then, at the beginning of 1998, fate came knocking—and Venter almost refused to open the door. "Celera started under sort of strange terms," he later recalled. "I got a couple of calls from senior management of what was then the Perkin-Elmer Corporation, saying that Mike Hunkapiller developed a new sequencing machine, and by the way, they were thinking of putting up $300 million to sequence the genome . . . was I interested? I thought they were crank calls and I hung up on them. Finally, out of frustration, Mike called me himself and said it was real, that the new instrument was going to be really fantastic, and they were thinking of funding the formation of a company and he thought this would work perfectly with our whole-genome shotgun strategy."

Even though Venter's initial reaction to Hunkapiller was "you've got to be crazy," he agreed to meet and discuss the idea further. Hunkapiller explained: "We spent a few days working through the math and came away thinking maybe it's doable. They went back and redid the calculations, and so did we." Venter, by contrast, claimed that he made up his mind in "about 15 minutes" that it was feasible: "We decided very quickly after seeing this [new sequencing] device that we would form Celera to sequence the human genome."

Venter was lucky—not so much that Hunkapiller had persisted despite Venter's initial rebuffs, but that he had been offered the chance to sequence the human genome at all. Initially, Hunkapiller had someone else in mind for the job. "He actually talked to me about doing something similar," Leroy Hood says. Hood was the clear first choice: a multifaceted scientist, he had not only helped develop the sequencers manufactured by Perkin-Elmer, but had been a tireless advocate of a human genome project since the earliest days. He had also been Hunkapiller's mentor. Despite this compelling pedigree, Hood turned down his former colleague. "If you were going to do this," Hood says, "you had to make a total commitment to the company: I didn't want to do that. I've always been in the delightful position of being an academic who's really done a lot of start-up kind of things, but in the end what I can focus on are long-term things, the future. I didn't want to compromise." His concerns proved characteristically prescient.

Although Hood says that he did not offer any particular suggestions as to who might fit the bill, "it was pretty obvious who [Hunkapiller] would go to next," he notes. "Craig was, I think, a really good candidate in the sense that he'd shown that he could organize a very large-scale operation in The Institute for Genomic Research, and he had the kind of personality that wasn't going to be intimidated by dominant characters in centrally-funded projects." This was important if the scientific aspects were not to be completely subservient to the business concerns.

Even if Hood would have been the most logical choice, it was still highly appropriate that Perkin-Elmer's Applied Biosystems division should team up with Venter. It had been Venter who had received one of the first sequencing machines, back in 1987, and had helped sort out "teething" problems. It had been Venter who had used these machines to obtain thousands of ESTs in the early 1990s, a success which doubtless encouraged many other labs to buy ABI machines. By 1997, the company had sold 6,000 of them. The entire whole-genome shotgun approach developed by Venter depended critically on the availability of high-throughput sequencing technology.

This connection between Celera and ABI was emphasized by the two press releases that Perkin-Elmer issued on May 9, 1998. The first announced the formation of Celera, and made the symbiosis explicit: "The new company's goal is to become the definitive source of genomic and associated medical information that will be used by scientists to develop a better understanding of the biological processes in humans and deliver improved healthcare in the future. Using breakthrough DNA analysis technology being developed by Perkin-Elmer's Applied Biosystems Division, applied to sequencing strategies pioneered by Dr. Venter and others at TIGR, the company will operate a genomics sequencing facility with an expected capacity greater than that of the current combined world output."

The second press release unveiled the machines that would make this possible: "The Perkin-Elmer Corporation announced today that it was nearing the end of development of a breakthrough DNA analysis technology that should enable the generation of sequencing data at an ultra-high throughput level. The Company is designing the 3700 DNA Analyzer to provide the catalyst for a major new genomics initiative."

The key advance of the ABI 3700 was the substitution of the traditional gel slabs, through which DNA sequence fragments moved in parallel lanes, by 96 thin capillary tubes. Venter explained later the key advantages of this approach. "Most of the sequencing up until then had been on slab gels, and we would try to cram as many samples [as possible] into these slab gels, but as they ran down the gels quite often they would get mixed. . . . The switch from slab gels to capillaries, where each DNA was in a small glass tube, . . . totally eliminated that problem. The other major change is the fully automated machine. We have six people that run 300 of these, and they run 24 hours a day, 7 days a week. This is in contrast to the usual situation of having two to three people running one machine. So it changed the cost factors very dramatically."

Less than a month after Celera's launch, a paper in *Science*, written jointly by Venter, Hunkapiller, and several key TIGR people who would soon be joining the start-up, gave more details of the venture. "The new human genome sequencing facility will be located on the TIGR campus in Rockville, Maryland, and will consist of 230 ABI PRISM 3700 DNA sequencers with a combined daily capacity of [approximately] 100 Mbp of raw sequence." That is, Celera aimed to produce 100 million DNA letters daily, roughly the equivalent of the entire nematode genome.

Such a phenomenal throughput would be needed to produce the high level of multiple coverage that the whole-genome shotgun method required. The

Science paper foresaw over 35 million clones (fragments of DNA), ranging in size from 2,000 bases to 150,000, being sequenced at both ends, to produce 70 million sequences. These would then be compared and fitted together in what was to be the greatest jigsaw puzzle in history.

Matching the $70 million spent on the sequencing facility—each ABI 3700 cost $300,000—was another massive investment in high-tech hardware: the world's most powerful civilian computer, surpassed only by Sandia National Laboratories' ASCI Red, used for modeling nuclear explosions. Celera's Compaq system employed 1,200 64-bit Alpha processors, was capable of 1.3 teraflops—1,300 billion mathematical calculations per second—and came with a nominal price tag of $80 million (Celera got a big discount). The running costs of all this hardware were pretty spectacular, too. For the sequencing facility alone, Venter said, "It is a million dollar a year electric bill, mostly for the air-conditioning to cool off the lasers" used to excite the fluorescent dyes as they passed the detectors.

At the time of Celera's launch, Venter estimated that the costs of its human genome project would be "between $200 and $250 million, including the complete computational and laboratory infrastructure to develop the finished sequence and informatics tools to support access to it." The obvious question was: How would Celera make money—and ABI recoup its investment?

Venter himself was acutely aware that Celera straddled two very different worlds. "The scientific community thinks this is just a business project," he said, "and the business community thinks it's just a science project. The reality is, it's both." But this marriage of science and business brought with it an inevitable tension between Venter's personal desire to publish his results and his company's need to make money from its data.

This was a key issue from the start. When Hunkapiller had approached him with the idea, Venter had only been free of the restrictions imposed by HGS on data release for a few months. Ideally, Venter would have liked to sequence the human genome as a scientist working at a public institute, but he realized this was an impossible dream. "Seeing as that the money wasn't likely to come from the government, and that the people who had tied up the government funds wanted to use them for their methods, not my methods, I'm glad I was able to do it in industry. It was much better than not doing it all," he later said.

Nonetheless, after his experiences with HGS, Venter was not about to go back to being in thrall to another commercial outfit. So this time, he tackled this issue of data access head-on: "Once we had sequenced the genome, we weren't going to keep it secret," he explained, and he made this clear to his backers at Perkin-Elmer. They put the ball back in Venter's court, saying to him: "If you want to use a couple of hundred million dollars and sequence the human genome and give it away, come up with a business model that allows you to do that."

How to make money from something that is given away: in a sense, this was to remain the Great Celera Conundrum for Venter. The answer seemed to vary according to whether science or business had the upper hand. In his *Science* article of June 1998, it was clearly the former: "An essential feature of the business plan is that it relies on complete public availability of the sequence data," Venter wrote. He then described a number of areas in which Celera would be active, including contract sequencing, gene discovery, and database services.

He emphasized the open nature of these data. "Because of the importance of this information to the entire biomedical research community, key elements of this database, including primary sequence data, will be made available without use restrictions. In this regard, we will work closely with national DNA repositories such as National Center for Biotechnology Information," which ran GenBank. "We plan to release contig data"—the preliminary assemblies—"into the public domain at least every 3 months and the complete human genome sequence at the end of the project."

On the basis of these promises, some were already writing GenBank off. "The new company's database seems likely to rival or supersede GenBank," was the view of a story in *The New York Times* that announced Celera to the world. Its second paragraph had been even more doubtful about the worth of the public Human Genome Project in the wake of Venter's new company: "If successful, the venture would outstrip and to some extent make redundant the government's $3 billion program to sequence the human genome by 2005"—not least because the article noted that Celera aimed to carry out the project in three years, for $150 to $200 million.

The writer also added that "the $3 billion federal program, by contrast, is now at the halfway point of its 15-year course, and only 3 percent of the genome has been sequenced." This overlooked two things: the huge amount of preliminary work that the Human Genome Project had carried out in mapping and sequencing model organisms, and the fact that the HGP had intentionally planned to leave the bulk of the sequencing until the final phase of the project.

Still, for a powerful media vehicle to paint such an overwhelmingly negative picture of the public efforts was both a personal triumph for the "outsider" Venter, who must have enjoyed inflicting a little discomfort on the officials that had so often thwarted him, and a very real threat to the continued provision of the large-scale funding for the Human Genome Project. After all, if Celera was going to do everything faster and cheaper, and yet put its results into the public domain, who needed a slow and expensive research organization to do the same?

By a stroke of good fortune that was perhaps the counterbalance to Venter's own luck, shortly before Celera's plans became public, and independently of it, the Wellcome Trust in the UK had been considering a massive increase in the funding of the Sanger Centre. Venter's announcement, coupled with the despondency it engendered among the U.S. members of the HGP consortium, encouraged Wellcome to go ahead with its plans to double its grant to the Sanger Centre in order to allow it to take on fully one-third of the entire human genome. There were even indications that it was prepared to go further and fund up to one half of the entire sequencing project at the Sanger Centre.

Despite this boost, many were still calling for HGP's case to be reexamined in the light of Celera. On June 17, 1998, the Subcommittee on Energy and the Environment of the House of Representatives' Committee on Science heard statements from a number of individuals on the grave matter of "The human genome project: how private sector developments affect the government program."

To his credit, Venter vigorously defended the public project. "I have heard from different sources that our new venture indicates that the federally-funded program has been a waste of money," he said in his prepared statement. "I cannot state emphatically enough that our announcement should not be the basis for this claim." Meditating on his favorite theme, he added: "By increasing the speed with which the sequence of the human genome will be obtained, we have not brought any program to completion. We have only helped get everyone to the starting line a little bit sooner."

Francis Collins, head of the HGP project at the NIH, and Ari Patrinos, head of the genome project at the Department of Energy, spent much of their time being conciliatory—they were clearly on the defensive. Only Maynard Olson offered forthright views on the shortcomings of Celera's plans.

Speaking of "the likelihood that [Celera's data] will be of poor quality," Olson went on to make a bold statement. "Specifically, I predict that the proposed technical strategy for sampling the human DNA sequence will encounter catastrophic problems at the stage at which the tens of millions of individual tracts of DNA sequence must be assembled into a composite view of the human genome," foreseeing "over 100,000 'serious' gaps." Venter was more sanguine: "It is likely that several thousand gaps will remain, although we cannot predict with confidence how many unclonable or unsequenceable regions may be encountered."

Given the prevailing pro-Celera mood at the time, Olson's scientific analysis was brave, but largely a restatement of the comments made by his colleague Philip Green. In some ways more original was Olson's analysis of the commercial rather than the technical side. "Perkin-Elmer is adopting, in this venture, an overtly 'biotech' style of operation. . . . As is a hallmark of biotech research, time is of the essence and publicity is a key tool for influencing events. . . . The excitement generated by the well-orchestrated public-relations campaign surrounding the Perkin-Elmer announcement should not disguise that what we have at the moment is neither new technology nor even new scientific activity: what we have is a press release. I believe that I speak for many academic spectators when I say that I look forward to a transition from plans to reality. In short, 'show me the data'."

Fortunately for the public project, the politicians on the committee seemed inclined to accentuate the positive. At the start of the hearing, one member waxed lyrical. "Here we have the possibility, a golden possibility, of a private-public partnership that could result in phenomenal return for science and in phenomenal return for the taxpayer." At the end of the hearing, having had its hopes of a politically neat solution tickled by numerous affirmations on both sides that science and business were not just compatible but complementary, the subcommittee indicated benignly that it was unlikely that Congress would cut funding for the public HGP as a result of Celera's entry.

The Human Genome Project may have escaped cuts this time, but as an experienced administrator, Francis Collins knew that he could hardly continue as if Celera did not exist. Whatever the deeper scientific issues, he understood that from the day of that fateful article in *The New York Times* the public, but above all the media, had before them one of those spectacles they loved best—a contest—and that henceforth he and his colleagues would be judged in part by how they fared in comparison to Venter. As Olson had perceptively noted, "Publicity is the key tool for influencing events," and Collins needed something to shout about.

At that time, it was almost exactly five years since Francis Collins had written his original road map for the HGP: this meant the next five-year plan statement could be used as a platform to launch at least the beginnings of a counterattack on Celera. In October 1998, *Science* published a paper from the massed forces of the HGP administrators. Entitled "New goals for the U.S. Human Genome Project: 1998–2003," it not only promised a "working draft" of the human sequence by the end of 2001, but also the finished version by the end of 2003, two years ahead of the original schedule. The paper itself referred to this as "a highly ambitious, even audacious goal," but the HGP leaders knew that matching Venter's legendary capacity to take risks with an equivalent boldness was the only way they could stay in the publicity race.

Shortly after taking a gamble in this way, Collins had something else to celebrate: the completion of the nematode sequencing project. He made the most of it. In the accompanying press release, he emphasized: "The commitment of these [worm] groups to make their sequence data available to the research community right from the start is admirable." And just in case people missed the significance, Collins added, "It typifies the spirit of the Human Genome Project and is exactly how we plan to operate our sequencing program on the human genome and other model organisms."

The sequencing of the nematode even drew a warm response from *The New York Times*: "Completion of the worm's genome," it wrote, "a 10-year project that was finished on schedule, also reinforces the credibility of the federal human genome project, which is locked in an undeclared race with a formidable new rival, a private enterprise named Celera." This private enterprise, meanwhile, was busily finalizing plans for its own project that would not only "reinforce its credibility," but would also handily trump the achievement of Sulston and Waterston—and provide it with a much-needed test of both its approach and facilities.

"Going straight from microbial to human genome was a very big step," Venter later explained, "because when we set this up we didn't really know for sure that the DNA sequencers would work. We had only seen an engineering prototype. But I had extreme confidence in the capabilities of the engineers and was sure that it would work eventually. The mathematics were a big challenge. We couldn't use the algorithm we had developed at TIGR because it wouldn't work at the scale we needed to do it. So we developed a whole new algorithm for putting the genome together. We decided to try it with the *Drosophila* genome which was the largest genome being attempted."

There were several reasons for choosing the fruit fly *Drosophila melanogaster* as the first test of Celera's approach. First, with around 180 million base pairs, it represented a challenge that was significantly harder than anything tried before using the whole-genome shotgun method, and yet still easier than attempting the human genome immediately. As perhaps the model organism *par excellence*, its genome promised great scientific riches. And finally, Venter must surely have enjoyed the fact that not only would he be sequencing the last and in some ways most important of the Human Genome Project's original model organisms, but he would use it as a demonstration that the Celera model worked.

Venter made his first move as soon as Celera had been announced. "I met Gerry Rubin [head of the public fruit fly sequencing project] at a Cold Spring Harbor meeting where we were first introducing our plan to the human genetics community," he recalled, "and I pulled him out in the hallway and I asked if he would be interested in collaborating with us on the fruit fly genome. I said Harold Varmus (head of the NIH) was pushing us to do another worm, I didn't really want to do a worm. As a neurobiologist, I wanted to do *Drosophila*"—since the fruit fly had a far better developed nervous system than worms. "Was he interested? It took him roughly five seconds to make up his mind. He said he would collaborate with us and I asked him why he decided so quickly. He said the *Drosophila* community would kill him if we sequenced a worm after he turned us down."

Gerald Rubin explained why he had no hesitation. "At this time the publicly-funded effort (to sequence the fruit fly) had only completed about a fifth of the genome and we were eager to speed up our project. . . . By combining our efforts, it seemed likely that we could get the science done better and faster than either group working alone." As a result, "in early 1999, with the full support and encouragement of the NIH and DOE, I signed a Memorandum of Understanding formalizing this collaboration."

In a sense, the *Drosophila* project was the realization of that "golden possibility" of a partnership between science and business that the politicians had been dreaming of back in June 1998. But the reason the partnership proved possible was that Rubin was able to insist on making the sequence freely available. "We agreed that in the end all the data would be made public without restriction," he said, "and we would share credit in the scientific papers that resulted from our work." Since Celera regarded this as a test run, and the fruit fly genome sequence was not critical to its business plans, Venter was able to agree to these terms.

Initially, Rubin recalled, "many colleagues were not enthusiastic about a collaboration with a for-profit company on the genome project, despite the fact that academic researchers develop partnerships with the pharmaceutical and biotechnology industry all the time." But he later reported that it was "both highly successful and enjoyable. Celera honored all the commitments they made to me in this collaboration and they have behaved with the highest standards of integrity and scientific rigor." Venter, too, would later look back on this period with nostalgia: "It turned out to be one of the best collaborations that I have ever participated in science."

In the January 27, 1999 press release announcing the signing of the Memorandum of Understanding, Francis Collins held it up as "an important pilot for the development of a similar partnership effort to obtain the human sequence." He told *Science* at the time that: "active discussions are going on right now on how to put together a memorandum of understanding on the human genome," but noted that there was still "some tension" over the issue of data release. At the same time as making these efforts, he wisely continued to force the pace of the Human Genome Project.

In March 1999, the NIH announced: "Based on experience gained from the pilot projects, an international consortium now predicts they will produce at least 90 percent of the human genome sequence in a 'working draft' form by the spring of 2000"—some 18 months ahead of the schedule announced in October 1998. But just as these pilot projects had marked the emergence of an elite among the academic genomic community, so the new acceleration was bought at the price of winnowing down this group even further, to just five institutions worldwide.

These were the UK Sanger Centre (whose annual funding from the Wellcome Trust was increased to $77 million, up from $57 million), the DOE's Joint Genome Institute, and three NIH-funded research teams, led by Waterston, Gibbs, and Lander. Notably, Lander's group received even more than Waterston's ($34.9 million compared to $33.3 million), signaling the former's continuing ascent in the U.S. sequencing pantheon.

Although this concentration of grants on the institutions with the highest throughput—that is, those which most resembled Celera's sequencing factory approach—disappointed the researchers who were left out, its efficacy in terms of its public impact was proved by a story in *The New York Times* a few days later. In it, commenting on the new timetable that potentially placed the HGP ahead of Celera, an obviously rattled Venter sniffed that it had "nothing to do with reality," and that it was merely "projected cost, projected timetables." This was rather ironic coming from a man who had almost closed down the entire public Human Genome Project with his own projected costs and timetables.

A press release at this time from PE Biosystems, the division of Perkin-Elmer that manufactured its sequencers, puts this spending in an interesting context. PE Biosystems announced at the end of March 1999 that it had received more than 500 orders for the ABI PRISM 3700 unit that had made Celera possible in the first place. Among these were 230 installed at Celera, but also 36 ordered by the Sanger Centre. Confirmation that the race between the HGP and Celera was boosting sales of the new sequencing came later that year, when PE Biosystems announced that it had shipped its 1,000th ABI PRISM 3700—making a total of $300 million in sales in just 18 months.

Against this background, and assuming that the whole-genome approach would work at least in part, Perkin-Elmer could hardly lose. Either Celera succeeded—in which case it ended up with a monopoly on some or all of the human genome—or else the public sequencing centers would be forced to buy large numbers of the new machine to match Celera's efforts. As it happens, it was the latter scenario that played out.

Collins managed to do even better in the publicity race in May 1999; *The New York Times* published a story that made encouraging noises about the HGP purely on the basis of a statement from NIH officials that the publicly-financed effort was "on track to meet its goal of finishing a first draft of the genome" within a year. Fortunately for Venter, his fruit fly collaboration was began to show its worth even before it was fully completed. In part, this was due to an astute campaign waged through a steady stream of press releases. On May 6, 1999, Celera announced that it had begun sequencing the fruit fly. On July 28, it had completed one million sequences—around 500 million base pairs.

By September 9, 1999, Celera announced that it had completed the "sequencing phase" of the *Drosophila* project—it still had to assemble the 1.8 billion base pairs that had resulted. Since the fruit fly genome contains around 180 million bases, this represented what is known as "10X" coverage—each DNA letter was sequenced ten times, on average, in the genome fragments produced by the whole-genome shotgun method. The better the coverage, the fewer the gaps that were likely to result. At this stage, however, it was still not clear how easy that assembly would be. As Venter said: "Sequence assembly is a challenging process," but "we are optimistic about our ability to complete this phase in the near future." He added, with a certain emphasis: "The completion of *Drosophila* will validate the effectiveness of Celera's whole-genome shotgun approach in deciphering complex genomes."

Some were already convinced, judging by an article that appeared in October 1999 in *Nature*, which wrote that thanks to the continuing success in sequencing *Drosophila*, Venter seemed "poised to score a victory over skeptics who predict that shotgun sequencing will not work with large, complex genomes." According to the story, Michael Ashburner, a fruit fly expert and joint head of the European Bioinformatics Institute, was won over: "I'm now fairly convinced the technique works," while Philip Green, the bioinformatics expert who had been so critical of Weber and Myers' whole-genome shotgun approach to the human genome, remained skeptical. "If they get it right in *Drosophila* I'll be impressed, but it will not persuade me that they will succeed in humans," he said.

In the *Nature* piece, Gene Myers, the mathematician heading Celera's bioinformatics group, said that *Drosophila* proved that "we are not being confounded by the repeats"—of which the fruit fly had a significant number. "We are able to identify all the unique stretches of the genome, assemble them and order them without any mistakes." However, in an otherwise upbeat piece in *The New York Times*, Myers noted that while Celera's computer could assemble the *Drosophila* genome in just 12 hours, it would need three months for the human sequence. This was a hint at the enormous difference in scale between the two projects and of the challenges that still lay ahead for Celera.

Despite these technical hurdles, the growing success of the *Drosophila* project meant that more and more people came to believe that Venter would pull off what just 18 months before had seemed impossible: sequencing the human genome using the whole-genome shotgun approach. As a result, the public effort came under increasing pressure once more to collaborate with Celera. Reflecting this new mood, a story in *The New York Times* noted: "The collaboration idea has been prompted by Celera's recent completion of a pilot project, deciphering the genome of the laboratory fruit fly, which seems to validate the company's daring shortcut approach for sequencing the human genome."

A couple of weeks later, an issue of *Nature* saw the publication by the HGP of the first finished sequence of a human chromosome: number 22. While an editorial applauded this achievement, it argued that the fruit fly project had shown the complementary qualities of the rival sequencing approaches and that "hostilities over data release policies should be reexamined" in order to realize the "significant benefits of closer cooperation between Celera and the publicly funded project."

These "hostilities" were not just reexamined at a crucial meeting on December 29, 1999 held at Dulles International Airport, Washington D.C., when representatives from both Celera and the public project met in a final attempt to hammer out an agreement for a formal collaboration; they seem to have been reenacted and reemphasized to a point of total breakdown. The public group had gone prepared to make a major concession: to allow Celera exclusive commercial use of the human genome for six months, or even a year if need be. It turned out, however, that Celera wanted much more.

Details of the meeting would only emerge some months later, but there was a visible shift in Celera's attitude immediately afterwards. On January 10, 2000, Celera issued another of its many press releases, in which it noted, almost incidentally, that the human genome data "will be made freely available to researchers around the world under a non-redistribution agreement." The addition of the words "under a non-redistribution agreement" seemed to confirm the worst suspicions of many in the public consortium that the "complete public availability of the sequence data," as Venter had promised in his *Science* article immediately after the announcement of Celera, would eventually be sacrificed to commercial necessity. Philip Green called this move a "significant departure from previous promises made by Celera."

This move may not have come as a surprise to many, but the main announcement of the press release certainly did—at least to those who managed to read past the extremely skillful presentation of the situation. Under the heading "Celera compiles DNA sequence covering 90 percent of the human genome," the text conveyed to the casual reader the sense that Celera had sequenced 90 percent of the human genome in just four months, beginning on September 9, 1999—the day it finished sequencing the fruit fly. *Nature* spotted the real story. "Celera Genomics Corporation appears to have cut back on its plans to single-handedly complete a high-quality sequence of the human genome," it wrote on January 13, 2000. "The company now says that it intends to achieve the same end by combining lower-quality sequence with data from the international, publicly funded Human Genome Project."

The Celera press release contained some telling figures. "Celera's DNA sequence is from more than 10 million high quality sequences, generated at Celera in the world's largest DNA data factory. The sequence, developed from randomly selected fragments of all human chromosomes, contains over 5.3 billion base pairs"—since each fragment had around 500 DNA letters— "at greater than 99 percent accuracy. The 5.3 billion base pairs represent 2.58 billion base pairs of unique sequence"—that is, if one takes out all the over-lapping regions.

The difference from the fruit fly sequence was striking. There, Celera had produced 1.8 billion bases to cover 180 million unique base pairs—10X coverage. For the human genome, it had 5.3 billion containing 2.58 billion unique base pairs—not even 2X coverage of 3 billion bases. Of course, this was only an interim figure, but according to the *Nature* news item: "Craig Venter . . . said the company plans to stop sequencing the human genome at the '4X' level in June—meaning that four bases of the sequence have been generated for every base of the genome—instead of 10X, as originally planned." To compensate for this greatly reduced coverage, Celera was taking all the data from the Human Genome Project, in what Venter slyly called a "*de facto* collaboration."

One reason why this startling change of plans appears to have been large-ly overlooked was that the general press and the public were too busy cheering on biotech companies as their share prices shot up to want to hear negative statements. As another news story in *Nature* on January 13, 2000 noted, the price of shares in some biotechnology companies had increased "threefold or fourfold within a few weeks." Celera's apparent success in sequencing the human genome, as trumpeted by the January 10 press release, seemed to pro-voke an even greater enthusiasm among investors: "The company's announcement on Monday that it has compiled sequence data from its own and publicly funded efforts covering 90 percent of the human genome sent its stock soaring," *Nature* wrote, "at one point reaching a value of $258, com-pared with $186 the previous Friday." These were shares that had opened at $10.65 (allowing for stock splits) on their first day of trading.

The recent torrent of press releases from parties on both side of the science-business divide certainly fed this investment feeding frenzy. But the *Nature* story suggests another interesting reason for the sudden take-off of biotech stocks. "Analysts say that many of those who have been buying up genomics stocks at such speed seem to be individuals who have already prof-ited from the recent growth in the value of Internet stocks," the journal reported, "and have been attracted to genomics because of the similarities between the two fields."

Celera benefited enormously and directly from the apparently insatiable thirst for genomics stocks, whatever their price. On March 1, 2000, PE

Corporation announced a follow-on public stock offering of 3.8 million shares in Celera Genomics, which it estimated would raise $820 million. But even at an astonishing $225 per share, investors wanted more: on March 3, 2000, PE Corporation announced that it would be allotting a further 570,000 shares, boosting the expected net proceeds to $944 million.

One consequence of this bubble was that the public consortium felt unable to definitively break off talks of collaboration with Celera. A letter had been prepared which detailed the unresolved issues and the unsuccessful efforts of Francis Collins to contact Craig Venter. As Sulston recalled, "for two whole months Craig became mysteriously unable to return phone calls or emails." The letter also gave a deadline for Celera to respond to these overtures if it really wanted to work with the public HGP. The deadline chosen was March 6, 2000. "We felt we could not release the letter until the [share] issue closed, as it might have been seen as an act of deliberate and illegal sabotage," Sulston noted in his memoirs.

The final release of this letter was botched—perhaps due to the inexperience of the scientists leading the Human Genome Project in the subtle world of public relations. The letter was leaked to the press a day before the deadline that had been given; this gave Celera the opportunity to cry foul, which it did to great effect. On March 6, 2000, the day of the deadline, *The Los Angeles Times* wrote: "Tony L. White, chairman and chief executive of PE Corp., the parent company of Celera Genomics, reacted angrily to the letter's release, saying it was a breach of trust that would probably doom prospects for any further discussion of a joint effort"—implying that the breakdown in talks was entirely the fault of the HGP. White also came up with some graphic language for his views. "Sending that letter to the press is slimy," he told the paper.

Reports at the time of what Celera was demanding during the negotiations over a possible collaboration were confused. In *Science*, the quoted terms were that "shared company data may not be redistributed to others or used in a commercial product without Celera's permission," which sounds reasonable enough. *The Los Angeles Times* reported, however, that according to the HGP letter, "Celera bargainers said they needed five years of exclusive rights to give commercial users the data produced by merging the two sides' efforts. They said this had to include not only the data existing at the time of the merger but also any improvements made subsequently by the public researchers"—which sounds totally unreasonable. Whatever took place behind closed doors at Dulles airport, the merger was clearly off once the letter from Francis Collins was published. In some ways, this was probably just as well, since some careful lobbying over the previous year (initiated by Mike Dexter at the Wellcome Trust) to bolster the position of the public Human Genome Project was about to come to fruition with consequences that would have devastated any tie-up.

On March 14, 2000, yet another genomics press release appeared—but with a difference. This one came from The White House; it was a joint statement with the United Kingdom's Prime Minister, Tony Blair. It offered a ringing endorsement of the HGP way: "Raw fundamental data on the human genome, including the human DNA sequence and its variations, should be made freely available to scientists everywhere. Unencumbered access to this information will promote discoveries that will reduce the burden of disease, improve health around the world, and enhance the quality of life for all humankind. Intellectual property protection for gene-based inventions will also play an important role in stimulating the development of important new health care products.

"We applaud the decision by scientists working on the Human Genome Project to release raw fundamental information about the human DNA sequence and its variants rapidly into the public domain, and we commend other scientists around the world to adopt this policy."

The "decision . . . to release raw fundamental information about the human DNA sequence" had been made four years before, at a conference in Bermuda. The conference took place from February 25 to 28, 1996, and was sponsored by the Wellcome Trust. There were two key elements of what came to be called the Bermuda Principles. One was that "sequence assemblies should be released as soon as possible; in some centres, assemblies of greater than 1 Kb [thousand bases] would be released automatically on a daily basis." The other was that "finished annotated sequence should be submitted immediately to the public databases." These were far more stringent than the previous HGP policy, which was that data and resources should be made available no later than six months after they were generated.

The driving force behind these new principles was John Sulston. He and Bob Waterston not only believed passionately in the free release of all DNA data, but had practiced it with great success on the worm sequencing project. It is rather ironic that this high-minded altruism was made possible largely through the generous support of the Wellcome Trust, whose enormous resources were the result of the commercial success of the pharmaceutical giant Burroughs Wellcome.

As Sulston later recalled: "Bob and I were running the session in Bermuda, and I found myself standing there in front of a horseshoe of chairs, making my pitch. I thought it pretty unlikely that everyone would agree; several of those present, who included Craig Venter of TIGR, already had links to commercial organizations and might oppose the idea of giving everything away for nothing." And yet they did: "I was amazed that in the end everyone put their hands up to this," Sulston said. "I had no idea that it was going to go so far."

The same might have been said with justice about the Clinton-Blair state-ment. In the context of the public relations battle between Celera and the HGP, it should have been a masterstroke: explicit backing for open data access by two of the most powerful politicians in the world. But the over-heated stock market had already responded negatively to the news that the debated public-private collaboration would not go ahead. The sudden—if coincidental—appearance of the Clinton-Blair statement, coupled with early mistaken reporting that it represented an intent to ban gene patents, caused one of the biggest falls ever in the main NASDAQ index, which reflects U.S. technology stocks. Thirty billion dollars were wiped off the cumulative value of biotech companies.

As a result of this turmoil, the U.S. Patent and Trademark Office felt com-pelled to intervene by issuing its own press release. It stated that "United States patent policy remains unaffected by Tuesday's historic joint statement [by Clinton and Blair]," adding "that genes and genomic inventions that were patentable last week continue to be patentable this week, under the same set of rules."

The Clinton-Blair declaration is one of the emblematic events in the his-tory of genomics, because for that brief media moment, it united many of the currents flowing through the new world of digital biology. A press statement that was about a central issue regarding DNA—access to the underlying data—was misunderstood by journalists keen to play up an area that was becoming of increasing interest to their readers. A stock market that had become carried away by its own genomic fever overreacted to the release, especially in its initial, misreported form. And the reason the biotech business took so badly what was meant to be a statement about the practice of genomic science was that it inflamed what has emerged as the rawest point of contact between the two domains: gene patents.

The battle over gene patents had been brewing for 20 years, since the first patent on a living organism was granted to molecular biologist Ananda Chakrabarty. He had spliced extra DNA into a bacterial genome to create a genetically-modified organism that produced an oil-dissolving enzyme. The courts had decided that this met the requirements for U.S. patents that they have novelty, utility, and be non-obvious.

DNA sequences were also considered artificial products and therefore patentable. It is important to note, however, that in these early days of recom-binant DNA, such sequences generally consisted of actual chains of chemi-cals, not—as was later to be the case—simply the representation of them as a text written in four letters. Before the development of large-scale DNA databases and bioinformatics tools to search through them, such digital code on its own had no value; techniques for isolating a gene and splicing it into a bacterium, on the other had, clearly did, and were non-obvious, at least initially.

The first sign that the situation was changing was when Walter Gilbert announced that his Genome Corporation would not only be sequencing the human genome, but routinely patenting the genes as it found them. This raised the possibility of one company effectively owning the human genome—something that had never presented itself when isolating individual genes was a slow and expensive process. As it turns out, Gilbert's plans never came to fruition, so the legal status of mass patents on genetic data obtained in an industrial fashion was never tested.

In 1991, however, what Gilbert had failed to achieve was finally brought to pass by a relatively unknown researcher named J. Craig Venter. At the time, he was still working for the National Institute of Neurological Disorders and Stroke, and had just developed his new EST strategy for finding genes on an unprecedented scale. It was a technique that, significantly, drew heavily on the DNA databases and powerful tools like BLAST that were missing when gene patents were first awarded. As *Science* reported in October 1991: "While describing his new project to sequence partially every gene active in the human brain, Venter casually mentioned that his employer, the National Institutes of Health, was planning to file patents applications on 1,000 of these sequences a month." Clearly, even in these early days, Venter loved springing little surprises on his colleagues.

An article in *The New York Times* explained what the problem was: "Until now, researchers have applied for patents only after they have determined a gene's role in the body and its potential commercial uses. In a sharp departure from that practice, officials of the National Institutes of Health applied in June for a patent that would cover rights to 340 pieces of genetic code, most of which have yet to be deciphered. Officials said they may soon apply for a second patent that would cover an additional 1,500 sequences." Even though these DNA sequences might be novel and non-obvious, they seemed to fail the utility test for patentability because no one really knew what they did.

James Watson, at that time head of the still very young Human Genome Project at the NIH, called the plan "sheer lunacy," adding that thanks to the new generation of sequencing machines, "virtually any monkey" could do what Venter had done. Comments such as these—even if meant only as off-the-cuff remarks—undoubtedly played a part in motivating Venter in his future audacious plans.

There was, however, a kernel of truth in Watson's words. More or less anyone with the same technology could produce thousands of such ESTs. If NIH's patents were allowed, there was a real danger of a mad race for patents, as Watson pointed out to *Science*: "If Craig can do it, so can the UK." This, in its turn, would have serious consequences, as *The New York Times* noted:

"Scientists fear that such a race could cripple international collaboration in mapping the genome because scientists would not share techniques, and could stifle commercial research because companies that uncovered the role of a particular gene could be forced to pay royalties to those that had merely isolated it."

There was a political dimension to this, though, and Venter found himself something of a pawn in a larger game. The new head of the NIH, Bernadine Healy, was keen to commercially exploit the research carried out there. A story in *Science* explained that Watson was offended because "Reid Adler, the director of technology transfer at NIH, filed the application [for the EST patents]—presumably with Healy's blessing—without bothering to inform him, even though it had major ramifications for the Genome Project." Healy, for her part, was "enraged when Watson began denouncing the plan as idiotic and destructive to the project, the biotech industry, and international relations."

Watson found himself accused of conflicts of interests (discussed in Chapter 3) and resigned, while Healy herself left in 1993. This allowed the issue of EST patenting to be resolved, at least as far as the NIH was concerned. *Science* later reported: "In 1993, the PTO [U.S. Patent and Trademark Office] rejected NIH's application in a preliminary ruling, largely because NIH had not explained how the gene fragments, whose biological function was unknown, would be used commercially. Harold Varmus, who became director of NIH in 1993—and who had come under pressure to abandon the claim—decided not to appeal." But even if the NIH had managed to extricate itself from a tricky situation, the gene patent problem remained.

Once again, it was Venter who found himself at the epicenter of the next EST earthquake. The funding of his new institute TIGR was in return for granting exclusive commercial rights to the company Human Genome Sciences under William Haseltine. As the previous chapter described, however, there were tensions between Venter and Haseltine almost immediately—and it was issues of data access and gene patents that formed the bones of contention.

H GS was not alone in applying for patents on large numbers of ESTs. Incyte Genomics started in 1991 as a company specializing in blood cell proteins, but it soon broadened its scope. As its annual report for the year ending 1996 explained: "The Company engages in the high-throughput automated sequencing of genes derived from tissue samples followed by the computer-aided analysis of each gene sequence to identify similarities, or homologies, to genes of known function in order to predict the biological function of newly identified sequences." Incyte then used the information gleaned from these homology searches in order "to file patent applications on what it believes to be novel full-length cDNA sequences and partial sequences obtained through the Company's high-throughput computer-aided gene sequencing efforts."

Although it was not clear whether the U.S. PTO would grant these patents (given their dubious utility), there were widespread fears in the genomic community that large numbers of human genes could be locked up in patent portfolios. And it was not just researchers who were concerned: the big pharmaceutical companies that had not signed up for one of the early exclusive deals with a genomic company to supply gene sequences—as SmithKline Beecham had with HGS—viewed the prospect of having to pay royalties for using basic genomic information with alarm.

It was partly for this reason that Merck decided to create its Merck Gene Index in September 1994. By placing in the public domain the many hundreds of thousands of ESTs that people like Bob Waterston obtained with Merck funding, the pharmaceutical giant could limit the competitive advantage that rivals like SmithKline Beecham derived from their deals. With a collection of key DNA sequences freely available, Merck not only gained access to that information, but it made it much harder for anyone to apply for patents. Although counterintuitive, Merck's bankrolling of the open database was a shrewd move.

The Merck Gene Index may have limited the scale of the damage that EST patents might cause the pharmaceutical industry, but it did not help resolve the outstanding question about the general patentability of ESTs—or stem the flood of EST patent applications. The U.S. PTO did address the latter problem with a minor technical fix: at the end of 1996, a ruling was issued that no patent application could contain more than 10 DNA sequences. Until then, companies had routinely included large numbers in a single application. Other measures were taken by the leaders of the genomics community. For example, when the NHGRI launched its pilot study of large-scale sequencing in 1996, it stated that "NHGRI is discouraging pilot project scientists from seeking patents on the raw genomic sequence. The scientists are free to apply for patents if they have done additional biological experiments that reveal convincing evidence for utility of the sequence—a standard criterion for patenting."

Meanwhile, to people like John Sulston who believed passionately in the right to access the human genome sequence without intellectual property constraints, the best defense was simply to get DNA sequence into the public domain, so that, "in patent office jargon, as much as possible became 'prior art' and therefore unpatentable by others," as he wrote in his memoirs. This was one of the motivations behind the Bermuda Principles that he helped to craft.

Despite such grassroots activity to preempt gene patents, it was clear that the U.S. PTO still needed to offer more guidance in this new area. It finally did so at the end of 1999, when it published a draft of Utility Examination Guidelines for its examiners in the area of gene patents. Although these were not officially introduced until January 5, 2001, they were effectively in force before that time. The key change was that there were now three criteria for utility: it must be "specific, substantial and credible." This was to catch gene patent applications that tried to meet the utility requirement by claiming that the protein for which the gene coded could be used as an animal feed supplement—regardless of what the protein was. Now, applicants would need to know something more detailed about the gene or EST they were trying to patent.

In March 2000, the head of the HGP, Francis Collins, explained his view of things. "The Patent Office is seeing fewer of what they call 'generation one' patents, where there's just a sequence and no clue as to what it does. PTO intends to reject those. They are seeing a reasonable number of 'generation two' applications, where there's a sequence, and homology suggests a function. NIH views such applications as problematic, since homology often provides only a sketchy view of function. Increasingly, PTO is seeing more in the 'generation three' category, which I think most people would agree is more appropriate for patent protection. These are gene sequences for which you have biochemical, or cell biological, or genetic data describing function."

This may be an overly optimistic assessment of the situation. What is noteworthy about Collins' categories, however, is that they define a suggestive tendency. What might be called 'generation zero' patents—those in the early biotech years—were strictly analogue, and often required extensive biochemical manipulations to produce the molecule in question. By contrast, the 'generation one' patents—just a sequence—which popped up in the early 1990s, are essentially digital entities, pure information written in four chemical letters without any known biochemical function. And as the U.S. PTO Utility Examination Guidelines explain: "A DNA sequence—*i.e.*, the sequence of base pairs making up a DNA molecule—is simply one of the properties of a DNA molecule. Like any descriptive property, a DNA sequence itself is not patentable."

'Generation two' patents that used homology to infer function may be "problematic," but they are also interesting in that they are implicitly moving away from the purely digital DNA sequence and towards the functional manifestation of that sequence. This shift towards the analogue aspect of a sequence, not its information, is even clearer in 'generation three.' Whatever the immediate consequences of the U.S. PTO guidelines, it may well be that this growing distinction between digital and analogue, between the DNA sequence information and the chemical consequences of that sequence—for example, the protein it codes for—will prove increasingly important in helping determine exactly what may or may not be patented when it comes to genomes.

NOTES

The author conducted interviews included in this chapter in May 2003 with the following individual: L. Hood.

1. p. 79 *he and his team had done seven of them* Celera Genomics press release, May 9, 1998.

2. p. 79 *he had opened up* "TIGR terminates relationship, releases data," *Human Genome News* 9 (January 1998): 1–2.

3. p. 79 *Venter would forgo the $38 million* N. Wade, "Team that put genome sequencing on the map splits," *The New York Times*, June 24, 1997.

4. p. 79 *I just walked away from more* G. Taubes, "TIGR's J. Craig Venter takes aim at big questions," *ScienceWatch* (September/October 1997).

5. p. 79 *Celera started under sort of strange terms* J.C. Venter, Lecture at Marine Biological Laboratory. Online at *http://www.mbl.edu/videofiles/lecture5/ transcript-print.html.*

6. p. 80 *You've got to be crazy* N. Wade, "Beyond sequencing of human DNA," *The New York Times*, May 12, 1998.

7. p. 80 *We spent a few days* N. Wade, "Beyond sequencing of human DNA," *The New York Times*, May 12, 1998.

8. p. 80 *about 15 minutes* E. Marshall and E. Pennisi, "Hubris and the human genome," *Science* 280 (1998): 994–995.

9. p. 80 *We decided very quickly after seeing this device* J.C. Venter, Lecture at Marine Biological Laboratory. Online at *http://www.mbl.edu/videofiles/ lecture5/transcript-print.html.*

10. p. 81 *the company had sold 6000 of them* J.C. Venter, Prepared statement before the Subcommittee on Energy and Environment, U.S. House of Representatives, June 17, 1998. Online at *http://www.house.gov/ science/venter_06-17.htm.*

11. p. 81 *The new company's goal is to* Celera Genomics press release, May 9, 1998.

12. p. 81 *Most of the sequencing up until then* J.C. Venter, Lecture at Marine Biological Laboratory. Online at *http://www.mbl.edu/videofiles/ lecture5/transcript-print.html.*

13. p. 81 *The new human genome* J.C. Venter, et al., "Shotgun sequencing of the human genome," *Science* 280 (1998): 1540–1542.

14. p. 82 *1,200 64-bit Alpha processors* E. Marshall, "A high-stake gamble on genome sequencing," *Science* 284 (1999): 1906–1909.

15. p. 82 *It is a million dollar a year* J.C. Venter, Lecture at Marine Biological Laboratory. Online at *http://www.mbl.edu/videofiles/lecture5/ transcript-print.html.*

16. p. 82 *between $200 and $250 million* J.C. Venter, et al., "Shotgun sequencing of the human genome," *Science* 280 (1998): 1540–1542.

17. p. 82 *The scientific community thinks* E. Marshall, "A high-stake gamble on genome sequencing," *Science* 284 (1999): 1906–1909.

18. p. 82 *Seeing as that the money wasn't likely to come* M. Herper, "The DNA of capitalism." Forbes.com, June 26, 2002. Online at *http://www.forbes.com/ 2002/06/26/0626genome.html.*

19. p. 82 *Once we had sequenced the genome* E. Marshall, "A high-stakes gamble on genome sequencing," *Science* 284 (1999): 1906–1909.

20. p. 82 *If you want to use a couple of hundred* E. Marshall, "A high-stakes gamble on genome sequencing," *Science* 284 (1999): 1906–1909.

21. p. 83 *An essential feature of the business plan* J.C. Venter, et al., "Shotgun sequencing of the human genome," *Science* 280 (1998): 1540–1542.

22. p. 83 *The new company's database* N. Wade, "Scientist's plan: map all DNA within 3 years," *The New York Times*, May 10, 1998.

23. p. 84 *I have heard from different sources* J.C. Venter, Prepared statement before the Subcommittee on Energy and Environment, U.S. House of Representatives, June 17, 1998. Online at *http://www.house.gov/ science/venter_06-17.htm.*

24. p. 84 *the likelihood that* M.V. Olson, Prepared statement before the Subcommittee on Energy and Environment, U.S. House of Representatives, June 17, 1998. Online at *http://www.house.gov/ science/olsen_06-17.htm* [sic].

25. p. 84 *It is likely that several thousand gaps* J.C. Venter, et al., "Shotgun sequencing of the human genome," *Science* 280 (1998): 1540–1542.

26. p. 85 *Here we have the possibility* Transcript of Subcommittee on Energy and Environment, U.S. House of Representatives, June 17, 1998. Online at *http://commdocs.house.gov/committees/science/hsy168180.000/ hsy168180_0.htm.*

27. p. 85 *a highly ambitious, even audacious goal* F.S. Collins, et al., "New goals for the U.S. Human Genome Project: 1998–2003," *Science* 282 (1998): 682–689.

28. p. 85 *The commitment of these [worm] groups* NHGRI press release, December 11, 1998.

29. p. 86 *Completion of the worm's genome* N. Wade, "Animal's genetic program decoded, in a science first," *The New York Times*, December 11, 1998.

30. p. 86 *Going straight from microbial* J.C. Venter, "Whole-genome shotgun sequencing." Talk at Conference of the Max Planck Society, Ringberg Castle, October 4–7, 2000. Online at *http://www.mpiwg-berlin. mpg.de/ringberg/Talks/venter/venter.html.*

31. p. 86 *I met Gerry Rubin* J.C. Venter, Lecture at Marine Biological Laboratory. Online at *http://www.mbl.edu/videofiles/lecture5/ transcript-print.html.*

32. p. 87 *At this time the publicly-funded effort* G.M. Rubin, Prepared statement before the Subcommittee on Energy and Environment, U.S. House of Representatives, April 6, 2000. Online at *http://www.house.gov/ science/rubin_040600.htm.*

33. p. 87 *We agreed that in the end* G.M. Rubin, Prepared statement before the Subcommittee on Energy and Environment, U.S. House of

Representatives, April 6, 2000. Online at *http://www.house.gov/science/rubin_040600.htm*.

34. p. 87 *many colleagues were not enthusiastic* G.M. Rubin, Prepared statement before the Subcommittee on Energy and Environment, U.S. House of Representatives, April 6, 2000. Online at *http://www.house.gov/science/rubin_040600.htm*.

35. p. 87 *It turned out to be one* J.C. Venter, Lecture at Marine Biological Laboratory. Online at *http://www.mbl.edu/videofiles/lecture5/transcript-print.html*.

36. p. 87 *an important pilot* Berkeley Drosophila Genome Project press release, January 27, 1999. Available online at *http://www.fruitfly.org/about/news/celera.html*.

37. p. 87 *active discussions are going on right* E. Pennisi, "Fruit fly researchers sign pact with Celera," *Science* 283 (1999): 767.

38. p. 87 *Based on experience gained from the pilot projects* NIH press release, March 15, 1999.

39. p. 88 *Lander's group received* E. Pennisi, "Academic sequencers challenge Celera in a sprint to the finish," *Science* 283 (1999): 1822–1823.

40. p. 88 *nothing to do with reality* N. Wade, "One of 2 teams in genome-map race sets an earlier deadline," *The New York Times*, March 16, 1999.

41. p. 88 *PE Biosystems announced at the end of March* PE Biosystems press release, March 25, 1999.

42. p. 88 *PE Biosystems announced that it had shipped* PE Biosystems press release, November 30, 1999.

43. p. 88 *on track to meet its goal* N. Wade, "Decoding of human genome likely to be finished soon," *The New York Times*, May 22, 1999.

44. p. 88 *Celera announced that it had begun* Celera Genomics press release, May 6, 1999.

45. p. 89 *it had completed one million sequences* Celera Genomics press release, July 28, 1999.

46. p. 89 *it had completed the "sequencing phase"* Celera Genomics press release, September 9, 1999.

47. p. 89 *Sequence assembly is a challenging process* Celera Genomics press release, September 9, 1999.

48. p. 89 *poised to score a victory* D. Butler, "Venter's *Drosophila* 'success' set to boost human genome efforts," *Nature* 401 (1999): 729–730.

49. p. 89 *Myers noted that while Celera's computer* N. Wade, "Rivals reach milestones in genome race," *The New York Times*, October 26, 1999.

50. p. 90 *The collaboration idea has been* N. Wade, "Talk of collaboration on decoding of the genome," *The New York Times*, November 14, 1999.

51. p. 90 *hostilities over data release policies* Editorial, "Human chromosome 22 and the virtues of collaboration," *Nature* 402 (1999): 445.

52. p. 90 *at a crucial meeting on December 29, 1999* P.G. Gosselin and P. Jacobs, "Rush to crack genetic code breeds trouble," *The Los Angeles Times*, March 6, 2000.

53. p. 90   *The public group had gone prepared*   P.G. Gosselin and P. Jacobs, "Rush to crack genetic code breeds trouble," *The Los Angeles Times*, March 6, 2000.

54. p. 90   *will be made freely available*   Celera Genomics press release, January 10, 2000.

55. p. 90   *significant departure from previous promises made by Celera*   D. Butler and P. Smaglik, "Celera genome licensing terms spark concerns over 'monopoly'," *Nature* 403 (2000): 231.

56. p. 90   *Celera compiles DNA sequence covering 90 percent*   Celera Genomics press release, January 10, 2000.

57. p. 90   *Celera Genomics Corporation appears*   P. Smaglik and D. Butler, "Celera turns to public genome data to speed up endgame . . . ," *Nature* 403 (2000): 119.

58. p. 91   *Celera's DNA sequence is from more*   Celera Genomics press release, January 10, 2000.

59. p. 91   *Craig Venter . . . said the company plans*   P. Smaglik and D. Butler, "Celera turns to public genome data to speed up endgame . . . ," *Nature* 403 (2000): 119.

60. p. 91   de facto *collaboration*   P. Smaglik and D. Butler, "Celera turns to public genome data to speed up endgame . . . ," *Nature* 403 (2000): 119.

61. p. 91   *threefold or fourfold within weeks*   D. Dickson, ". . . as Internet fervour hits genomics," *Nature* 403 (2000): 119–120.

62. p. 91   *The company's announcement on Monday*   D. Dickson, ". . . as Internet fervour hits genomics," *Nature* 403 (2000): 119–120.

63. p. 91   *Analysts say that many of those*   D. Dickson, ". . . as Internet fervour hits genomics," *Nature* 403 (2000): 119–120.

64. p. 92   *PE Corporation announced a follow-on*   Celera Genomics press release, March 1, 2000.

65. p. 92   *on March 3, 2000*   Celera Genomics press release, March 3, 2000.

66. p. 92   *A letter had been prepared*   J. Sulston and G. Ferry, *The Common Thread* (London/New York: Bantam Press, 2002), 216.

67. p. 92   *for two whole months Craig*   J. Sulston and G. Ferry, *The Common Thread* (London/New York: Bantam Press, 2002), 216.

68. p. 92   *We felt we could not release*   J. Sulston and G. Ferry, *The Common Thread* (London/New York: Bantam Press, 2002), 217.

69. p. 92   *The letter was leaked to the press*   J. Sulston and G. Ferry, *The Common Thread* (London/New York: Bantam Press, 2002), 217.

70. p. 92   *Tony L. White, chairman and chief*   P.G. Gosselin and P. Jacobs, "Rush to crack genetic code breeds trouble," *The Los Angeles Times*, March 6, 2000.

71. p. 92   *shared company data may not*   E. Marshall, "Talks of public-private deal end in acrimony," *Science* 287 (2000): 1723–1725.

72. p. 92   *Celera bargainers said they needed*   P.G. Gosselin and P. Jacobs, "Rush to crack genetic code breeds trouble," *The Los Angeles Times*, March 6, 2000.

73. p. 92 *some careful lobbying* J. Sulston and G. Ferry, *The Common Thread* (London/New York: Bantam Press, 2002), 219.

74. p. 93 *Raw fundamental data on the human genome* The White House press release, March 14, 2000.

75. p. 93 *sequence assemblies should be released* Summary of principles agreed at the International Strategy Meeting on Human genome sequencing, February 25–28, 1996. Online at *http://www.gene.ucl.ac.uk/hugo/bermuda.htm.*

76. p. 93 *Bob and I were running the session* J. Sulston and G. Ferry, *The Common Thread* (London/New York: Bantam Press, 2002), 145.

77. p. 94 *United States patent policy* U.S. PTO press release, March 16, 2000.

78. p. 94 *since the first patent on a living organism* E. Marshall, "Intellectual property: companies rush to patent DNA," *Science* 275 (1997): 780–781.

79. p. 95 *While describing his new project* L. Roberts, "Genome patent fight erupts," *Science* 254 (1991): 184–186.

80. p. 95 *Until now, researchers have applied* E.L. Andrews, "U.S. seeks patent on genetic codes, setting off furor," *The New York Times*, October 21, 1991.

81. p. 95 *sheer lunacy* L. Roberts, "Genome patent fight erupts," *Science* 254 (1991): 184–186.

82. p. 96 *Scientists fear that such a race* E.L. Andrews, "U.S. seeks patent on genetic codes, setting off furor," *The New York Times*, October 21, 1991.

83. p. 96 *Reid Adler, the director of technology transfer at NIH* L. Roberts, "Why Watson quit as project head," *Science* 256 (1992): 301–302.

84. p. 96 *enraged when Watson began denouncing* L. Roberts, "Why Watson quit as project head," *Science* 256 (1992): 301–302.

85. p. 96 *In 1993, the PTO* E. Marshall, "Intellectual property: companies rush to patent DNA," *Science* 275 (1997): 780–781.

86. p. 97 *to file patent applications* Incyte annual report, 1996.

87. p. 97 *at the end of 1996, a ruling* E. Marshall, "Intellectual property: companies rush to patent DNA," *Science* 275 (1997): 780–781.

88. p. 97 *NHGRI is discouraging pilot project scientists* NHGRI press release, April 1996.

89. p. 97 *in patent office jargon, as much as possible* J. Sulston and G. Ferry, *The Common Thread* (London/New York: Bantam Press, 2002), 269.

90. p. 98 *specific, substantial and credible* United States Patent and Trademark Office, Utility Examination Guidelines, online at *http://www.uspto.gov/web/offices/com/sol/notices/utilexmguide.pdf.*

91. p. 98 *The Patent Office is seeing fewer* "In the crossfire: Collins on genomes, patents and 'rivalry'," *Science* 287 (2000): 2396–2398.

CHAPTER 6

Showing the Data

On April 6, 2000, the Energy and Environment Subcommittee of the U.S. House of Representatives Committee on Science heard testimony from a number of witnesses, including Gerald Rubin, the head of the *Drosophila* sequencing project, Bob Waterston, and Craig Venter. Under discussion was the Human Genome Project in general, but gene patents were also on the agenda. The opening statement of the chairman made clear what had prompted the legislators' interest:

> *This Committee has always encouraged the government to take a role in high-risk basic research and then transfer the fruits of that knowledge to the private sector where they can be developed and brought to market. This model worked splendidly with the Internet and appeared to be working quite well in the nascent field of biotechnology until the morning of March 14th. CBS News, quoting the White House Spokesperson, stated that the President would announce a ban on gene patents later that day. This unexpected and unprecedented announcement sent biotech stocks into a $30 billion tailspin.*

Craig Venter clearly relished the opportunity to testify again. He lost no time revisiting the previous occasion: "One of the witnesses on that day said, 'show me the data!' He predicted we would fail—fail 'catastrophically.' He was wrong—and I am happy to again show the Subcommittee and the world the data." The data to which he was referring were the complete genome sequence of the *Drosophila*, published as part of a series of articles in the March 24, 2000 issue of *Science*. The fruit fly was on the cover. In addition to the main feature describing the fruit fly genome, there was a separate article, with Gene Myers as the lead author, that described the whole-genome shotgun process in loving detail. One paper looked at the comparison of the *Drosophila* genome with those of the nematode worm, yeast, and humans, while others considered various aspects of the fruit fly research community.

Entitled "Flying to new heights," *Science*'s editorial gushed: "Even the most cynical spectator of the genome races will be inspired by the accomplishments presented in this special issue." It was particularly impressed by the bioinformatics results: "The similarities between *Drosophila* genes and genes involved in human physiological processes"—how the body works—"and disease are staggering." It also had some comments on the whole-genome shotgun approach, which, it noted, "was met with serious skepticism and indeed declared unfeasible given the large genome size and the number of repetitive regions, which would preclude an accurate reassembly. Although there are certain to be debates over the definition of completeness it is clear that the approach will be viable for the mammalian genomic efforts that are now well along."

With this kind of panegyric ringing in his ears, no wonder Venter was feeling good during his testimony a couple of weeks later. He was probably pleased for another reason, too. For Venter, the second advantage of the HGP's commitment to placing all of its raw data in the main databanks—the first being that Celera could combine it with its own to improve its overall coverage—was that he had a very good idea of how things were going in the public project.

"On Monday it was reported in *Time* magazine that the public effort was 'done' and that the race to complete the genome sequence was over," he told the subcommittee. "I have read that Dr. Collins said that the draft human genome sequence they are about to announce has only a few gaps and is 99.9 percent accurate. However, analysis of the public data in GenBank reveals that it is an unordered collection of over 500,000 fragments of average size 8,000 base pairs. This means that the publicly funded program is nowhere close to being 'done'." From what Venter could see in GenBank, the public consortium's data were even more fragmented than his own, and it looked like Celera's imminent assembled sequence would not only be first—it would be the only one.

But Eric Lander, who would be the lead author of the paper on the Human Genome Project's sequence when it was eventually published, says that things were not as bad as they seemed. In a way, the HGP had already done the hard part by virtue of the sequencing method it had adopted. This was essentially the same as that employed for the nematode. First, the genome was split up into fragments, which were copied in the form of BAC clones. "BAC" (bacterial artificial chromosome) simply refers to the copying method. A set of BAC clones, or BACs as they are generally known, was chosen so that the whole genome was covered by the fragments they contained. Each was sequenced using the shotgun method to produce several hundred short fragments, and these were assembled into larger contiguous sequences for each BAC.

"The truth was that because you have the individual BACs," Lander tells me, "the genome was in some sense already assembled at the level of the BACs" because it was known where they were in the whole genome. "It was just a question of pasting them together." Actually, there was a little more to it than that: "Because the BACs aren't finished—they each consist of maybe 20 chunks—what you have to do is figure out how to connect the chunks to each other," Lander explains.

The person who began this task was the bioinformatics expert, David Haussler, at the University of California at Santa Cruz. He had been asked by Lander to help find genes in the sequence; he decided he needed a full assembly to do so. Haussler set to work creating a program to sort through and assemble the 400,000 sequences grouped into 30,000 BACs that had been produced by the laboratories of the HGP. But in May 2000, when one of his graduate students, Jim Kent, inquired how the programming was going, Haussler had to admit: "Jim, it's looking grim." Kent had been a profession-al programmer before turning to research. His experience in writing code against deadlines, coupled with a strongly-held belief that the human genome should be freely available, led him to volunteer to create the assembly pro-gram in short order.

He later explained why he took on this task: "I needed it for my research. David Haussler needed it for his research. Bob Waterston needed it for his research. Pretty much everyone needed it. There was not a heck of a lot that the Human Genome Project could say about the genome that was more informative than 'it's got a lot of As, Cs, Gs, and Ts' without an assembly. We were afraid that if we couldn't say anything informative, and thereby demon-strate 'prior art,' much of the human genome would end up tied up in patents by Celera and their subscribers." The raw sequence on its own was probably insufficient to undermine patent applications; what was needed was annota-tion, too—and this required an assembly.

Kent set to work creating what became the GigAssembler program. "Jim in four weeks created the GigAssembler by working night and day," Haussler explained. Like the program that Celera was using around the same time to piece together the human genome, GigAssembler takes the sequence frag-ments, along with auxiliary information such as ESTs that can help put the pieces together in the right order, to create the best overall fit. Kent called this the Golden Path. And like Celera, Kent had some serious hardware: "100 800 MHz Pentium processors with 256 Mbyte RAM," he later recalled.

By June 22, 2000, Kent had completed his first assembly of the human genome. Celera finished its own first version three days later. This means that despite finding himself playing David to Celera's computational and analytical Goliath, it was Kent who was the first to make visible—and presumably see—the human genome, or at least 70 percent of it. The HGP was still working on producing additional sequence fragments to cover more of the genome. In retrospect, it is fitting that the first large-scale assembly of the human DNA sequence was achieved at the University of California at Santa Cruz, the place where the seed of the idea was first planted by Robert Sinsheimer back in 1985.

Lander emphasizes that it was not all coincidental that Jim Kent finished around the same time as Celera: they were both working with the same deadline. "If the deadline had been two months later," he explains to me, "Jim would have kept writing and finished something two days before that deadline. You've got to remember that you use every available moment" to produce the best result possible. In fact, even without Kent's sterling effort, "there would easily have been a solution," Lander notes, "not as good as Jim's program, but a solution."

The deadline had emerged following secret negotiations between Francis Collins and Craig Venter to arrange a joint announcement on the human genome. The matchmaker was Ari Patrinos, who was in charge of the Department of Energy's sequencing team. Collins later explained: "When I called him up in late April and said, can we try this [meeting], he was quick to say, yes, let's give it a shot, and put together that first discussion," which took place on May 7. There were three further meetings, all at the house of Ari Patrinos. Collins pointed out two key ingredients at these meetings: "He served beer and pizza, which was an important part of the good outcome here."

This "good outcome" was not only an agreement to announce what was formally termed "the completion of the first survey of the entire human genome." It was one that would take place in The White House under the aegis of President Clinton and with the virtual presence of the British Prime Minister by satellite. The date chosen, June 26, had nothing to do with the respective state of the genome assemblies: according to John Sulston, it was picked "because it was a day that happened to be free in both Bill Clinton's and Tony Blair's diaries."

It had been largely political pressure that had finally brought the two rivals together; the continued bickering between the public project and Celera was threatening to become something of a blot on the record of public science. Leaving aside the fact that the White House had manufactured an occasion that was otherwise an arbitrary moment, though, it was highly appropriate that the race between the two sides should officially end in this manner.

This race—a race in public relations terms rather than scientific ones—had begun, as Maynard Olson pointed out, with a press release announcing the formation of Celera. It had continued with a barrage of further press releases, as each side tried to gain advantage by putting its own achievements in the best possible light. It culminated in a recent press statement, from Clinton and Blair themselves, that had nearly brought the entire biotech industry to its knees. So it was fitting that this first era of "science by press release" should reach its conclusion in "science by press conference."

As might have been expected given these origins, the speeches were full of platitudes. Clinton spoke of the human genome as "the most important, most wondrous map ever produced by humankind," and how, through it, we were "learning the language in which God created life." There were also pious hopes: "I am so pleased to announce that from this moment forward, the robust and healthy competition that has led us to this day and that always is essential to the progress of science, will be coupled with enhanced public-private cooperation." At least Clinton tried to moderate expectations as to what might flow from the announcement, he noted that "today's historic achievement" was "only a starting point."

But it was not even that. What was being celebrated that day was the triumph of appearance over substance. The HGP had managed to assemble 82 percent of the human genome as a "draft sequence," which, as Venter pointed out, was "a term introduced by the public effort but without scientific meaning." Celera, on the other hand, was announcing "a first assembly" of the human genome. But since its sequence was not deposited in any public database, there was no way of telling exactly what that meant or how good it was. As Maynard Olson might have said once again: "Show me the data."

Venter, of course, had no illusions about what remained to be done. "This is an exciting stage," he said at a press conference after The White House announcement. "It's far from being the end-stage. . . . In fact, annotating this, characterizing the genes, characterizing the information, while that's, in reality, going to take most of this century we plan to make a very significant start on that between now and later this year, when Francis and I agreed to have the two teams try to simultaneously publish the results of the different efforts. At that stage, they'll be really able to be compared in detail." This joint "showing of the data" was perhaps the most concrete achievement of the agreement brokered by Patrinos. It would not only allow the different results to be compared; it would also permit a joint victory to be declared with a certain plausibility. Getting to this simultaneous publication, however, was no simple matter.

To begin with, there was the technical issue of annotating the genome sequences each group had obtained. In the middle of 2000, what both had was, as Kent had memorably put it, "a lot of As, Cs, Gs, and Ts"—that is, a vast quantity of data and not much information. Annotation consists of sifting through the three billion DNA letters and elucidating some of the structures they contain, starting with the genes. This is akin to reading a computer printout of unknown software, written in a programming language whose rules are only partially known, and trying to discern which parts are just comments or spacing to make the layout look tidy and which parts are the subroutines that code for specific functions.

There are three main ways of doing this. The first involves looking for characteristic elements that generally signal the presence of a gene; this is equivalent to looking for keywords in a computer program that are commonly used in functional units. Another takes longer sequences of code in order to find stretches that have a certain kind of distinctive "feel." This corresponds to parts of a program that might contain an above-average number of brackets, for example, reflecting the way that the subunits that actually do something are written, in contrast to the comments, which are more "Englishlike." Finally, there is the technique of comparing raw sequence with holdings in databases like GenBank. Like a skillful programmer, Nature tends to reuse its code, slightly modified if necessary, rather than start from scratch in each species. This is logical: if you have a piece of software that is debugged and works, it is generally more sensible to try to adapt it slightly for a related function than to throw it out and begin again.

All of these techniques lend themselves to automation. Because DNA can be represented as a text written in four letters (and proteins one written in twenty), given fast enough hardware it is easy to compare even entire genomes against vast databases like GenBank. One of the advantages of this approach is that it gets better all the time simply by virtue of the increasing size of GenBank. It means that there are more annotated sequences against which to compare, with a greater likelihood of catching genes in the new sequence. It is also relatively straightforward to search through these texts for particular structures or distributions that indicate the presence of genes.

For this reason, people started writing gene-finding software almost as soon as there were sequences to which it could be applied. Pioneers in the early 1980s include Rodger Staden, who was also working on shotgun assembly programs at the time, and a group under Andrzej Ehrenfeucht at the University of Colorado. Ehrenfeucht was a colleague of another mathematician interested in the structures of DNA sequences, Stan Ulam, and also the mentor of David Haussler and Gene Myers, who studied together at Colorado. There is a certain symmetry in their ending up on opposite teams of the human genome race—Myers employed by Celera, and Haussler a leading member of the HGP analysis team.

One of the most famous later attempts to automate gene-finding by computer was GRAIL, published in 1991. Ten years later, a whole host of other programs, with names like GeneFinder, Genie, GenScan, Genview, Glimmer, HMMgene, and MZEF, were available to the annotators of the human genome, and able to tease a surprising quantity of information from the apparently formless sequences of DNA letters. In addition, Celera developed a tool called Otto, an attempt to "simulate in software the process that a human annotator uses to identify a gene and refine its structure."

Once putative genes had been found, together with their likely homologies and functions, researchers need a way of making this information available in the most useful way. The model here was AceDB, the software used for storing information about the nematode worm. It had acquired a graphical interface that allowed researchers to explore visually the various kinds of information that were held on the database. One of the people who built on this approach for the human genome was the indefatigable Jim Kent. He wrote a piece of software that allows tracks of genomic information—genes, ESTs, STSs, etc.—to be displayed at the appropriate point as a kind of overlay to the linear DNA sequence. Users could zoom out to get the bigger picture or move in closer to examine the details. Suggestively, this kind of software came to be known as a genome browser, making a clear analogy with Web browsers that allowed navigation through another, more complex informational space. A similar tool was produced by the Sanger Centre and the nearby European Bioinformatics Institute. Appropriately enough for a collaboration, their browser is called Ensembl; it adopts a similar approach of displaying tracks of information anchored at various points along the underlying DNA sequence.

The second issue that needed to be addressed to achieve simultaneous publication—alongside the primary one of completing a preliminary annotation—was accommodating the wishes of both groups in terms of choosing a journal. The obvious choice was *Science*: this had seen the unveiling of the *E. coli*, nematode and *Drosophila* genomes, and was effectively the "house journal" of the U.S. genomics community.

A leading authority on the fruit fly and its genome, Michael Ashburner was joint head of the European Bioinformatics Institute on the Wellcome Trust Genome Campus. He had also been a member of *Science*'s Board of Reviewing editors. This seems to have given him some inside knowledge as to the publishing plans of Celera. For on December 6, 2000, Ashburner sent an urgent email to the members of the Board of Reviewing editors, informing them that Celera was indeed hoping to publish its human genome paper in *Science*, and warning about the rather particular terms under which it was intending to do so. "The editorial staff of *Science* has, I understand, agreed to Celera's request that their paper be published without there being the usual submission of the sequence data to GenBank," Ashburner wrote. "Rather, *Science* and Celera have negotiated a form of public release of the data which falls far short of submission to the public databases." Instead, Celera would be allowed to "publish" the data on its own Web site.

Ashburner then went on to explain why this was problematic: "Let us imagine that I have just sequenced a new cDNA from flies and now wish to compare this sequence with all others known in the public domain. Today what do I do? I go to a single site (and there are several such sites) which offers a service to compare my sequence with all of the others known (e.g. with BLAST). . . . following the establishment of the Celera site, what I will have to do is to do a BLAST on _both_ a public site (e.g. at the NCBI AND at Celera). Otherwise I cannot guarantee having searched all of the available data." As a result, he continued, "the data will fragment across many sites and today's ease of searching will have gone, and gone forever. Science will be the MUCH poorer, and progress in this field will inevitably be delayed. Surely that cannot be an objective of *Science*?"

Ashburner's criticisms were sufficient to call forth a response from *Science*, which attempted to justify its special case: "Although traditionally publication of sequence data has been taken to require deposition in GenBank or one of the other centers of the International Nucleotide Sequence Database Collaboration"—at the European Molecular Biology Laboratory or the DNA Database of Japan—"our Information to Contributors has never stipulated a particular database." But as two leading researchers in the bioinformatics field, Sean Eddy of Washington University and Ewan Birney of the European Bioinformatics Institute, pointed out in "An open letter to the bioinformatics community," "this is a conveniently revisionist view of their own policy."

"Our view," they wrote, "is simply that the genome community has established a clear principle that published genome data must be deposited in the international databases, that bioinformatics is fueled by this principle, and that *Science* therefore threatens to set a precedent that undermines bioinformatics research." They then went on to give a concrete example of how things have worked from the very earliest days: "A classic example of how our field began to have an impact on molecular biology was Russ Doolittle's discovery of a significant sequence similarity between a viral oncogene"—a gene in a virus that can cause cancer—"and a cellular growth factor. Russ could not have found that result if he did not have an aggregate database of previously published sequences."

Their letter also contained an interesting possible explanation by Eddy and Birney of why *Science* was taking this approach: "*Science* believes that the deal is an adequate compromise because it provides us the right to download the data and publish our results. We believe *Science* is thinking in terms of single gene biology, not large scale bioinformatics." When genes were essentially analogue objects—chemicals—obtaining their sequence was a major achievement and warranted a paper in a scientific journal. Today, though, genes are digital substructures of a larger entity—the entire genome. As such, they do not warrant a paper on their own. Instead, researchers have moved on to finding homologies, connections between genes—in short, to annotating the information. But as Eddy and Birney pointed out in their letter, "we can't usefully annotate a genome we can't freely redistribute" because the annotation needs to be hung on a sequence that provides the underlying structure, as in genome browsers.

In part, this situation had arisen because, as Eddy and Birney put it, Celera was seeking a "special deal that lets them have their cake and eat it too." Ashburner agreed. In his email, he had written: "The problem comes, of course, because Celera want the best of both worlds. They want the commercial advantage of having done a whole human shotgun sequence and they want the academic kudos which goes with it." Once again, Venter's desire for scientific recognition clashed with his need to find a way to make money.

Ashburner continued: "Many other companies are far more straightforward—they sequence on a very large scale and make money selling access to these data, but they (e.g. Incyte, HGS) make no claims whatever to academic credibility. I have nothing whatsoever against the idea that Celera sequence the human genome and sell it; I have nothing whatsoever against their 'Drosophila model' (where their behavior was exemplary, Celera kept the very letter and went beyond the spirit of the formal agreement they made with the public domain). But I am outraged and angry with the idea that they can simply flout the strong conventions of their peers, conventions established only for the greater good of the scientific community. I am, similarly, outraged and angry that *Science*, of all journals, should enable them to do this."

Many others, too, were "outraged and angry" that one of the fundamental principles of scientific progress—the publication and free access of data—should be undermined in this way. And whereas all that most scientists could do was to write to the editor-in-chief expressing their concern, those on the Human Genome Project had another option. The day after Ashburner's stinging condemnation of the *Science*-Celera deal, the leaders of the public genome project voted to submit their paper to *Nature*, the rival publication to *Science*. The decision was not unanimous. Ari Patrinos, head of the DOE's sequencing effort, said: "It's no secret that I was advocating back-to-back publication in one journal, *Science*." What swayed the vote seems to have been the British members of the consortium, whose earlier advocacy of openness had largely determined the agenda for data release ever since John Sulston helped frame the Bermuda Principles in 1996.

As Ashburner rightly noted, other business leaders in the genomics field had none of Venter's hankering after academic credibility. The CEO of Incyte bluntly told *The New York Times*: "We're trying to run a business here, not put things in *Science* magazine." Whatever its motivations, the fact remains that Celera was attempting to make its sequence data available to scientists. Moreover, it did not add onerous conditions like "reach-through rights" that would have given it the option to commercialize any discoveries made using its data. So the firestorm that greeted its plans seems a little harsh, to say the least. Part of the reason was that Celera's access restrictions hit another raw nerve in the scientific community—one that, in truth, probably worried researchers in the field of genomics even more than the issues surrounding gene patents, because it affected them more directly in their day-to-day work.

Public access to data lay at the heart of the scientific tradition as it had evolved over the centuries. Without the data, other scientists could not check the conclusions drawn from them, rendering scientific claims less valuable, and less likely to be incorporated in subsequent research. In their open letter criticizing the terms under which Celera's data would be made available, Eddy and Birney touched on this aspect: "We have no issue with Celera's commercial data gathering, and their right to set their own access terms to their data. We do feel, though, that scientific publications carry a certain ethical responsibility. The purpose of a paper is to enable the community to efficiently build on your work. There is always a tension between disclosing your work to your competitors (this is not unique to private companies!) and receiving scientific credit for your work via publication."

Allowing the community to build on partial or incomplete results had worked well—thanks to what Waterston calls the "societal contract"—when the intermediate data were clearly separate from the result and simply part of the process of obtaining the latter. In the digital genomic world, however, the scientific result—the sequence of all or some of a genome—is no different from the data used to produce it. Indeed, thanks to the power of bioinformatics, much useful information could be extracted even from the raw data of researchers.

This posed increasing problems for those involved in large-scale sequencing. Already in June 2000, *Nature* had fretted over the issue: "Researchers who devote themselves to sequencing genomes often lack the time to interpret their results. Others don't. . . . the problem, from the point of view of those doing the sequencing, occurs on occasions when they are getting on with their sequencing while others, perhaps better placed to annotate the sequence, are free to use it to publish biologically useful information. What rights of first publication do the sequencers have?"

Later that year, a group of scientists, including one of the pivotal figures in the genomic world, Leroy Hood, wrote a letter to *Science* discussing some of the issues surrounding preliminary and final data: "Official notification that the data are final is often captured by publication of comprehensive analyses in peer-reviewed journals. Publication of such analyses by third parties before the data producers have officially signed off preempts what producers consider to be their prerogative." The letter also offered an interesting observation: "In the past, etiquette has guided decisions about publishing analyses of other people's sequences or annotations. Often, informal contacts have resulted in permission to publish, co authorship, back-to-back papers or other agreeable options. However, the Web fosters a climate of anonymity, in which data content is divorced from the context of its acquisition, with the result that credit is often not properly given to data producers."

Aside from shifts brought about in the scientific community by the Internet, one of the underlying reasons that the nature of sequencing had changed was due to an industrialization of the process. The main architect of this was none other than Hood, who came up with a way to automate the dideoxy technique Sanger had invented. Successive refinements in Hood's approach resulted in the ABI PRISM 3700 that had made projects involving billions of bases—such as the human genome—feasible in the first place. So there is a certain irony that Hood himself pointed out some of the problems with this development.

Hood made various suggestions as to how the tensions could be eased, including a way of flagging up of sequences that indicated whether the sequencer required permission for analyses based on that data. Taking the high-throughput revolution that Hood initiated to its logical conclusion, it may be that sequencing and analysis will gradually become divorced entirely, with the former produced in a completely industrial way, perhaps under contract, for everyone to use, while the focus of original research shifts entirely to annotation.

This issue was still very much up in the air when the two human genome projects published their respective papers, the public consortium in *Nature* on February 15, 2001, and Celera in *Science*, on February 16, 2001. They represent the culmination of a long tradition of papers describing first sequences, and later entire genomes, of progressively more complex organisms. As such, they also offer the ultimate in attempts by editors and journalists to provide substitutes for the reams of raw, unprintable sequence with a kind of people's annotation—converting the dry stuff of the genome's digital code into that most analogue of media, the printed word.

Not surprisingly, perhaps, given that it had staked its reputation on the value of the Celera sequence, *Science* devoted practically every page of its issue to the human genome in some form or other. Alongside the main paper by Venter and his team, and ancillary ones analyzing various aspects of it, even the book reviews all had a genomic theme. An unusual and attractive 30-page News Focus section presented over 20 short items that deal with the past, present, and future as a series of vignettes. Some of these were amplified in further, more in-depth, articles covering scientific, medical, and ethical issues.

But these were rather overshadowed by the dozen analysis pieces in *Nature*. They focused on the practical implications of the human genome. Most were first attempts to pull out new information from the draft sequence, an interesting experiment in publishing science as it happened. *Nature*'s coverage also devoted considerable space to the physical mapping of the human genome, some 14 pages. In doing so, the journal paid tribute to the historical development of the public project, which moved from early physical maps to final sequencing. Indeed, it is notable and perhaps under-standable that *Nature* aligned itself closely with the methodology and ethos of the Human Genome Project. The introduction to the main papers was called—presumably with intentional ambiguity—"Everyone's genome," while the editorial pondered issues of data release and the norms of scientif-ic publication.

In its own editorial, *Science* attempted to justify its actions partly through an invocation of Darwin, the anniversary of whose birthday fell during the week of the double human genome publication. "Darwin's message that the survival of a species can depend on its ability to evolve in the face of change is peculiarly pertinent to discussions that have gone on in the past year over access to the Celera data," *Science* wrote hopefully, but with tenuous logic. *Science*'s main editorial did, however, boast the wittier writing of the two journals. Suggesting that the two rival projects contributed to one another, *Science* allowed itself a little orotundity: "The inspired vision that launched the publicly funded project roughly 10 years ago reflected, and now rewards, the confidence of those who believe that the pursuit of large-scale funda-mental problems in the life sciences is in the national interest. The technical innovation and drive of Craig Venter and his colleagues made it possible to celebrate this accomplishment far sooner than was believed possible." It then added: "Thus, we can salute what has become, in the end, not a contest but a marriage (perhaps encouraged by shotgun) between public funding and pri-vate entrepreneurship."

To its credit, *Science* also carried a piece by David Roos that was openly critical of its deal with Celera. In particular, he noted that the terms are not good enough for all kinds of scientific research: "*Science* has taken care to craft a policy which guarantees that the data on which Celera's analyses are based will be available for examination. But the purpose of insisting that primary scientific data be released is not merely to ensure that the published conclu-sions are correct, but also to permit building on these results, to allow further scientific advancement. Bioinformatics research is particularly dependent on unencumbered access to data, including the ability to reanalyze and repost results. Thus the statement [from *Science* in December 2000] that '. . . any scientist can examine and work with Celera's sequence in order to verify or confirm the conclusions of the paper, perform their own basic research, and publish the results' is inaccurate with respect to research in bioinformatics." Both *Science* and *Nature* devoted a number of pages to bioinformatics and its fundamental role in the world of genomics. In many ways, the two main human genome papers themselves, permeated as they are with computations, stand as monuments to the new digital age of molecular biology.

Celera's paper began with names—a wall of them filling an entire page in a continuous stream, starting, of course, with Craig Venter's, followed by those of Mark Adams, Gene Myers, and so on down the list. The public con-sortium's paper began with a summary of the results; the facing page was purely names, but broken down by sequencing center, and ordered merito-cratically by total genomic sequence contributed. The first center on the list was the Whitehead Institute—Eric Lander's—and Lander himself was the lead author of the entire paper. Evidently the automation he installed at his lab paid off, enabling him to pull past both the Sanger Centre and Bob Waterston's Washington University Genome Sequencing Center, respectively numbers 2 and 3 in the ranking, even though these had formed the mainstay of the HGP. Also worth noting is the fact that John Sulston (Sir John, thanks to a knighthood from Queen Elizabeth II in January 2001), the man who con-tributed in so many ways—technical and ethical—nonetheless with typical modesty placed himself second in the Sanger Centre team.

Both papers started their long expository journey with a potted history of genomics and sequencing, each reflecting their own bias. The public project concentrated on mapping and what it calls the 'hierarchical shotgun ap-proach': generating a set of bacterial artificial chromosome (BAC) clones that cover the human genome, and then applying the shotgun approach to each of these. Celera, of course, filled in the background to the whole-genome shotgun strategy, reviewing the technological breakthroughs that made it possible.

Celera had already announced in January 2000 that it would be using the freely-available HGP data deposited in GenBank to supplement its own. But the paper in *Science* revealed how Celera would be drawing even more deeply on the public HGP data: "In addition to the WGA [whole-genome assembly] approach, we pursued a localized assembly approach that was intended to subdivide the genome into segments." This compartmentalized shotgun assembly (CSA), as Celera termed it, took place across shorter regions of the genome that had been defined partly using sequences from the BAC clones, and did not use the whole-genome shotgun approach at all.

Later in the Celera paper the two approaches are compared: "The CSA assembly was a few percentage points better in terms of coverage and slight-ly more consistent than the WGA, because it was in effect performing a few thousand shotgun assemblies of megabase-sized problems, whereas the WGA is performing a shotgun assembly of a gigabase-sized problem. When one considers the increase of two-and-a-half orders of magnitude in problem size, the information loss between the two is remarkably small." So far, so good. But then the paper went on: "Because CSA was logistically easier to deliver and the better of the two results available at the time when downstream analyses needed to be begun, all subsequent analysis was performed on this assembly."

This was the bombshell. For the final analysis, Celera had jettisoned its whole-genome shotgun approach in favor of one that was based around local assembly, rather like that of the HGP. If, as the paper states, the difference between the WGA and CSA sequences was just "a few percentage points," why did Celera not use the sequence obtained using the whole-genome shotgun approach—the cornerstone of the company's scientific approach? Perhaps the explanation lies in Venter's uneasy straddling of science and business. As a scientist, he wanted to be innovative, as he had been with the whole-genome shotgun assemblies of bacteria and the fruit fly. As a businessman, his assembly had to be demonstrably better than that of the public consortium. If it were worse, or even only as good, there would be little reason for customers to pay Celera significant sums for accessing its data when more or less the same could be had for nothing direct from GenBank or EMBL.

After this startling U-turn, the results of the Celera paper were something of an anticlimax. As might be expected—since they were both dealing with the same underlying data—the analyses of Celera and the Human Genome Project writers did not differ substantially. Both found far fewer genes than had generally been expected: Celera suggested that there was strong evidence for 26,588 of them, and weaker evidence for another 12,000. The public project came up with a similar number: 30,000 to 40,000. What was shocking about these estimates, which were significantly lower than the 100,000 figure that had generally been quoted before the human genome sequence was available for analysis, was that the figure was only around twice as many as the nematode worm (19,000 genes) or fruit fly (14,000). From an anthropocentric viewpoint, this hardly seemed a big enough factor to explain the observed physical and mental differences. Of course, this simply reflects current ignorance about how genes actually produce the cells that go to make up an organism—as well as our own inflated sense of self-importance.

Both papers offered extensive analysis of these genes, their probable similarities to those in other organisms, and the proteins that they produce. Celera's paper, in particular, offered detailed tables comparing proteins in humans, fruit flies, worms, yeast, and a plant. Only the HGP paper, however, went beyond this basic level to look at some of the practical implications of the human genome. Its authors noted that they were able to do so thanks to the early release of all data: "In most research papers, the authors can only speculate about future applications of the work. Because the genome sequence has been released on a daily basis over the past four years, however, we can already cite many direct applications." One of these was the location of 30 genes involved in diseases that had been pinpointed thanks to the availability of sequence data.

It was precisely the lack of sequence data that made gene-finding such an arduous undertaking even ten years ago. As Venter ruefully explained: "I spent more than a decade attempting to isolate and purify the adrenaline receptor protein from heart and brain to finally have enough protein to enable gene isolation and sequencing. Because of the availability of the human genome sequence and advances in technology and computing, that work can now be done in a ten-second computer search for any human gene." From ten years to ten seconds: there could be no better symbol of how genomics coupled with bioinformatics is revolutionizing biological research. This combination promises to do the same for medicine in due course. For Venter, though, the transition brought with it a characteristic regret: "I look back and think of all the things I could have done with that decade of research."

The HGP paper reminded readers that "the human sequence will serve as a foundation for biomedical research in the years ahead, and it is thus crucial that the remaining gaps be filled and ambiguities be resolved as quickly as possible." It then offered some final thoughts. "In principle, the string of genetic bits holds long-sought secrets of human development, physiology and medicine. In practice, our ability to transform such information into understanding remains woefully inadequate. . . . Fulfilling the true promise of the Human Genome Project will be the work of tens of thousands of scientists around the world, in both academia and industry." And then, as if unable to resist the temptation to take a final dig at Celera and *Science*, the authors added: "It is for this reason that our highest priority has been to ensure that genome data are available rapidly, freely and without restriction."

The paper then ended with one of those little jokes that academics so love: "Finally, it has not escaped our notice that the more we learn about the human genome, the more there is to explore." This is an obvious reference to the concluding thought of Watson and Crick's first DNA paper: "It has not escaped our notice that the specific pairing we have postulated immediately suggests a possible copying mechanism for the genetic material." In rounding off the first genomic age that was opened up with the revelatory double-helix structure of DNA, the scientists behind the HGP clearly wished to signal with their paper the start of the next one, which has at its heart the full digital code implicit in Watson and Crick's proposal.

By comparison, the Celera paper was curiously muted. There were no grand speeches of what lay ahead, just a matter-of-fact statement of the next steps; there were not even any sly jokes. Instead, the whole Celera paper was very businesslike, in the same way that the HGP had more of an academic feel—it even provided a handy "genome glossary." The last paragraph of the Celera paper was mainly of interest because in its unusual emphases it surely bore the stamp of the man who made it possible: Craig Venter. It warned that "there are two fallacies to be avoided: determinism, the idea that all characteristics of the person are 'hard-wired' by the genome; and reductionism, the view that with complete knowledge of the human genome sequence, it is only a matter of time before our understanding of gene functions and interactions will provide a complete causal description of human variability."

Finally, it suggested: "The real challenge of human biology, beyond the task of finding out how genes orchestrate the construction and maintenance of the miraculous mechanism of our bodies, will lie ahead as we seek to explain how our minds have come to organize thoughts sufficiently well to investigate our own existence." This rather touching return to the area where Venter's career began—brain research—offered, like the HGP paper's nod in the direction of Watson and Crick, a neat if partial sense of closure.

Anyone who thought that the simultaneous publication of human genome papers in *Nature* and *Science* would mark a reconciliation between the Human Genome Project and Celera was very much mistaken. For on March 19, 2002, the scientific leaders of the public consortium—Eric Lander, John Sulston and Bob Waterston—published a paper in the journal *Proceedings of the National Academy of Sciences of the United States of America* (*PNAS*) entitled "On the sequencing of the human genome." Despite its neutral title, this was anything but a bland review of the subject. For this book, Bob Waterston explains why he and the other leaders felt impelled to stir things up again: it was "because of the impression in the scientific community that the whole-genome shotgun was the way to proceed. We felt that that misconception was going to create difficulties for future genomes." In their paper they sought to underline what they saw as the shortcomings in Venter's approach—notably that "the Celera paper provides neither a meaningful test of the WGS [whole-genome shotgun] approach nor an independent sequence of the human genome," as they put it.

Their main points were that the way Celera incorporated data from the public sequence into their whole-genome approach implicitly included key positional information that made it easier to assemble the genome, and that the so-called compartmentalized sequence assembly (CSA) amounted to little more than the HGP sequence with some Celera data added. "The CSA thus provides a revised version of the HGP assembly based on the addition of WGS reads to the individual clone contigs," they wrote. The paper ends with a couple of comments that are typical of those operating in the academic world with its subtle and not-so-subtle put-downs. First, the three authors cheekily use the fact that Celera based its paper on the CSA version, drawing heavily on public data, to underline that "although the Celera paper leaves open many methodological issues, it does demonstrate one of the HGP's core tenets, the value of making data freely accessible before publication. As the analysis above shows, the availability of the HGP data contributed to Celera's ability to assemble and publish a human genome sequence in a timely fashion." Then as a final comment, they add: "When speed truly matters, openness is the answer." This is clearly a reference to Celera's motto: "Speed matters—discovery can't wait."

The next issue of the *PNAS* contains two articles on the subject. The first, with the witty title "Whole-genome disassembly," was written by Philip Green. It is not surprising that given his previous comments, he, too, was unimpressed by Celera's approach. He went even further to condemn the whole "race" mentality that it engendered on both sides. "Competition is of course a basic fact of nature that we cannot and should not eliminate," he wrote. "The undesirable results it may have produced in this case—widespread misinformation, exaggerated claims, and a compromised product—are mostly due to the high-profile nature of the contest, and perhaps also to the fact that a significant amount of corporate money was riding on the perceived success of one team."

Venter and his team were admirably restrained in answering the points of the public consortium's leaders. The title was matter-of-fact—"On the sequencing and assembly of the human genome"—and the tone measured. Myers, the lead author, suggested that the earlier paper was wrong in places, their simulations misleading, the HGP dataset contained misassemblies that reduced its usefulness, and that the "data from Celera's whole-genome libraries was the driving force for assembly by both methods. . . . Thus while neither the Compartmentalized Shotgun Assembly (CSA) nor Whole-Genome Assembly (WGA) represents a completely 'pure' application of whole-genome sequencing, the whole-genome sequence dataset produced at Celera determined the structure and content of the genome assemblies."

Green had concluded his paper: "The best that those of us on the sidelines can do is to continue to scrutinize the results." But for the vast majority, this is easier said than done. The points raised are extremely technical—Green himself had noted that "issues surrounding sequencing strategies will no doubt seem arcane to most readers"—and with eminent scientists arguing diametrically opposite views it has hard to know what to think. What is particularly striking is that the world of science, which is supposed to be based on the binary distinction true/false, can nonetheless harbor gray areas.

One thing is certainly clear: neither the public's nor Celera's sequence was in any way definitive. Both had dubious readings and many significant stretches missing. Waterston explains why it was imperative to attain the 99.99 percent accuracy required for "finished" sequences. When scientists have problems understanding what the genome means, they need to know whether these problems arise from imperfections in the data or from a deeper ignorance. "There are always questions," he says. "Is it because it's missing—is there an out?" For this fundamental reason, which goes to the heart of the scientific process, the Human Genome Project was committed to producing a finished version. But Celera was a business: getting a draft out to its customers quickly was more important than waiting until it had some final version. Because its sequence was proprietary it was not possible for others to step in and finish the Celera sequence.

The fruit fly was different. The sequence was in the public domain, and so researchers were able to pick up where Celera left off. On January 6, 2003, Baylor College of Medicine announced that in collaboration with the U.S. Department of Energy's Lawrence Berkeley Laboratory they had finished the *Drosophila* sequence. This meant that they had closed thousands of gaps and corrected errors and misassemblies using a variety of painstaking direct sequencing methods.

The finished sequence was highly important, since it not only gave the *Drosophila* community the fruit fly genome with a very low level of error—most of it less than one base pair in 100,000—but it also provided useful confirmation that it was possible to finish a large genome to this degree. Moreover, as the authors of the paper reporting the work noted, this finished genome also provided a benchmark—effectively the "right" answer—against which the whole genome shotgun (WGS) method employed for the previous version could be measured. This allowed some objectivity to be brought into the debate over whether the WGS method should be employed more widely in the future. The results must have been gratifying for Venter who, along with Myers and Adams, was among the authors of the paper. The researchers found that "with the exception of a larger number of gaps, overall sequence quality [of Celera's WGS fruit fly genome] approaches the NHGRI standard for finished sequence"—which had been set at an error rate of one base pair in 10,000.

This was an important paper, then, and one that had a significance that went beyond its undoubted scientific value. For it appeared neither in *Science*, as the previous *Drosophila* papers had done, nor in *Nature*, the obvious alternative. Instead, it was published in *Genome Biology*. This describes itself as "a journal, delivered over the web." That is, the Web is the primary medium, with the printed version offering a kind of summary of the online content in a convenient portable format. The originality of *Genome Biology* does not end there: all of its main research articles are available free online.

Although *Genome Biology* comes from a commercial publisher—which makes money from the journal by selling access to commentaries and additional content—the idea that primary research should be freely available, rather than locked up in often expensive journals, originally arose in the public sphere. In January 1999, *Nature* reported that David Lipman, the director of the National Council for Biotechnology Information (NCBI), together with Patrick Brown, one of the pioneers in the study of gene expression (see chapter 10) proposed creating "an e-print archive similar to that established for physics at the Los Alamos National Laboratory in New Mexico by Paul Ginsparg in 1991," where physicists could publish papers online much more rapidly than in conventional hardcopy journals. As *Nature* explained: "The life science e-print archives would be established at a single website. Papers could be automatically posted, archived and distributed, with authors retaining copyright over their work. Articles would either be posted without refereeing, or peer reviewed by third-party professional societies or electronic journals, and labeled as such."

In a way, this was simply a logical extension of the NCBI's work with GenBank and other databases, where sequences were deposited for free distribution. As Brown tells me, "The single most under appreciated and important thread that runs through the history of genomics is the essential role played by the free, open, unrestricted availability of every sequence that's been published." He adds: "Virtually none of the useful things that you take for granted about sequences would happen if it weren't for the fact that they are a free, open, public resource, and there's no reason why that shouldn't also be the case for every other kind of published result in biology."

But there is a stark contrast between the automatic and immediate data release of the human genome, for example, and the world of scientific publishing, where papers are jealously guarded by the journals in which they appear. This means that scientists who want to build on the results and work of others—the essence of the scientific method—have to pay publishing houses for journal subscriptions in order to do so. Reflecting this proprietorial approach, journals generally require that authors hand over copyright to them. The new e-print archive aimed to improve the efficiency of information distribution and give ownership and power back to the scientists who wrote the papers.

In April 1999, Harold Varmus, director of the U.S. NIH, took up the idea and proposed to create something even more ambitious: a centralized electronic publishing site, which he provisionally called E-biomed. The proposal explained that "the essential feature of the plan is simplified, instantaneous cost-free access by potential readers to E-biomed's entire content in a manner that permits each reader to pursue his or her own interests as productively as possible." The online nature of the project was key. The proposal's summary noted that "the advent of the electronic age and the rise of the Internet offer an unprecedented opportunity to change scientific publishing in ways that could improve on virtually all aspects of the current system."

Not everyone was as enamored of this opportunity as Varmus. In May 1999, *Nature* reported that there was a "mixed response to NIH's web journal plan," and the final form of the repository, which was called PubMed Central, was rather different when it came into being in February 2000. Instead of trying to take over the functions of commercial publishers, the NCBI's new arm became a central archive for accessing some of it, and the idea of posting unrefereed papers was gone. Although it offered unrestricted access to it contents, participation by publishers was voluntary.

But this was not the end of the story. In October 2000, Patrick Brown helped set up the Public Library of Science, "a non-profit organization of scientists and physicians committed to making the world's scientific and medical literature a public resource." One of its first acts was to circulate "an open letter calling on scientific publishers to make the primary research articles they publish available through online public libraries of science such as PubMed Central" not more than six months after their initial publication date. The threat was that those signing the letter would boycott any journals that failed to comply. Even though over 30,000 scientists signed the letter, only a handful of publishers committed themselves. Moreover, few scientists proved willing or able to follow through with the boycott.

Once again, though, matters did not rest there. Brown, joined by his colleague Michael Eisen and Harold Varmus, obtained "a $9 million grant from the Gordon and Betty Moore Foundation to launch a non-profit scientific publishing venture, controlled and operated by scientists for the benefit of science and the public." Using these funds, the Public Library of Science (PLoS) "will publish two new journals—*PLoS Biology* and *PLoS Medicine*—that will compete head-to-head with the leading existing publications in biology and medical research, publishing the best peer-reviewed original research articles, timely essays and other features." Journal content will be "immediately available online, with no charges for access or restrictions on subsequent redistribution or use." Costs will be covered by charging scientists a basic fee when their papers are published.

What is particularly interesting about this development is how once more it was the Internet that had acted as the catalyst, and how it was the genomic community that was in the vanguard of change—"it certainly has led the way," Brown says. Moreover, after *PLoS Biology* and *PLoS Medicine*, the idea will be extended to other areas of science—planned titles include *PLoS Chemistry* and *PLoS Computer Science*, as well as field-specific journals like *PLoS Genetics*. "Once we get some traction with that," Brown explains, "either we or someone else will pick up the model to expand way beyond life sciences and medicine into other scientific and other academic disciplines."

One of the few commercial publishers sympathetic to the ideas behind the original E-biomed and the later Public Library of Science is the Current Science Group. On April 26, 1999, it announced that it would become "the first commercial publisher to offer all research reports (primary papers) in medicine and biology free of charge, from now on, to individuals through the web." The initiative had been taken "in response to the new opportunities offered by technological developments, and to a strong feeling among some leading biologists that the way scientific reports are published must change." One of the fruits of this new initiative was *Genome Biology*.

Of course, such gestures are easy to make; the question was whether a journal operating on these principles could attract top-rank scientists. This question was answered definitively in the affirmative with the publication of the announcement and analysis of the finished *Drosophila* sequence in January

2003. This key opening paper's list of authors included not only Venter, Myers, and Adams, but equally stellar representatives of the academic world of science, such as Gerald Rubin, the boss of the fruit fly genome project, and Richard Gibbs, head of sequencing at Baylor College. Alongside this paper were no less than nine other weighty contributions, including one on Apollo, a new tool for viewing and editing sequence annotation. For its own *Drosophila* extravaganza of March 2000, *Science* had marshaled seven papers in total. Clearly, *Genome Biology* had arrived, and with it a new commercial publishing model based on the latest way of showing the data.

NOTES

Interviews included in this chapter were conducted by the author between November 2002 and June 2003 with the following individuals: E. Lander, R. Waterston, P. Brown.

1. p. 105 *This Committee has always encouraged*   Opening statement, Subcommittee on Energy and Environment, Committee on Science, U.S. House of Representatives, April 6, 2000. Online at *http://www. house.gov/science/sensenbrenner_040600.htm.*

2. p. 105 *One of the witnesses on that day*   J.C. Venter, Prepared statement before the Subcommittee on Energy and Environment, U.S. House of Representatives, April 6, 2000. Online at *http://www.house.gov/ science/venter_040600.htm.*

3. p. 106 *Even the most cynical spectator*   B.R Jasny and F.E. Bloom, Editorial, *Science* 287 (2000): 2157

4. p. 106 *On Monday it was reported in* Time *Magazine*   J.C. Venter, Prepared statement before the Subcommittee on Energy and Environment, U.S. House of Representatives, April 6, 2000. Online at *http://www. house.gov/science/venter_040600.htm.*

5. p. 107 *Jim, it's looking grim*   N. Wade, "Grad student becomes gene effort's unlikely hero," *The New York Times,* February 13, 2001.

6. p. 107 *I needed it for my research*   B. Stewart, "Keeping genome data open." O'Reilly Network, April 5, 2002. Online at *http://www.oreillynet.com/ pub/a/network/2002/04/05/kent.html.*

7. p. 107 *Jim in four weeks created the GigAssembler*   N. Wade, "Grad student becomes gene effort's unlikely hero," *The New York Times,* February 13, 2001.

8. p. 107 *100 800 MHz Pentium processors*   B. Stewart, "Keeping genome data open." O'Reilly Network, April 5, 2002. Online at *http:// www.oreillynet.com/pub/a/network/2002/04/05/kent.html.*

9. p. 107 *By June 22, 2000, Kent had completed*   N. Wade, "Grad student becomes gene effort's unlikely hero," *The New York Times,* February 13, 2001.

10. p. 107 *Celera finished its own first version three days later*   J.C. Venter, Lecture at Marine Biological Laboratory. Online at *http://www.mbl.edu/videofiles/ lecture5/transcript-print.html.*

11. p. 108 *When I called him up in late April* Press Briefing, The White House, June 26, 2000. Online at *http://www.ornl.gov/hgmis/project/clinton3.html.*

12. p. 108 *He served beer and pizza* Press Briefing, The White House, June 26, 2000. Online at *http://www.ornl.gov/hgmis/project/clinton3.html.*

13. p. 108 *because it was a day* J. Sulston and G. Ferry, *The Common Thread* (London/New York: Bantam Press, 2002), 224.

14. p. 109 *the most important, most wondrous map* W. Clinton, Remarks at The White House, June 26, 2000. Online at *http://www.ornl.gov/ hgmis/project/clinton2.html.*

15. p. 109 *a term introduced by the public effort* J.C. Venter, Prepared statement before the Subcommittee on Energy and Environment, U.S. House of Representatives, April 6, 2000. Online at *http://www.house.gov/ science/venter_040600.htm.*

16. p. 109 *This is an exciting stage* Press Briefing, The White House, June 26, 2000. Online at *http://www.ornl.gov/hgmis/project/clinton3.html.*

17. p. 110 *simulate in software the process* J.C. Venter, et al., "The sequence of the human genome," *Science* 291 (2001): 1304–1351.

18. p. 111 *The editorial staff of* Science *has* M. Ashburner, "Email to members of Science's Board of Reviewing Editors," December 6, 2000. Online at *http://www.marywaltham.com/ashburner.htm.*

19. p. 112 *Although traditionally publication of sequence* Online at *http://www. sciencemag.org/feature/data/announcement/genomesequenceplan.shl*

20. p. 112 *this is a conveniently revisionist view* S. Eddy and E. Birney, "An open letter to the bioinformatics community." Online at *http://www.genetics.wustl.edu/eddy/people/eddy/openletter.html.*

21. p. 113 *the leaders of the public genome project* E. Marshall, "Sharing the glory, not the credit," *Science* 291 (2001): 1189–1193.

22. p. 113 *It's no secret that I was advocating* E. Marshall, "Sharing the glory, not the credit," *Science* 291 (2001): 1189–1193.

23. p. 113 *We're trying to run a business here* G. Kolata, "Celera to charge other companies to use its genome data," *The New York Times*, December 8, 2000.

24. p. 114 *Researchers who devote themselves* Opinion. *Nature* 405 (2000): 719.

25. p. 114 *Official notification that the data are final* L. Rowen, et al., "Publication rights in the era of open data release policies," *Science* 289 (2000): 1881.

26. p. 116 *Darwin's message that the survival* Editorial, "The human genome," *Science* 291 (2001): 1153.

27. p. 116 Science *has taken care to craft a policy* D.S. Roos, "Bioinformatics—trying to swim in a sea of data," *Science* 291 (2001): 1260–1261.

28. p. 117 *In addition to the WGA* J.C. Venter, et al., "The sequence of the human genome," *Science* 291 (2001): 1304–1351.

29. p. 118 *In most research papers* International Human Genome Sequencing Consortium, "Initial sequencing and analysis of the human genome," *Nature* 409 (2001): 860–921.

30. p. 118 *I spent more than a decade*   J.C. Venter, Talk at the Commonwealth Club, March 5, 2002. Online at *http://www.commonwealthclub.org/archive/02/02-03venter-speech.html.*

31. p. 120 *the Celera paper provides neither a meaningful test*   R.H. Waterston, E.S. Lander, and J.E. Sulston, "On the sequencing of the human genome," *Proc. Natl. Acad. Sci. USA* 99 (2002): 3712–3716.

32. p. 121 *Competition is of course a basic fact of nature*   P. Green, "Whole-genome disassembly," *Proc. Natl. Acad. Sci. USA* 99 (2002): 4143–4144.

33. p. 121 *data from Celera's whole-genome libraries*   E.W. Myers, et al., "On the sequencing and assembly of the human genome," *Proc. Natl. Acad. Sci. USA* 99 (2002): 4145–4146.

34. p. 122 *On January 6, 2003, Baylor College of Medicine announced*   Baylor College of Medicine press release, January 6, 2003. Online at *http://public.bcm.tmc.edu/pa/fruitflygaster.htm.*

35. p. 122 *with the exception of a larger number of gaps*   S.E. Celniker, et al., "Finishing a whole-genome shotgun: Release 3 of the *Drosophila melanogaster* euchromatic genome sequence," *Genome Biology* 3 (12) (2002): 0079.1–0079.14.

36. p. 122 *a journal, delivered over the web*   Genome Biology FAQ. Online at *http://genomebiology.com/information/faq/faq2.asp.*

37. p. 122 *an e-print archive similar to that established for physics*   D. Butler, "U.S. biologists propose launch of electronic preprint archive," *Nature* 397 (1999): 91.

38. p. 122 *the life science e-print archives*   D. Butler, "U.S. biologists propose launch of electronic preprint archive," *Nature* 397 (1999): 91.

39. p. 123 *the essential feature of the plan is simplified*   H. Varmus, "E-biomed: a proposal for electronic publication in the biomedical sciences." Online at *http://www.nih.gov/about/director/pubmedcentral/ebiomedarch.htm.*

40. p. 123 *mixed response to NIH's web journal plan*   D. Butler and M. Wadman, "Mixed response to NIH's web journal plan," *Nature* 399 (1999): 8–9.

41. p. 123 *when it came into being in February 2000*   PubMed Central FAQs. Online at *http://www.pubmedcentral.gov/about/faq.html.*

42. p. 124 *a non-profit organization of scientists and physicians committed*   Public Library of Science. Online at *http://www.plos.org/about/index.html.*

43. p. 124 *an open letter calling on scientific publishers to make*   Public Library of Science History. Online at *http://www.plos.org/about/history.html.*

44. p. 124 *a $9 million grant from the Gordon and Betty Moore Foundation*   Public Library of Science History. Online at *http://www.plos.org/about/history.html.*

45. p. 124 *will publish two new journals*   About the PLoS Journals. Online at *http://www.plos.org/journals/index.html.*

46. p. 124 *the first commercial publisher to offer all research reports*   Genome Biology press release, April 26, 1999.

CHAPTER 7

A Very Different Animal

The first stage in understanding the underlying logic of the complete sequence of the human genome is to find the genes, which are the basic functional units. What might be called "classical" bioinformatics has proved a powerful tool, but it can only go so far. The results obtained by different groups using various kinds of gene-finding software on the same data are by no means unanimous. And beyond the genes there are other structures within the genome that cannot be found in this way because they lack the telltale signs or signatures of genes. These include many of the key regulatory sequences that determine when and how much genes are expressed.

In computer terms, the genes can be thought of as program subroutines that carry out well-defined tasks; such subroutines typically display a well-defined structure, with opening and closing keywords. Regulatory sequences, which represent the lines of programming code that call the subroutines, tend to be more free form and thus harder to spot. Nonetheless, such code contains clues about how the genome produces the organism, and locating it is vital for any comprehensive understanding of how the genome operates—particularly in light of the lower-than-expected overall human gene count.

One way to find out where such regulatory sequences are is to compare the genomes of two species that are reasonably closely related, an approach that is known as comparative genomics. "Closely related" in this context means that the species in question diverged from each other relatively recently—tens of millions of years ago. One of the guiding principles of comparative genomics is that key regulatory sequences are likely to be preserved over such time scales. The reason is that they represent critical code that cannot be fiddled with too radically without causing a catastrophic program crash: cell death.

The animal generally chosen as the semi-official close relative for humans is the mouse; it has a number of advantages as a subject for genomic study. As Eric Lander and collaborators wrote in a 1993 paper: "Historically, the mouse has been the mammal of choice for genetic analysis primarily because of its short gestation period and large litter sizes, the availability of inbred strains"—those containing a restricted set of genes, hence displaying their effects more clearly—"and the ability to perform controlled matings" to obtain particular combinations of genes. For these and other reasons, as Lander noted, the goals of the Human Genome Project included the development of a high-resolution physical map of the mouse, with the intention to eventually sequence the mouse for the purposes of comparative genomics.

This was made explicit in Francis Collins' second five-year plan for the HGP, published in *Science* in 1998. Comparative Genomics was listed as Goal 5, and alongside the completion of the sequencing of the worm and fruit fly model organisms, the mouse makes an appearance. "The mouse is currently the best mammalian model for studies of a broad array of biomedical research questions," Collins and his team wrote. "The complete mouse genome sequence will be a crucial tool for interpreting the human genome sequence, because it will highlight functional features that are conserved, including noncoding regulatory sequences as well as coding sequences. . . . Therefore, this is the time to invest in a variety of mouse genomic resources." The importance of the mouse to the HGP can be gauged from the fact that even while Collins was trying to bolster the public project in the face of Celera's bold irruption into the field, he nonetheless wrote that "the centers sequencing human DNA are encouraged to devote up to 10 percent of their capacity to sequencing mouse DNA." The eventual aim was to produce a finished sequence by 2005.

Sequencing the mouse for comparative purposes was just as pertinent for Celera. As Venter explained in April 2000: "One of Celera's founding principles is that we will release the entire consensus human genome sequence freely to researchers on Celera's Internet site when it is completed. . . . Annotation of the data by Celera scientists using an array of bioinformatics tools will act as the platform for developing a range of products and services." The essence of Venter's model was that Celera would make money not so much from the raw data as their annotation; this meant that anything that helped annotate the human genome was a priority.

It was no surprise, then, that on April 6, 2000, when Celera announced that it had completed the sequencing phase of the human genome project, it switched immediately to the mouse, just as it had gone straight on to sequencing the human genome as soon as it had enough data for the fruit fly. The company explained: "A key feature of Celera's business model will be the ability to compare genomes from various organisms (comparative genomics).

The comparison of the mouse, *Drosophila*, and human genomes is expected to open many new avenues of research into the mechanisms of gene conservation and regulation, which could lead to a better understanding of gene function and disease." In its usual fashion, Celera then issued periodic press releases detailing its progress. For example, on June 1, 2000, a press release revealed that the company had sequenced more than one billion base pairs from the mouse.

Meanwhile, during this particularly competitive period, the public project was fighting back with its own mouse announcements, just as it had done with the human genome. On August 7, 2000, the National Human Genome Research Institute (NHGRI) upped the stakes by declaring a restructuring of its model organism projects: "NHGRI is now accelerating its program, initiated in 1999, to determine the genomic sequence of the mouse." The most dramatic element was the almost casual announcement that the two main centers carrying out the mouse sequencing, those of Bob Waterston and Eric Lander, "plan to use a hybrid DNA sequencing strategy that combines the advantageous features of the 'hierarchical' (BAC or map-based) shotgun strategy"—as used by the main HGP project—"with those of the 'whole genome' shotgun" espoused by Celera.

This was amazing news, for it apparently represented an admission by some of its sharpest critics that the whole-genome shotgun (WGS) method was, after all, valid. A closer reading however, shows that the public project was not being hypocritical: the new mouse strategy was indeed a hybrid, and it involved generating a rapid rough sequence of the genome thanks to the WGS approach, orienting that data using a series of overlapping clones, and then moving on to produce the finished sequence by more traditional means. Nonetheless, the adoption of Venter's approach (even partially) was an important move and a significant signal for the future.

Shortly afterwards, another announcement was made. On October 6, 2000, the Mouse Sequencing Consortium (MSC) was formally unveiled. This was a joint public and private grouping, consisting of the NIH, the Wellcome Trust, the pharmaceutical companies SmithKline Beecham and Merck, as well as Affymetrix, the leading player in the increasingly important DNA chip market (see Chapter 10). Although the NIH was footing over half the $58 million bill for the Mouse Sequencing Consortium, with the Wellcome Trust picking up just under $8 million, the presence of private funding is another instance of major companies deciding to support open release of materials collectively rather than to compete individually. This had first manifested itself in Merck's public EST database; there would be more examples in due course.

This release also gave some details about exactly which of the main varieties of mouse would be sequenced. The strain of mouse chosen was known as C57BL6/J; fortunately, this particular breed also has the rather cooler name of "Black 6." Tucked away at the end of the release was another important announcement: "The data release practices of the MSC will continue the international Human Genome Project's sequencing program's objective of making sequence data available to the research community as soon as possible for free, unfettered use. In fact, the incorporation of the whole genome shotgun sequencing component has led to adoption of a new, even more rapid data release policy whereby the actual raw data (that is, individual DNA sequence traces, about 500 bases long, taken directly from the automated instruments) will be deposited regularly in a newly-established public database" to be operated by NCBI and the Sanger Centre/EBI, and called respectively the Trace Archive and Trace Server.

Hitherto, data had been released by the HGP centers not as traces—raw reads from the sequencing machines—but as larger continuous sequences. This was possible since each center worked on its own batch of clones; they could be sequenced and assembled separately. In adopting the WGS method, however, which was necessarily global, the MSC was not able to release assemblies immediately. It needed good overall coverage before such an assembly could be attempted. This technical limitation would have brought it into conflict with its own data release principles, so establishing special trace archives, where the raw digital data could be accessed, was a tidy solution to the problem. Even though no one had thought to use raw traces before, it was soon realized that thanks to the power of computers, there was no reason why searches should not be made against even this preliminary data. For example, GenBank adapted BLAST to produce MegaBLAST, a Web-based search tool for making cross-species comparisons against discontiguous data—the unordered traces.

As well as adding still more weapons to the armory of genomics, the trace repositories also highlighted a problem that was becoming more acute. By moving data release ever closer to data acquisition, it necessarily gave less time for the researchers producing them to investigate their own results. This was obviously the reason that the Ensembl Trace Server included the following among its "Conditions of Data Release": "The Centers producing the data reserve the right to publish the initial large-scale analyses of the dataset . . . large-scale refers to regions with size on the order of a chromosome (that is 30 Mb or more)."

Celera responded to the Mouse Sequencing Consortium by announcing less than a week later that it had already sequenced 9.3 billion base pairs, giving it 3X coverage—the mouse and human genomes are roughly the same size—spread over three different mouse strains. It added: "Celera now intends to continue sequencing and combine all of its sequence information with publicly available data when it is generated to assemble the most complete picture of the mouse genome."

A few months later, during the news conference for the joint publication of the human genome, Celera mentioned, almost as an aside, that it had assembled the mouse genome, too. But it took another two months before Celera formally announced the fact, on April 27, 2001. Reading the press release, it is not hard to guess why. After noting that it had sequenced more than 15.9 billion base pairs, and was now annotating the mouse genome, it went on: "Celera has sequenced and assembled the mouse genome with data generated exclusively from Celera's high-throughput sequencing factory, proprietary algorithms, and the whole genome shotgun technique"—no public data, that is. And just in case anyone had failed to get the message, Venter was quoted as saying: "This is another validation of Celera's Whole Genome Shotgun sequencing and assembling strategy. The sequence and assembly process was based entirely on Celera's proprietary data and bioinformatics expertise."

Clearly, Venter had been stung by the criticism that greeted the Celera human genome paper in *Science*—which not only used HGP data, but also based its entire analysis on the Compartmentalized Shotgun Assembly. Even though in business terms it would have made far more sense to offer its subscribers the public mouse data as well, he was obviously determined to provide the "validation of Celera's Whole Genome Shotgun sequencing and assembling strategy" that rather unwisely he had failed to deliver in the human genome paper. This time, he used only Celera data and techniques.

Of course, one problem with Celera's mouse sequence was that scientists had to pay to see it, which meant that few were in a position to comment on its quality. It was certainly further along, though, than the Mouse Sequencing Consortium's at that point. On May 8, 2001, the MSC announced that it had completed the first phase of its project and had covered the mouse genome three times on average, "bringing the amount of mouse sequence available to about 95 percent of the total." The press release then added: "albeit in small, unordered fragments"—15 million of them. What researchers needed ideally was a fully-assembled mouse sequence that was freely available, and neither Celera's nor the MSC's offered this.

Perhaps for this reason, the first paper comparing human and mouse genomes came from the independent sequencing and assembly of mouse chromosomes that were related to human chromosome 19, one of the smallest and most gene-dense of the entire genome. It was carried out by a team under Lisa Stubbs at the Department of Energy's Joint Genome Institute—one of the other major sequencing powerhouses along with the three NIH-funded laboratories and the Sanger Centre. Stubbs' paper appeared in *Science* on July 6, 2001; it confirmed that human genes were "overwhelmingly conserved in mouse."

The paper from Stubbs provided a hint of the kind of treasures that the full mouse sequence would provide when compared computationally against the full human sequence. Meanwhile, the Mouse Sequence Consortium was ploughing ahead. First, it finished the shotgun sequencing: by December 2001 there were 30 million reads, and by January 2002, 40 million. Then, it tackled the assembly, using two different programs: Arachne from the Whitehead

Institute, and Phusion from the Wellcome Trust Sanger Institute, renamed from the Sanger Centre in October 2001. On May 6, 2002, the "advanced draft sequence" was formally announced, based on the Arachne assembly, which had taken eight days of nonstop computing time on a single-processor machine.

The Mouse Sequencing Consortium naturally placed the assembled sequence in GenBank immediately. Rather surprisingly, Celera announced on 30 May that it, too, had deposited mouse DNA in the public databases. This was to accompany the publication of a major paper in *Science* comparing the mouse genome with that of the human sequence. There were no special arrangements this time, but then Celera was only giving away some of its proprietary sequence: mouse chromosome 16.

The reason for this was probably commercial in part. By displaying its wares in this public fashion, it was allowing potential buyers to inspect the goods. There was surely another motivation, however, for submitting the paper to *Science* in December 2001, in that it once again allowed Venter to prove that his approach worked. Even the rather ungainly title—"A comparison of whole-genome shotgun-derived mouse chromosome 16 and the human genome"—alluded to the fact. No public data were used: the paper noted that the four strains sequenced by Celera "complemented the C57BL/6J strain"—Black 6—that the public project studied. Just to make sure that everyone got the message, a little further on in the paper, the authors assured the readers that the data set was "generated solely at Celera," and also noted as if parenthetically, that they were "analyzed with the whole-genome assembler previously used to produce the sequence of the *Drosophila* and human genomes." As with the Stubbs' paper a year before, the main result was the "high degree of similarity between the mouse and human genomes": among the 731 genes predicted using bioinformatics, only 14 seemed to have no human counterpart.

This tantalizingly small difference naturally made the full comparative analysis of the two genomes even more eagerly awaited. It finally appeared in another *Nature* blockbuster, on December 5, 2002. Once more, a clutch of ancillary articles swirled around the jewel in the crown, the 42-page article entitled "Initial sequencing and comparative analysis of the mouse genome." As with the human genome, it was the work of some of the world's top bioinformaticians, forming what an NHGRI news release called a "virtual genome analysis center," which met across the Internet.

Their paper begins with a perfect summary of why comparative genomics is important: "With the complete sequence of the human genome nearly in hand, the next challenge is to extract the extraordinary trove of information encoded within its roughly 3 billion nucleotides. This information includes the blueprints for all RNAs and proteins, the regulatory elements that ensure proper expression of all genes, the structural elements that govern chromosome function, and the records of our evolutionary history. Some of these features can be recognized easily in the human sequence, but many are subtle and difficult to discern. One of the most powerful general approaches for unlocking the secrets of the human genome is comparative genomics, and one of the most powerful starting points for comparison is the laboratory mouse."

Along with the usual discussion of Sanger's pioneering work and the strengths and weaknesses of hierarchical shotgun and whole-genome shotgun, one incidental fact to emerge from the details of the sequencing strategy was that the chosen Black 6—whose 2.5 billion nucleotide genome is 14 percent smaller than that of humans—was a female. There were two main reasons for this. One was that females have pairs of all 20 of their chromosomes, including two X chromosomes; applying the shotgun process would ensure that an equal coverage of the X and autosomes (non-sex chromosomes) was obtained. Had a male been chosen, there would have been an X-Y pair alongside the 19 other autosome pairs, resulting in only half the coverage for both X and Y—and thus lower accuracy. The other reason was that the mouse chromosome Y has multiple duplicated regions, which is precisely the kind of thing that the whole-genome shotgun method finds tricky. It was decided to deal with it using just the HGP's clone-based hierarchical shotgun approach.

One of the most important aspects of comparative genomics is *synteny*, the presence of stretches of extensive sequence similarity in two species. Because the human and mouse genomes diverged only relatively recently, they have in common not only many similar genes, but entire blocks of digital DNA. As the *Nature* paper explained: "Starting from a common ancestral genome approximately 75 Myr [million years ago], the mouse and human genomes have each been shuffled by chromosomal rearrangements. The rate of these changes, however, is low enough that local gene order remains largely intact. It is thus possible to recognize syntenic (literally, *same thread*) regions in the two species that have descended relatively intact from the common ancestor." The Mouse Sequencing Consortium team found that the mouse genome could be divided up into 342 conserved blocks for which there is a corresponding block in the human genome. The patterns of the segments differed substantially across chromosomes. For example, the human and mouse X chromosomes are single, syntenic blocks of each other's code, while human chromosome 20 corresponds entirely to part of mouse chromosome 2. This cutting and pasting of code as the two species diverged gives a fascinating glimpse of the kind of processes brought about by evolution.

Despite this very striking level of rearrangement of the same basic building blocks—90 percent of the mouse DNA could be lined up with a region of the human genome—only 40 percent of the mouse and human sequences can be lined up base by base, at least roughly. That is, although the overall structure in terms of syntenic segments is highly similar, the sequence details are not. The stretches where detailed similarities can be found—if only by computers able to spot even distant relationships—seem to be the sequences that remain from the common ancestor of mice and humans; the rest have been deleted in one or both genomes since that time.

The mouse appears to confirm that the number of genes in mammals is only around 30,000, and not the 100,000 once thought. The high proportion of genes in common—over 99 percent—is in agreement with the general figure of the earlier Celera mouse paper. What this means is that the basic building blocks—the protein machines—are almost identical in humans and mice. The manifest differences must therefore lie in the way these building blocks are deployed.

This was confirmed by another result to emerge from comparing the two genomes closely. It was found that, overall, the areas of high conservation between the two genomes, where the sequences match well, form about 5 percent of the total. These are regions of both genomes that seem to be resistant to change compared to the rest of the sequence, since they have stayed roughly the same for 75 million years. One obvious explanation is that they contain crucially important functions that cannot be tampered with much. Because genes are now believed to form only a third of this amount, it seems to offer evidence that there are vital non-genic structures in the DNA sequence that have not been revealed by traditional annotation methods. These elements include key parts of the digital code that control genes, as well as other undiscovered features.

The importance of this result is reflected in a project set up by the NHGRI as part of its post-Human Genome Program work. Called the ENCyclopedia Of DNA Elements (ENCODE), the goal is "to identify and precisely locate all of the protein-coding genes, non-protein coding genes and other sequence-based functional elements contained in the human DNA sequence." The pilot project, analyzing 1 percent of the genome (30 megabases), was launched on March 4, 2003, with a budget of $12 million.

The closing paragraphs of the mouse genome paper also focused on this aspect: "Comparative genome analysis is perhaps the most powerful tool for understanding biological function. Its power lies in the fact that evolution's crucible is a far more sensitive instrument than any other available to modern experimental science: a functional alteration that diminishes a mammal's fitness by one part in [10,000] is undetectable at the laboratory bench, but is lethal from the standpoint of evolution."

"Comparative analysis of genomes should thus make it possible to discern, by virtue of evolutionary conservation, biological features that would otherwise escape our notice. In this way, it will play a crucial role in our understanding of the human genome and thereby help lay the foundation for biomedicine in the twenty-first century."

"The initial sequence of the mouse genome reported here is merely a first step in this intellectual programme. The sequencing of many additional mammalian and other vertebrate genomes will be needed to extract the full information hidden within our chromosomes. Moreover, as we begin to understand the common elements shared among species, it may also become possible to approach the even harder challenge of identifying and understanding the functional differences that make each species unique."

By the time the mouse genome was published, the sequencing of these additional mammalian and other vertebrate genomes was already well underway. One of these is the rat. In February 2001, the NIH expanded its rat genome program with grants totaling $58 million—the more complete mouse genome had cost $130 million. The grants were awarded to Baylor College of Medicine, the University of British Columbia, The Institute for Genomic Research, and two companies: Genome Therapeutics Corporation and Celera. In the Celera press release, Craig Venter is quoted as saying "we are pleased to be collaborating on this NIH-funded project." Just a few months earlier it would have seemed inconceivable that NIH would pay $21 million to Celera to carry out sequencing.

The rat genome is doubly important. Because the rat diverged from the mouse around 44 million years ago, it represents a kind of genomic triangulation point for the mouse and human genomes. By comparing all three, it is possible to tell which differences were introduced by which organisms. The rat is also important as the proverbial laboratory test animal. The rat genome was assembled by Richard Gibbs' team at Baylor College in November 2002, using yet another assembler, called ATLAS. Before this, however, and even before the mouse genome, another organism had been sequenced and the results published in August 2002.

It was Sydney Brenner who had spotted the potential of the pufferfish, *Fugu rubripes*, early on—just as he had for the nematode worm. The pufferfish's special attraction lies in its particularly compact genome (under 400 megabases). Since it is a vertebrate (an animal with a backbone) the pufferfish shares the majority of its genes with humans. The discrepancy in genome size—the human genome is seven times larger—is due to the fact that the pufferfish lacks the huge swathes of repetitive DNA found in humans and other mammals like the mouse or rat. This makes it more easy to find pufferfish genes and regulatory sequences, which can then be used to aid the analysis of fellow vertebrates. The pufferfish's ancestor diverged from the forebear of mammals around 450 million years ago, so its evolutionary distance from humans is much greater than that of rodents, and thus offers quite a different comparative view of the human genome.

Aside from its genomic information, the pufferfish project is also of note because it used only the whole-genome shotgun approach. As the authors of the pufferfish paper (who included Sydney Brenner) wrote: "The feasibility of assembling a repeat-dense mammalian genome with whole-genome shotgun methodology is currently a matter of debate. However, using this approach, we have been able to sequence and assemble *Fugu* to a level suitable for preliminary long-range genome comparisons" and for the relatively modest cost of $12 million. "It suggests that even in the absence of mapping information, many vertebrate genomes could now be efficiently sequenced and assembled to levels sufficient for in-depth analysis."

This was an important point. It drew a distinction between finished sequence, correct to 99.99 percent, as was the aim of the human and mouse projects, and sequences that were "sufficient for in-depth analysis." For projects where completeness is paramount, the traditional clone-by-clone method is probably the way to go. For most genomes, however, the quicker and cheaper whole-genome shotgun method may well be best. In particular, for the purposes of comparative genomics, where overall similarities rather than individual details are examined, the whole-genome shotgun method is generally good enough.

Venter's approach came across as something of a damp squib in his *Science* paper, since the detailed analysis was not based on it. But the fact that the genomic community has overwhelmingly adopted the whole-genome shotgun approach for nearly all species other than human shows that Venter was right in general. The whole-genome shotgun method has emerged phoenix-like from the ashes of the *Science* paper after its roasting by scientists like Lander, Sulston, and Waterston to take flight as the sequencing strategy of choice for comparative genomics.

Which variant of the whole-genome shotgun approach is employed depends mostly on the particular project. For example, in addition to *Fugu rubripes*, another fish, *Tetraodon nigroviridis*, is being sequenced, this time by Eric Lander's group, using a pure whole-genome shotgun technique. A major project by the Sanger Institute to sequence the zebrafish (*Dario rerio*) uses clones and whole-genome shotgun together. The zebrafish is an example of an organism chosen not so much for the light its genome might shed on the human code directly, but for the fact that it will allow the function of sequences homologous to human genes to be investigated experimentally in a way not possible with the mouse or rat. The zebrafish has special characteristics that make it well-suited for this: it can produce a hundred eggs each week which develop into transparent embryos. These embryos mature to hatchlings in just three days. As with the nematode worm, this allows the development of the internal organs of genetically modified variants to be observed without needing to dissect the animal.

Fish are not the only organisms for which genomes of closely related species have been obtained. Alongside the K-12 variant of *E. coli* that Fred Blattner and his team had sequenced back in 1997, researchers detailed in January 2001 a strain called O157:H7—one that is a serious threat to human health, leading even to death in some cases. The two strains diverged about 4.5 million years ago, and by comparing the two genomes it is possible to gain a greater understanding of what makes O157:H7 so deadly. The nematode worm, *Caenorhabditis elegans*, acquired a sequenced cousin, *Caenorhabditis briggsae*, as did *Drosophila melanogaster* in the shape of *Drosophila pseudoobscura*. However, the clearest demonstration of the power of comparative genomics analyses of closely-related species has come from yeast studies.

A group at the Whitehead Institute under Eric Lander used a 7X whole-genome shotgun approach to obtain high-quality draft sequences of three yeast species that are related to the original *Saccharomyces cerevisae*, but separated by 5–20 million years of evolution. By aligning all four genomes, and comparing them computationally, Lander and his team were able to spot those parts of the sequence that had been conserved. Most of these were genes that had been located in the 1996 yeast sequence. Using the new genomes to check those earlier results, however, produced some surprises. The Whitehead group found that around 500 of the 6,000 genes in *Saccharomyces cerevisae*—nearly 10 percent—were probably erroneous, caused by the gene-finding programs misinterpreting random DNA as protein-coding sequences.

Being able to check gene prediction was a useful by-product of comparative genomics, but more exciting perhaps was the identification of some of the regulatory elements that controlled the genes. Finding these had been difficult in the past, but by comparing the four sequences, Lander and his coworkers located around 70 short sequences used repeatedly around the genomes that were highly conserved across the four varieties of yeast. Because they were not genes themselves, it was therefore likely that they played a role in controlling gene expression.

All in all, this paper, published in *Nature* in May 2003, provided ample confirmation of what scientists had long believed: "that comparative genome analysis of a handful of related species has substantial power to identify genes, define gene structures, highlight rapid and slow evolutionary change, [and] recognize regulatory elements," as the Whitehead team wrote. It was also a "dry run" for carrying out the same analysis on the human genome, Lander says, using the mouse and rat sequences, plus any other available mammals.

Some of these had already been chosen. In October 2001, the NHGRI gave two reasons for coming up with a list of additional organisms. One was theoretical: "The genomic sequence information (from model organisms) has kindled a revolution in biomedical and biological research, leading scientists to propose large-scale genomic projects for even more animal models as they explore the mysteries of human health and disease." The other was more practical, as a quotation from Francis Collins in the press release explained: "The NHGRI and its partners have built a tremendous capacity for sequencing genomic DNA . . . As we approach the completion of the human sequence, we need to think about the best ways to continue to use this capacity to advance human health." In other words, having spent huge sums creating sequencing factories, it was necessary to find something useful for them to do after the human and mouse genomes were completed. Not that there was a shortage of ideas. According to the NHGRI: "Researchers already have informally suggested sequencing a wide range of animal genomes, including the chimpanzee, macaque, dog, frog, cat, cow, chicken, kangaroo, opossum, rabbit, earthworm, and even the house fly and the platypus."

The NHGRI decided to employ a competitive system whereby researchers would write proposals championing an organism for sequencing. A review board would then decide which ones were the most appropriate, bearing in mind the likely "contribution to the improvement of human health, the scientific utility of the new data, and technical considerations." The first papers were submitted in February 2002 and reviewed in March. The lucky winners were announced in May. "The organisms designated as high priority for having their genome analyzed include chicken, chimpanzee, several species of fungi, a sea urchin, a microscopic animal commonly used in laboratory studies called *Tetrahymena* and the honey bee." However, as the press release explained: "The decision does not specifically launch large-scale sequencing on any of these organisms. Rather, it creates a pool of candidate organisms on which the institute-supported sequencing centers can choose to begin working as capacity becomes available."

The pressure for a chimpanzee project had been steadily mounting as the human genome project neared completion. In 2000, Ajit Varki, one of its keenest proponents, had written an article entitled "A chimpanzee genome project is a biomedical imperative" in which he listed some medical reasons why a chimpanzee genome would be a valuable tool. Of note was how the lower incidence of major diseases like Alzheimer's and cancer in chimps compared to humans might shed light on the genetic factors involved. A few months later, Varki helped pen a letter to *Science*, signed by an illustrious list of the scientific world's great and good, including Francis Crick, with a similar title: "A primate genome project deserves high priority." As well as the biomedical benefits Varki had cited before, two other reasons were given. The first was for its use in comparative genomics, and the second was for the benefit of great apes themselves, particularly those kept in captivity. The letter suggested that "if the HGP officially embraces a primate genome project, public awareness of the close evolutionary distance between humans and other primates will improve."

One of the two teams submitting an official chimpanzee proposal to the NHGRI included Varki; Maynard Olson was the lead author. Once more, the medical differences between the two species were listed, but this time with a thought-provoking twist. The authors of the paper suggested that "it is plausible that much of the distinctive pattern of human disease—our propensity to obesity, diabetes, cardiovascular disease, epithelial cancers [those involving cells lining the internal and external surfaces of the body] and neurodegenerative disease—is the downside of the rapid evolutionary success of the human lineage." In a sense, the human genome has evolved certain advantageous characteristics so quickly that it has not been debugged properly. The major diseases afflicting humans are the outstanding faulty modules in genomic software that Nature was unable to fix in the time since humans evolved as a species. Looked at in this light, chimpanzees can be regarded as a kind of healthy version of humans, but without the turbo brain code. If this is true, then sequencing their genome might provide clues as to how to fix the problems that humans developed when they diverged from their better-designed cousins.

Another crucial benefit, Olson and his colleagues wrote, was that "a carefully executed chimp genome sequence would provide an ideal tool for cleaning up the human sequence." The similarities are likely to be so great that information from each would be invaluable in helping sort out the remaining gaps and misassemblies, particularly in the area of sequence repeats. A full, finished sequence was necessary, the authors insisted, "to test the classical hypothesis that major evolutionary changes during the human-chimp divergence"—dated around five million years ago—"may have been due to regulatory mutations." Supporters of the chimp genome were suggesting that the sequence regions coding for genes might be practically identical: after all, 99 percent of the mouse genes were essentially the same as those of humans. It was already known that around 98.8 percent of the entire chimp genome— not just the small portion coding for genes—was the same as the human version. It was clear, then, that the important differences would be found in the as-yet poorly understood regulatory regions. To investigate the latter, a high-quality sequence rather than a draft was required. This meant the cost would be close to $100 million, according to the proposal led by Olson.

The second chimpanzee submission included Eric Lander as one of its authors, and largely echoed Olson's, but with one important difference. For the initial phase at least, Lander and colleagues suggested using a fairly light whole-genome shotgun strategy, with finishing reserved for "regions of particular interest or complexity."

The chicken genome proposal included some digs at other sequencing projects already underway or completed, such as those for the zebrafish and pufferfish: references to chickens in the literature were many times more common, its backers noted. Scientific citations aside, the chicken genome would be useful as the first bird genome, offering a different comparative genomics viewpoint to the ones of the mouse, rat, or fish: "The chicken is well positioned from an evolutionary standpoint to provide an intermediate perspective between those provided by mouse and *fugu* [pufferfish]." The chicken, or at least its chicks, were important for medical research: "the premier non-mammalian vertebrate model organism," as the proposal proudly proclaimed.

Last, and by no means least, is the fact that the chicken is big business. The submission rattled off a series of impressive statistics: "Chickens provide one of the most important and rapidly growing sources of meat protein in the world and in the U.S. ([approximately] 41 percent of meat produced). U.S. broiler production has grown over 65 percent in the last decade to about 30.4 billion pounds in 2000. Per capita broiler consumption in the U.S. has grown nearly 30 percent over the same period." Partly as a result of this, the U.S. Department of Agriculture "expressed interest in helping to support the project," which would come in handy when footing the $30 million bill to sequence the 1.2 billion base pairs.

The Department of Agriculture was similarly interested in one of the other proposals picked by the NHGRI, the rather smaller honey bee genome project, whose 270 megabases would cost $7 million. Its proponents suggested that the sequence of the honey bee's DNA would benefit human health and medicine in many areas, including the study of poisons, parasites, old age, mental illness, allergies and infectious diseases. Another plus of using the honey bee was that its "small brain but cognitive sophistication" endows bee societies with a complexity that rivals our own, according to its fans, including the use of the only non-primate symbolic language.

The other choices were more obscure. The sea urchin, *Strongylocentrotus purpuratus*, with a genome size of 800 megabases, was chosen because it was already an important model system, particularly in developmental biology. The single-celled organism *Tetrahymena thermophila* was useful for detailed studies of chromosomes thanks to its double genome. The clutch of fungi proposed by another group, including the apparently omnipresent Eric Lander, was important because many fungi represent serious threats to human health, as well as offering useful comparative genomic information to other species.

In September 2002, the NHGRI announced that it had given permission to various laboratories to begin sequencing these approved organisms. Bob Waterston's team at Washington University genome center would work on the chicken and chimpanzee; the latter project was to be shared with Eric Lander's team at the Whitehead Institute and with labs in Germany and Asia. Richard Gibbs' Human Genome Sequencing Center at Baylor College won the right to start on the honey bee and sea urchin. The NHGRI also revealed that two new high priority animals would be added to the first division DNA list—the cow and the dog.

The cow was unusual in that there was already a full set of clones covering the genome, which would speed the project and reduce costs. According to the cow proposal, "comparative genetic maps have indicated that the bovine and human genomes are more similarly organized than when either is compared to the mouse." The size of the cow genome is also closer. The cow's fans believed that its sequence would catalyze the entire field of human genomics— and to emphasize the point, they subtitled their proposal: "Cattle-izing the human genome." The proposal's authors even presumed to question the value of sequencing either primates like the chimpanzee or rodents like the mouse or rat: "We propose that genomes of different primate species are not sufficiently diverged to identify many biologically significant elements and that human and rodent genomes are too far removed on the molecular clock to find others. The genome of at least one non-primate, non-rodent placental mammal"—that is, not a marsupial such as a kangaroo—"must be sequenced to triangulate the comparative sequencing strategy for finding biologically important sequences."

This kind of heavy selling was probably unnecessary, since once more the U.S. Department of Agriculture was naturally very interested in the $50 million cow genome. It even helped to write the proposal, along with Baylor College scientists who, together with Bob Waterston's team and Eric Lander's Whitehead Institute, were fast emerging as the champs of comparative genomic sequencing. Because there are only a few major centers, sharing out genomes has not been a problem. "We do get together and chat with each other," Lander explains to me, "and say, ah well, if you guys are planning to do the fish, we'll not do the fish, we'll do the dog." Moreover, he notes, "the truth is, there's so darn much to do, it's not like we're battling over narrow territory."

It was indeed Lander's group who offered to "do the dog." His name appeared on the dog sequencing proposal, along with an impressive number of others representing the "canine genome mapping community." As their proposal pointed out, "dogs are unique among mammalian species in the extent of variation they show in morphological traits such as height, weight, mass, shape, and behavior, yet within each breed, key traits are inherited within extremely narrow limits. The Chihuahua is less than six inches high at the shoulder; the Irish wolfhound close to three feet. The Pomeranian weighs between four and five pounds; the St. Bernard may weigh 150 pounds. The Collie has a small, narrow head like that of a fox; the Pug has a massive head with a short, blunt muzzle."

However, this extraordinary diversity came at a steep price for dogs, as the paper noted: "Given the aggressive breeding programs needed to reproducibly generate animals of distinctive size, shape and behavior, it is not surprising that purebred dog fanciers have also produced closed breeding populations, characterized by over 400 inherited disorders. Genetic diseases are predicted to occur with high frequency in populations with closed gene pools and in which breeding of close relatives is used to propagate desired traits. Breeds established from a small number of founders and expanded rapidly to meet breeders' and consumers' demands suffer the most." The list of diseases includes many serious ones: the proposal mentioned "cancer, heart disease, deafness, blindness, motor neuron disease, skin disorders, and a host of autoimmune disorders." In this respect, the canine genome is like that of humans—full of unfixed bugs due to rushed coding—only more so.

What is bad news for dogs, however, turns out to be good news for humans. The highly inbred nature of dogs means that inherited disorders afflicting particular breeds are much more common than their human analogues. The dog genome would enable these genes to be found more easily, and hence by homology the corresponding human genes, too.

The breed of dog chosen for the $50 million project is the boxer. The NHGRI explained that "analyses of 120 dogs representing 60 breeds showed it was one of the breeds with the least amount of variation in its genome and therefore likely to provide the most reliable reference genome sequence. The actual choice of breed is not terribly important," it pointed out, "since all dog breeds are more than 99 percent identical at the DNA level." One of the interesting aspects of dogs is the great physical variation they show despite this close genomic similarity. After completing the 2.8 gigabase (billion bases) boxer genome, researchers plan to sample and sequence DNA from 10 to 20 other breeds to throw light on the regulatory mechanisms responsible for this variety.

One breed has already been sequenced. In September 2003, a paper in *Science* described the genome of a male standard poodle called Shadow. His owner was Craig Venter, who had evidently decided to add the sequence of one of his dogs as a kind of pendant to his own genome. The paper showed that even a very light whole-genome shotgun approach—just 1.5X coverage—could still provide valuable insights when its fragmentary sequences were compared with other, more complete genomes. This was a significant result that would help guide sequencing strategies for future comparative genomics projects.

Although often unjustly overshadowed by its larger partner (the NHGRI), another important player in the U.S. sequencing world is the Department of Energy's Joint Genome Institute (JGI). Like the NHGRI, the JGI has been following up its work on the human genome by sequencing other organisms of interest. On December 12, 2002, *Science* published a report on the draft sequence of the sea squirt, *Ciona intestinalis*, carried out by a consortium of researchers led by the JGI. Despite its nondescript appearance as an adult—it consists of a squishy tube that sieves water for nutrients and oxygen—it is closer to vertebrates like humans and mice than nematode worms or fruit flies are. The last common ancestor of mammals and the sea squirt existed around 500 million years ago.

Its kinship to other vertebrates is most evident after an egg is fertilized. The result is a small tadpole, consisting of some 2,500 cells. Most importantly, the tadpole has a kind of rod running down the length of its back called a notochord, the forerunner of our backbone, as well as a primitive nervous system. These early features of vertebrates, together with its small genome—around 160 megabases—make it extremely valuable for comparative genomics purposes. The *Science* paper reported that the sea squirt had around 16,000 genes, of which 80 percent are related to those found in humans and other vertebrates.

While the JGI was finishing the sea squirt, it announced that it would be taking on two other projects. One was the African frog *Xenopus tropicalis*—an obvious model organism to sequence given its popularity with scientists—and the other was a pair of microbes responsible for the dramatically named sudden oak death syndrome and soybean root rot. Although the microbes were to be sequenced, this is a useful reminder that all of the genomes mentioned so far are either bacteria, single-celled eukaryotes (like yeast), or animals. A hugely important class not represented among these is that of plants. The twin emphasis on laboratory animals and life-threatening bacteria was natural enough in the early days of genomics, but once the model organism sequencing projects were drawing near to a close, the case for sequencing a plant became overwhelming.

The final choice for the model organism was not one of the well-known species, but something of an outsider: *Arabidopsis thaliana*, a diminutive mustard-like weed, commonly known as thale cress, and a relative of many familiar plants such as cabbage and cauliflower. It was chosen largely for practical reasons. One of these becomes apparent when *Arabidopsis* is compared with the victim of sudden oak death syndrome. Experimental genome research typically requires thousands of variant organisms to compare and investigate genetic variation. A thousand *Arabidopsis* plants would fit on a standard piece of office paper; a thousand oak trees would require rather more space. Similarly,

Arabidopsis has a conveniently rapid life cycle that allows many generations to be studied in a way that is not possible with centenarian oaks.

Arabidopsis also shares a key feature with the pufferfish: it has a very compact genome, running to around 125 megabases. This is not only small compared to the human genome, but tiny compared to some other common plants: maize/corn, for example, is roughly the same size as the human genome—2.5 gigabases—while barley is nearly double the size (4.8 gigabases). Wheat, however, has a stunning 16 gigabases in its sequence. This is due to often large sections of DNA that are duplicated across the genome.

After four years of work, the *Arabidopsis* genome was published in *Nature* in December 2000. One of the most interesting revelations concerned these gene duplications. As an accompanying analysis piece explained: "The rapid rise of *Arabidopsis* as the model experimental flowering plant was based on the argument that it had but one copy of each gene and less than 10 percent repetitive DNA. With the complete *Arabidopsis* genome sequence in hand, however, the major surprise is the amount of genetic redundancy. About 26,000 genes have been identified in the sequence. But, astonishingly, at least 70 percent of the genome had been duplicated. In all, there are fewer than 15,000 different genes—a figure that could shrink again as researchers recognize duplicated genes whose sequences have diverged further."

A rabidopsis may be perfect as a model organism, but there is little disagreement as to what is the most important plant genome. Rice is the staple food for half of the world's population. Moreover, large-scale synteny between rice and commercially valuable cereals like maize, barley, sorghum, and wheat make the former extremely important from the viewpoint of comparative plant genomics. As a result, obtaining its DNA became a race between public and private groups, and something of a replay of the HGP versus Celera match—only more complex.

First to get started was an international nonprofit consortium led by the Rice Genome Research Program in Japan, which built on earlier mapping work carried out there. Like the Human Genome Project, the International Rice Genome Sequencing Project (IRGSP) adopted the hierarchical shotgun approach, with a series of overlapping clones covering the entire genome. Work began in 1998, and was proceeding slowly but surely when scientists were surprised to learn on April 3, 2000, that the agrochemical giant Monsanto had secretly funded Leroy Hood and his group to produce a draft sequence of the same variety of rice, known as *japonica*, and that this was now finished. The researchers were probably even more amazed to find that Monsanto would be turning the data over to the public consortium for anyone to use, enabling the finished rice genome to be produced in just a couple of years with a savings of around $100 million.

However, before then, another company, the Swiss-based Syngenta, had produced its own draft sequence in collaboration with Myriad Genetics, the company set up by Walter Gilbert among others. The project was completed six months ahead of schedule, and under budget, triggering a nice $3 million cash bonus for Myriad. As Myriad's Rice Genome FAQ (Frequently Asked Questions) explained, it had used Celera's whole-genome shotgun strategy to produce its sequence. Like Celera, it intended to seek patent protection for inventions relating to specific gene uses. *Science* reported at the time that the rice genome would be publicly available only "through scientific collaborations, in return for a share of any commercial inventions stemming from the research."

Also like Celera, Syngenta's scientists wanted to publish their results, but once more, questions of data access proved an issue. Rumors began circulating that *Science* was prepared to make yet another exception, and leading scientists, including Michael Ashburner, wrote a letter condemning such a move. The Syngenta paper did indeed appear in *Science*, on April 5, 2002. The editorial explained: "The value of the sequence, which is of high quality and of a rice variety used widely in the temperate world, qualified it for an exception in our view. Having decided that this resource was a uniquely valuable one, we worked with TMRI [Syngenta's research institute] so that the data would be made available to the scientific community under terms essentially identical to those we allowed for the human genome sequence" from Celera. Two factors, however, helped lessen the outcry this time.

One was that Syngenta announced shortly before the *Science* article was published, on March 29, 2002, that it would release the rice genome unconditionally for noncommercial users. "Academic researchers will be able to access the data, without reach-through rights, through the TMRI website or, with the consent of their research institution, via a CD-Rom. Additionally, Syngenta has offered the sequence to the International Rice Genome Sequencing Project (IRGSP) to aid in the public effort to finish the sequence. Data will be provided to commercial researchers through an agreement with Syngenta." Of course, any data passed to the IRGSP would eventually end up in GenBank anyway.

The other factor was the publication in the same issue of *Science* of another rice genome, this time of a slightly different subspecies, *indica*. It is widely grown in southeast Asia, notably in China. This is where the sequencing was carried out, at the Beijing Genomics Institute (BGI). Although only a draft sequence, the *indica* genome was an important resource. Its quality and the speed at which it had been produced—using the whole-genome shotgun method—were also signals that China had now joined the front ranks of the world's sequencing community.

The BGI's work had a double importance: it had intrinsic worth and served as a spur to Syngenta. "It seems likely that the release of TMRI's sequence (assembled in early 2000, but initially only available to the public sector research community with certain restrictions) was motivated by the rapid progress of the BGI program," an analysis accompanying the two rice genomes in *Science* suggested. The rapid progress of both Syngenta and the BGI also put pressure on the slower-moving IRGSP. As with the Human Genome Project, it was initially decided to produce a draft rice sequence (by December 2002) so as to be able to show something for all its years of work. Thanks to this increasing cooperation between the private and public sectors, however, the IRGSP in fact found itself in a position to publish two finished chromosomes out of rice's 12—numbers 1 and 4—before this, in November 2002.

Despite the friendlier relations between the two sides, in the first *Nature* paper the IRGSP could not resist taking a few jabs at their colleagues' work, noting that "the complete genomic sequence of chromosome 1 has yielded several findings that would be observed only using a clone-by-clone se-quencing strategy." The paper concluded: "Our results and those from the sequencing of rice chromosome 4 show clearly the importance of finished se-quence," as opposed to the whole-genome shotgun technique employed by Syngenta and the BGI.

All this rather frenzied competition and then cooperation in the field of plant genomics indicates how high stakes can complicate scientific endeavors. One name strikingly absent from this saga, though, is the company that more than most straddled the business-science divide: Celera. And yet, back in April 1999, Celera was reportedly planning to polish off the rice genome in just six weeks. Answering claims that such a move would damage the public rice genome project, Venter replied: "We have the set-up and the technology to proceed with the sequencing work, and although we do not mean to compete with the public initiative, we can't wait until they get their act together." Speed matters, in other words.

The six-week sequencing blitz never took place. In December 2000, a company spokesman explained, "We never started it because the other or-ganizations that we approached to cooperate all had their own programs." Rice was not the only genome, however, that Celera somehow never got around to sequencing. In the early days of the company, Venter declared to *The New York Times* that the first five genomes he intended to sequence would be those of humans, mice, fruit flies, rice, and *Arabidopsis*; together these would form the core of Celera's biomedical and agricultural database. But his long-term plans were much more ambitious, the newspaper reported: "His wider plan is to sequence the genomes of a thousand major species in the next

10 years and to make this fountain of genetic information the centerpiece of an electronic information empire."

There had been signs quite early on that this ambitious "electronic information empire"—similar to Gilbert's original Genome Corporation, but on an even grander scale—might not come to pass. Initially, Celera formed one of two operating groups of the Applera company, the other being Applied Biosystems, which made sequencers and other tools. In a press release dated December 6, 2000, which announced the submission of its human genome paper to *Science*, there was still the following mantra: "The Celera Genomics group . . . intends to become the definitive source of genomic and related medical information." Barely a month later, though, Celera quietly sprouted a couple of new business units. In addition to its online information business, there are the Discovery Sciences and Discovery Services units.

O n June 13, 2001, there was an even more significant addition when Celera acquired Axys Pharmaceuticals. The accompanying press release explained the rationale: "Over the past three years, Celera has established expertise in generating, integrating, and analyzing genomic data—demonstrating the value of an industrialized approach to understanding biological processes. This information has been the basis for Celera's On-line Information Business. Celera is now leveraging its high-throughput and integrated approaches in bioinformatics, genomics, and proteomics to create a next-generation diagnostic and therapeutic company. Axys is expected to complement Celera's existing capabilities."

This was clearly a radical shift from the original vision of a business that was based squarely on becoming "the definitive source of genomic and related medical information," but was not necessarily incompatible with it. However, signs that things were likely to tilt even further towards drug development emerged on December 4, 2001, when Celera announced that Paradigm Genetics would acquire Celera's plant genomics business. Venter is quoted as saying: "By working with Paradigm, we should realize value from services for the plant-based agricultural industry, while focusing our internal resources on activities related to Celera's therapeutic discovery and online business."

The fact that Celera's therapeutic discovery business is mentioned before the online business is intriguing, but there was no hint of the shocking move that was to follow a few weeks later. On January 22, 2002, it was announced that Craig Venter would be stepping down as president and chief scientific officer, taking up the comparatively unimportant role of chairman of Celera's scientific advisory board. Although tight-lipped at the time, Venter later said bluntly: "I got fired! I was fired from Celera because I said I was leaving in another six months. So it became, 'You can't leave; we're firing you!'" Venter said that he was intending to leave because he had achieved the two goals he had set himself when he agreed to help found Celera: "One was the sequencing and the genome. The other was to build the endowment of my foundation so I could go back and do science when it was done." This is, of course, precisely why he had agreed to the earlier deal involving Human Genome Sciences—to carry out experiments that the public funding bodies had declined to support.

The "reinvention" of Celera continued apace. On March 4, 2002, Celera announced that it was selling its animal genomics business. On April 22, the parent company Applera appointed Kathy Ordoñez as president of Celera. She had joined in November 2000 to lead what was described then as "a major initiative by the company in the field of molecular diagnostics." She was an experienced manager in the pharmaceutical industry, and her appointment was an apt symbol of the transformation that Celera was undergoing. The same day that Ordoñez' appointment was announced, an even more fateful change took place. The task of selling subscriptions to the main genomics databases, the Celera Discovery System, passed from Celera to its sister company, Applied Biosystems. As the press release explained, this was to "free Celera's executive team to focus on therapeutic discovery and development."

What this all meant was made clear on April 25, 2002, when Tony White, Applera's CEO, stated simply: "Celera Genomics' core mission is the discovery and development of new therapeutic targets and drugs." He went further: "in today's [press] release, we also emphasized our intention not to pursue new sequencing grants and contract services agreements that are unrelated to therapeutic discovery." The unthinkable had happened: the company that had more or less invented industrial-scale sequencing was getting out of the business. A spokesman for Celera later confirmed: "whole genome sequencing is not something we'll be doing in the future."

Celera was not alone in making this huge shift. Reporting in February 2002 on a rather dismal preceding financial year, the head of Incyte noted that the company was "poised to develop a first-rate capability in therapeutic discovery and development." On November 12, 2002, Incyte acquired Maxia Pharmaceuticals and made 37 percent of its 700-person workforce redundant. Finally, on December 16, 2002, Incyte Genomics became Incyte Corporation, "reflecting the company's broader mission as both a drug discovery company and a leading provider of discovery research products."

Another pioneering genomics company, Millennium Pharmaceuticals, followed a similar trajectory, leading to 103 redundancies just after Incyte announced its own. Unlike Celera or Incyte, Millennium's early strategy was not to sell raw information but to identify specific targets for pharmaceutical partners. Initially, this was highly successful. From 1994 on, it forged more than 20 alliances that provided nearly $2 billion of funding. However, as a document on the company's Web site explained: "Millennium leadership also recognized that discovering new drug targets was only one step in the pathway toward the ultimate goal of providing breakthrough therapeutic products. . . . In February 2002, a merger with COR Therapeutics—among the largest such mergers in the history of the biotech industry—helped to further solidify our standing as a leading biopharmaceutical company."

Eric Lander, among those who founded Millennium in 1993, says that this evolution "was always part of the plan from the beginning." He comments: "You can't possibly stay a tool developer for ever. It's not a sustainable business. The only thing that actually makes money is drugs. And so what Millennium did was I think a reasonably well-executed ten-year plan to start with nothing and to turn it into a pharmaceutical company."

Like Millennium, Human Genome Sciences (HGS) had planned to become a drug company all along, and had wisely decided to exploit its EST database—produced first by Venter and later in-house—as a way of generating much-needed early revenue without losing control over its intellectual property. It ended up with the best of both worlds: the $125 million deal with SmithKline Beecham that started the investment world's genome delirium in 1993 was revised in July 1996 to allow HGS to sell access to other companies, too. Moreover, on June 30, 2001, all of these exclusive deals expired, enabling HGS to exploit the information directly in drugs that it developed and sold itself. On top of this shrewd deal-making, HGS also had the good fortune to offer shares at just the right time. In October 2000, it needed to make even more available than originally planned, so great was the demand. As a result, the company raised $950 million—trumping the $118 million raised by a previous offering in April 1997, which had also been oversubscribed and extended.

In a letter to shareholders dated August 2003, the canny Chairman and CEO of HGS, William Haseltine, announced that the company had cash and short-term investments totaling $1.38 billion. Even though this was $110 million lower than six months before, this still gave HGS many years of funding at the current rate should it require it. This seemed unlikely, given the ten drugs that it had in clinical development—further proof of Haseltine's astute handling of the genomics data at his disposal.

The wisdom of moving from information-based services to drug development is underlined by the fate of a genomics pioneer that never attempted the transition. Pangea was founded in 1991 and began as a consultancy providing database integration and analysis. In February 1997, when it received $10 million in financing from top venture capitalists including Kleiner Perkins Caufield & Byers—the firm that backed early Internet winners like Netscape, Amazon.com and AOL—its future looked rosy. In September 1999, *The New York Times* gave it star billing in a major feature called "Surfing the human genome." The article explained: "Pangea Systems Inc. is a small but leading company in 'bioinformatics,' a hot new field that combines the two keystone technologies of the 1990s—computing and biotechnology. But its products are expensive"—$500,000 is the figure mentioned—"and difficult for mortals to use, which limits Pangea's potential market and reduces the prospects for a public stock offering."

"What to do?" *The New York Times* writer asked rhetorically, and answered: "This being 1999, the answer if you are Pangea is to dot-com yourself." More precisely, Pangea had decided to metamorphose itself into DoubleTwist.com, "the first Web portal that enabled scientists to do molecular research," as Pangea's president and CEO, John Couch, explained. An Apple Computer veteran, Couch provided a perfect analysis of what was wrong with the original business model of Pangea and other bioinformatics hopefuls: "Only a few select pharmas can afford the tools, and if they can, then in some cases they can also afford to produce their own software." The latter problem was also an issue for the very first bioinformatics company, IntelliGenetics, some 20 years before. In a (double) twist of fate, Doug Brutlag, cofounder of Intelli-Genetics, was on Pangea's scientific advisory board.

With hindsight, Pangea's plans to "dot-com" itself and to create a Web "portal"—an online point of reference providing consolidated and cross-linked information—were clear warning signals that the company did not have an alternative business plan other than hoping that Net mania would somehow carry it along. It came as no surprise, then, that in March 2002, *Nature* reported the demise of DoubleTwist—"once one of the most dynamic bioinformatics companies of the dotcom age"—a death that came "after a prolonged decline" and that "was barely noticed outside the world of bioinformatics."

The *Nature* news item also suggested another key reason why the original business model of selling high-price bioinformatics tools to major customers was not viable in the long term: "Some Pangea Systems software sold quite well, but the company was up against a stream of free genome-analysis tools flowing out of academic institutions where student programmers had begun doing thesis work in biology labs." And the more that genomics took center stage in molecular biology, the more student programmers there were turning out such free tools.

DoubleTwist's downfall provides important clues as to why Celera's original business model was problematic, and why companies like Incyte and Millennium Pharmaceuticals all became very different animals from their original incarnations. Since the source of DoubleTwist's core data was the public sequencing projects, it depended on its bioinformatics software to add value that customers would pay for. As the *Nature* story in March 2002 noted, however, this model was undermined by the increasing numbers of free genome-analysis tools, which allowed scientists to analyze the publicly available data directly, bypassing DoubleTwist's offerings.

Celera faced the same problem, but enjoyed one important advantage: it generated its own sequences, rather than drawing solely on those in the public domain. As digital data, though, there is no qualitative difference between the two. The genomes obtained by Celera and the public projects differed only in the extent to which Celera offered more data, and more computational analysis, sooner. It was probably the need to stay ahead that led Celera to prefer the marginally more complete compartmentalized shotgun assembly of the human genome over its main whole-genome shotgun version. Early subscribers to Celera's database were well aware of what they were paying for. One told *Science* in 1999: "It's not so much what the information is . . . it's getting the first look."

In this sense, Celera's motto—"Speed matters"—was more profoundly true, and its name more apposite, than most people realized. This driving necessity for speed explains why Celera bought the specialist company Paracel for $283 million of its stock in March 2000. According to the press release issued at the time, Paracel's products included "the world's fastest sequence comparison supercomputer (GeneMatcher)." Celera's thirst for ever-faster hardware also lay behind the announcement the following year that Celera, Compaq, and the U.S. Sandia Labs would work together on a project to "develop the next generation software and computer hardware solutions that will be specifically designed for the demands of computational biology." The project had as its ultimate goal the creation of a machine capable of 100 teraflops (100 trillion computing operations per second)—50 times faster than Celera's current supercomputer—with hopes of reaching even a fabulous "petacruncher" level (1,000,000,000,000,000 computing operations per second).

O ne reason why Celera Genomics changed its business model is that the company was doomed to lose this kind of race. The huge biocomputing system put together by Compaq for Celera was a dinosaur—the last, rather than the first, of its kind. It was becoming increasingly clear that the way to create raw computing power of the kind that Celera needed to stay ahead of the competition—both public and private—was not to use proprietary systems like those sold by Compaq. Modular systems built around open source software solutions were far more cost-effective. In particular, so-called Beowulf clusters of computers—groups of machines working in a coordinated fashion—running the freely available GNU/Linux operating system were fast making inroads into the supercomputer market. Appropriately enough, Jim

Kent had used a GNU/Linux cluster to assemble the HGP's sequence shortly before Celera had put together its own. Even Celera was moving in this direction: in May 2001, its Paracel subsidiary introduced a software and hardware solution called the BlastMachine, which was "based on a clustered architecture with Intel Pentium processors and the [GNU/]Linux operating system," and ran a special optimized version of BLAST.

Beyond clusters lie grids, geographically separate computers connected by fast links that enable the entire system to work as a single system. Once again, the operating system of choice for the grid nodes is GNU/Linux, and the coordinating program is the open source Globus Toolkit. The scalability of grids means that it was almost impossible for Celera to maintain a competitive advantage based largely on information technology. However great its computing firepower, the academic world could always create a virtual computer whose capabilities were greater.

The Celera model was doomed, then, for two quite separate but congruent reasons: the ready availability of both DNA code in the public databases and free computer code in the form of open source software like GNU/Linux that made high-performance computing available to anyone who had enough low-cost commodity hardware.

This does not mean that the original Celera could not have made a respectable profit—for a time, at least. In the early days of the company, its rapidly assembled genome sequences led those of the public groups, and proprietary computer hardware still had a slight edge over emerging freely available solutions. Celera could have made money from its genomics model based on these temporary advantages as it worked its way through the 1,000 species Venter had spoken of in 1999. As Celera press releases emphasized, it was selling an increasing number of subscriptons to its database services. Spare sequencing capacity might have been used for contract sequencing, as was envisaged at the time of Celera's foundation.

But however great the number of subscriptions and the revenue they generated, and however much sequencing the company had carried out for paying customers, they would never been enough to justify the extraordinary valuation placed on Celera during its heyday. At one point its capitalization hit $14 billion, making it one of the most valuable in the world. Venter himself had no doubts that it was this utterly unrealistic figure that destroyed the genomics company he was creating, and forced Celera to deny its origins and transform itself into a drug discovery machine. In such a business, a single successful treatment could generate sales worth billions of dollars a year, justifying the kind of share price Celera had briefly achieved and that its investors now demanded.

Celera made a sudden and painful transition from the iconic company of the genome age, offering pure data, to a rather more conventional pharmaceutical firm selling a range of chemicals. This transition was born therefore not only of the enduring difference between the digital and analogue worlds, but also from something much more ephemeral: the dot-com boom and bust. As chapter 5 noted, money made from the crazy valuations of Internet stocks was finding its way into genomics, inflating prices there to similarly unjustified levels. It is ironic that the first major scientific field that came to depend so completely on the Internet for its accelerating progress should see its brightest business hope dashed low by dot-com excesses.

NOTES

The author conducted interviews included in this chapter in June 2003 with the following individual: E. Lander.

1. p. 130 *Historically, the mouse has been*   N.G. Copeland, et al., "A genetic linkage map of the mouse: current applications and future prospects," *Science* 262 (1993): 57–66.

2. p. 130 *Francis Collins' second five-year*   F.S. Collins, et al. "New goals for the U.S. Human Genome Project: 1998–2003," *Science* 282 (1998): 682–689.

3. p. 130 *One of Celera's founding principles*   J.C. Venter, Prepared statement before the Subcommittee on Energy and Environment, U.S. House of Representatives. April 6, 2000. Online at *http://www.house.gov/ science/ venter_040600.htm.*

4. p. 130 *A key feature of Celera's*   Celera Genomics press release, April 6, 2000.

5. p. 131 *the company had sequenced more than*   Celera Genomics press release, June 1, 2000.

6. p. 131 *NHGRI is now accelerating its program*   NHGRI release, August 7, 2000.

7. p. 131 *the Mouse Sequencing Consortium (MSC) was formally unveiled*   Mouse Sequencing Consortium press release, October 6, 2000.

8. p. 132 *The Centers producing the data*   Ensembl Trace Server, online at *http://trace.ensembl.org.*

9. p. 132 *Celera now intends to continue*   Celera Genomics press release, October 12, 2000.

10. p. 132 *Celera mentioned, almost as an aside,*   N. Wade, "Genetic sequence of mouse is also decoded," *The New York Times*, February 13, 2001.

11. p. 133 *Celera has sequenced and assembled*   Celera Genomics press release, April 27, 2001.

12. p. 133 *bringing the amount of mouse sequence available*   NHGRI press release, May 8, 2001.

13. p. 133 *overwhelmingly conserved in mouse*   P. Dehal, et al., "Human chromosome 19 and related regions in mouse: conservative and lineage-specific evolution," *Science* 293 (2001): 104–111.

14. p. 134 *advanced draft sequence*   Sanger Institute press release, May 6, 2002.

15. p. 134 *Even the rather ungainly title*   R. Mural, et al., "A comparison of whole-genome shotgun-derived mouse chromosome 16 and the human genome," *Science* 296 (2002): 1661–1671.

16. p. 134 *virtual genome analysis center*   NHGRI press release, December 4, 2002.

17. p. 134 *With the complete sequence of the human genome*   R. Waterston, et al., "Initial sequencing and comparative analysis of the mouse genome," *Nature* 420 (2002): 520–562.

18. p. 136 *to identify and precisely locate*   NHGRI press release, March 4, 2003.

19. p. 137 *with grants totaling $58 million*   Baylor College press release, February 28, 2001. Online at *http://public.bcm.tmc.edu/pa/ratdna.htm*.

20. p. 137 *we are pleased to be collaborating*   Celera Genomics press release, February 28, 2001.

21. p. 137 *NIH would pay $21 million*   J. Billis, "Government gives Celera $21 million to map rat genome," *Washington Post*, March 1, 2001.

22. p. 138 *The feasibility of assembling a repeat-dense*   S. Aparicio, et al., "Whole-genome shotgun assembly and analysis of the genome of *Fugu rubripes*," *Science* 297 (2002): 1301–1310.

23. p. 138 *it can produce a hundred eggs each week*   D.R. Beier, "Zebrafish: genomics on the fast track," *Genome Research* 8 (1998): 9–17.

24. p. 139 *that comparative genome analysis of a handful*   M. Kellis, et al., "Sequencing and comparison of yeast species to identify genes and regulatory elements," *Nature* 423 (2003): 241–254.

25. p. 139 *The genomic sequence information*   NHGRI press release, October 2001.

26. p. 140 *researchers would write proposals*   the proposals are online at *http://www.genome.gov/10002154*.

27. p. 140 *contribution to the improvement of human health*   NHGRI press release, October 2001.

28. p. 140 *The first papers were submitted in February 2002*   NHGRI press release, May 22, 2002.

29. p. 140 *if the HGP officially embraces a primate*   E.H. McConkey, et al., *Science* 289 (2000): 1295–1296.

30. p. 142 *expressed interest in helping to support the project*   NHGRI press release, May 22, 2002.

31. p. 142 *In September 2002, the NHGRI announced*   NHGRI press release, September 11, 2002.

32. p. 144 *analyses of 120 dogs representing 60 breeds*   NHGRI press release, May 29, 2003.

33. p. 145 *The result is a small tadpole*   JGI press release, December 12, 2002.

34. p. 145 *One was the African frog*   JGI press release, August 20, 2002.

35. p. 145 *the other was a pair of microbes*   JGI press release, October 16, 2002.

36. p. 145 *a relative of many familiar plants*   V. Walbot, "A green chapter in the book of life," *Nature* 408 (2000): 794–795.

37. p. 145 *A thousand Arabidopsis plants*   V. Walbot, "A green chapter in the book of life," *Nature* 408 (2000): 794–795.

38. p. 146 *maize/corn, for example,*   D. Adam, "Now for the hard ones," *Nature* 408 (2000): 792–793.

39. p. 146 *the Arabidopsis genome was published*   The *Arabidopsis* Genome Initiative, "Analysis of the genome sequence of the flowering plant *Arabidopsis thaliana*," *Nature* 408 (2000): 796–815.

40. p. 146 *The rapid rise of* Arabidopsis *as the model* V. Walbot, "A green chapter in the book of life," *Nature* 408 (2000): 794–795.

41. p. 146 *Rice is the staple food* B. Antonio, et al., "Rice at the forefront of plant genome informatics," *Genome Informatics* 11 (2000): 3–11.

42. p. 146 *scientists were surprised to learn* E. Pennisi, "Stealth genome rocks rice researchers," *Science* 288 (2000): 239–241.

43. p. 147 *The project was completed* Myriad Genetics press release, January 26, 2001.

44. p. 147 *through scientific collaborations* R.J. Davenport, "Syngenta finishes, consortium goes on," *Science* 291 (2001): 807.

45. p. 147 *The value of the sequence* D. Kennedy, "The importance of rice," *Science* 296 (2002): 13.

46. p. 147 *Academic researchers will be able to access* Syngenta press release, March 29, 2002.

47. p. 148 *It seems likely that the release* J. Bennetzen, "Opening the door to comparative plant biology," *Science* 296 (2002): 60–63.

48. p. 148 *the complete genomic sequence of chromosome 1* T. Sasaki, et al., "The genome sequence and structure of rice chromosome 1," *Nature* 420 (2002): 312–316.

49. p. 148 *Celera was reportedly planning* A. Saegusa, "US firm's bid to sequence rice genome causes stir in Japan. . ." *Nature* 398 (1999): 545.

50. p. 148 *We never started it because* D. Adam, "Now for the hard ones," *Nature* 408 (2000): 792–793.

51. p. 148 *His wider plan is to sequence* N. Wade, "Dr. J. Craig Venter: the genome's combative entrepreneur," *The New York Times*, May 18, 1999.

52. p. 149 *The Celera Genomics group . . . intends* Celera Genomics press release, December 6, 2000.

53. p. 149 *Over the past three years* Celera Genomics press release, June 13, 2001.

54. p. 149 *By working with Paradigm* Celera Genomics press release, December 4, 2001.

55. p. 149 *Craig Venter would be stepping down* Celera Genomics press release, January 24, 2002.

56. p. 149 *I got fired!* K. Davies, et al., "John Craig Venter unvarnished," *Bio-IT World* (November 2002).

57. p. 150 *One was the sequencing* K. Davies, et al., "John Craig Venter unvarnished," *Bio-IT World* (November 2002).

58. p. 150 *a major initiative* Applera press release, November 6, 2000.

59. p. 150 *free Celera's executive team to focus* Celera Genomics press release, April 22, 2002.

60. p. 150 *Celera Genomics' core mission* Applera Corporation Teleconference (April 25, 2002). Online at *http://www.applera.com/press/prccorp0:4:2502.html*.

61. p. 150 *whole genome sequencing is not* A. Coghlan, "Celera abandons gene sequencing," *New Scientist* (June 13, 2002). Online at *http://www.newscientist.com/news/news.jsp?id=ns99992401*.

62. p. 150 *poised to develop a first-rate capability*   Incyte press release, February 13, 2002.

63. p. 150 *Incyte acquired Maxia Pharmaceuticals*   Incyte press release, November 12, 2002.

64. p. 150 *reflecting the company's broader mission*   Incyte press release, December 16, 2002.

65. p. 150 *leading to 103 redundancies.*   "Millennium Pharmaceuticals laying off," *The Boston Globe*, December 17, 2002.

66. p. 151 *from 1994 on, it forged more than 20*   "About Millennium, history." Online at *http://www.mlnm.com/about/history/index.asp.*

67. p. 151 *Millennium leadership also recognized*   "About Millennium, history." Online at *http://www.mlnm.com/about/history/index.asp.*

68. p. 151 *was revised in July 1996*   HGS press release, July 2, 1996.

69. p. 151 *all of these exclusive deals expired*   HGS press release, July 2, 2001.

70. p. 151 *it needed to make even more*   HGS press release, October 31, 2001.

71. p. 151 *trumping the $118 million raised*   HGS press release, April 17, 1997.

72. p. 151 *founded in 1991*   Pangea press release, February 11, 1997.

73. p. 152 *when it received $10 million in financing*   Pangea press release, February 11, 1997.

74. p. 152 *Pangea Systems Inc. is a small*   L.M. Fisher, "Surfing the human genome," *The New York Times*, September 20, 1999.

75. p. 152 *the first Web portal that enabled scientists*   L.M. Fisher, "Surfing the human genome," *The New York Times*, September 20, 1999.

76. p. 152 *Doug Brutlag, cofounder of IntelliGenetics*   DoubleTwist press release, August 18, 1997.

77. p. 152 *once one of the most dynamic bioinformatics*   J. Knight, "Software firm falls victim to shifting bioinformatics needs," *Nature* 416 (2002): 357.

78. p. 153 *It's not so much what the information is*   E. Marshall, "A high-stakes gamble on genome sequencing," *Science* 284 (1999): 1906–1909.

79. p. 153 *Celera bought the specialist company*   Celera Genomics press release, March 20, 2000.

80. p. 153 *develop the next generation*   Celera Genomics press release, January 19, 2001.

81. p. 154 *based on a clustered architecture*   Celera Genomics press release, May 8, 2001.

82. p. 154 *its capitalization hit $14 billion, making it one*   Questions and Answers after Commonwealth Club lecture, March 5, 2002. Online at *http://www.commonwealthclub.org/archive/02/02–03venter-qa.html.*

83. p. 154 *it was this utterly unrealistic figure*   Questions and Answers after Commonwealth Club lecture, March 5, 2002. Online at *http://www.commonwealthclub.org/archive/02/02–03venter-qa.html.*

CHAPTER 8

People's Genes

Craig Venter's departure from Celera meant that he was no longer in the spotlight and headlines as much as he had been during the golden years of the great Human Genome Race that the media had reported on with such glee. Though down, he was certainly not out of the publicity game—as a typical Venter moment in 2002 proved.

On April 17, he mentioned casually on the U.S. TV program *60 Minutes II* that the Celera human genome was principally his. This rather nullified the careful procedures employed for selecting the pool of 21 donors that were enrolled by Celera, whittled down to five for the final sequencing—two males and three females. It also undermined the solemn statement in the Celera paper that "the decision of whose DNA to sequence was based on a complex mix of factors," since the dominant one was clearly Venter's desire to see his own genome.

Amusingly, the NIH-DOE guidance on selecting human subjects for DNA sequencing addressed this issue explicitly. "Staff of laboratories involved in library construction and DNA sequencing may be eager to volunteer to be donors because of their interest and belief in the HGP." However, the guidelines warned, "there is a potential that the choice of persons so closely involved in the research may be interpreted as elitist," and so "it is recommended that donors should not be recruited from laboratory staff, including the principal investigator."

Accusations of elitism would hardly have worried Venter, whose hide had grown thick under a barrage of unflattering epithets during his genomic career. And, in a way, it was perhaps appropriate that the final result of Celera's human genome project should be the ultimate and most intimate manifestation of the man whose dominant personality had informed and driven it from start to finish.

Poetic justice aside, Venter's little surprise in 2002 served to emphasize something that had often been overlooked in all the grand rhetoric about sequencing the human genome: the fact that it does not exist. Rather than *the* human genome, there are billions of different human genomes, of which Venter's was but one example, distinguished in this case by the fact that it belonged to the first person to have the bulk of his DNA sequenced. The Human Genome Project's sequence, by contrast, is truly a mosaic: individual BAC clones were drawn from several people—two predominantly, but with contributions from others mixed in.

For most people, it is precisely the differences between human genomes that are interesting, not what they have in common, which is more relevant to scientists. It is the unique set of several million DNA letters that defines large parts of who we are and plays a major role in determining our health and illnesses. It is this kind of variation that lies at the heart of genetics. Mendel's original experiments with peas involved crossing plants with different pairs of traits—two colors or two sizes, for example. Each of these traits corresponded to two different versions, known as *alleles*, of a particular gene—two stretches of DNA that differ for that gene.

Genetics has been most successful investigating so-called Mendelian disorders: those that are due to changes in one gene. Typically, this means that there is an allele that causes a genetic disease, while the other allele (or alleles, since sometimes there is more than one variant at a given position) does not. Victor McCusick started putting together a directory of such Mendelian disorders in 1966; in 1987, it became the Online Mendelian Inheritance in Man. In April 2003 it contained encyclopedic references to over 8,500 locations on the human genome sequence that are involved in these kinds of diseases.

Nearly all human cells come with 46 chromosomes, 23 from each parent. During *mitosis*—cell division—all of these DNA sequences are copied as exactly as possible before being redistributed evenly between the two new cells. But during the creation of special cells called *gametes*—the ovum and spermatozoon—a more complex process occurs. Corresponding chromosomes, one from the mother and father, pair up and then swap stretches of DNA to produce a kind of banding, with alternating sections from each parent. This process, known as *meiosis*, allows genetic variation to be introduced. Gametes have only one copy of these "banded" chromosomes, so when the sperm fuses with the ovum, each set of 23 chromosomes joins—but does not mix—with the other to give the full set of 46 chromosomes in the new cell, which then begins dividing to produce the embryo.

As these sequence swaps take place, they mix the sets of the various alleles—the variant forms of the genes—that are found in an interbreeding population. It seems that the shuffling only takes place at certain points, so relatively large blocks of code are exchanged, rather than just a few DNA letters. As a result, a marker on the genome—a readily identifiable stretch of DNA, for example—that is near a particular gene will tend to stay near it, even after many meioses. The nearer it is, the more likely it is to stay on the same block. This forms the basis of what is called *linkage analysis*, which aims to pinpoint the approximate position of genes that have alleles associated with a particular medical condition.

If a particular marker sequence turns up among those affected by a disease more often than among their unaffected relatives, this suggests that the marker is close to the disease-causing allele in question, and that both have been inherited by some of the family group. Linkage analysis therefore allows the position of a likely gene to be narrowed down enormously, certainly to a particular chromosome, and perhaps to just a few million bases. This is still a huge stretch to explore, but far less than the 3 billion letters of the entire human genome.

Because of this potential, in the early 1980s a kind of proto-HGP began—not to sequence DNA, but to create what is called a genetic map. This map shows the relative position of markers, in this case a type known as RFLPs (Restriction Fragment Length Polymorphisms). Since such a map, if dense enough, would speed the location of medically important—and hence valuable—genes, creating it also had clear commercial value. This led to a race between a company, Collaborative Research, and a public group, headed by Raymond White at the Howard Hughes Medical Institute at the University of Utah.

This competition to create a genetic map even finished with the same kind of unscientific bickering that characterized the end of the first phase of the human genome sequencing projects, in what came to be known as the "map flap." As *Science* wrote in 1987: "This tiff is the most public in a long-simmering and acrimonious feud—some call it a war—between the two research groups. . . . The normal, if intense, scientific rivalry seems to be heightened by a sort of clash of cultures between an academic researcher and a biotech company with its understandable need for publicity and eye towards profits."

The map flap and Collaborative Research are largely forgotten today, but the company's influence in the early days of genomics was felt in many fields. As well as creating the earliest human genetic map, Collaborative—which was founded in 1961 and changed its name to Genome Therapeutics Corporation (GTC) in 1994—was also one of the first to work on sequencing bacteria. A story in *Science* in January 1995 reported that on December 9, 1994, "Genome Therapeutics Corp. . . . announced in a press release that it had sequenced the genome of *Helicobacter pylori*, the bacterium that causes most peptic ulcers. A letter accompanying the press release, which the letter says was sent to a 'few knowledgeable writers,' refers to the sequencing of *H. pylori* as a 'milestone'." However, this was hard to verify, since "GTC has no intention of going through peer review and publishing the sequence or depositing the data in public data banks," *Science* noted.

This lack of data or peer review provoked considerable skepticism from scientists at the time, especially those working on sequencing organisms themselves. One told *Science* that GTC's press release and the accompanying letter was "science by press conference" and an example "of the worse part of the commercialization" of science. Oddly enough, it was precisely these charges that were later leveled against the speaker, a certain J. Craig Venter, then working at TIGR on what came to be the official first sequenced organism, *H. influenzae*.

Controversy aside, Collaborative was noteworthy for the impressive roster of scientists it had assembled to help it carry out the genetic mapping with RFLPs. David Botstein, who had come up with idea of using RFLPs in the first place, was on its scientific advisory board, while two young researchers destined for greater things were handling the practical details.

"The actual mapping involves determining the linkages among the markers," *Science* wrote, "their arrangement along the chromosomes, and the distances between them. This entails a massive number-crunching exercise, for which Collaborative used two new computer algorithms for multilocus linkage analysis"—that is, for finding particular markers that seem to be correlated with the presence or absence of disease alleles—"one developed by Eric Lander of MIT's Whitehead Institute, the other by Collaborative scientist Philip Green." The latter, of course, went on to create a number of key bioinformatics programs, while Lander—who stepped down from his position as consultant to Collaborative over the map flap—became one of the leading figures in the public Human Genome Project.

Although Lander is best known for his high-profile work in turning the Whitehead Institute/MIT Center for Genome Research into the top public sequencing laboratory in the United States as part of the Human Genome Project, it is the study of genetic variation that has always been at the heart of his work. In a sense, perhaps, even his work on the human genome was a means to this end, albeit a rather grand and important means.

Born in 1957 in Brooklyn, New York, Lander received his undergraduate degree in mathematics from Princeton, then was a Rhodes scholar at Oxford, where he earned a PhD in 1981. On his return to the United States, he became Assistant, then Associate professor in the Graduate School of Business at Harvard. His heart seems not to have been in this field, however, even if his studies of organization probably stood him in good stead when running his big sequencing factory. Lander soon became passionately interested in biology; he began studying molecular biology and practicing his wet-lab skills alongside his work at Harvard.

Lander later explained how the move to biology came about: "Although I trained as a pure mathematician, when I was finishing a set of work in pure mathematics I began casting about for something else to apply my interests to, and a good friend suggested I go study the human brain. There are lots of great mathematical problems in the human brain. Being hopelessly naive and having a spare summer, I started reading about it. And I came away at the end of the summer realizing I didn't even know enough biology to understand what the problems were. So being even more naive, I started learning biology in my spare time. And you know how these things are—one thing led to another, I began moonlighting in labs, cloning genes late at night, and eventually took a leave of absence for a while to go down to visit at MIT and learn more about this and I guess I got hooked."

Lander became a Visiting Scientist at MIT's Department of Biology in 1984 while still retaining his post at the Harvard Business School. It was a chance encounter that really set his genetics career in motion. "I met David Botstein in 1985 outside of a seminar, at MIT," Lander explains, "and Botstein launched into a whole series of questions about how you could ever use genetics to dissect complex diseases. He'd heard I was a mathematician who had been learning genetics for the past couple of years, and we immediately fell to arguing about this, talking about it, working on it." Underlying Lander's move to genetics was the idea that "biology was not just molecules, it was information." In particular, he says, "What captivated me was the notion that the information about what genes cause disease was hiding in the genome, was hiding in the transmission pattern in families, was hiding in the distribution of variation in populations." Given all this information just waiting to be revealed, "the trick is to read it, to mine it, to decode it."

In 1986, Lander secured a position as a Fellow of the Whitehead Institute for Biomedical Research. Remarkably, by 1987 he had won a MacArthur Fellowship commonly called the "genius award"—for his genetics work. It was a testimony to the rapid rate at which he was making significant contributions to this field and the already evident promise that he would contribute much more in the future. In 1989, Lander became a Member of the Whitehead Institute and Associate Professor at MIT. Finally, in 1990, he became Director of the new Whitehead Institute/MIT Center for Genome Research.

The center was involved in major projects like producing genetic maps for the mouse and humans, both of which required huge amounts of lab work, as well as the invention of techniques to allow large-scale automation. For example, the physical map of the human genome, produced by Lander and his colleagues in December 1995 (discussed in chapter 4), involved the creation of the Genomatron, a robotic system capable of 300,000 chemical reactions per day.

In addition to this practical work, however, Lander continued to produce papers grappling with the theory of genetics. A good example of the drier side of Lander's work is a major paper that was published with Nicholas Schork in *Science* in September 1994. Its title not only laid down the subject matter for the 12-page review, but also encapsulated perhaps the single most important theme of Lander's work: "Genetic dissection of complex traits." Lander and Schork sketched the background to complex traits as follows: "The key breakthrough [in genetic mapping] was the recognition that naturally occurring DNA sequence variation provided a virtually unlimited supply of genetic markers—an idea first conceived by Botstein and colleagues. . . . These ideas soon led to an explosion of interest in the genetic mapping of rare human diseases having simple Mendelian inheritance." They noted that, at the time of writing in 1994, "more than 400 such diseases have been genetically mapped in this manner, and nearly 40 positionally cloned." A gene is "mapped" once its approximate location on the genome is established, and "positionally cloned" when its exact location and sequence have been obtained.

They then moved on to their paper's subject. "Human geneticists are now beginning to explore a new genetic frontier, driven by an inconvenient reality: Most traits of medical relevance do not follow simple Mendelian monogenic inheritance. Such 'complex' traits include susceptibilities to heart disease, hypertension, diabetes, cancer, and infection." That is, several genes may play a role, or there may be a subtle environmental component that interferes with traditional Mendelian inheritance in such a way that it is hard to locate the gene or genes involved using traditional methods like linkage analysis.

A couple of years later, in 1996, Lander himself tried to apply what might be termed classical linkage analysis to a complex disease: adult-onset diabetes. He added a refinement designed to amplify any weak genetic correlation that might be present. Instead of choosing families from the usual places—major cities in the United States or Western Europe, he opted to screen some 4,000 individuals in an isolated region in Finland.

As the press release that was issued to accompany the publication of the results explained: "The Botnia region on the western coast of Finland is ideal for genetic studies because the population is unusually homogeneous—it was settled over 1,000 years ago and there has been little immigration since the middle of the 14th century—and it has many large, stable families. In addition, local health centers maintain excellent medical records. The scientists asked all previously identified diabetic patients in the Botnia region to complete questionnaires concerning family history and then recruited families with a particular history to participate in clinical studies."

"Twenty-six families, comprising 217 individuals (120 diabetes patients and 97 unaffected relatives), were deemed to meet the research criteria: that is, they had at least three affected family members, including one patient who developed diabetes before age 60 and another before age 65."

"The scientists performed a complete genome scan on all 217 subjects, analyzing DNA spelling differences at 387 sites distributed across all 46 human chromosomes. The goal was to locate one or more spelling differences that occurred with greater frequency in diabetes patients than their unaffected relatives. Such spelling differences provide crucial signposts, narrowing the search for new disease-related genes to tiny fragments of a single human chromosome." Those "crucial signposts"—genomic markers—eventually pinpointed a gene, but only one that "may be involved in a significant fraction of adult-onset diabetes tied to low insulin secretion," as the press release cautiously put it.

Linkage studies depend on finding many affected families—something that is difficult and time-consuming—and even when these are available, the results are often tentative and provisional, as Lander's work on diabetes had shown. An alternative is to use association studies, which do not require families, but simply compare those affected by the disease and others, known as controls, who are not. As Lander and Schork explained in their 1994 review article: "Association studies do not concern familial inheritance patterns at all. Rather, they are case-control studies based on a comparison of unrelated and unaffected individuals from the population. An allele A at a gene of interest is said to be associated with the trait if it occurs at a significantly higher frequency among affected compared with control individuals." In practice, association studies compare the prevalence of a set of genetic markers between affected and unaffected groups, looking for a marker that turns up significantly more often in the affected group, since this is likely to be near the gene in question.

This is clearly much easier than finding enough affected families, but there is a downside. As Lander and his colleague noted: "Association studies are not well suited to whole-genome searches in large, mixed populations." The difficulty is that "one would need tens of thousands of genetic markers to 'cover' the genome." If there are not enough markers, the gene whose allele is linked with the disease may be missed. The problem, then, is shifted from locating the families to finding enough markers.

It was Lander himself who sketched out a solution to this problem, in an article published in *Science* in 1996. Called rather grandly "The new genomics: global views of biology," it proposed ten goals for the next phase of genomics "with success in sight" for the Human Genome Project. One of these goals was the "systematic identification of all common variants in human genes." As Lander explained, although genes have thousands of alleles—because simple DNA letter changes can occur at multiple points throughout the often tens of thousands of bases that code for a protein—in practice, only a handful of common variants in their coding regions are found very often. "The effective number of alleles," Lander wrote, "is rather small, often two or three. This limited diversity reflects the fact that modern humans are descended from a relatively small population that underwent exponential explosion in evolutionary recent time."

The big benefit of compiling a catalog of common variants, Lander explained, was that it would "transform the search for susceptibility genes through the use of association studies. . . . They are logistically simpler to organize and potentially more powerful than family-based linkage studies, but they have had the practical limitation that one can only test a few guesses rather than being able to systematically scan the genome." A large number of markers are needed for association studies, and hitherto it had been difficult to find enough for large-scale scans. As Lander noted, though, "in the post-genome world, however, it would be possible to test disease susceptibility against every common variant simultaneously," once a catalog of them had been drawn up.

Although Lander did not use the term, the key to association studies is the use of single nucleotide polymorphisms—SNPs, pronounced "snips"—defined as positions in the DNA sequence at which two alternative bases occur at an appreciable frequency (generally greater than one percent). For example, for a SNP at a certain point in the genome, the letter A might be found in the vast majority of the population, with T in a few percent, and C or G in very rare cases. There were believed to be around 3 million SNPs in every human genome, or one every 1,000 bases on average. Most of these have no effect since they occur in noncoding regions; however, a small but important minority do. In fact, these apparently trivial differences in DNA largely determine who we are. In theory, then, SNPs would be a perfect way of providing an extremely dense map of markers for association studies.

The potential of SNPs to allow powerful association studies to be carried out on populations was one reason why the head of the HGP, Francis Collins —himself an expert in genetics—and two colleagues wrote in 1997 that "the time is now right to begin the systematic cataloging of human sequence variation," just as Lander had suggested. There was another, more ominous reason, however. "Although it may seem odd that common variation in the human genome could be claimed as intellectual property," Collins wrote, "some patent experts consider SNPs (particularly those found in protein-coding regions, or cSNPs) to have sufficient defining features of novelty, utility, and nonobviousness to be patented. If SNP development continues without guidance or public funding support, substantial numbers of SNPs and cSNPs could be generated in private collections."

Over the next few years, the momentum behind SNPs began to build. First came a landmark paper in *Science* in 1998 from a large group of researchers from the Whitehead Institute, including Lander, and from the company Affymetrix, a pioneer in the development of DNA chips (see chapter 10). Lander and his colleagues explored the feasibility of creating a dense map of SNPs. The map was to be not for the whole genome, since this would be a vast project taking teams around the world many years, but for some 24,000 STSs (sequence-tagged sites), comprising a total of over 2 million bases. The STSs, which had been developed for the physical map of the human genome put together by the Whitehead Institute in 1995, were used as a convenient way to provide thousands of small snippets from it. Comparing the same snippet from different individuals allowed the common single base variants—the SNPs—to be located for those particular parts of the genome.

Over 3,000 possible SNPs were identified, and around 2,000 of these could be placed on a genetic map of the human genome, which provided a rough indication of their location. Finally, Lander and coworkers created DNA chips that allowed the genotype for each SNP—the particular letter—to be measured automatically. Although the chip contained just 500 SNPs, the work showed that not only could a dense map of SNPs be generated, but that it could then be used to genotype individual genomes—establish the particular SNP pattern—in a highly automated fashion. Lander knew from his previous experience in mapping and sequencing the human genome that the ability to automate was crucially important; it allowed tasks to be scaled up to new levels and to tackle new problems. This, then, was the significance of the paper: it showed that "large-scale screening for human variation is clearly feasible," as Lander and his team wrote.

Parallel to this work investigating how SNPs might be found and used on a large scale, public databases were created to aid the process of discovery and dissemination. Collins' National Human Genome Research Institute (NHGRI) assembled the DNA Polymorphism Discovery Resource, which held samples from 450 U.S. residents with ancestry from all the major regions of the world. Lander's study, by contrast, had drawn on donors from Amish, Venezuelan, and Utah populations.

In collaboration with NHGRI, the National Center for Biotechnology Information (NCBI) launched its dbSNP database in September 1998. As with DNA sequences, the SNPs in this database came from many different sources, and were not a systematic attempt to cover the human genome, for example, with a dense map of markers. This, however, was precisely the aim of The SNP Consortium, announced on April 15, 1999.

As the accompanying press release explained: "The two-year, $45 million initiative to create a high-quality map of genetic markers is being funded by the Wellcome Trust and ten pharmaceutical companies: AstraZeneca PLC, Bayer AG, Bristol-Myers Squibb Company, F. Hoffmann-La Roche, Glaxo Wellcome PLC, Hoechst Marion Roussel AG, Novartis, Pfizer Inc, Searle, and SmithKline Beecham PLC. . . . Through the collaboration, it is expected that a high-density, high-quality map will be created more quickly, and with shared financial risk and less duplication of effort than if each company pursued development of a SNP map on its own."

A news story in *Nature* offered more background. "The idea that pharmaceutical companies could fund a more comprehensive map emerged from discussions two years ago"—in 1997, around the time that Collins first aired the idea for such a project. "Pharmaceutical companies were initially approached with the idea of forming a profit-making consortium, which would charge for the use of the map. But those companies that agreed to the idea surprised most observers by insisting that the data should be made available free," just as Merck had done with its EST database. "The Wellcome Trust's involvement was also conditional on full and free access to the data."

The goals of The SNP Consortium were ambitious. As the Chairman of The SNP Consortium later wrote: "The objectives of the Consortium are as follows. 1. Identify 300,000 SNPs within two years of launch of the scientific work plan. 2. Map 150,000 of the SNPs over the two-year term of the program. 3. Manage publication of the resulting SNP map in a manner intended to maximize the number of SNPs that enter the public domain (as that term is understood in the patent law)"—the last of these to prevent anyone else from patenting them.

The figure of 150,000 in two years was significantly higher than the 100,000 SNPs that Collins had hoped would be available in 2003 as part of his 1998 five-year plan for the Human Genome Project. The SNP discovery and mapping would be carried out by the Whitehead Institute, Bob Waterston's Washington University School of Medicine, and the Wellcome Trust's Sanger Centre. The main technique would be shotgun sequencing—not of the whole genome this time, but of many small sections drawn from samples donated by 24 unrelated individuals.

In fact, things progressed even more briskly than The SNP Consortium had expected. The public work on SNPs culminated in a joint paper that combined the work of The SNP Consortium with that of the Human Genome Project, which, following Collins' edicts, was generating SNPs alongside its main sequencing work. It appeared on February 15, 2001, in the same issue of *Nature* as the public sequence of the human genome, and was inevitably rather overshadowed by it.

The paper drew on all the SNPs that were publicly available in November 2000. It described nearly one and half million SNPs that had not only been discovered, but mapped to a specific location, too. That so many had been placed on the genome was due to one central fact: the availability of the draft human genome sequence. This meant that placing a SNP was simply a matter of matching the DNA sequence surrounding a SNP with one on the assembled genome. The relative ease with which this was achieved compared to the considerable efforts required from Lander and colleagues to map their 3,000 SNPs provided an early hint of the transformative effect that the elucidation of the complete human genome sequence was going to have.

Genomic companies, too, were offering SNP collections. For example, Incyte introduced its SNP database in January 2000. Celera was slower off the mark, launching its own SNP Reference Database in September of that year as part of its Web-based Celera Discovery System. The SNPs were derived from comparing the sequences of all five donors whose sequences collectively went to make up Celera's human genome sequence. Presumably this time, however, Craig Venter's DNA did not dominate, because the whole point of SNPs is to pinpoint variation, which necessarily implies comparison of at least two individuals.

Even though Celera claimed at the launch that it had 2.4 million unique, proprietary SNPs—excluding the usual borrowing of public database material, which added a further 400,000 non-overlapping entries—it effectively faced the same situation here as it did with the human genome. For its SNP database to be competitive in the face of the free SNPs on offer from dbSNP, it needed to continually produce more of them faster than the public projects. This was reflected in its announcement of the Applera Genome Project— not, be it noted, the Celera Genome Project, since this was in the wake of Venter's departure and the reorientation of the company towards drug development.

Speaking on April 25, 2002, Kathy Ordoñez, Celera Genomics' new boss, gave some details. "The Applera Genome Project, involving the re-sequencing of the coding and regulatory regions of approximately 40 individuals plus a chimpanzee, is proceeding rapidly," she said. "The Project's aim is to identify novel SNPs in and around genes that have the potential to alter patterns of gene expression and protein products." Among other uses, Ordoñez explained that Celera Genomics' sister company, Celera Diagnostics, "is using these discoveries to conduct association studies to identify novel diagnostic markers, which it intends to configure into tests to diagnose and monitor disease."

Celera may have the advantage in terms of technological firepower—after all, it must be doing something with all those sequencers it used for the fruit fly, human, and mouse genomes—but it came late to the game of looking for associations between markers and diseases. A number of companies already have well-established track records in this area.

For example, Myriad Genetics made the search for genes that can play important roles in diseases the basis of its strategy for most of the 1990s. Its first major breakthrough was locating the *BRCA1* gene in 1994, variants of which predispose carriers to breast cancer. It followed this up in 1995 with *BRCA2*, another gene involved in breast cancer. Later successes included genes with alleles conferring predispositions to diabetes, prostate cancer, high cholesterol, and hereditary obesity.

Accounts for the financial year ending June 30, 1997 mention one reason why Myriad Genetics was more successful finding genes for complex traits like diabetes than other players in this market: "A key competitive advantage of the Company's gene discovery process is the information derived from the genetic analysis of large, multi-generational Utah families. The early Utah population was characterized by many large families with a dozen or more children, hundreds of grandchildren and thousands of descendants. By using the extensive and detailed genealogical records kept by the families themselves, the Company is better able to resolve the ambiguities caused by interactions between environmental factors and multiple predisposition genes."

This was the approach that Eric Lander and his team had employed in Botnia, Finland. Myriad Genetics employed it on a far larger scale: "Researchers have collected over 25,000 DNA samples from extended families with breast cancer, ovarian cancer, colon cancer, prostate cancer, lung cancer, bladder cancer, brain cancer, leukemia, lymphoma, and melanoma. In the cardiovascular and obesity fields, the Company is currently working with researchers at the University of Utah's Cardiovascular Genetics Research Clinic, which has an extensive collection of data from extended families with cardiovascular disease and obesity, with over 10,000 DNA samples collected to date." Even the scale of these resources, however, pales in comparison to those of another gene-discovery company that can draw on the entire population of Iceland—some quarter of a million people—for its DNA samples and corresponding linkage analyses.

This company is called deCODE, and the driving force behind it is someone who, as much as Craig Venter with Celera, has made his company a manifestation of his own personality: Kári Stefánsson. He received his medical training in his native Iceland before holding positions in neurology, neuropathology, and neurosciences at the University of Chicago from 1983 to 1993. From 1993 until April 1997, he was professor in the same field at Harvard University. One of Stefánsson's areas of research there was multiple sclerosis.

As he later explained: "During my days as a researcher in academe studying the genetics of multiple sclerosis, I concluded that the scarce item in human genetics is not technology but the availability of a sample population with a sufficiently homogeneous genetic background to identify genetic variations. Iceland's highly homogenous population, along with the vast amount of accumulated information on the genealogy of its citizens and the high quality of the country's medical care—a national health-care system since 1915 with universal access and very good record-keeping—makes it a unique resource for such an endeavor."

Homogeneous populations without significant immigration are valuable because the range of genetic variation is limited to that present in the so-called "founders"—those making up the original forebears. This makes finding particular alleles that are linked to predispositions for certain illnesses easier than in general populations, where there are more variant forms. It was for this reason that Lander chose the isolated region of Botnia in Finland when searching for a gene linked to diabetes, and why Myriad Genetics is based in Salt Lake City, so as to be near to the Utah populations, which also are relatively homogeneous. Some have cast doubts on the homogeneity of the Icelandic population. Even Stefánsson seems to have backpedaled on this aspect: "I think that genetic homogeneity is overrated. It helps," he said in an interview in 2001. The other advantages he cited, though—the genealogical and medical records—have remained at the heart of deCODE's approach.

Because of a national obsession with genealogy—reflected even in the structure of Icelandic names, where the surname is a patronymic, formed from the father's first name—the future deCODE would be able to create a computerized database of the Icelandic nation. This database would go back not the usual two or three generations, but a thousand years in some cases. In 1999, Stefánsson said that the database held 600,000 names out of the 800,000 Icelanders who had ever lived.

It was during a visit home that Stefánsson had his insight into the unique value of this genealogical information. Genomics was no longer the hot investment area it had been a few years before, but Stefánsson's energetic advocacy of the idea enabled him to raise $12 million in just a few months. deCODE genetics was launched in August 1996 as a U.S. company registered in Delaware, but with its headquarters in Reykjavik, Iceland's capital.

deCODE's application of classical linkage analysis to the Icelandic population rapidly paid off. On August 25, 1997, just a year after its creation, the company published a paper in *Nature Genetics* on familial essential tremor (FET). An accompanying press release explained: "Essential tremor is a disease characterized by shakiness of the hands and arms and, occasionally, the head and voice as well. The disease affects an estimated 5-10 percent of the elderly population, making it more common than Parkinson's disease, a disease that produces a different type of tremor in affected individuals."

Stefánsson commented: "The disease is passed from generation to generation in affected families, but no group has been able to locate a causative gene until now." Thanks to the excellent clinical records kept by Iceland's public health system, deCODE had been able to identify 16 families with 75 affected individuals. Drawing up a family tree of these individuals was relatively easy because of the unparalleled genealogical records in Iceland. Genotyping a series of markers across the genomes of the affected and unaffected individuals, coupled with the known relationships of individuals, allowed deCODE's computers to calculate that one allele of a particular gene on chromosome 13 turned up more often in affected individuals than chance alone would produce.

Proving quickly that its approach worked was indispensable for the company. The way for deCODE to make money was by signing deals with pharmaceutical companies, just as Human Genome Sciences had done initially. The EST method that HGS employed, however, had already proved itself in Venter's widely-praised work; deCODE's linkage analysis may have been standard, but there was no guarantee that it would discover anything of interest in the Icelandic population, which might have turned out to have a seriously atypical gene pool.

The FET gene paper doubtless proved very handy as a calling card when it came to selling the deCODE approach to pharmaceutical companies. Certainly, F. Hoffmann-La Roche seems to have been impressed: on February 2, 1998, deCODE announced that it had signed a "research collaboration that will focus on the discovery of disease genes to facilitate the development of new therapeutic and diagnostic products."

"The total value of the five-year deal, the largest between a genomics company and a major pharmaceutical company in human genomics, could exceed US $200 million and includes an equity investment, research funding and milestone payments. The research will focus on the discovery of genes with alleles or mutations that predispose people to the development of up to twelve common diseases." Roche was banking on deCODE's ability to use the people of Iceland to find genes for non-Mendelian diseases that had so far eluded researchers.

Given the central role of the Icelanders in the Roche deal, it was appropriate that there should be a little thank-you gift for them, too. Quoting Stefánsson, the press release explained: "We are excited that Roche has agreed to give to the Icelandic nation, at no charge, all medications that will be developed on the basis of the discoveries resulting from our collaboration."

In March 1999, deCODE unveiled the first fruits of its collaboration with Roche: the mapping of a gene linked to osteoarthritis. In September of that year, deCODE announced the mapping of a gene linked to preeclampsia, a common condition—three to seven percent of pregnancies—that can be fatal for mothers and infants alike. In March 2000, another gene was mapped for Roche, one that was implicated in common forms of stroke, the third leading cause of death in the industrialized world. A few months later, deCODE followed this up with another major find, the mapping of a gene contributing to the occurrence of the late-onset form of Alzheimer's disease, the most common cause of dementia in the elderly, which affects about 5 percent of people over 65.

Two months later, deCODE announced not just the mapping—finding the rough location—but the identification of a gene linked to schizophrenia. Moving beyond mapping was by no means a trivial exercise, and deCODE employed a two-tier approach for carrying it out.

For the mapping, it used 1,000 microsatellite markers spread throughout the genome. A microsatellite marker is a segment of DNA that contains a variable number of short repeats; it represents a more powerful form of the original RFLP markers that were used in the early days of linkage analysis. By genotyping each microsatellite marker and comparing the pattern of repeats at each point, it was possible to determine which portion of the genome is shared among most or all of the patients whose illness is being studied.

At this point, when the gene had been mapped to a region of around 2 or 3 million base pairs (since there are 1,000 microsatellite markers spread across the 3 billion base pairs of the human genome), deCODE switched to using SNPs to create a denser set of markers. By genotyping enough SNPs across the mapped region it was possible to narrow down the portion where a gene was likely to be located to well under a million bases. This was sequenced using standard techniques; the resulting DNA code was fed into gene-searching programs. The stretches that were likely to code for genes could then be examined in detail. By screening them for mutations that were common in the affected members of the family but rare in those unaffected, a gene that may confer a predisposition to the disease in question could be pinpointed.

A month after locating the schizophrenia gene, deCODE had mapped a gene whose variants appeared to contribute to peripheral arterial occlusive disease, a narrowing of the arteries of the arms and legs that affects between two and five percent of those over 65. The disease results in pain, diminished mobility, and even amputation of the affected limbs. The same day also saw the unveiling of a chromosomal region that contained a gene with alleles that contributed to osteoporosis, the progressive thinning and weakening of the bones.

In 2001, the company isolated the gene involved with strokes that it had mapped the year before, as well as mapping a gene involved in adult-onset diabetes—the kind that is most prevalent among the severely obese and people over the age of 40. To round off a good year for gene finding, deCODE announced that it had mapped one gene linked to obesity and another to anxiety. As the head of global research at Roche, Jonathan Knowles, said in the accompanying press release, "deCODE's success in localizing disease-contributing genetic factors even in such complex disorders as anxiety and obesity marks once more achievements that we believe could not easily be obtained by anyone else."

The same might be said of another deCODE triumph in 2001, the location of a long sought-after gene linked to late-onset Parkinson's disease, a degenerative neurological disorder that leads to trembling and a progressive loss of control of motor function, to a region of chromosome 1. The press release quoted Stefánsson as saying, not without a certain self-satisfaction, that "many scientists and funding agencies had recently concluded that there was no identifiable component to late-onset Parkinson's. We are very pleased to have been able to counter this skepticism."

Stroke, diabetes, Alzheimer's, Parkinson's, obesity, anxiety—to which hypertension (high blood pressure), schizophrenia, and asthma were added in 2002: the list read like a roll call of every serious common disease affecting mankind. It seemed at times as though deCODE had single-handedly solved the problem of non-Mendelian diseases that top researchers like Eric Lander had been grappling with for a decade.

It was difficult to tell, however. As *The New York Times* noted just before deCODE added high blood pressure to its collection, "The claims of the company are hard for others to assess because so far it has published articles on only two of the disease locations it has found"—in contrast to the Celera-like stream of press releases trumpeting its achievements. However, Roche's Jonathan Knowles told *The New York Times* that "13 of the disease gene locations, found under contract to Roche, had been verified for Roche by independent experts."

Compliments were not the only thing that Roche was paying to deCODE: under the terms of their collaboration, milestone payments were due as deCODE delivered on its side of the bargain. Since Roche had "verified" 13 gene locations, it had presumably been happy to pay up. Brilliantly successful as it seemed to be, though, deCODE had to face an unpleasant truth: that milestone payments alone would not be enough.

In particular, deCODE found itself under the same kind of investor pressure that eventually defeated Venter. deCODE had made a successful initial public offering in the United States, while the stock market was still reasonably buoyant, raising nearly $200 million gross. Shares were priced at $18, and finished up at over $25 on the first day of trading, July 18, 2000. After hovering around this level for a few months, however, the share price fell steeply, and spent most of 2001 under $10—just half of the opening price. Clearly, something needed to be done. The solution turned out to be the same as Celera's: deCODE would become a drug company.

The first sign that something was up at deCODE was in November 2001, when the company announced that its scientists had discovered 350 genes in key drug target classes, and that it was filing patents on them. However, deCODE had a major advantages over most companies trying to patent human genes: it could draw on its powerful bioinformatics system—called the deCODE Clinical Genome Miner—to place these genes in the context of over 40 common diseases, hence assigning a more specific utility to each. Almost as an aside, the press release mentioned that "deCODE will integrate these targets into its growing in-house drug discovery program."

What this in-house program was became a little clearer on January 29, 2002, when deCODE and Roche unveiled a new, three-year alliance "focused on turning the landmark achievements of their gene discovery collaboration into novel treatments for common diseases." Roche would fund deCODE to carry on its research work, but on just four of the diseases covered by the previous agreement. This allowed deCODE to "recapture for its proprietary drug development" the other eight diseases that Roche was not pursuing.

deCODE's proprietary drug development had been boosted a few weeks before by the announcement that it would be acquiring MediChem Life Sciences, "a pioneer in providing drug discovery and development services," as the press release put it. Buying MediChem would add "integrated chemistry capabilities to accelerate deCODE's growth into a fully-integrated biopharmaceutical company," rather as the acquisition of Axys Pharmaceuticals had done for Celera six months before.

In many respects, then, deCODE's evolution from a company selling information to one developing drugs mirrors that of Celera: both realized that however successful they were providing their respective services to pharmaceutical companies, it was the latter that would make the big money from their work. The ineluctable logic, therefore, was that the drug discovery programs should be brought in-house so that they rather than their clients reaped the main benefits.

Along with a larger-than-life leader, the two companies also have in common the fact that by their actions they helped make concrete abstract questions that until then had been vaguely debated without much sense of urgency. As such, they forced people to confront new and important issues. In the case of Celera, these issues concerned whether a company should be allowed to establish a monopoly on the human genome—for example, through the patenting of the genes it found there. deCODE's case, too, was about the ownership of genomic information, but on a vastly expanded scale: that of an entire nation.

The controversy arose over Stefánsson's plans to move far beyond the simple application of linkage analysis to families drawn from the Icelandic people. Even though this had led to some potentially important results in locating key genes involved in complex diseases, the process was rather low-tech. For example, the genealogical information was stored in a database and the linkage analysis itself was performed using computers, but the initial lists of patients for a given investigation were drawn up manually in consultation with various medical specialists in Iceland. Ideally, this aspect would be automated, too, allowing an unprecedented pooling of genetic information.

As Stefánsson explained in 1999: "We would like to create a database that would contain anonymous information that could be queried to create new knowledge about human disease. The Icelandic Healthcare Database would link medical information together with genealogy, genotypes (genetic fingerprints), and environmental exposure information. It would also link healthcare data to resource use information, with records documenting how much the single-payer healthcare system in Iceland spent for each procedure, clinic visit, and hospitalization."

He also gave some examples of how such a totally-integrated digital repository might be applied. "The database will be useful for modelling disease risk as a function of genetic and environmental factors. Moreover, unknown relationships between three primary parameters—genetics, environment, and disease—might be discovered by querying the database for patterns, suggesting new hypotheses that may be specifically tested in other populations. The synergy of genealogy, genetic, environmental, and medical information holds enormous potential for creating medical knowledge in a new model-independent way. Sophisticated informatics tools would help the user to search for patterns and relationships among these components in the database, even those completely unanticipated, in a way analogous to the data-mining tools companies use to search inventory and sales records for trends."

Clearly, creating the Icelandic Healthcare Database could only occur with the support of the Icelandic government, since it meant being granted full access to the nation's health records. Stefánsson was obviously persuasive, because "at the initiative of deCODE Genetics," a government bill authorizing the creation of the Icelandic Health Sector Database (IHSD) was introduced by the Minister of Health in March 1998. As *Science* noted, however, this was "withdrawn just weeks later after a storm of protest from Icelandic doctors, scientists, and patients' groups."

After a second draft was sent out for comments, a third draft was placed before the Althingi, the Icelandic parliament, on October 9, 1998. *Science* reported: "Even after the most recent refinements, critics maintain that the bill is unacceptable. They have focused in particular on provisions that would permit people's medical data to be used for research without their informed, written consent. They also argue that safeguards to protect patients' privacy are inadequate and that it is unfair to grant one company use of the data while denying it to outside researchers whose studies might harm that company's commercial interests."

Regarding privacy, Stefánsson said in 1999: "The database will be irreversibly encrypted by independent groups, and direct access to its content will be very restricted. Only information involving groups of at least 10 individuals will be revealed during database queries in order to prevent someone from illegally attempting to identify any one individual using a set of known characteristics."

However, an internationally-respected computer security expert, Ross Anderson, wrote in a 1998 report for the Icelandic Medical Association, that "the proposed database falls outside the boundaries of what would be acceptable elsewhere in Europe. If established as proposed, it would likely cause serious conflict with the ethical principle that identifiable health information should only be made available with the consent of the patient."

Stefánsson pointed out: "If one wished to obtain medical information about someone in Iceland, it would be orders of magnitude easier to obtain that information from the hospital computer systems where original data lie unencrypted." This may well be true, but the deCODE database, with its consolidated data, would represent a much more attractive target. Once its defenses had been breached—either through technical or other means, like bribery—information would be available on every aspect of every Icelander who did not opt out.

Stefánsson's justification for deCODE's approach to consent is interesting. In 1999, he said: "The Icelandic Parliament and the Health Ministry—which oversees the healthcare system in Iceland—have agreed to allow irreversibly encrypted medical data to be transferred to the database without explicit informed consent by individuals in Iceland. This 'permission' is in the form of a government bill . . . which entitles the Icelandic Ministry of Health the right to grant a license to a company to build a database containing medical records of all Icelanders that could be linked to genetic and genealogical information."

Implicit in this statement is the idea that the official representative of the Icelandic nation—the Icelandic government—has a natural right to exploit the people's genes as it thinks best. The issue of who owned the genetic patrimony of a nation, however, was so new—and the implications so profound—that many felt it was too soon to accept such an assumption as blithely as the Icelandic government.

For example, in October 1999, the Nordic Committee on Bioethics organized a conference called "Who owns our genes?" As the introduction noted: "The information DNA reveals is very valuable for the person, the society and the future generations—especially as genetic research moves quickly forward. . . . Should human genes be seen as a part of the person, as property, as a gift (common property) or as something in between, requiring a separate status?" It also commented that "the Icelandic Centralized Health Database illustrates different aspects of use of genetic information including controversies on 'ownership'."

One reason why the Icelandic government seems to have felt happy with deCODE's plans was the shrewd way that Stefánsson had emphasized how it was all in the national interest. For example, the early deal with Roche stipulated that Icelanders would receive free medications as a result of any discoveries made from their DNA. Similarly, Stefánsson often underlined the fact that deCODE, though registered in the United States, was based in Iceland, had created hundreds of jobs there, and even engineered a reverse brain-drain, with many Icelandic scientists returning from abroad to work for the company.

More subtly, deCODE's whole business plan was based on the idea that for historical reasons the Icelandic population was special. For the Icelanders, then, not to support deCODE would have been both unpatriotic and a negation of their own specialness. Indeed, opinion polls conducted at various times during the debates over deCODE showed a high level of public support for the company's plans.

There was certainly plenty of backing in the Icelandic parliament when the final version of the bill was presented. It passed on December 17, 1998, despite continuing opposition from some quarters—notably from a new organization called the Association of Icelanders for Ethics in Science and Medicine, or "Mannverd" ("Human Protection"), set up specifically to fight deCODE. And in due course, on January 22, 2000, deCODE was granted the exclusive license to create, run, and market the database for 12 years. Winning the license was really just the beginning, though.

As the prospectus for deCODE's U.S. IPO in July 2000 warned potential investors at painful length, deCODE still faced a number of obstacles before it could exploit the potential riches of the linked databases. Of note was the ability to collect the necessary data from possibly reluctant hospitals and other health centers, and managing to create the database quickly enough to derive revenues from it.

In some sense, then, deCODE remains a fascinating experiment in large-scale population genomics and massive cross-linked databases. Whatever its future success, however, and regardless of the rights and wrongs of its particular approach, one enduring contribution that deCODE has already made is alerting others to the key ethical issues—and perhaps even suggesting ways of avoiding at least some of the controversy surrounding them.

The Estonian Genome Project, for example, has much in common with deCODE. It, too, hopes to enroll almost the entire nation as participants—the target is up to 1,000,000 out of a population of 1.4 million—who will give blood samples and answer detailed questionnaires concerning health status, genealogy, lifestyle, and environmental factors.

The idea has been sold partly on the basis that from it will flow "the achievement of a new level in Estonian health care," as well as an "increase in the international competitiveness of the Estonian economy," including "investments in high technology and the creation of new jobs." For these reasons, the Estonian Genome Project comes with as much political backing from the top as deCODE: the Estonian prime minister was reported by *Science* as being "a big supporter" in October 2000. The differences from the Icelandic company, though, are just as striking.

The Estonian project was the brainchild of a professor of biotechnology at the University of Tartu, Andres Metspalu. Those behind the project have gone out of their way to draw on relevant experience around the world. The basic idea was formulated by "a group of scientists under the supervision of the Estonian Genome Foundation, a non-profit body founded in January 1999 by Estonian scientists, doctors, and politicians to support genetic research and biotechnology in Estonia." The legislation, passed in December 2000, was prepared by "an international working group and guidance was obtained from all available international documents dealing with genetic research, such as the UNESCO Universal Declaration on the Human Genome and Human Rights (1997) and the Council of Europe's Convention on Human Rights and Biomedicine (1997)."

There is a commercial side to the venture, but it is completely separate. EGeen International is headquartered in the United States and has been granted exclusive commercial access to all data emerging from the Estonian Genome Project in return for financing the latter and the grant of a stake in the company to the Estonian Genome Project Foundation. An independent Ethics Committee has the task of overseeing the project and all its research.

Participation is on a purely voluntary basis, and gene donors will have "the right to demand deletion of the data that enable identification of his or her person or, in certain cases, of all the information stored in the Gene Bank about him or her," which will be separate from personal data. "After deletion of the given data, it will not be possible to associate a blood sample and a gene donor."

There are some notable technical differences, too. For example, unlike deCODE, which has tended to emphasize the specialness of its people, the Estonian Genome Project draws attention to the fact that "recent research has demonstrated that the Estonian population is perfectly representative of all European (Caucasian) populations. . . . Meaning that if the research will be carried out based on the genetic data of Estonians, it can be generalized for other Europeans as well."

Lacking the much-vaunted Icelandic homogeneity and in-depth genealogical data, the Estonian project will not use linkage analysis, but the other main approach: association studies. They try to find areas of the genome that turn up more frequently in unrelated groups of people with a given condition. This will require an extremely dense set of markers: "genotyping will be performed using most efficient technology available to ensure that project cost is low enough to analyze approximately 60,000–100,000 SNPs (single nucleotide polymorphisms) per individual."

This is an extraordinary number—deCODE has typically used 1,000 markers spread across the genome, although each of these is as informative as several SNPs—and is indicative of the fact that, in its way, the Estonian gene bank is as much of an experiment as its Icelandic rival. The same might be said in the ethical arena, too.

In signing the Gene Donor Consent Form for the Estonian Genome Project, participants confirm that they are aware of ten key points. The sixth one forms part of the project's scrupulous attempt to avoid accusations that it is simply appropriating the genomic information of a nation. It states simply: "I have the right to know my genetic data," and guarantees that participants can share in the ownership of their genetic make-up in the most fundamental way possible: by knowing it.

This is no mere sop to those concerned about genetic exploitation. Providing such personal genotypes to participants is an integral part of the Estonian Genome Project, which has two goals: "First, to identify disease genes by comparing genotypes within a group of patients with a given disease. Second, to set up a health care database that would give Estonians access to their own data, so they can benefit from the personalized medicine of the future." Individually-tailored medicine promises to become one of the most direct ways in which genomic information affects the lives of ordinary people. As with so many advances, however, the blessings that it brings are mixed.

NOTES

The author conducted interviews included in this chapter in June 2003 with the following individual: E. Lander.

1. p. 159 *he mentioned casually on the U.S. TV program* N. Wade, "Scientist reveals genome secret: it's his," *The New York Times*, April 27, 2002.

2. p. 159 *the decision of whose DNA to sequence* J. Craig Venter, et al. "The sequence of the human genome," *Science* 291 (2001) 1304–1351.

3. p. 159 *Staff of laboratories involved in library construction* NIH-DOE guidance on human subjects issues in large-scale DNA sequencing. Online at *http://www.ornl.gov/hgmis/publicat/97pr/08_3appc.html.*

4. p. 160 *Victor McCusick started putting together* A. Hamosh, et al., Online "Mendelian Inheritance in Man (OMIM), a knowledgebase of human genes and genetic disorders," *Nucleic Acids Res.* 30 (2002): 52–55.

5. p. 161 *This tiff is the most public in a long-simmering and acrimonious feud* L. Roberts, "Flap arises over genetic map," *Science* 238 (1987): 750–752.

6. p. 161 *Genome Therapeutics Corp. . . . . announced in a press release* R. Nowak, "The gold bug: *Helicobacter pylori*," *Science* 267 (1995): 173.

7. p. 162 *science by press conference* R. Nowak, "The gold bug: *Helicobacter pylori*," *Science* 267 (1995): 173.

8. p. 162 *was on its scientific advisory board,* R. Cook-Deegan, *The Gene Wars* (New York/London: Norton, 1995), 41.

9. p. 162 *The actual mapping involves determining the linkages* L. Roberts, "Flap arises over genetic map," *Science* 238 (1987): 750–752.

10. p. 163 *Although I trained as a pure mathematician,* E. Lander, interview. Online at *http://www.accessexcellence.org/AB/CC/lander.html.*

11. p. 164 *The key breakthrough [in genetic mapping] was the recognition* E.S. Lander and N.J. Schork, "Genetic dissection of complex traits," *Science* 265 (1994): 2037–2048.

12. p. 164 *The Botnia region on the western coast of Finland* Whitehead Institute Center for Genome Research press release, September 2, 1996.

13. p. 165 *Association studies do not concern familial* E.S. Lander and N.J. Schork, "Genetic dissection of complex traits," *Science* 265 (1994): 2037–2048.

14. p. 165 *with success in sight* E.S. Lander, "The new genomics: global views of biology," *Science* 274 (1996): 536–539.

15. p. 166 *defined as positions in the DNA sequence* D.G. Wang, et al., "Large-scale identification, mapping, and genotyping of single-nucleotide polymorphisms in the human genome," *Science* 280 (1998): 1077–1082.

16. p. 166 *the time is now right to begin the systematic* F.S. Collins, et al., "Variations on a theme: cataloging human DNA sequence variation," *Science* 278 (1997): 1580–1581.

17. p. 166 *First came a landmark paper . . . from a large group of researchers* D.G. Wang, et al., "Large-scale identification, mapping, and genotyping of single-nucleotide polymorphisms in the human genome," *Science* 280 (1998): 1077–1082.

18. p. 167 *large-scale screening for human variation is clearly feasible,* D.G. Wang, et al., "Large-scale identification, mapping, and genotyping of single-nucleotide polymorphisms in the human genome," *Science* 280 (1998): 1077–1082.

19. p. 167 *which held samples from 450 U.S. residents* "A DNA polymorphism discovery resource for research on human genetic variation," F.S. Collins, et al., *Genome Research* 8 (1998): 1229–1231.

20. p. 167 *The two-year, $45 million initiative to create a high-quality map* Wellcome Trust press release, April 15, 1999.

21. p. 168 *The idea that pharmaceutical companies could fund* E. Masood, ". . . as consortium plans free SNP map of human genome," *Nature* 398 (1999): 545–546.

22. p. 168 *The objectives of the Consortium are as follows.* A.L. Holden, "The SNP Consortium: summary of a private consortium effort to develop an applied map of the human genome," *BioTechniques* 32 (2002): S22–26.

23. p. 169 *Incyte introduced its SNP database* Incyte Genomics press release, January 10, 2000.

24. p. 169 *Celera claimed at the launch that it had* Celera Genomics press release, September 13, 2000.

25. p. 169 *The Applera Genome Project, involving the re-sequencing* Transcript of Applera Corporation teleconference, April 25, 2002.

26. p. 170   *Researchers have collected over 25,000 DNA samples*   Myriad Genetics annual report 1997.

27. p. 170   *He received his medical training in his native Iceland*   deCODE company information, online at *http://www.decode.com/main/view.jsp?branch=11729.*

28. p. 170   *During my days as a researcher in academe*   K. Stefánsson, "Opportunity, not exploitation" (October 1998). Available online at *http://news.bmn. com/hmsbeagle/40/people/op_ed.htm.*

29. p. 171   *I think that genetic homogeneity is overrated.*   H. Breithaupt, "Health care and privacy," *EMBO Reports* 2 (2001): 964–967.

30. p. 171   *In 1999, Stefánsson said that the database held*   K. Stefánsson, "The Icelandic healthcare database: a tool to create knowledge, a social debate, and a bioethical and privacy challenge." Included in proceedings of conference "Who owns our genes?" October 1999, Tallinn, Estonia. Available from *http://www.ncbio.org/Html/Whoowns.pdf.*

31. p. 171   *enabled him to raise $12 million in just a few months.*   M. Specter, "Decoding Iceland," *New Yorker* (February 18, 1999).

32. p. 171   *Essential tremor is a disease characterized by shakiness*   deCODE press release, August 25, 1997.

33. p. 172   *research collaboration that will focus on the discovery of disease genes* deCODE press release, February 2, 1998.

34. p. 172   *In September of that year, deCODE announced*   deCODE press release, September 20, 1999.

35. p. 172   *In March 2000, another gene was mapped*   deCODE press release, March 29, 2000.

36. p. 172   *A few months later, deCODE followed*   deCODE press release, August 18, 2000.

37. p. 173   *the identification of a gene linked to schizophrenia*   deCODE press release, October 20, 2000.

38. p. 173   *For the mapping, it used 1000 microsatellite*   deCODE IPO prospectus, July 17, 2000.

39. p. 173   *deCODE switched to using SNPs to create*   deCODE IPO prospectus, July 17, 2000.

40. p. 173   *contribute to peripheral arterial occlusive disease,*   deCODE press release, November 14, 2000.

41. p. 173   *The same day also saw the unveiling*   deCODE press release, November 14, 2000.

42. p. 173   *deCODE's success in localizing disease-contributing*   deCODE press release, September 11, 2001.

43. p. 174   *many scientists and funding agencies had recently concluded*   deCODE press release, October 23, 2001.

44. p. 174   *to which hypertension (high blood pressure),*   deCODE press release, June 2002.

45. p. 174   *asthma*   H. Hakonarson, et al., "A major susceptibility gene for asthma maps to chromosome 14q24," *Am J Hum Genet* 71 (2002): 483–491.

46. p. 174 *The claims of the company are hard for others to assess* N. Wade, "A genomic treasure hunt may be striking gold," *The New York Times* (June 18, 2002).

47. p. 174 *13 of the disease gene locations,* N. Wade, "A genomic treasure hunt may be striking gold," *The New York Times* (June 18, 2002).

48. p. 174 *the company announced that its scientists* deCODE press release, November 7, 2001.

49. p. 175 *deCODE will integrate these targets into its growing in-house drug discovery program.* deCODE press release, November 7, 2001.

50. p. 175 *focused on turning the landmark achievements* deCODE press release, January 29, 2002.

51. p. 175 *recapture for its proprietary drug development* deCODE press release, January 29, 2002.

52. p. 175 *a pioneer in providing drug discovery and development services,* deCODE press release, January 8, 2002.

53. p. 176 *We would like to create a database that would contain* K. Stefánsson, "The Icelandic healthcare database: a tool to create knowledge, a social debate, and a bioethical and privacy challenge." Included in proceedings of conference "Who owns our genes?" October 1999, Tallinn, Estonia. Available from *http://www.ncbio.org/Html/Whoowns.pdf.*

54. p. 176 *The database will be useful for modeling* K. Stefánsson, "The Icelandic healthcare database: a tool to create knowledge, a social debate, and a bioethical and privacy challenge." Included in proceedings of conference "Who owns our genes?" October 1999, Tallinn, Estonia. Available from *http://www.ncbio.org/Html/Whoowns.pdf.*

55. p. 176 *at the initiative of deCODE Genetics,* K. Stefánsson, "The Icelandic healthcare database: a tool to create knowledge, a social debate, and a bioethical and privacy challenge." Included in proceedings of conference "Who owns our genes?" October 1999, Tallinn, Estonia. Available from *http://www.ncbio.org/Html/Whoowns.pdf.*

56. p. 176 *withdrawn just weeks later after a storm of protest* M. Enserink, "Opponents criticize Iceland's database," *Science* 282 (1998): 859.

57. p. 176 *The database will be irreversibly encrypted by independent groups,* K. Stefánsson, "The Icelandic healthcare database: a tool to create knowledge, a social debate, and a bioethical and privacy challenge." Included in proceedings of conference "Who owns our genes?" October 1999, Tallinn, Estonia. Available from *http://www.ncbio.org/Html/Whoowns.pdf.*

58. p. 177 *Ross Anderson, wrote in a 1998 report* R. Anderson, "The deCODE proposal for an Icelandic health database." Online at *http://www.cl.cam.ac.uk/users/rja14/iceland/node1.html.*

59. p. 177 *If one wished to obtain medical information* K. Stefánsson, "The Icelandic healthcare database: a tool to create knowledge, a social debate, and a bioethical and privacy challenge." Included in proceedings of conference "Who owns our genes?" October 1999, Tallinn, Estonia. Available from *http://www.ncbio.org/Html/Whoowns.pdf.*

60. p. 177 *The Icelandic Parliament and the Health Ministry*　K. Stefánsson, "The Icelandic healthcare database: a tool to create knowledge, a social debate, and a bioethical and privacy challenge." Included in proceedings of conference "Who owns our genes?" October 1999, Tallinn, Estonia. Available from *http://www.ncbio.org/Html/Whoowns.pdf.*

61. p. 177 *The information DNA reveals is very valuable for the person,*　L. Nielsen and C. Holm, "Introduction." Included in proceedings of conference "Who owns our genes?" October 1999, Tallinn, Estonia. Available from *http://www.ncbio.org/Html/Whoowns.pdf.*

62. p. 178 *It passed on December 17, 1998,*　deCODE IPO prospectus, July 17, 2000.

63. p. 178 *the target is up to 1,000,000*　"Estonian Genome Project, 7." Online at *http://www.geenivaramu.ee/mp3/trykisENG.pdf.*

64. p. 178 *the achievement of a new level in Estonian health care,*　"Estonian Genome Project, 4." Online at *http://www.geenivaramu.ee/mp3/trykisENG.pdf.*

65. p. 179 *a big supporter*　L. Frank, "Estonia prepares for national DNA database," *Science* 290 (2000): 31.

66. p. 179 *a group of scientists under the supervision of the Estonian Genome Foundation,* "Estonian Genome Project, 3." Online at *http://www.geenivaramu.ee/mp3/trykisENG.pdf.*

67. p. 179 *an international working group and guidance was obtained*　"Estonian Genome Project, 3." Online at *http://www.geenivaramu.ee/mp3/trykisENG.pdf.*

68. p. 179 *exclusive commercial access to all data*　"Estonian Genome Project, 10." Online at *http://www.geenivaramu.ee/mp3/trykisENG.pdf.*

69. p. 179 *the right to demand deletion of the data that enable identification*　"Estonian Genome Project 5." Online at *http://www.geenivaramu.ee/mp3/trykisENG.pdf.*

70. p. 179 *recent research has demonstrated that the Estonian population*　"Estonian Genome Project, 10." Online at *http://www.geenivaramu.ee/mp3/trykisENG.pdf.*

71. p. 179 *genotyping will be performed using most efficient technology*　"Estonian Genome Project, 8." Online at *http://www.geenivaramu.ee/mp3/trykisENG.pdf.*

72. p. 180 *I have the right to know my genetic data,*　"Estonian Genome Project," Gene Donor Consent Form. Online at *http://www.geenivaramu.ee/index.php?lang=eng&sub=74.*

73. p. 180 *First, to identify disease genes by comparing genotypes*　"Estonian Genome Project, 3." Online at *http://www.geenivaramu.ee/mp3/trykisENG.pdf.*

CHAPTER 9

Getting Personal

Personalized medicine is built around the idea that detailed knowledge about an individual's genome can be used to identify potential problems—for example, a susceptibility to a certain condition—even before they begin to manifest themselves. This knowledge can also be used to tailor courses of treatment that are most effective for a given genetic make-up.

Realizing this vision will require the ability to genotype individuals—to establish which particular alleles they possess—on an unprecedented scale. The Estonian Genome Project, for example, envisages analyzing 60,000 to 100,000 SNPs for each participant. At the time the Estonian project was first proposed, genotyping costs were typically $1 per genotype measurement, implying a cost of as much as $100,000 per person—clearly an impossible figure. An article published in June 2002 wrote of the "plummeting" prices of genotyping, but even then, only to a figure of around 10 or 20 cents per genotype.

For comprehensive personalized medicine to be viable on a large scale—as opposed to the use of one or two targeted tests—either the costs of current genotyping technologies need to be brought down dramatically, or an alternative way of characterizing individual genomes has to be found. The first of these is quite likely: companies are working on a variety of different approaches, including the use of mass spectrometry (discussed in chapter 12) and DNA chips (chapter 10). Alongside such applications of existing technologies, however, a completely new approach looks likely to play an important role.

One reason that large-scale association studies like those in Estonia planned to genotype up to 100,000 SNPs for each person was the belief that a very dense map of markers—roughly one every 30,000 DNA bases—would be needed. Both computer simulations and some empirical data indicated that the average range over which there was correlation between a marker and a region implicated in a medical condition—known as the linkage disequilibrium (LD)—was quite short. In other words, the genome seemed to have been "chopped up" quite finely by the repeated combinations of ancestral chromosomes. As a result, SNP-based association studies had typically only been used to narrow down the region where a gene was to be found once it had been mapped through linkage analysis.

It was a series of important papers from Eric Lander and his team at the Whitehead Institute that began to chip away at the conventional wisdom that the linkage disequilibrium in the general population was short. This helped lead to the introduction of a powerful new way of analyzing individual genomes.

The first of these papers appeared in *Nature* in May 2001 and was called "Linkage disequilibrium in the human genome." In its brief explanation of linkage disequilibrium, the paper employed another key concept: "LD refers to correlations among neighbouring alleles, reflecting 'haplotypes' descended from single, ancestral chromosomes." A haplotype, then, is a kind of block of DNA that is passed down intact from generation to generation during the exchanges between maternal and paternal chromosomes. The critical issue was the size of such haplotypes.

Lander and his colleagues looked at 19 regions across the human genome using the DNA of 44 unrelated individuals from Utah. They carried out a computational analysis of how big the blocks of SNPs were that statistically tended to be inherited together. They found that the linkage disequilibrium typically extended over 60 kilobases from common alleles—far further than previously thought.

The question, then, was: Why was the LD far greater than expected? "The simplest explanation for the long range LD," the researchers wrote, "is that the population under study experienced an extreme founder effect or bottleneck: a period when the population was so small that a few ancestral haplotypes gave rise to most of the haplotypes that exist today." In other words, there were so few founders at one point in the distant past that a correspondingly low number of haplotypes formed the basis of those found in their descendants. Fewer haplotypes than originally thought meant less mixing down the years and thus larger haplotype blocks today.

This was exciting because the population under study was essentially a typical northern European one—not normally thought of as descending from relatively few individuals, which was what the long-range LD implied. To check that the figure was not just an artifact of the particular regions they had chosen to analyze—always a danger for these kind of studies—Lander's team repeated the exercise with two very different populations: 48 Swedes and 96 Yorubans, (a West African people from Nigeria). The results were dramatic: for the Swedes, the LD pattern was nearly identical to that of the Utah population. For the Nigerians, however, the LD extended far less: just 5 kilobases.

This confirmed the initial Utah result and the hypothesis of a population bottleneck: "The vast difference in the extent of LD between populations points to differences owing to population history, probably a bottleneck or founder effect that occurred among the ancestors of the north Europeans after the divergence from the ancestors of the Nigerians." It was even possible to put some rough figures on this bottleneck: "an effective population size . . . of 50 individuals for 20 generations; 1000 individuals for 400 generations; or any other combination with same ratio."

As well as these thought-provoking figures—which implied that the entire indigenous population of northern Europe may be descended from just a few hundred individuals—the paper also noted another important consequence of its results. "The presence of large blocks of LD in northern European populations suggests that genome-wide LD mapping is likely to be possible with existing SNP resources." If DNA code is inherited in relatively large blocks, a less dense set of SNP markers would suffice to find genes using association studies.

A paper in *Science* in July 2001 provided further hints of the hitherto unsuspected power of haplotypes. Written by a team of scientists at Genaissance Pharmaceuticals, the paper looked at haplotype variation and linkage disequilibrium in 313 genes, rather than in random regions as Lander and his colleagues had done. 82 individuals whose ancestors had come from various regions of the world were studied.

In total, 3,899 variable sites were discovered in nearly 720 kilobases—one SNP every 185 bases across the whole group. This was far more than previously thought and meant that for each gene there might be millions of different haplotypes. Genes are typically thousands of bases long and therefore contain dozens of SNPs, each of which could, theoretically, vary independently. Yet the researchers found just 14 different haplotypes per gene on average, testimony to the fact that SNPs do indeed tend to be passed down through the generations in just a few extended blocks. Also noteworthy was the statistic that over a third of the genes studied did not have a single haplotype that occurred more than half the time in the sample population study. That is, there was no such thing as a "typical" haplotype that occurred more often than all the others put together.

The next Whitehead paper appeared in October 2001. Building on earlier work that a gene conferring susceptibility to Crohn disease, an inflammatory disease of the bowel, was to be found on chromosome 5, the team sought to localize it using linkage disequilibrium. Initially, 156 microsatellite markers were used, spread across the fairly large region that had been implicated previously. These markers were genotyped for 256 families in which a child had Crohn disease and at least one parent was unaffected.

Although this provided a smaller region that was statistically linked with the disease, it was not possible to locate one gene in particular. So even finer markers were used across a core region of 285 kilobases. A total of 651 SNPs was found in this region, and genotyping was carried out across 301 of them.

This ultra-fine SNP map allowed the haplotypes for that region to be determined. The statistical analysis of which SNPs tend to be found together showed that the region could be broken up into haplotype blocks that came only in two, three, or four main types. Together, though, they accounted for 90 to 98 percent of all the chromosomes examined. Potentially there was a huge number of haplotypes, formed by choosing different combinations from among the hundreds of SNPs that were found in that region. The fact that in reality there were just a few common haplotypes confirmed the results of the researchers from Genaissance Pharmaceuticals and underlined the potential of this new way of looking at genomic information.

Just one of these haplotypes seemed to be a risk factor for Crohn disease—what might be called the *risk haplotype*. Ironically, the very power that allowed such a risk haplotype to be identified also meant that it was not possible to say which of the SNPs might be responsible. As the Whitehead team wrote: "We have not been able to implicate a single causative mutation, because the tight LD across the region results in at least 11 SNPs having equivalent genetic information. Most of these SNPs are likely to simply be fellow travelers on the risk haplotype." Since they were on the same haplotype, they were generally inherited together, and so there was no way of discriminating between the SNP that conferred the susceptibility and those nearby with this method.

Finding the specific cause would therefore require a different approach. Despite this failure at one level, Lander and his fellow researchers grasped that something much more important had emerged than the location of a particular gene from their work: the power and simplicity of haplotype structures. This was spelled out in a paper in the journal *Nature Genetics* immediately following the one detailing the work on the Crohn risk haplotype.

Here, Lander and his team examined the region found in the paper on Crohn disease in greater detail. This time they were interested not in the causative factor located there, but the overall haplotype structure of the region, which spanned about 500 kilobases—a relatively small fraction of the human genome. It was one, though, that proved to be enormously rich in terms of the hidden structures that statistics and computers could reveal.

For this particular section of DNA, 103 SNPs were genotyped for several hundred individuals. A computer program compared the genotypes for each position and extracted the haplotype blocks based on the groups of SNP values that tended to vary in a coordinated fashion. The result was striking: each haplotype block came in at most four common variants, which together accounted for over 90 percent of all the cases in the sample. For one block, which spanned 84 kilobases—a considerable distance for linkage to be observed—just two distinct haplotypes represented 96 percent of all the measurements.

Moreover, the haplotype blocks themselves also tended to come in just a few combinations—what the paper called "ancestral long-range haplotypes." Fully 38 percent of the DNA sequences in the study turned out to be one of the four most common ancestral haplotypes that spanned the entire region. Despite more than 100 SNPs that were present in the region (SNPs that potentially could have varied more or less independently to create billions of different haplotypes), over a third of the sequences examined belonged to one of just four basic patterns, each with a unique set of SNPs.

Having established the usefulness of the haplotype idea, the authors pointed out that "once the haplotype blocks are identified, they can be treated as alleles and tested for LD." That is, the SNPs can be clumped together to create blocks that come in just a few major variants—the haplotype "alleles"—that can then be tested for linkage disequilibrium to search for correlations in the presence of disease. This was the great promise of haplotypes: that they could be used in association studies to locate genes, replacing the more time-consuming and costly SNP approach.

Lander and his colleagues then noted an important shortcut in defining haplotypes: "Once the haplotype blocks are defined . . . it is straightforward to examine a subset of SNPs that uniquely distinguish the common haplotypes of each block." Because it turned out that so many SNPs were inherited together, it was not necessary to know all of them to deduce which particular haplotype they represented. This made establishing which particular haplotypes an individual possessed much easier.

Another paper in the same issue of *Nature Genetics*, this time from a group in the UK, described how this might be done, using what it called "haplotype tag SNPs." These allow the common haplotypes to be defined by a minimal set of SNPs—a kind of bar code for haplotypes—and significantly reduce the effort of genotyping involved. For the 135 kilobase sequence of DNA studied in the paper, 122 SNPs could be reduced to just 34 without any loss of discriminatory power.

More boldly, the Whitehead team suggested in its paper that its approach "provides a precise framework for creating a comprehensive haplotype map of the human genome. By testing a sufficiently large collection of SNPs, it should be possible to define all of the common haplotypes underlying blocks of LD. Once such a map is created, it will be possible to select an optimal reference set of SNPs"—a set of bar codes covering the whole genome—"for any subsequent genotyping study."

Although highly suggestive, the paper of Lander and his colleagues examined only 500 kilobases out of the human genome's 2.9 gigabases. There was always the danger that they had chosen an unrepresentative region and that haplotype blocks were not so useful elsewhere. A paper that appeared in *Science* in June 2002, from a Whitehead group led by David Altshuler and which also included Lander, addressed this issue directly. It reported on the haplotype patterns across 51 different regions of DNA spanning 13 megabases. Some 275 individuals from four population groups—Nigerian, European, Asian (Japanese and Chinese), and African-American—were genotyped for nearly 4,000 SNPs.

Reassuringly, the results were unequivocal. As the paper put it: "Our data provide strong evidence that most of the human genome is contained in blocks of substantial size; we estimate that half of the human genome exists in blocks of 22 kb or larger in African and African-American samples and in blocks of 44 kb or larger in European and Asian samples." This confirmed the results of Lander's paper a year before that showed significant linkage disequilibrium in the human genome, but with notable differences between European and Yoruban populations. The Whitehead group continued: "Within each block, a very small number of common haplotypes (three to five) typically capture [approximately] 90% of all chromosomes in each population. Both the boundaries of blocks and the specific haplotypes observed are shared to a remarkable extent across populations."

As if to celebrate this achievement, the next work on haplotypes involving a Whitehead team under Lander moved on to a practical demonstration of their power. The idea was to seek regions of the genome that had changed as a result of recent natural selection. To do this involved probing the underlying structures to an unprecedented depth, using haplotype patterns as the key tool.

The paper that was published in *Nature*—just a few months after the one in *Science* had established the validity of the haplotype idea—commented: "The ability to detect recent natural selection in the human population would have profound implications for the study of human history and for medicine." It continued: "Our method relies on the relationship between an allele's frequency and the extent of linkage disequilibrium (LD) surrounding it. . . . Under neutral evolution"—that is, one where there is no natural selection— "new variants require a long time to reach high frequency in the population," since they only spread slowly through successive generations. At the same time, however, "LD around the variants will decay substantially during this period owing to recombination" caused by the constant mixing of genomes in the gametes down through the generations. The more generations there are, the more mixing occurs, and the less linkage disequilibrium remains in the DNA sequence.

"As a result, common alleles will typically be old and will have only short-range LD. Rare alleles may be either young"—and so have not had time to spread through a population—"or old"—on their way out as they are displaced by other alleles—"and thus may have long- or short-range LD," respectively. The paper then revealed the core of its approach: "The key characteristic of positive selection, however, is that it causes an unusually rapid rise in allele frequency"—driven by the preferential selection—"occurring over a short enough time that recombination does not substantially break down the haplotype on which the selected mutation occurs. A signature of positive natural selection is thus an allele having unusually long-range LD given its population frequency." That is, natural selection can be spotted acting on a particular allele when a gene variant displays an anomalous combination of being relatively common and yet having long-range LD. Normally, it is an "either/or" scenario.

Lander's team applied this idea to two genes that are involved in resistance to the malaria parasite *Plasmodium falciparum* (see chapter 14), known by the somewhat cryptic names of *G6PD* and *TNFSF5*. The approach involved several layers of analysis. First, a set of SNPs in a small region around each gene were genotyped for three African and two non-African groups to allow the core haplotypes to be established. An allele known as *G6PD-202A*, which previous work had shown was associated with protection from malaria, was carried on only one core haplotype. The Whitehead analysis showed that it did indeed have unusually long-range linkage disequilibrium for its relative frequency— the signature of recent natural selection. The same was true for one of the core haplotypes around the *TNFSF5* gene.

Lander's team also estimated when the two alleles conferring some degree of malaria resistance arose. The results were about 2,500 years ago for *G6PD* and 6,500 years ago for *TNFSF5*, consistent with previous estimates obtained using microsatellite markers rather than SNPs. They were confident, however, that the technique could be pushed back even further: "Selective events occurring less than 400 generations ago (10,000 years assuming 25 years per generation) should leave a clear imprint," the researchers wrote. Revealing the impact of natural selection that occurred thousands of years ago is an impressive feat, one that gives a foretaste of what deep statistical analysis of sequence information is likely to provide in the years to come.

What is striking about this *tour de force* of computational genomics is the way that it constantly extracts levels of information: first by finding SNPs, then by comparing genotypes to establish haplotype structures, and finally by comparing the different properties of the main haplotypes. This is quintessential Lander, who freely admits: "what I live for are papers that present some interesting new angle on how to find information hiding—like that malaria paper."

It seems appropriate that just a few days after "that malaria paper" appeared in *Nature*, on October 29, 2002, the National Human Genome Research Institute announced a three-year, $100 million project "to create the next generation map of the human genome": the International HapMap Project. As the accompanying press release explained: "The human genome is thought to contain at least 10 million SNPs, about one every 300 bases. Theoretically, researchers could hunt for genes using a map listing all 10 million SNPs, but there are major practical drawbacks to that approach," notably the cost of genotyping people on that scale.

"Instead, the HapMap will find the chunks into which the genome is organized, each of which may contain dozens of SNPs. Researchers then only need to detect a few tag SNPs to identify that unique chunk or block of genome and to know all of the SNPs associated with that one piece. This strategy works because genetic variation among individuals is organized in 'DNA neighborhoods,' called haplotype blocks."

"Because of the block pattern of haplotypes, it will be possible to identify just a few SNP variants in each block to uniquely mark, or tag, that haplotype. As a result, researchers will need to study only about 300,000 to 600,000 tag SNPs, out of the 10,000,000 SNPs that exist, to efficiently identify the haplotypes in the human genome. It is the haplotype blocks, and the tag SNPs that identify them, that will form the HapMap." One of the main proponents of the HapMap idea, Eric Lander, says: "It was really clear that this was just the next efficient step" for studying the human genome.

The haplotype blocks and haplotype tag SNPs will be identified from blood samples taken from "200 to 400 people from four large, geographically distinct populations: the Yorubas in Nigeria, the Japanese; the Han Chinese; and U.S. residents with ancestry from northern and western Europe." As well as the NIH, a number of public research institutions around the world are providing funding, as are the Wellcome Trust and private companies, working through The SNP Consortium (TSC).

TSC would also organize the construction of the HapMap, while the analysis would be carried out by RIKEN/University of Tokyo, The Wellcome Trust Sanger Institute, the McGill University in Quebec, and the Beijing Genomics Institute (which had earlier produced the draft rice genome). In the United States, the main groups were located at the Whitehead Institute, Baylor College, the University of California, and the Johns Hopkins School of Medicine.

Despite this impressive array of international support, the HapMap, like the Human Genome Project before it, was not without its critics. As *The New York Times* reported: "Other population geneticists do not yet agree on the nature or the extent of the haplotypes in the human genome, and some doubt that the hapmap approach will be very useful in tracking down the variant genes that cause common diseases."

Tracking down variant genes through association studies—searching for particular haplotypes that tend to crop up more often in people with a certain disease—is not the only application of the HapMap. As the press release announcing the project explained: "Mapping an individual patient's haplotypes also may be used in the future to help customize medical treatment. Genetic variation has been shown to affect the response of patients to drugs, toxic substances and other environmental factors. Some already envision an era in which drug treatment is customized, based on the patient's haplotypes, to maximize the effectiveness of the drug while minimizing its side effects."

This important new area is now generally known as *pharmacogenomics*; it represents an extension of the earlier term, pharmacogenetics, with a greater emphasis on genomics. The premise of pharmacogenomics—that different alleles of particular genes result in altered response to drugs—is clearly close to that implicit in the search for genetic variations that result in heightened susceptibility to medical conditions.

Although linkage studies are possible, most pharmacogenomics research is based on association studies. These might employ dense maps of SNPs or— if the HapMap project is successful—haplotypes. There were doubters about the latter's usefulness here, however, as there had been for gene hunting. Shortly after the HapMap project was launched, a group of researchers at the pharmaceutical giant GlaxoSmithKline wrote an extended letter to the journal *Nature Genetics* commenting on the move.

"The scientific community is currently divided regarding the perceived need for genome-wide maps of common haplotype blocks," they wrote. "Most support the proposal of constructing haplotype maps to maximize information content and to minimize the number of SNPs required for whole-genome genotyping. The scope of its utility is, however, bounded." After reviewing some experiments they had carried out on the application of SNP mapping to pharmacogenomics/pharmacogenetics, where subsequent analysis indicated that haplotype blocks did not offer a quick way of locating alleles associated with adverse drug reactions, the writers concluded: "The increased knowledge generated by the haplotype map will be a welcome stride forward. . . . For applying pharmacogenetics in the short term, it will provide not a panacea, but rather a valued addition to the analysis toolkit."

Whatever the genotyping system employed—whether based on traditional SNPs or the new haplotypes—the potential of pharmacogenomics is not in doubt. For example, research published in 1998 suggested that in 1994, more than two million patients in U.S. hospitals had adverse reactions to drugs— and over 100,000 of these cases were fatal. These reactions were between the fourth and sixth leading cause of death. Even allowing for some overreporting, these figures indicate the scale of the problem. Once a genetic profile— a set of genotypes or haplotypes—associated with a particular adverse drug reaction has been established to a given level of statistical significance, it is then possible to test patients for that profile before deciding whether or not to give them that particular drug.

The benefits of such personalized medicine for patients are clear: the likelihood that the treatment will be beneficial is increased, while the risk that they will experience an adverse drug reaction is reduced. Pharmaceutical companies also stand to gain. As Allen Roses, one of the authors of the *Nature Genetics* letter and a leading advocate of pharmacogenomics, wrote in 2002: "Attrition of drugs during development"—that is, the elimination of candidate drugs from trials—"due to safety concerns is one of the main problems in the pharmaceutical pipeline." Profiling patients in drug trials may allow particular genotypes (or haplotypes) to be identified as associated with a high risk of an adverse drug reaction. Excluding them could allow the trial to proceed to a successful conclusion, increasing the chance that the drug will eventually be approved.

If serious adverse reactions start to crop up as the drug is used more widely, pharmacogenomics could be used to establish particular genomic profiles—until then not encountered in large enough numbers to show up—that ought not to be prescribed the treatment. Similarly, drugs that previously failed during trials—perhaps in the final stages—might now be reexamined, with the emphasis on finding a subset of the general patient population that could, in fact, take the medicine without side effects.

There is also a downside to this kind of winnowing of users. It may well turn out that significant proportions of the target patients have genotypes that preclude them from taking a particular drug. This means that the potential market for the drug is reduced. On the other hand, it may be possible for pharmaceutical companies to gain a competitive advantage with a carefully-targeted drug since patients would presumably prefer to take a medicine that is less likely to cause adverse reactions. They may even be prepared to pay premium prices for such products.

As targeting becomes more common and its benefits more clear, this, in its turn, might put pressure on companies developing drugs to provide profiling information as a matter of course. If they do not, and there are serious unexpected reactions after approval—perhaps even fatal ones—they might be judged negligent for not using advanced genotyping techniques to investigate potential susceptibilities and develop tests to screen out patients at risk.

Finally, the drug approval authorities such as the U.S. Food and Drug Administration (FDA) might start to expect gene testing to be carried out as a standard part of the drug trials process. Already, an article coauthored by the FDA's Director, Office of Clinical Pharmacology and Biopharmaceutics, has appeared bearing the significant title "Pharmacogenomic-guided drug development: regulatory perspective." One of its closing thoughts seemed to hint at things to come: "We continue to be concerned that despite the widespread availability of simple [pharmacogenomics/pharmacogenetics] tests to determine a patient's phenotype and/or genotype with regard to polymorphism in drug metabolizing enzymes"—that is, to find out whether they have particular allele (genotype) that affects their drug response (phenotype)—"there has been little use of this information to tailor drug doses and dosing regimens to individual patient subgroups in clinical practice before using the drug." The message seems clear: medicine needs to get personal, and pharmacogenomic tests are the way to do it.

Moreover, as Rebecca Eisenberg, professor of law at the University of Michigan and one of the most astute commentators on the legal aspects of genomics, has written: "If the determination that a drug is safe and effective depends critically on patient genotype, the law may at some point require coordinated development and marketing of a pharmacogenomic test along with the therapeutic product." That is, pharmacogenomics and genetic testing are intimately bound up together. Eisenberg noted: "In anticipation of this development, many institutions are seeking patent claims on advances in pharmacogenomics that they hope will permit them to share the wealth from future products. The bargaining position of the parties may depend on the strength of their patent positions." Unfortunately, this means that patents based on the use of genotypes for testing are likely to be fiercely contested.

A foretaste of what might ensue regarding patents is provided by the example of Myriad Genetics, one of the earliest of the new-style genomic companies. It had been set up by Walter Gilbert with Mark Skolnick of the University of Utah. Myriad used the extensive genealogical information about large Utah families to track down genes, some of whose alleles conferred susceptibility to various ailments. One of these diseases was breast cancer. According to the American Society of Clinical Oncology, it is the second most common cancer in women and the second leading cause of cancer death among women. In October 1994, Myriad announced the discovery of the *BRCA1* breast and ovarian cancer disposing gene. Since this did not account for all families with an inherited susceptibility, researchers began looking for another such gene.

Mark Skolnick had been collaborating with a group at the Institute of Cancer Research in the United Kingdom, led by Mike Stratton. Like his British colleague John Sulston, Stratton was concerned about the effect of business on science in this area. According to Sulston's autobiography, Stratton asked Skolnick what Myriad would do if their collaboration managed to map and locate the second breast cancer gene. As Sulston explained: "The answer was that Myriad would patent it and own exclusive rights to exploit it both for diagnosis and therapy." Stratton was unhappy with this situation; he ended the collaboration with Myriad after they had published the rough location of the gene now known as *BRCA2*. As a result, yet another race between public and private researchers began: to pinpoint the gene exactly, and to obtain its sequence. Stratton enlisted the help of the Sanger Centre, which decided to sequence one million bases around where the gene had been located. Because of the Sanger Centre's data release policy, once the region was sequenced, the DNA would be entered into public databases for anyone—including Myriad—to see and use.

Nonetheless, Stratton's team was able to locate a mutation from one of their breast cancer families that was located in the region of the new breast cancer gene, *BRCA2*, and then another five. As Sulston recounted: "Mike [Stratton] moved fast to publish the group's discovery in *Nature*, while keeping it secret even from his collaborators until the last possible minute. But despite his efforts, enough information about the discovery reached Skolnick to enable him to locate the gene himself and bang in a patent application—the day before the [Institute of Cancer Research] paper came out in *Nature*." Myriad's work was published in the March 1996 issue of *Nature Genetics*. An editorial in that issue under the headline "Behold *BRCA2*!"—filled in some details.

"Last December, the race to unearth the second hereditary breast and ovarian cancer gene, *BRCA2*, was concluded. Michael Stratton and colleagues reported that they had identified part of the massive *BRCA2* gene on chromosome 13 and identified six mutations in families with breast and ovarian cancer, including some cases of male breast cancer. . . . Not to be outdone, however, scientists at Myriad Genetics, who had isolated *BRCA1* in 1994, rushed to submit a patent application for *BRCA2* coinciding with the publication of the *Nature* paper. In remarkably little time, the group and its collaborators had managed—with the help of the 900 kilobases of publicly available genomic DNA sequence—to assemble the complete gene sequence." That is, Stratton and his team got there first, but with only part of the coding sequence—68 percent is the figure mentioned in the editorial. Since it built on "900 kilobases of publicly available genomic DNA sequence"—thanks to a data release policy that had just been enshrined in the Human Genome Project's Bermuda principles—the main achievement of the Myriad scientists seems to have been their extraordinary speed in filling in the missing areas.

As *Nature Genetics* pointed out, the result of this complicated situation was that "two rival patent applications have been submitted in the United Kingdom and United States. Each group obviously feels it has a case: the European group was the first to publish evidence that *BRCA2* had been cloned"—its exact position and extent determined—"by virtue of documenting a handful of mutations in affected families. By contrast, the Myriad team points to having been the first to compile the full-length sequence of the gene."

Predictably, things soon turned nasty. As *Science* reported in December 1997, "What began a decade ago as a race to find genes that increase a woman's risk for breast cancer (*BRCA1* and *BRCA2*) has evolved into a bitter court battle over who owns the right to exploit these genes commercially." The central issue for many people was whether Myriad should be allowed to stop public laboratories from carrying out their own breast cancer tests. This came to a head at the end of 2001. *Nature* reported that "a European rebellion against the patent on a gene for breast cancer held by US company

Myriad Genetics is gathering pace." Leading the revolt was Paris's Curie Institute, which filed a formal objection to the patent. According to *Nature*, "scores of geneticists and dozens of diagnostic labs throughout Europe are still doing their own *BRCA1* testing. They say they are reluctant to concede their independence to a firm whose costs substantially exceed their own." *Nature* gives a figure of $2,680 as the price of Myriad's test at the time.

One of the European scientists interviewed for the *Nature* story is quoted as saying: "The substance patents [on genes] are inappropriate and endanger research and medicine." At first glance, this might seem to be the kind of blanket criticism that is routinely made against gene patents. Work published in *Nature* just a few months later, however, highlighted the very real threat that patents represented for genetic testing in particular. As the February 2002 paper noted, "setting aside the debate about the ethics of allowing any patenting of human gene sequences, many are concerned about the ramifications of gene patents for biomedical research and clinical medicine. Unfortunately, there are few empirical data about the effects of patents on the translation of genomic discoveries into medical advances, so it is not clear how justified these concerns are. Here, we present the results of a survey of US laboratories' adoption and use of genetic testing for hereditary haemochromatosis."

The sequence for the gene, one of whose alleles gives rise to the disease, was only elucidated in 1996; the result was published in the August issue of *Nature Genetics*. The editorial gave some background to the disease. "Haemochromatosis develops in mid-adulthood," the writer explained, "but despite its prevalence is widely under diagnosed. As excessive iron accumulates in various organs including the pancreas, liver and heart, patients suffer from conditions that include diabetes, cirrhosis, liver cancer and cardiac dysfunction, often culminating in early death. Ironically, there is a simple and effective treatment—regular episodes of bleeding, or phlebotomy, as practiced for hundreds of years, to deplete surplus iron." Since, as the editorial noted: "Among whites, haemochromatosis occurs in about 1 in 400 people," the potential market for genetic testing is relatively large.

Against this background, the results of the survey of laboratories offering haemochromatosis testing were disturbing. The authors of the paper in *Nature* wrote: "We have found that US laboratories have refrained from offering clinical-testing services for haemochromatosis because of the patents" that were awarded for the diagnostic test. This matters, because "a lot of clinical study is needed to validate and extend the early discovery of a disease gene such as that for haemochromatosis, so our results give reason to fear that limiting clinical testing will inhibit further discovery as well as the understanding that emerges naturally from broad medical adoption."

The survey data indicated that there was a rapid adoption of the haemochromatosis testing by laboratories soon after the *Nature Genetics* paper was published. "It is clear," the *Nature* article commented, "as is typical with genetic tests, that the patents were unnecessary for rapid translation of the [haemochromatosis] discovery into clinical-testing services." Proponents of gene patents often cite the need to encourage this kind of translation as a justification for awarding temporary exclusive rights to what many regard as the common heritage of humanity. "On the contrary, our data show that the patents inhibited adoption, perhaps by creating a financial risk for laboratories, and a disincentive to develop and validate a clinical assay [test] that could be stopped by patent enforcement."

The authors added: "Of course, without the potential value of the patented discovery, the investment of venture capital in Mercator Genetics"—the company that discovered the haemochromatosis gene—"might not have been made and the gene discovery delayed." This is certainly not always the case, however: nothing would have been lost had Myriad not been working on *BRCA2*. Stratton's group located most of the gene first, and would doubtless have found the rest of it, too, had the Sanger Centre not, with scrupulous fairness, published the full sequence data. Myriad then used these data in its own completion of Stratton's work.

The deadening effect of patents on haemochromatosis testing is particularly ironic because Francis Collins, head of the Human Genome Project, held it up as a shining example in a lecture he gave after receiving an award from the Association of American Physicians in 2000. *The New York Times* reported on Collins' predictions about the impact of the HGP over the next 40 years. One was that "by 2010, the genome will help identify people at highest risk of particular diseases, so monitoring efforts can focus on them." It then went on: "A disorder of iron metabolism is likely to become the model for such screening. . . . By 2010, studies will have found the most effective combination of biochemical and genetic tests to detect people who are susceptible." Unfortunately, if the *Nature* paper is right, genetic tests are likely to remain bogged down in the quagmire of patents for longer than that, and not just for haemochromatosis. And in the absence of readily available diagnostic tests, personalized medicine, too, is likely to be delayed.

In the same speech, Collins touched on another key issue affecting pharmacogenomics. "Using genetics to tailor and improve health care will be the genome project's main legacy if effective laws are passed to protect privacy, prevent use of genetic information to deprive an individual of health insurance or a job, and prohibit other forms of genetic discrimination, Dr. Collins said," according to *The New York Times*.

Collins has consistently used his preeminent position as head of the U.S. Human Genome Project to alert scientists and policy makers to the danger that genetic discrimination could nullify potential benefits of genomics. In 1995, for example, he was coauthor of a paper in *Science* reporting on the results of the

NIH-DOE Joint Working Group on Ethical, Legal and Social Implications (ELSI) of the Human Genome Project. James Watson had wisely decreed that monies be set aside for ELSI as part of the HGP from the start.

Under the headline "Genetic discrimination and health insurance: an urgent need for reform," Collins and his colleagues wrote: "We all carry genes that predispose to common illnesses. In many circumstances knowing this information can be beneficial, as it allows individualized strategies to be designed to reduce the risk of illness. But, as knowledge about the genetic basis of common disorders grows, so does the potential for discrimination in health insurance coverage for an ever increasing number of Americans."

They pointed out that this was no mere theoretical possibility. "In the past, genetic information has been used by insurers to discriminate against people. In the early 1970s, some insurance companies denied coverage and charged higher rates to African Americans who were carriers of the gene for sickle cell anemia. Contemporary studies have documented cases of genetic discrimination against people who are healthy themselves but who have a gene that predisposes them or their children to a later illness such as Huntington's disease. In a recent survey of people with a known genetic condition in the family, 22% indicated that they had been refused health insurance coverage because of their genetic status, whether they were sick or not." This can be a critical matter, especially in countries like the United States. As the *Science* paper said, "Because of high costs, insurance is essentially required to have access to health care in the United States." But it added: "Over 40 million people in the United States are uninsured."

As Collins and his coauthors explained, the problem for insurers is the "fear that individuals will remain uninsured until, for example, they receive a genetic test result indicating a predisposition to some disease such as breast or colon cancer. In the absence of the ability to detect hereditary susceptibility to disease, the costs of medical treatment have been absorbed under the current health insurance system of shared risk and shared costs." Since it has not been possible to predict accurately who might develop a disease, everyone pays an average price. Although this might seem unfair, it means that those unlucky enough to develop a disease are subsidized by those who are lucky enough not to. Most people would probably rather end up paying a little more rather than developing the disease, so in practice the system works well.

Problems arise as the accuracy of genetic testing improves and it becomes feasible to pick out those who have a predisposition to a disease. The *Science* paper continued: "Today our understanding of the relation between a misspelling in a gene and future health is still incomplete, thus limiting the ability of insurers to incorporate genetic risks into actuarial calculations"—those that use the probabilities of events to work out the likely payments—"on a large scale. As genetic research enhances the ability to predict individuals' future risk of diseases, many Americans may become uninsurable on the basis of genetic information." People in other countries are also likely to be adversely affected.

Building on the 1993 recommendations of an earlier ELSI Working Group, which advocated "a return to the risk-spreading goal of insurance"—one where everyone paid the same premiums—the Collins group drew up a set of uncompromising recommendations. These included that insurance providers should be prohibited from using genetic information to deny or limit any coverage, from establishing differential rates or premium payments based on genetic information, and requesting or requiring collection or disclosure of genetic information.

Two years later, another ELSI group including Collins addressed the related issue of genetic discrimination at work in the United States. As the paper explained, "Employers are increasingly concerned about the spiraling cost of health insurance as well as the possibility of genetic susceptibility to illness caused by exposure to workplace toxins"—the last point adding an interesting new environmental dimension to the issue of testing. It might be, for example, that people with certain genotypes are susceptible to an industrial carcinogen even at low doses, while others are relatively immune.

In many ways, the situation in 1997 regarding genetic discrimination at work in the United States was even worse than that for insurance: "Employers in most jurisdictions are not prohibited from requiring genetic testing, even though there is insufficient evidence to justify the use of any existing test for genetic susceptibility as a basis for employment decisions," Collins and his coauthors wrote. "Even if employers do not use genetic testing, they still may have access to the medical records of their employees, and thus will be able to find out if these individuals have certain predispositions to disease. Employers may be reluctant to hire or promote individuals they believe will become prematurely unable to work."

Once more, Collins' group drew up a series of recommendations, notably that "employment organizations should be prohibited from using genetic information to affect the hiring of an individual or to affect the terms, conditions, privileges, benefits, or termination of employment unless the employment organization can prove that this information is job related and consistent with business necessity."

Happily, Collins was able to speak some years later of progress on preventing genetic discrimination. "Largely on the basis of recommendations formulated in workshops held by the Human Genome Project and the National Action Plan on Breast Cancer," he said when he gave a lecture in 1997, "the Clinton administration endorsed the need for congressional action to protect against genetic discrimination in health insurance and employment. In 1996, Congress enacted the Health Insurance Portability and Accountability Act, which represented a large step toward protecting access to health insurance in the group-insurance market but left several serious gaps in the individual-insurance market that must still be closed."

"In the area of workplace discrimination," he continued, "the Equal Employment Opportunity Commission has interpreted the Americans with Disabilities Act as covering on-the-job discrimination based on 'genetic information relating to illness, disease or other disorders.' But no claims of genetic discrimination have been brought to the commission, and the guidance has yet to be tested in court, so the degree of protection actually provided by the act remains uncertain."

Naturally, the insurance industry is keen to minimize the legislation that regulates their activities in this area. "Such laws may serve a useful symbolic purpose," wrote William Nowlan of the U.S. National Life Insurance Company in *Science* in 2002, "but the rationale for their enactment is flawed—the erroneous belief that the threat of genetic discrimination by health insurers represents a clear and present danger."

In a letter to *Nature* the following year, Nowlan argued that "health insurers are not inclined to discriminate on the sole basis of a theoretical risk of future disease. In contrast, an individual who already has a serious illness presents the insurer with an altogether different magnitude of risk, because costly claims are almost inevitable. If an applicant for individually underwritten health insurance is worried about discrimination, it makes more sense to fear a mammogram [breast screening], for example, than being tested for a *BRCA* mutation, because tests that detect actual disease are vastly more likely to trigger an adverse underwriting decision."

The situation for life insurance is different, as Nowlan wrote in *Science*: "It . . . might seem reasonable to worry that genetic risk will be of greater interest to life insurers than health insurers, because a policy will often stay in force many decades. But, except for the gene associated with Huntington's disease, genetic risk in an otherwise healthy adult does not preclude affordable coverage." Leaving aside the question of what exactly "affordable" means in this context, it is instructive to consider the UK experience here.

In December 1997, the Association of British Insurers (ABI), the main industry body, launched its Code of Practice for genetic testing. Its three basic principles were that "insurers should not require applicants to undergo a genetic test to obtain insurance; insurers may require disclosure of existing test results under certain circumstances; applications for life insurance up to £100,000 [$150,000] linked to a mortgage will not be asked for test results."

This three-point summary comes from a report by the Select Committee on Science and Technology, a powerful group of British Members of Parliament that periodically reviews important areas on behalf of the UK House of Commons. The Fifth Report was published on March 26, 2001, and contained the results of some probing questions that had been put to representatives of the British insurance industry on the use of genetic tests.

As the report noted: "One of the most difficult aspects of the inquiry has been to discern, with any degree of certainty, exactly what each company's attitude was to the use of tests. [One of the leading UK insurers] Norwich

Union, for example, told us in their initial memorandum that they would use tests for 'rare monogenetic disorders . . . only when approval has been given by GAIC'." The Genetics and Insurance Committee (GAIC) was the key body that evaluated and approved genetic tests for use by the insurance industry. In October 2000, GAIC had announced that the genetic test for Huntington's disease could be used by insurance companies; this was the only such test approved at that time.

"Yet at the oral evidence session," the report continued, "the company's Chief Actuary . . . admitted that the Norwich Union is using tests prior to approval by GAIC. In a similar manner, after submitting their original memorandum, the Prudential [another major insurance company] discovered an 'inconsistency' in their policy and submitted a further memorandum to clarify their position. We could speculate that had more insurers been summoned to give oral evidence, various other *inconsistencies* might have emerged, especially as we had received several memoranda that did very little to clarify their company's position."

In other words, the committee was of the view that the ABI Code of Practice was being widely flouted, and that results from unapproved genetic tests were being used by insurers. No wonder that it wrote: "There must be doubts whether the ABI, a trade organization funded by insurers to represent their own interests, is the right body to regulate the use of genetic test results." Aside from questions of who should oversee the use of such tests, though, an even more important issue emerged from the committee's questioning.

"It does not appear to be certain, at present, that the information obtained from positive genetic tests is relevant to the insurance industry," the report said simply. For example, it noted, one of its eminent witnesses had informed them that "even for Huntington's Chorea, which is generally considered to be one of the most straightforward of the purely genetic disorders, he was unaware of any scientists who believed that the age of onset of the condition could be predicted to any really accurate degree. . . . In effect, we were told, genetic tests can tell you whether, or not, a person has a particular gene defect you are looking for but cannot say, with any degree of certainty, whether they will actually get the disease, when they will get it, how severe it will be, and how responsive to treatment they will be."

These were precisely the kinds of information that insurers needed in order to calculate premiums for individuals; the lack of them rendered current genetic tests useless for that purpose. In the committee's opinion, "Insurers appear to have been far more interested in establishing their future right to use genetic test results in assessing premiums than in whether or not they are reliable or relevant." As a result, "We suggest that at present the very small number of cases involving genetic test results could allow insurers to ignore all genetic test results with relative impunity," the authors of the report wrote, "allowing time to establish firmly their scientific and actuarial relevance."

Given the drubbing they had received at the hands of the Select Committee and the threat that they might be regulated by law rather than a voluntary code of practice, the British insurers were probably relieved that the main recommendation of the committee was a "voluntary moratorium on the use of all positive genetic tests by insurers for at least the next two years." In fact, on October 23, 2001, the ABI agreed with the British Government on a five-year moratorium, which would be used "to develop a lasting consensus between different stakeholders and Government about what should replace it."

A s in the United States, then, the situation regarding the use of genetic tests in the United Kingdom remained up in the air. One central point to emerge from the detailed work by the parliamentary Select Committee was doubt about the extent to which genetic tests were useful as accurate predictors of future medical conditions. The issue had already been raised back in 1997, when a U.S. task force presented its report "Promoting safe and effective genetic testing in the United States." The fear then was that "the rapid pace of test development combined with the rush to market them may create an environment in which tests are available to health care consumers before they have been adequately validated."

Both the "rapid pace" and the "rush to market" have continued. At the beginning of 2003, the publicly-funded US site Genetests.org listed tests for nearly 1,000 diseases. In September 2002, an ABCNews.com commentary by an ethicist at the University of Virginia reported that "Myriad Genetics, the company that owns the patent for the BRACAnalysis test, which tests for genetic alterations that can lead to breast cancer, has announced a new advertising drive. Like other successful campaigns that bypass doctors and go directly to consumers, the effort will place advertisements in major media outlets where the target audience will be most likely to take note." The writer commented: "With the BRACAnalysis test this is the first time that ads will try to sell consumers a test for a genetic disease. Medical testing is usually done for diseases people already have, but genetic screens are about future conditions that carry uncertain risks. When the symptoms will appear, how serious they will be, or even if the disease will manifest itself at all, cannot always be predicted. So an important precedent is being set."

Just how uncertain these risks are is clear from information on Myriad Genetics' Web pages for its breast cancer tests. As a section "Understanding inherited breast and ovarian cancer" explains, around ten percent of the 200,000 cases of breast cancer and 25,000 cases of ovarian cancer are believed to be hereditary—the result of certain alleles. Some of these involve *BRCA1* and *BRCA2*. For women with such alleles the chance of developing breast cancer by age 50 is between 33 percent and 50 percent according to Myriad's figures, compared with two percent in the general population. While the relative risk is greatly increased, the outcome is far from certain, even for those with harmful mutations (rarer alleles).

Moreover, the range of options for reducing this risk is circumscribed. Myriad's Web site mentions increased surveillance, preventive drug therapies, or a prophylactic mastectomy (removal of the breasts). The first of these does not reduce the risk, but may allow a tumor to be caught more quickly. Drug treatment with Tamoxifen halves the chance of developing breast cancer for women with *BRCA* mutations. The most effective option is mastectomy, which can decrease the risk for women with a *BRCA* mutation by 96 percent according to Myriad. This, however, is clearly a drastic solution.

Not only is the benefit of genetic testing limited, but there exists a real downside, too. A 1997 paper in *Science* pointed out that genetic test results form a special kind of "dangerous knowledge," for "once given, it cannot be retrieved. Most clinicians who have dealt with *BRCA* gene testing can recount anecdotes of individuals who have been severely affected by the news that they had inherited the gene, and of individuals in whom the news that they had not inherited it produced not reassurance but agonies of guilt, perhaps toward a sister who was less fortunate." Similarly, "the failure to find a *BRCA* mutation may also be interpreted wrongly as a lack of risk, and women may fail to follow population screening programs as a result."

If genetic testing can give rise to this kind of "dangerous knowledge" for a relatively well-defined physical condition such as breast cancer, it can be imagined how much more problematic it is likely to be for, say, mental illnesses. This is an area examined in a 1998 report issued by the independent Nuffield Council on Bioethics, entitled "Mental disorders and genetics: the ethical context." In a letter to *Nature* at the time of the report's publication, members of the working party emphasized their main conclusion: "The Nuffield inquiry concluded that genetic tests for the diagnosis of the common mental disorders with more complex causes will not be particularly useful in the near future. Even if a number of susceptibility genes were identified for a particular disorder, the Nuffield Council takes the view that, without an understanding of their interaction, they would not be adequate for predicting individual risk in a clinical setting. It has therefore recommended that genetic testing for susceptibility genes which offer relatively low predictive or diagnostic certainty be discouraged unless and until there is clear medical benefit to the patient."

Four years later, another Nuffield Council report broadened the field of inquiry to consider the impact of genetics on all human behavior, and not just on those involved in mental disorders. Once again, the report concluded that "genetic tests will have a low predictive capacity because of the myriad other factors that influence our behaviour and the vastly complex interactions between genetic factors themselves." Nonetheless, the report noted: "In the future it may become possible to make predictions, albeit limited ones, about behaviour based on genetic information and to design useful applications of that knowledge." It also noted, however, that there is a particular risk if such a development takes place.

"Traits such as sexuality, aggression and intelligence have in the past been thought of as outcomes of inheritance, family background, socio-economic environment, individual choice and even divine intervention. If research in behavioural genetics identifies the influence of genes on such traits, these traits may be mistakenly come to be thought of as being fundamentally determined by genetic factors and even aspects of life which belong to one's 'fate'." The authors of the report were quick to emphasize that "fatalism about genetics is a misconception. Even when behavioural traits are influenced by genes, there are always other influences, and the existence of genetic influences does not show that we are powerless to change or modify our character. Nonetheless, this misconception is pervasive."

The issue of genetic determinism had been raised a year before, by Craig Venter, in the concluding paragraph of the Celera human genome paper, where "determinism, the idea that all characteristics of a person are 'hardwired' in the genome" was singled out as one of two fallacies to be avoided (the other being reductionism). His abiding interest in the deeper ethical implications of genomics was amply demonstrated by the direction he chose to take after he left Celera. On April 30, 2002, Venter announced that he was using money he had made from his shares in HGS and Celera to set up three not-for-profit organizations: the TIGR Center for the Advancement of Genomics (TCAG), the Institute for Biological Energy Alternatives (IBEA), and the J. Craig Venter Science Foundation. The last of these supports the other two, as well as the original TIGR, run by his wife, Claire Fraser. IBEA hopes to come up with clean energy production by applying microbial genomics, while TCAG is a not-for-profit policy center dedicated to advancing genomics through "education and enlightenment of the general public, elected officials, and students," as its Web site puts it.

To help them realize their respective goals, in August 2002, TIGR, IBEA and TCAG announced "their plan to create a next generation, high-throughput DNA sequencing facility." Venter wanted to make a leap beyond the current throughput levels, just as he had done with TIGR and Celera. As the press release pointed out: "While the cost to sequence a species has rapidly declined from billions to millions of dollars, there is still a need to substantially reduce these costs so that everyone can benefit from the great promise that genomics holds." Venter defined the incredibly ambitious objective he and his organizations had set themselves: "One of our goals in building this facility is to make genomic sequencing of the six billion people on this planet technologically feasible so that everyone can benefit and be empowered by this information."

A couple of months later, Venter helped make this idea more concrete through his participation in one of TIGR's series of international Genome Sequencing and Analysis Conferences (GSAC). It was held in Boston from

October 2–5, 2002, and Venter cochaired a session with the thought-provoking title "The future of sequencing: advancing towards the $1000 genome." In the accompanying press release, Venter is quoted as saying: "Genomics has advanced rapidly over the past decade and is now playing a major role in scientific and medical research. However, in order for genomics to revolutionize everyone's life we need to make advances in sequencing technology so that the work can be done rapidly and cost-effectively. This new panel session at GSAC will bring together developers of new sequencing technologies to discuss what their technologies have to offer and the likely time line for getting them on line."

Companies that made presentations included U.S. Genomics, Solexa, Amersham Biosciences, VisiGen Biotechnologies, and 454 Corporation. Each hoped that its own innovative technology would be successful in breaking the $1,000 barrier for sequencing the entire human genome. The first of these is notable for the fact that Craig Venter sits on its board, but whether it is U.S. Genomics or one of the other hopefuls in the sub-$1,000 genome race that is ultimately successful, and when, is not clear. One thing does seem certain: at some point, it will be possible to sequence any genome for $1,000 or less.

The history of computers offers an interesting parallel. During the early years, when mainframe computers were extremely costly, it was widely believed that only a few would ever be built. They were for exceptional users like the government or the military, who were the only ones likely to have any use for such number crunchers. The arrival of the personal computer, or PC, however, in the early 1980s showed not only that people wanted their own computer, but that PCs could be applied in ways never dreamt of in the beginning. In the same way, although many find it hard to imagine now why people would routinely want access to their entire DNA sequence—call it the personal genome, or PG—uses will certainly be found that go far beyond the obvious applications.

For example, genetic tests costing thousands of dollars would be redundant: the results of every possible test would already be present, stored in the complete genome sequence. Before prescribing a new medicine, a doctor could check the patient's PG against the accompanying profiles for the drug in order to minimize adverse reactions. As new discoveries about drugs, genes or alleles, came along, people could either go to their doctors to review the implications for their own particular genome or perhaps just access online services that performed the analysis in the comfort of their own home. This seems to have been part of Venter's original vision for Celera: "You'll be able to log on to our data base and get information about yourself," he had told *The New York Times* in September 1999.

Couples thinking about starting a family might run their PGs jointly through programs designed to check on genomic compatibility. Even if both adults are healthy, they might share alleles that, brought together in their children's DNA, would cause serious medical conditions. More contentiously, dating agencies could offer the option to find partners with complementary PGs that were more likely to produce healthy offspring, while responsible parents might want to check out the PGs of prospective sons- and daughters-in-law to make sure that there were no genetic skeletons in the genome's closet. The result would be a kind of genteel eugenics. Unlike the earlier discredited attempts at selective breeding, though, this would be based not on subjective views of what is genetically "good," but on scientific facts about digital DNA sequences and their consequences. It would thus be all the more dangerous for its apparently objective nature.

Because the three billion bases contained in a PG represent less than a gigabyte of computer data, it will soon fit easily on a small memory card that could be carried by everyone to allow doctors and hospitals to access key information in the case of accidents or emergencies. Such cards would obviously need several layers of strong encryption to prevent unauthorized access. Ultimately, as the price of sequencing the genome falls further, even the cards would become unnecessary. The information could be obtained almost as simply by taking a few cells from the individual and sequencing them, if only partially, on the spot. The DNA they contain would form not only a complete genetic description of its owner, but also the ultimate digital fingerprint of that person. For countries that require such things, the genome would be the perfect national identity number—one that could never be lied about, forged, or lost.

Even though its owner could never part with it, a virtual identity card could still be stolen—or rather its data can. Once PGs can be obtained cheaply, there will be the danger that our genomes could be recovered from a huge range of trivial, everyday objects—the comb we brush our hair with, the towel we wipe our hands on, the cup we drink from—that contain a few cells with our telltale DNA. Given the intimate nature of the information our DNA reveals, such genomic pickpockets could become a serious threat, especially for the rich and powerful. Imagine the impact if it were revealed that a world leader or business tycoon had an allele conferring a susceptibility to mental illness.

These apparently futuristic privacy issues are closer than most people might think. In May 2002, the Human Genetics Commission, an official group of experts offering advice to the British government, published a report entitled "Inside information—balancing interests in the use of personal genetic data." One of its recommendations was that "it should be a criminal offence to test someone's DNA or access their genetic information without their knowledge or consent for non-medical purposes, except as allowed by law," because existing legislation offered insufficient protection from what was obviously perceived as a growing potential threat.

Meanwhile, the rise of biobanks—massive collections of DNA that may, like those in Iceland and Estonia, encompass an entire nation—will create tempting targets for data thieves. Governments do not even need to resort to underhand methods: they can simply arrogate to themselves the right to access such confidential information wherever it is stored. One of the questions addressed by the FAQ of a biobank involving half a million people, currently under construction in the United Kingdom, is: "Will the police have access to the information?" The answer—"only under court order"—does not inspire confidence.

The greatest privacy challenge posed by the ready availability of personal genomes, however, is not this public kind. As the examples discussed show, even existing genetic tests, based as they are on relatively old technologies, provide "dangerous knowledge" about what might happen to us. The arrival of PGs will make that knowledge more complete, and potentially more problematic. A comprehensive, personalized list of alleles that are associated with future medical problems may be to hand, but what the list provides is only a probability that we will in fact develop those conditions at some point in the future. This turns the personal genome into something of a twenty-first century sword of Damocles, suspended perilously above us by the thinnest of threads—that of our own DNA.

Do we really want to know that we have a genetic susceptibility to a disease that is currently incurable? Would that change how we live? Similarly, do we wish to carry around with us the knowledge that we have a certain constellation of alleles that could, if combined with those of someone with another particular set through an unlucky throw of the DNA dice, potentially cause grave difficulties for the children bearing them? Would that affect who we marry? Above all, do we want to have to deal with not just these present quandaries, but all the future unknown ones that will surely arise as genomics continues its spectacular advance and is able to mine ever more dangerous knowledge from that huge string of chemical letters?

So far, the only person who has had to face this issue was uniquely wellplaced to deal with it. After Craig Venter became the first human to know (most of) his genome—the first owner of a PG—he decided to start taking medication to lower his cholesterol—a practical example of the new-style pharmacogenomics that $1,000 genomes may one day allow for all. Few of us have the genomic expertise of Venter, though, or are able to think through as he has what it means to know our own genome. Magnifying the seriousness of these implications is the same central fact that gives bioinformatics its extraordinary power: that all genomes are related, derived by evolution from a common ancestor. Everything you glean about your own DNA is likely to have an impact, to a greater or lesser degree, on those who share parts of it: your family. Your dangerous knowledge is unavoidably theirs, too, at least in part. As a consequence, it may be that most people will opt for another way.

As chapter 8 related, the sixth point of the Gene Donor consent form for the Estonian Genome Project states: "I have the right to know my genetic data." But immediately before this—negating it almost—is a stark warning of the reality of such knowledge: "Data on hereditary characteristics and genetic risks obtained as a result of genetic research may be unpleasant for me." It adds as a corollary: "I have the right to not know my genetic data." Until medicine offers the assurance that it can cure or—better still—preempt the consequences of any adverse genetic condition, total genomic knowledge may prove to be simply too personal for most people to handle.

NOTES

Interviews included in this chapter were conducted by the author in June 2003 with the following individual: E. Lander.

1. p. 185 *An article published in June 2002 wrote* M. Branca, "Genotyping prices to plummet," *Bio-IT World*, June 12, 2002.

2. p. 186 *LD refers to correlations* D.E. Reich, et al., "Linkage disequilibrium in the human genome," *Nature* 411 (2001): 199–204.

3. p. 187 *The vast difference in the extent of LD* D.E. Reich, et al., "Linkage disequilibrium in the human genome," *Nature* 411 (2001): 199–204.

4. p. 187 *A paper in* Science *in July 2001* J. Claiborne Stephens, et al., "Haplotype variation and linkage disequilibrium in 313 human genes," *Science* 293 (2001): 489–493.

5. p. 188 *We have not been able to implicate a single causative mutation,* J.D. Rioux, et al., "Genetic variation in the 5q31 cytokine gene cluster confers susceptibility to Crohn disease," *Nature Genetics* 29 (2001): 223–228.

6. p. 189 *once the haplotype blocks* M.J. Daly, et al., "High-resolution haplotype structure in the human genome," *Nature Genetics* 29 (2001): 229–232.

7. p. 189 *haplotype tag SNPs* G.C.L. Johnson, et al., "Haplotype tagging for the identification of common disease genes," *Nature Genetics* 29 (2001): 233–237.

8. p. 190 *Our data provide strong evidence that most of the human genome* S.B. Gabriel, et al., "The structure of haplotype blocks in the human genome," *Science* 296 (2002): 2225–2229.

9. p. 190 *The ability to detect recent natural selection* P.C. Sabeti, et al., "Detecting recent positive selection in the human genome from haplotype structure," *Nature* 419 (2002): 832–837.

10. p. 191 *to create the next generation map of the human genome* NHGRI press release, October 29, 2002.

11. p. 191 *The human genome is thought to contain at least* NHGRI press release, October 29, 2002.

12. p. 192 *200 to 400 people from four large, geographically distinct* NHGRI press release, October 29, 2002.

13. p. 192 *Other population geneticists do not yet agree* N. Wade, "Gene-mappers take new aim at diseases," *The New York Times*, October 30, 2002.

14. p. 193 *The scientific community is currently divided regarding the perceived* E. Lai, et al., "Medical applications of haplotype-based SNP maps: learning to walk before we run," *Nature Genetics* 32 (3) (2002): 353.

15. p. 193 *research published in 1998 suggested that in 1994,* J. Lazarou, et al., "Incidence of adverse drug reactions in hospitalized patients: a meta-analysis of prospective studies," *JAMA* 279 (15) (1998): 1200–1205.

16. p. 194 *Attrition of drugs during development. . . . due to safety concerns* A. Roses, "Genome-based pharmacogenetics and the pharmaceutical industry," *Nat Rev Drug Discovery* 1 (2002): 541–549.

17. p. 194 *We continue to be concerned that despite the widespread availability* L.J. Lesko and J. Woodcock, "Pharmacogenomic-guided drug development: regulatory perspective," *The Pharmacogenomics Journal* 2 (2002): 20–24.

18. p. 195 *If the determination that a drug is safe and effective* R.E. Eisenberg, "Will pharmacogenomics alter the role of patents in drug development?" *Pharmacogenomics* 3 (5) (2002): 571–574.

19. p. 195 *In anticipation of this development, many institutions* R.E. Eisenberg, "Will pharmacogenomics alter the role of patents in drug development?" *Pharmacogenomics* 3 (5) (2002): 571–574.

20. p. 195 *The answer was that Myriad would patent it* J. Sulston and G. Ferry, *The Common Thread* (London/New York: Bantam Press, 2002), 140.

21. p. 196 *Mike [Stratton] moved fast to publish* J. Sulston and G. Ferry, *The Common Thread* (London/New York: Bantam Press, 2002), 141.

22. p. 196 *Last December, the race to unearth the second hereditary* Editorial, "Behold *BRCA2!*" *Nature Genetics* 12 (1996): 222.

23. p. 196 *What began a decade ago as a race to find genes* E. Marshall, "The battle over *BRCA1* goes to court; *BRCA2* may be next," *Science* 278 (1997): 1874.

24. p. 196 *a European rebellion against the patent on a gene* M. Wadman, "Testing time for gene patent as Europe rebels," *Nature* 413 (2001): 443.

25. p. 197 *setting aside the debate about the ethics of allowing* J.F. Merz, et al., "Diagnostic testing fails the test," *Nature* 415 (2002): 577–579.

26. p. 197 *Haemochromatosis develops in mid-adulthood* Editorial, "Haemochromatosis . . . definite maybe!" *Nature Genetics* 13 (1996): 375–376.

27. p. 198 *by 2010, the genome will help identify people* L.K. Altman, "Genomic chief has high hopes, and great fears, for genetic testing," *The New York Times*, June 27, 2000.

28. p. 199 *We all carry genes that predispose to common illnesses.* K.L. Hudson, et al., "Genetic discrimination and health insurance: an urgent need for reform," *Science* 270 (1995): 391–393.

29. p. 200 *a return to the risk-spreading goal of insurance* K.L. Hudson, et al., "Genetic discrimination and health insurance: an urgent need for reform," *Science* 270 (1995): 391–393.

30. p. 200 *Employers are increasingly concerned about the spiraling cost of health insurance* K. Rothenberg, et al., "Genetic information and the workplace: legislative approaches and policy challenges," *Science* 275 (1997) 1755–1757.

31. p. 200 *employment organizations should be prohibited from using* K. Rothenberg, et al., "Genetic information and the workplace: legislative approaches and policy challenges," *Science* 275 (1997): 1755–1757.

32. p. 200 *Largely on the basis of recommendations formulated in workshops* F.S. Collins, "Medical and societal consequences of the Human Genome Project," *N. Engl. J. Med.* 341 (1999): 28–37.

33. p. 201 *Such laws may serve a useful symbolic purpose* W. Nowlan, "A rational view of insurance and genetic discrimination," *Science* 297 (2002): 195–196.

34. p. 201 *health insurers are not inclined to discriminate* W. Nowlan, "Correspondence," *Nature* 421 (2003): 313.

35. p. 201 *insurers should not require applicants to undergo a genetic test* Fifth Report of Select Committee on Science and Technology, March 26, 2001. Online at *http://www.parliament.the-stationery-office.co.uk/pa/cm200001/cmselect/cmsctech/174/17402.htm.*

36. p. 203 *to develop a lasting consensus between different stakeholders* ABI press release, October 23, 2001.

37. p. 203 *the rapid pace of test development combined with the rush* National Human Genome Research Institute press release, October 1997.

38. p. 203 *Myriad Genetics, the company that owns the patent for the BRACAnalysis test,* J. Moreno, "Selling genetics tests," *ABCNews.com,* September 23, 2002.

39. p. 203 *Understanding inherited breast and ovarian cancer* "Myriad Tests, Understanding inherited breast and ovarian cancer." Online at *http://www.myriadtests.com/brac.htm.*

40. p. 204 *Myriad's Web site mentions increased surveillance* "Myriad Tests, Inherited breast and ovarian cancer FAQ." Online at *http://www.myriadtests.com/faq_brac.htm.*

41. p. 204 *Drug treatment with Tamoxifen* "Myriad Tests, Reducing the risk of breast and ovarian cancer." Online at *http://www.myriadtests.com/riski.htm.*

42. p. 204 *once given, it cannot be retrieved.* B. Ponder, "Genetic testing for cancer risk," *Science* 278 (1997): 1050–1054.

43. p. 204 *The Nuffield inquiry concluded that genetic tests* "Correspondence," *Nature* 395 (1998): 309.

44. p. 204 *genetic tests will have a low predictive capacity* "Nuffield Council on Bioethics—Genetics and human behaviour: the ethical context" (2002).

45. p. 205 *On April 30, 2002, Venter announced* The Center for the Advancement of Genomics press release, April 30, 2002.

46. p. 205 *their plan to create a next generation,* TIGR press release, August 15, 2002.

47. p. 206 *Genomics has advanced rapidly over the past decade* TIGR press release, September 23, 2002.

48. p. 206 *You'll be able to log on to our data base* L.M. Fisher, "Surfing the human genome," *The New York Times,* September 20, 1999.

49. p. 207 *it should be a criminal offence to test* HGC press release, May 21, 2002.

50. p. 208 *only under court order* "UK Biobank FAQ." Online at *http://www.biobank.ac.uk/FAQs.htm.*

51. p. 208 *he decided to start taking medication* J. Goldstein, "Venter's next move," *SunSpot.net,* September 16, 2002.

52. p. 208 *Data on hereditary characteristics and genetic* Estonian Genome Project, Gene Donor Consent Form.

CHAPTER 10

Free Expression

Traditional genetics started from physical characteristics—eye color in the fruit fly, say. By observing how these traits were propagated in cross-breeding experiments, it was possible to deduce information about the hidden structures called genes—the "particles" of heredity—such as their relative location, for example. Genomics turned this picture on its head. The flood of digital sequence data during the 1990s meant that the exact position and the full sequence of many of the genes in a growing number of organisms was known. Often what exactly they did, however, remained a mystery.

As a result, a new field came into being called functional genomics, which sought to establish the role for protein-coding structures within the DNA sequence. The main technique in the early days of functional genomics was gene disruption. Gene disruption involves introducing extraneous DNA into a particular gene sequence. The consequences are then observed—for example, whether there are physical changes or whether the organism fails to develop at all. Clearly, gene disruptions could not be applied directly to humans, since it would be not just impractical but unethical, too. Fortunately, the wide-ranging homologies that exist among higher animals meant that knowledge gained from gene disruption programs on model organisms often applied to humans.

As was so often the case, the fruit fly community was in the vanguard here. A paper published by Gerald Rubin and colleagues in 1995 explained the rationale of the gene disruption program operating under the auspices of the Berkeley Drosophila Genome Project (BDGP): "If the model organism projects are to be maximally useful in assigning function to human DNA sequences, they must be accompanied by genetic studies so that not only the sequences of the genes, but also their biological functions, are determined. To facilitate this end, BDGP has adopted a broad approach that combines the determination of the genomic sequence with the development and application of methods for large-scale functional analysis."

In the same year that the BDGP paper was published, Patrick Brown and his colleagues at Stanford University were investigating gene function through disruption. Born in 1954, Brown prepared himself for his scientific career with exemplary thoroughness. After a degree in chemistry from the University of Chicago, a PhD (in biochemistry), an M.D., and a residency in pediatrics at a local hospital, he moved on to postdoctoral work. In 1988, he went to Stanford University as professor of biochemistry, although his employer was the Howard Hughes Medical Institute, where he was a member of the elite band of 350 scientists known as investigators.

The chosen organism for Brown's functional genomics work was yeast, and the technique—called "genetic foot printing"—allowed high-throughput screening. It is "an efficient experimental approach," he and his team wrote, "designed to allow the biological roles of thousands of genes in the [yeast] genome to be studied economically." With thousands of genes to investigate, increasing the speed at which gene function could be assigned was an important advance, one that Brown and his team consolidated the following year by applying genetic foot printing to the whole of yeast's chromosome V. The paper concluded with the usual look forward to future possibilities: "We anticipate that simply extending the methods described above to the whole genome will enable us to assign mutant phenotypes"—the physical changes caused by gene disruption—"to more than half of the genes."

Despite this inviting prospect, the large-scale genetic foot printing work was only carried out much later: "Our attention got diverted," Brown admits to me. He had come up with something even better, which he described in a paper published in *Science* in October 1995 under the title "Quantitative monitoring of gene expression patterns with complementary DNA microarray." Although the paper was short—just three pages—it marked the start of a new phase in functional genomics, one that went far beyond the slow and painstaking gene deletion approach by allowing the direct study of the activity of thousands of genes simultaneously.

The DNA microarray came about in a rather circuitous way. In addition to the work on genetic foot printing, Brown's lab was also engaged in other projects, including the study of how the AIDS virus inserts its genome into host cells. Arising out of this, Brown was working on a method to carry out high-throughput genotyping, but in an inspired lateral shift he realized that the technique he was developing could be applied even more broadly to the burgeoning field of functional genomics.

Genes produce their corresponding protein—that is, are expressed—through the intermediate stage of messenger RNA (mRNA). This is a single-stranded version of the DNA sequence that codes for the protein. Physically, there is a slight difference in the sequences; in RNA, all the instances of the chemical thymine (T) in the DNA are replaced by a similar chemical uracil (U). The digital (informational) content is identical, however.

A way to monitor gene expression would be to extract all the mRNAs in a given tissue at a given time, and then measure which were present and in what quantities. One of Craig Venter's insights had been that a convenient technique for dealing with mRNA is to convert it back to the corresponding DNA sequence that gave rise to it—the complementary DNA (cDNA). Brown adopted this approach for studying gene expression.

Implicitly, his method built on the other key feature of Watson and Crick's proposed structure for DNA, alongside the double helix structure: the fact that the two strands are complementary to each other. That is, opposite every chemical letter A in one strand is a T in the other, and vice versa, with a similar pairing of Gs and Cs. This fact allows it to be copied perfectly in a conceptually simple way: the two strands separate and complementary chemical letters are added at each position in the sequence on both to create two identical double helices.

For the same reasons of chemical attraction that DNA forms the double helix, isolated single DNA strands can bind to strands with the complementary sequence, a process known as hybridization. For example, a single DNA strand consisting of the chemical letters ATTGACGTAGCCGTG would hybridize with TAACTGCATCGGCAC. As a result, the complementary sequence can be used to test for the presence of its corresponding strand. At the heart of this technique lies the digital nature of DNA code, which allows the matching to be far more specific than any analogue method could be.

Brown's approach was to place different and known single-stranded DNA sequences at pre-selected points on a surface to form an ordered array. A test sample containing single-stranded cDNAs derived from mRNAs is labeled in some way and then added to the array. After allowing sufficient time for the hybridization process to take place where complementary DNA sequences meet, the array is washed and then scanned for the label.

Since the DNA sequences at each point on the array are known, those points where hybridization is observed give exact information about which cDNA sequences are present in the sample being investigated, and thus which mRNAs are present. An important feature of this approach is that hybridization tests are carried out in parallel: the only limit is how many DNA strands can be placed on a given surface while keeping them separate. The ability to detect thousands of sequences simultaneously give DNA arrays the potential to show the pattern of gene expression changes across the entire genome, rather than for just a few genes.

As Brown and his frequent collaborator Michael Eisen later wrote, "The idea of using ordered arrays of DNAs to perform parallel hybridization studies is not in itself new; arrays on porous membranes have been in use for years. However, many parallel advances have occurred to transform these rather clumsy membranes into much more useful and efficient methods for performing parallel genetic analyses."

"First, large-scale sequencing projects have produced information and resources that make it possible to assemble collections of DNAs that correspond to all, or a large fraction of, the genes in many organisms from bacteria to humans." The genes were needed to provide the reference DNA on the array. "Second, technical advances have made it possible to generate arrays with very high densities of DNA, allowing for tens of thousands of genes to be represented in areas smaller than standard glass microscope slides. Finally, advances in fluorescent labeling of nucleic acids and fluorescent detection have made the use of these arrays simpler, safer and more accurate." There are analogies here to sequencing machines, which took the basic dideoxy technique of Sanger and applied it on a vastly-greater scale. The achievement of Brown's lab was similar to that of Leroy Hood's: to automate and make parallel what had previously been a slow, manual procedure.

A standard programmable robot that can pick up objects in one location and place them precisely in another is used to drop tiny spots of DNA solution onto standard microscope slides, typically 110 of them at a time, fixed to the robot's baseplate in a kind of grid. The DNA samples are held in 96 or 384 small wells—tiny depressions in a surface. The robot positions a cluster of specially-designed spring-loaded printing tips into several adjacent wells at once. The tips have a tiny cut at the end, rather like that in a fountain pen, which takes up around one millionth of a liter of DNA as it is dipped in the wells.

Brown explains: "We needed to be able to print thousands and thousands of different sequences, which meant that our printing device either would need a corresponding number of printing elements, or we would need the printing elements to be able to easily be rinsed and reloaded. It seemed to me like the perfect technology for that was the fountain pen: it's very robust, and simple."

The tips are then lightly tapped by the robot at identical positions on groups of slides, each of which has been specially coated, to leave a small drop with less than half a billionth of a liter of the DNA solution. After depositing DNA on every slide the tips are washed and dried and the process is repeated for the next set of DNA samples with the new spots separated by a small distance relative to previous spots. The distance between the center of the spots is typically one fifth of a millimeter, and can be half this. Despite this impressive density, the system was fast: in 1999, each cycle of wash, dry, load, and print on 110 slides, took about two hours. Using a print-tip cluster of 16 tips, it was possible to spot the entire genome of yeast—6,000 genes—on 110 slides in six hours. Once the spotting is complete, the slides are processed to maximize the amount of DNA stably attached to the surface. Finally, the DNA is denatured—converted from the double-stranded form to the single-stranded variety required for hybridization—by plunging the slides in water just off the boil.

When the mRNA in the test material is converted to single-stranded cDNA, one of the DNA bases—usually a T—is replaced with an equivalent one containing a fluorescent marker. Ideally, arrays would be used to measure the absolute levels of cDNA, but in practice this is seldom possible: there are too many variables that affect the strength of the signal from the marker and thus distort the reading. Instead, the relative gene expression of two different samples is calculated. As Brown and Eisen noted: "Fortunately, *differences* in gene expression between samples—i.e., where and when it is or is not expressed, and how it changes with perturbations, are what matters most about a gene's expression." This is one of the key ideas of Brown's DNA arrays: that the relative abundance of mRNA is measured. Doing so allows the significant features to emerge from confounding factors that have nothing to do with the experiment in hand, but are simply artifacts of how hybridization arrays work.

In practice, this comparison of two different samples is effected by labeling them with two distinct fluorescent dyes—generally red and green—and mixing the two samples together for simultaneous hybridization to one cDNA array. Once hybridization has taken place, the relative amount of a gene's mRNA in the two samples is obtained by measuring the ratio of the intensities of the two colors.

The first public outing for DNA microarrays, in *Science*, was modest in the extreme. A mere 45 random cDNAs from the humble *Arabidopsis thaliana* were spotted on a glass microscope slide. The paper contained one rather dull-looking image of six groups of spots—the microarrays in three different circumstances, each measured in two ways—and no results of any significance. *Science*, however, had no doubts about the importance of these small beginnings. An accompanying news analysis piece spoke of "Entering the postgenome era," no less, and explained: "As some teams are gearing up for the final push to spell out all 3 billion base pairs of the human genome, others are poised to step into the post genome era and find out how those genes act in concert to regulate the whole organism." Remarkably, the story referred to not one but two new techniques, noting that they allowed researchers to generate "in a matter of weeks information that might otherwise have taken years to gather."

Alongside the technique from Brown's laboratory came one from a team led by Kenneth Kinzler and Bert Vogelstein of Johns Hopkins University. The first author of the paper was Victor Velculescu, who had developed the technique for his thesis. One of the lead authors on the other paper, Dari Shalon, had devised a key element—the robot arrayer—as part of his thesis. In most other respects, though, the techniques were worlds apart.

The microarray technique required the creation of a new instrument, and was based on the measurement of analogue properties—the intensity of two levels of fluorescence. Velculescu's Serial Analysis of Gene Expression (SAGE), as it was called, was not only fundamentally digital, but used established laboratory techniques to offer a direct measurement of gene expression levels.

The basic idea makes use of a surprising fact about mRNAs and the cDNAs derived from them: that for a given organism, as few as nine DNA letters are generally sufficient to identify each one uniquely, provided they come from a known position within the overall gene sequence. Nine chemical letters such as AATGCGTGA might seem too few to identify uniquely a cDNA and hence the equivalent mRNA string, also known as the *transcript* of the gene. However, as Velculescu and his coauthors pointed out, nine letters give 4×4×4×4×4×4×4×4×4 or 262,144 different possibilities, which far exceeds the number of genes in the human genome, for example.

If a string of nine letters could be found from a fixed, known position in the cDNA, it could be used to identify the gene responsible for the mRNA transcript in question simply by searching through GenBank for corresponding sequences. Assuming the gene had been entered into the database, the nine letters would act as kind of bar code for the mRNA and its gene.

The next problem was how to read that bar code. The second idea of SAGE, and the part that explains its name, is to cut the bar codes out of the cDNA and to concatenate them—to join them together into a long chain of DNA letters. This chain could then be sequenced using standard techniques. If the tags were simply joined together directly, however, it would be impossible to tell where one ended and the next began when the tag chains were broken for shotgun sequencing, for example. This meant that it was crucial to have spacing elements that marked off the beginning and end of each nine-letter tag.

The secret to implementing the SAGE idea was to use one of Hamilton Smith's restriction enzymes as a way to create the tags at well-defined points in the cDNA sequence. For example, tags could be produced in such a way that they were known to lie next to the last occurrence of the sequence CATG in every cDNA transcript. An analogy would be to bar code books using the sequence of nine letters that were located immediately before the last occurrence of the word "also" in the text. Assuming an index of bar codes for every book had been set up, a title could be identified from its text by noting the sequence of letters found immediately before the last "also" in the book in question, and then looking these up in the bar code database.

For cDNAs, reading the sequence was slightly harder, and involved sequencing the concatenated tags and reading them off between the spacing elements. The tags could then be searched against the same part of the sequences that were held in GenBank, which would need to be generated using a computer—a fairly straightforward task. The result would be a list of matches to various genes expressed in the sample corresponding to all the different tags observed. Counting how many times a particular tag occurred provided a direct measurement of exactly how many mRNA molecules had been in the sample.

To demonstrate how SAGE worked in practice, Velculescu and his coauthors looked at the gene expression of the human pancreas. Out of some 840 tags that were analyzed—by no means all of them, but enough to be representative—351 tags occurred only once, while one tag (GAGCACACC) occurred 64 times—obviously from a protein that was particularly important for pancreatic cells. For this test, the tags were sequenced manually, but as the paper pointed out: "Adaptation of this technique to an automated sequencer would allow the analysis of over 1000 transcripts in a single 3-hour run." Just how powerful this high-throughput version of SAGE could be was shown by a paper from essentially the same team, published in the journal *Cell* at the beginning of 1997.

The paper was entitled "Characterization of the yeast transcriptome," where this new concept was defined as "conveying the identity of each expressed gene and its level of expression for a defined population of cells." The last was an important point: "Unlike the genome, which is essentially a static entity, the transcriptome can be modulated by both external and internal factors. The transcriptome thereby serves as a dynamic link between an organism's genome and its physical characteristics" since the latter are created by the proteins that are the result of the transcriptome.

Meanwhile, Brown and his team at Stanford had been making progress in extending the range of their own approach. In October 1996, they published a paper describing a microarray containing 1,046 randomly selected human cDNAs, which allowed parallel monitoring of genes when tissue was heated to an abnormally high temperature (heat shock). The same tissue at body temperature formed the control to allow the relative effect of heat shock to be observed. The paper marked a transitional point in DNA microarray technology. Brown and his team were within striking distance of placing all the genes for a eukaryote on a single slide—what is sometimes called "downloading the genome" on to an array. This allowed the transcriptome to be explored in a highly parallel fashion.

The Stanford group showed exactly the kind of thing that such microarrays were capable of in a paper that appeared in *Science* in October 1997. This time the array contained virtually every gene of yeast, which had become the first fully sequenced eukaryote a year earlier. Brown and his collaborators chose one of the most important processes in yeast, the so-called diauxic shift, when the organism switches from fermenting sugars—the basis of the alcohol industry—to breaking down the ethanol produced by fermentation once the sugars are depleted.

"We used DNA microarrays to characterize the changes in gene expression that take place during this process for nearly the entire genome," Brown and his colleagues wrote, "and to investigate the genetic circuitry that regulates and executes the program." This was the long-term aim of functional genomics: to understand how the genes worked in concert to create and run the cell—a level up from merely elucidating the function of single genes within the genome. A major advantage of using DNA microarrays was that they made it possible to eavesdrop on all the conversations that were taking place among the genes through the mRNAs simultaneously.

The yeast paper used a technique for exploring gene expression patterns that has since become widely adopted. After an initial nine hours of growth, samples were taken from the yeast culture every two hours to create a time series of gene expression levels for all of the genes. As Brown's team explained, "several distinct temporal patterns of expression could be recognized, and sets of genes could be grouped on the basis of the similarities in their expression patterns." Having picked out a few characteristic patterns for the gene expression changes, the Stanford researchers then proceeded to group the other genes according to their similarity to these.

Brown says that it was this set of experiments that alerted him to the true power of DNA microarrays: "The thing that was kind of an epiphany was we would see sets of genes that we knew in a sense belonged together functionally, would cluster together based on their expression patterns." That is, microarrays not only allowed one to monitor the expression levels of thousands of genes simultaneously—useful, to be sure—but also to find meaningful patterns among them, a far deeper kind of knowledge. "You take the data, you organize it in a systematic way and there is an emergent property to that large data set that comes from the intrinsic order from the genome's expression program."

In the case of the diauxic shift in yeast, the result of this organization was a set of graphs showing the coordinated behaviors of six major gene clusters. For example, one group showed steady gene expression until the diauxic shift, at which point the expression increased dramatically. Another group, by contrast, was steady but began to drop as the sugar was exhausted, and fell dramatically after the shift. The realization that these genome-wide patterns existed was a crucial insight, but as Brown points out, "those early analyses had the problem that they were kind of ad hoc for a particular data set. So we were looking for a more systematic method."

Exacerbating the situation was the sheer quantity of data involved. As Brown and his team noted in their diauxic shift paper: "Even conceptually simple experiments, as we described here, can yield vast amounts of information." Each of the thousands of spots on the array is measured several times, giving tens of thousands of data points for a single experiment. As a result, they concluded, "Perhaps the greatest challenge now is to develop efficient methods for organizing, distributing, interpreting, and extracting insights from the large volumes of data these experiments will provide." In principle, the solution was clear: to use bioinformatics. Computers could sift through what for humans were unmanageable quantities of data, picking out any patterns they found according to some predefined scheme. Dealing with this data deluge then became a question of finding the right computational approach.

Another major paper in *Science*—this time studying gene expression changes during yeast sporulation, or sexual reproduction—from a team including Brown, was published a year later in October 1998, and addressed this issue directly. "To facilitate visualization and interpretation of the gene expression program represented in this very large body of data," they explained, "We have used the method of Eisen *et al.* to order genes on the basis of similarities in their expression patterns and display the results in compact graphical format." The paper written by Michael Eisen with Patrick Brown, David Botstein, and Paul Spellman to explain their new approach, and published in December 1998, broke down the problem of dealing with gene expression data into two separate parts: cluster analysis and representation. The first is about grouping information in a useful way; the second is about how to present what are still very large data sets in a form that people can grasp easily.

To solve the first problem, Eisen and colleagues adopted a straightforward technique that consists of grouping together the closest pair of points—using a standard statistical definition of "closeness"—and replacing them by a single point that is their average. The next two closest points are then grouped and replaced by their average, and so on. "Relationships among objects (genes) are represented by a tree whose branch lengths reflect the degree of similarity between the objects." The tree is slightly unnatural in that every branch always splits into two smaller branches, each of which also splits in two; the "twigs" at the extremity of the tree are the data points, grouped at successively higher levels by the branches.

As the Eisen team noted, "The resulting ordered but still massive collection of numbers"—the data points measuring the gene expression arranged in a tree-like structure—"remains difficult to assimilate. Therefore, we always combine clustering methods with a graphical representation of the primary data by representing each data point with a color that quantitatively and qualitatively reflects the original experimental observations. The end product is a representation of complex gene expression data that, through statistical organization and graphical display, allows biologists to assimilate and explore the data in a natural manner."

In practice, what this means is that increases in gene expression relative to the control sample are represented as shades of red; relative decreases as shades of green. The lighter the red, the greater the increase; the lighter the green, the greater the decrease. Black is used when there is no observable difference. In this way, the most significant figures are represented by the brightest colors. Blocks of genes that show overall increases in gene expression appear reddish, while groups of genes that show decreases appear greenish. Although a simple idea, this highly visual approach has proved of crucial importance to the field of DNA microarrays. Brown comments: "When you're looking at a large data set where there's order in it but you don't know in advance what kinds of order you're looking for, there's no substitute to using your visual system."

The red and green mosaics that result have become commonplace in scientific journals that report work on gene expression—some researchers even started to call the characteristic appearance "Eisenized" clusters. Their widespread use has probably helped make the approach even more useful, since scientists have become through practice quite adept at taking in the salient points from these visual representations of data.

D espite the widespread adoption of this approach, it is not without its drawbacks. Indeed, Eisen and his group recognized that "the particular clustering algorithm we used is not the only, or even the best, method available." One group that agreed, and thought it could do better, was at the Whitehead Institute, led by Todd Golub. The group also included Eric Lander. Commenting on the approach taken by Eisen, the Whitehead group warned that the automatic, almost mechanistic way of imposing a tree-like structure might create patterns that were not there and miss those that were. Instead, they suggested using self-organizing maps (SOMs), a technique that the paper likened to an executive summary, to find the most representative patterns among the gene expression data.

The Whitehead team might well argue that SOMs were more mathematically appropriate than Eisen's approach, but there is no doubt that the eerily beautiful red and green mosaics produced by the hierarchical clustering technique win hands down when it comes to impact. Which is more helpful for researchers is ultimately a matter of taste. Golub's group pointed this out: "As with all exploratory data analysis tools, the use of SOMs involves inspection of the data to extract insights." In other words, for both techniques, the images still have to be interpreted.

A press release issued by the ever-efficient Whitehead publicity machine to accompany the SOM paper explained, "The study was supported in part by [a] consortium of three companies—Bristol-Myers Squibb Company; Affymetrix, Inc.; and Millennium Pharmaceuticals Inc.—that formed a unique corporate partnership to fund a five-year research program in functional genomics at the Whitehead/MIT Genome Center."

Announced in April 1997, the collaboration brought $8 million per year to the Whitehead Institute, making it one of the biggest functional genomics projects so far. This kind of scale was entirely in keeping with the man who was running the collaboration: Eric Lander. It also marked yet another logical step in the progression of his increasingly ambitious career, as he moved from genetics into mapping, and then into sequencing. At the same time his group was finishing off the basic sequence, Lander was also busy working on genomic variation, as Chapter 8 recounted. The $40 million grant from the industry consortium added functional genomics to his research collection.

In return, the companies involved received "certain licensing rights" to developments funded by the consortium or emerging from the use of contributed technology. It was also agreed that "Whitehead participants in the program will have the right to publish their research results promptly"—so there would be no question of holding back data while patents were obtained, for example.

As for the members of this collaboration, Millennium Pharmaceuticals is the start-up that Lander had helped to found, so the deal was in part simply an affirmation of their common history. Bristol-Myers Squibb is a pharmaceutical and related health care products company. The origins of the third partner, Affymetrix, go back to a paper that appeared in *Science* in February 1991. In it, the lead author Stephen Fodor and his team, then at the Affymax Research Institute in California, announced a remarkable chemical synthesis process that they had developed. "The revolution in microelectronics has been made possible by photolithography, a process in which light is used to spatially direct the simultaneous formation of many electrical circuits. We report a method that uses light to direct the simultaneous synthesis of many different chemical compounds."

The work of Fodor and his team is a generalization of the process used to lay down silicon on integrated circuits like the ones widely employed in computers. It allows various kinds of chemicals to be built up in layers at thousands or even millions of points simultaneously, including amino acids to make proteins, and sequences of DNA letters to create oligonucleotides (short stretches of single-stranded DNA). In doing so, it creates another kind of bioinformatics—not a symbolic one involving computation of biological information, but a literal coming-together of biology and information technology as a new kind of chip.

In ordinary integrated circuit design, a thin film with transparent and opaque areas—known as a mask—is used to expose or protect areas on the silicon chip. When a light is shone, the areas that are exposed are changed so that they can accept the next layer of the chip. Similarly, with Affymetrix' technology the pattern of exposure to light determines which regions of the chip's base are activated and able to accept the first building block. This might be one of DNA's four chemical letters (A, C, G, T) or one of the 20 amino acids. By using a series of different masks before applying successive chemical building blocks, it is possible to build up an array of different linear sequences that are attached at one end to the glass base of the chip.

Fodor and his team concluded their original paper by noting some uses for their new technology: "Oligonucleotide arrays produced by light-directed synthesis could be used to detect complementary sequences in DNA and RNA"—by hybridization. "Such arrays would be valuable in gene mapping, fingerprinting, diagnostics, and nucleic acid sequencing." It is hardly surprising that gene expression fails to get a mention: after all, even though 1991 was the year of "genome delight," things were still at a very early stage. The main emphasis was on sequencing and discovering the genes; finding out what they did could wait until later.

Affymetrix was founded the same year as the *Science* paper, as a division of Affymax N.V., a company set up in 1988 by the Uruguayan entrepreneur Alejandro Zaffaroni. Affymax was purchased by the pharmaceutical company Glaxo Wellcome in 1996, but in 1993, Affymetrix was spun out as an independent company. For the first few years of its life, the emphasis remained on the use of its novel chip-making process for DNA sequencing. For example, in May 1994, Fodor and his Affymetrix team published a paper entitled "Light-generated oligonucleotide arrays for rapid DNA sequence analysis." In October 1996, they published a paper in *Science* in which they described the use of DNA chips to investigate variation in the genome of the human mitochondrion—the main source of energy in the cell. Significantly, the paper notes that "the methods described here are completely generic and can be used to address a variety of questions in molecular genetics including gene expression, genetic linkage and genetic variability."

In November 1996, a paper was published on a refinement of the DNA chip process that allowed the individual feature size on the chip to be decreased from the then 5–10 millionths of a meter to around 1 millionth of a meter. This would permit even greater densities of oligonucleotides, which at that point had reached the already impressive figure of one million DNA sequences per square centimeter.

It was in December 1996, though, just a couple of months after the "postgenome" issue of *Science* detailing the cDNA microarray and SAGE techniques, that Affymetrix really made its mark. *Nature Biotechnology* carried a paper called "Expression monitoring by hybridization to high-density oligonucleotide arrays," while its sister title, *Nature Genetics*, had no less than two papers written with Affymetrix researchers—the first of them a joint effort between Stephen Fodor and Francis Collins—as well as an editorial entitled "To affinity . . . and beyond!"

The editorialist wrote: "Scientists are becoming increasingly enthralled with DNA microchip technology, especially as practiced by a young biotechnology company named Affymetrix, located in an unassuming industrial park complex just south of San Francisco. The company's GeneChip technology"—Affymetrix' commercial product, which first went on sale in April 1996—"has captured the imagination of a number of academic and corporate investigators."

Affymetrix further bolstered its credentials by the publication in December 1997 of a paper in *Nature Biotechnology* that reported on the monitoring of gene expression levels across the entire yeast genome, using four arrays containing 260,000 specially-chosen oligonucleotides. Like the papers in *Nature Genetics* a year before, this, too, was accompanied by something of a panegyric from the editor under the heading "The yeast genome yields its secrets." In its own whole genome analysis of gene expression in yeast using cDNA arrays, the Stanford team had beaten Affymetrix by a couple of months, but it was clear that the two were essentially neck and neck in terms of technical capabilities.

At first sight, they could hardly be considered rivals, since Brown's group was academic. The situation, however, was more complicated than it appeared. Back in 1994, Dari Shalon, one of the coauthors on the original cDNA paper in *Science*, had founded a company to sell microarrays and related services called Synteni, which later gained funding from the venture capital firm Kleiner, Perkins, Caufield & Byers, the group that also backed Pangea Systems/DoubleTwist. Synteni's main product was GEM—the Gene Expression Microarray—and by the end of 1997, when Affymetrix published its yeast studies in *Nature Biotechnology*, Synteni had a customer base of some 20 pharmaceutical and biotechnology companies.

On December 23, 1997, Incyte acquired Synteni and its patents for $80 million. As the press release announcing the deal explained: "The combined technology platforms [of Synteni and Incyte] will allow Synteni to put Incyte's genes on a microarray for direct sale to the pharmaceutical community as well as to build large gene expression databases." Just a few days after the Incyte-Synteni deal, Affymetrix filed a patent infringement suit against Synteni and Incyte, alleging infringement of one of Affymetrix' GeneChip patents.

Brown was the joint holder, along with Shalon, of the patent for microarray machines, and yet he was uninterested in making money from the technology; he was more concerned about helping others use it. In April 1998, just a few months after the start of the legal battle between Affymetrix and Incyte/Synteni, Joseph DeRisi, another graduate student in Brown's laboratory, and the lead author of the paper exploring yeast's diauxic shift, posted something called MGuide on the Internet. It was a manual explaining in great detail how to construct a microarray system, complete with a listing of parts, prices, and where one could get them.

A year later, DeRisi, Brown, and Michael Eisen gave a course that showed how to build a microarray. According to a report in *Science*, 16 people each paid $1,955 for this expertise; for an extra $30,000, four of them were able to take a unit home. *Science* put these figures in perspective: "Affymetrix sells a variety of standard kits for yeast, *Arabidopsis*, mouse, rat, and human genes, among others, which are listed at $500 to $2,000 per chip. (The chips are good for one use). The company donates equipment to collaborators at major genome centers, but few labs get free chips and few can afford the estimated $175,000 it costs to install an Affymetrix chip." Paying $30,000 for the capability to create cDNA arrays for any organism was a bargain.

In addition to saving money, at stake was a larger issue. By putting together its MGuide, the Brown lab was ensuring that there was an alternative to the commercial systems, and that scientists would at least have the option of building their own setup and doing exactly the experiments they wanted to. One advantage of this approach was that they could also carry out checks on the sequences before they were spotted on the array. This was not an option for those who depended on commercial chips. Instead, they had to rely on the manufacturer. In 2001, though, Affymetrix admitted that some of the sequences on its mouse DNA arrays were scrambled. As *Science* reported: "Affymetrix first disclosed the problem in a 7 March notice to the U.S. Securities and Exchange Commission (SEC). . . . When company researchers began to annotate genes and ESTs that had already been placed on chips, they discovered that most appeared to be reproduced correctly, but some were reversed. . . . Affymetrix plans to have replacement chips ready for those who want them in a matter of weeks."

In many respects, the Brown microarrays stand in the same relation to Affymetrix' GeneChips as the open source GNU/Linux operating system does to proprietary software such as Microsoft Windows. Companies naturally claim that their proprietary products are better, and hence worth the extra cost, but in one respect they are nearly always worse: there is no freedom to adapt or change them. The ability to do so lies at the heart of Brown's microarray and also of the free software movement.

Although Brown calls those in the open source world "kindred spirits," he says that placing MGuide online was motivated by more practical concerns. "It was just that this was a much more natural way of sharing a kind of information that wasn't best done by publishing in a conventional journal," he explains. MGuide can therefore be seen as an early example of Brown's interest in promoting the free dissemination of information, something that would culminate in the founding of the Public Library of Science, described in Chapter 6.

As is so often the case in patent battles, the legal tussle between Affymetrix and Incyte dragged on for a while and was eventually settled behind the scenes. An Incyte press release issued on December 21, 2001—almost exactly four years after it acquired Synteni—said laconically: "Incyte Genomics . . . and Affymetrix . . . today announced a comprehensive settlement of all existing infringement litigation between the two companies. . . . Financial terms were not disclosed."

In fact, as Affymetrix' annual filing for 2002 revealed, this was not quite the end of the matter, but things were finally ironed out after another year, as a press release from Affymetrix in December 2002 made clear. Entitled "Affymetrix, Stanford University and Incyte resolve patent oppositions and interferences," it consisted of a listing of the various cases that had been resolved, together with some background to the whole area of microarrays. The latter was adapted from an announcement in November 2002 that Brown and Fodor were among those being presented with the Takeda Award for that year.

The Takeda Foundation Website explains: "This award shall be presented to individuals who have demonstrated outstanding achievements in the creation and application of new engineering intellect and knowledge. . . . The awards will place an emphasis on three targeted fields—social/economic well-being, individual/humanity well-being, and world environmental well-being. . . . Each award will be accompanied by a monetary prize of 100 million yen"—roughly a million dollars. Winners of the 2001 award included Craig Venter and Michael Hunkapiller for the individual/humanity well-being class, and two of the key figures in the free software world, Richard Stallman and Linus Torvalds, for the social/economic well-being category.

The technical achievements of Brown and Fodor included the following points. Brown "disclosed the know-how, tools, and designs for the fabrication of DNA microarrays on the Internet so that scientists could make their own DNA arrays in their laboratories. This disclosure of information for the self-fabrication of DNA microarrays has promoted the widespread use of DNA microarrays with pre-synthesized probes." Similarly, Fodor "succeeded in manufacturing and selling the first DNA array, GeneChip. The mass-produced, off-the-shelf GeneChip has enabled the ready use of DNA microarrays in many research and diagnostic applications." Both, then, were honored for promoting, in their different ways, the uptake of DNA array technology.

Papers describing practical applications of the technology had started to flow almost as soon as it became possible to monitor gene expression. For example, as *Science* had remarked as far back as 1995, in its "Entering the postgenome era" piece: "The two gene-expression techniques"—cDNAs and SAGE—"are already being put through their paces in real-life research situations. Both groups are trying to use them to spot the differences between normal and cancer cells."

Cancer was a natural first choice. As a team of researchers, mostly from Stanford University and including Brown, later wrote: "The biology of tumors, including morphology [physical form], is determined in large part by gene expression programs in the cells comprising the tumor. Comprehensive analysis of gene expression patterns in individual tumors should, therefore, provide detailed molecular portraits that can facilitate tumor classification." Since tumors are, by definition, a growth pattern within a set of cells that is abnormal, it follows that the gene expression pattern—the instructions sent by the genome to the protein-making machinery—is also likely to be abnormal. By comparing normal cells and cancer cells it should be possible to pinpoint exactly which messages cause the change. This potentially allows two things to be done. First, the pattern of gene expression in cancer cells can be used to help classify the tumor; second, knowing more exactly what is wrong in a cancerous cell offers hope that it will be possible somehow to fix the problem at a molecular level.

Both of these possibilities were a long way off when the first paper was published looking at cancer gene expression patterns. Not surprisingly, it came from Brown and his team, and was published in December 1996. Like the first cDNA paper, published barely a year before, Brown's paper was more a test run or statement of intent than an in-depth study of tumors—the array included just 1,161 cDNAs. The first paper on cancer from the Johns Hopkins University research group, which followed a little later, in May 1997, offered considerably more detail—thanks in no small part to the SAGE technique itself. Over 300,000 transcripts derived from a variety of cancers were analyzed. "These transcripts represented about 49,000 genes that ranged in average expression from 1 copy per cell to as many as 5300 copies per cell," the authors wrote (this was when it was believed that there were approximately 100,000 human genes in total). The rest of the paper filled out the details of which genes were over- or under-expressed in cancer cells.

Then followed something of a lull in gene expression studies of cancer. As Michael Eisen and his colleagues wrote in early 1999: "The number of review articles on gene expression technologies probably exceeds the number of primary research publications in this field." They attributed this to "a limited number of efficient, publicly available tools for data processing, storing and retrieving the information and analyzing the results [of gene expression experiments] in the context of existing knowledge."

The paper from Eisen and his colleagues that appeared in December 1998 had made an important contribution in this area with its hierarchical clustering approach and graphical representation. It is tempting to ascribe some of the sudden interest in applying gene expression techniques to practical problems to the availability of an easy-to-use way of looking at and understanding the otherwise ungraspably large data sets the technology generated.

Although a paper published in June 1999 from a group at Princeton studying gene expression in tumor and normal colon tissue samples did not use Eisen's software, it did adopt a broadly similar approach that resulted in a familiar mosaic-like view of clustered data. The fact that this structure emerged from the data was a significant result on its own, as the authors pointed out. "Recent work," they wrote, "demonstrated that genes of related function could be grouped together by clustering according to similar temporal evolution under various conditions." That is, a series of measurements of gene expression at various time points could be clustered by gene to give meaningful groups. The present paper was different, though.

"Here, it was demonstrated that gene grouping also could be achieved on the basis of variation between tissue samples from different individuals." This was an important distinction: instead of measuring the expression of a gene at different times, the authors of the study had measured the same gene in different individuals. It might have been that clustering only made sense for measurements from one individual; instead, it turned out that gene expression readings from different individuals could be clustered together according to how similar they were overall. The individual genes within each sample could then be clustered according to how similar their expression patterns were across different samples.

This kind of double hierarchical clustering—by sample and by gene—was adopted contemporaneously by the Stanford team themselves in a study of breast cancer that appeared just after the paper from the Princeton group, in August 1999. As Brown explains: "It's very, very useful to have some way that uses intrinsic order in the data to produce visual order" by grouping tissues together. The hope was that normal cells and cancer cells, for example, would be distinguished automatically on the basis of their distinct gene expression profiles. The second clustering, by genes, could then be used to explore how the two groups differed at the level of gene expression.

What Brown and his colleagues were seeking was a set of gene expression profiles that could be used to group breast cancers into well-defined and distinct classes automatically. It is known, for example, that chemotherapy or hormonal therapy reduces the risk of breast cancer spreading to other parts of the body, but that 70–80 percent of patients would survive without this treatment. This clearly implied that there were different subtypes of breast cancer that respond very differently to treatment. Gene expression held out the hope that a relatively simple test could distinguish between those subtypes and allow treatment to be better targeted.

A couple of months after the Stanford paper appeared, a team at the Whitehead Institute, led by Todd Golub and Eric Lander, announced that they had devised precisely this kind of test for another cancer. Using Affymetrix GeneChips, they analyzed the gene expression in bone marrow samples from children suffering from two different types of acute leukemia—cancer of the blood-forming tissues—called acute myeloid leukemia (AML) and acute lymphoblastic leukemia (ALL). They were then able to come up with what they called a "class predictor." It was a way of assigning an unknown leukemia to ALL or AML solely on the basis of its gene expression profile. Distinguishing between them is crucially important because the chemotherapy used to treat them is very different in each case.

A few months later, in February 2000, a group of 32 scientists, including Brown and Eisen, applied the same general technique to a form of lymphoma—cancer of the lymphatic system. As they wrote: "40% of patients respond well to current therapy and have prolonged survival, whereas the remainder succumb to the disease." This suggested that there could be two different cellular processes involved, and that gene expression profiles might be able to distinguish between them.

The researchers created what they called a "Lymphochip"—a specialized microarray made up of genes that were particularly relevant to lymphoma. Using this, they analyzed 96 normal and malignant samples, and clustered the results using Eisen's techniques. The result of this and further analysis "strongly implies at least two distinct diseases" not detected or even suspected before, they wrote. These were evident from the two different patterns of expression observed across hundreds of different genes and made visible by Eisen's software. "Indeed," the authors went on, "the new methods of gene expression profiling call for a revised definition of what is deemed 'disease'," since it may often be possible to use gene expression studies to subdivide what were thought of as unitary diagnostic classes.

The success in characterizing cancers like leukemia and lymphoma at the molecular level led to a spate of similar studies for other tumors, including melanomas (cancers of the skin), bladder and prostate cancers, brain tumors, and lung cancer. The one that proved the most resistant to analysis, however, was breast cancer. In their 1999 paper, the Stanford team had indicated why: "The study of gene expression in primary human breast tumors, as in most solid tumors, is complicated for two major reasons. First, breast tumors consist of many different cell types," so obtaining a clear gene expression signature for just the tumor cells was difficult. "Second, breast carcinoma . . . cells themselves are morphologically and genetically diverse"—a complicated mix of different kinds.

This difficulty, coupled with the fact that it was the second leading cause of cancer-related death in women in the Western world, made elucidating the nature of breast cancer one of the key challenges for the new field of cancer gene expression. Within the space of one month in the autumn of 2001 three papers appeared that tackled the problem. Each of the main gene expression technologies—SAGE, Affymetrix GeneChips, and cDNA arrays—was represented. Despite this multipronged attack, none of them—not even Brown's group, which was approaching the problem for the second time—came up with the kind of neat classification by gene expression patterns that had been achieved for leukemia or lymphoma.

This was finally achieved by work published in January 2002 by Dutch researchers and scientists at Rosetta Inpharmatics, which had been founded in 1998 by Leroy Hood and others. It was acquired by the pharmaceutical giant Merck in 2001, in part for its novel gene expression technology: in 2002, Merck revealed it would be using 50,000 of its arrays that year. For the breast cancer study, Rosetta Inpharmatics' scientists employed their inkjet-based approach—yet another tool developed by Hood and his team—to create microarrays containing some 25,000 human genes. This was considerably more than the number on the Affymetrix chip (5,000) or cDNA array (8,000), which may go some way to explaining why Rosetta and its collaborators succeeded where the others had not.

When a double hierarchical clustering approach with graphical display was applied to the data, two distinct groups of tumors emerged. The real significance of the result, though, lay in the correlation of this division into two classes with clinical outcome. In one of the two groups, 34 percent developed cancer elsewhere in the body within five years, whereas in the other group it was 70 percent. Building on this result, the researchers then went on to define a prognosis profile—similar to the Whitehead group's class predictor—that allowed them to characterize unknown tumors on the basis of the expression profile of 70 marker genes. The prognosis profile was potentially a powerful tool for choosing the most suitable treatment. Applied in a clinical setting, it could greatly reduce the cost of breast cancer treatment, both in terms of adverse side effects and health care expenditure.

Gene expression signatures for cancers lay behind an even more ambitious approach, known as diagnosis by database. The idea is that if characteristic expression patterns could be found for every kind of tumor, these could be placed in a unified database. It would then be possible to compare the gene expression signature for any tumor against that database and discover exactly what kind of cancer it was, without needing any additional information—not even what tissue it came from.

A team at Whitehead, including Todd Golub and Eric Lander, took the first steps to turning this vision into reality in a paper published in December 2001. "We created a gene expression database containing the expression profiles of 218 tumor samples representing 14 common human cancer classes," they wrote. "By using an innovative analytical method, we demonstrate that accurate multiclass cancer classification is indeed possible, suggesting the feasibility of molecular cancer diagnosis by means of comparison with a comprehensive and commonly accessible catalog of gene expression profiles."

The authors made an interesting point about such a catalog: "Currently, diagnostic advances are disseminated into clinical practice in a slow and uneven fashion," so progress is uneven and unpredictable. "By contrast, a centralized classification database may allow classification accuracy to rapidly improve as the classification algorithm 'learns' from an ever-growing database." The more gene expression profiles that are entered, the better the system gets. This improvement is propagated instantly to anyone using the catalog—there is no time lag as the improvements spread into clinical practice.

There was just one problem with the otherwise highly-promising diagnosis by database idea. As the Whitehead team noted: "[Gene expression studies of cancers] have spanned multiple platforms"—SAGE, Affymetrix GeneChips, cDNA microarrays—"complicating comparison among different datasets." For the gene expression signature idea to work—and for it to improve through the constant aggregation of new data—a way had to be found to compare and unify data derived from different systems. This problem was not limited to the area of cancer, though this was where the need for a single database was felt most keenly. As gene expression analysis is applied to an increasingly wide range of situations—for example, understanding the effects of bacterial infections on the gene expression of human cells—so the inability to compare related experiments from different laboratories becomes more of a serious problem.

A comparison with the world of DNA sequences is helpful. There, the digital nature of the sequence means that all data is immediately compatible. It is precisely this fact that makes searches for homology among sequences derived from different sources so powerful. For gene expression data, however, there is nothing comparable: it is not, in general, possible to search for similarities across experiments unless, as in the case of the Whitehead group's work on molecular profiles, the work has been carried out with this end in mind from the start.

In September 1998, well before the work on diagnosis by database had begun to take shape, some of the top researchers in the field of gene expression had written: "As large-scale gene expression data accumulates, public data access becomes a critical issue. What is the best forum for making the data accessible? Summaries and conclusions of individual experiments will, of course, be published in traditional peer-reviewed journals, but electronic access to full data sets is essential." They enumerated three possible approaches: Web sites run by authors; journal Web sites; and a centralized public repository along the lines of GenBank.

A good example of the first category is the Stanford Microarray Database, set up Brown and his colleagues. Essentially this was to hold the results of their experiments and to release data when they were completed. As far as the second category is concerned, journals have proved unwilling to take on the task of providing a unified gene expression database, but the National Center for Biotechnology Information, which runs GenBank, opened a public central repository in 2000. As a paper describing it explained: "Our primary goal in creating the Gene Expression Omnibus [GEO] was to attempt to cover the broadest spectrum of high-throughput experimental methods possible and remain flexible and responsive to future trends, rather than setting rigid requirements and standards for entry."

Although GEO was valuable, it did not address the problem of data standards or exchange that many felt was crucial if the field was to progress. Writing a commentary piece in *Nature* in February 2000, Alvis Brazma, Alan Robinson, Graham Cameron, and Michael Ashburner of the European

Bioinformatics Institute (EBI) said: "It is time to create a public repository for microarray data, with standardized annotation." They had no illusions about the magnitude of the task: "This is a complex and ambitious project, and is one of the biggest challenges that bioinformatics has yet faced. Major difficulties stem from the detail required to describe the conditions of an experiment, and the relative and imprecise nature of measurements of expression levels. The potentially huge volume of data only adds to these difficulties. However, it is this very complexity that makes an organized repository necessary"—for without it, there is no hope of being able to compare data sets meaningfully.

Fortunately, the first steps towards such a public repository had been taken at the end of 1999, at an international meeting organized by the EBI. "Progress towards such standards was made last November," Brazma and his colleagues wrote, "when many of the main academic and commercial users and developers of microarray technology accepted a list of recommendations for data representation and annotation."

One direct consequence of that November meeting was a proposal called MIAME: minimum information about a microarray experiment. As its 24 authors—led by Alvis Brazma—wrote: "We believe that it is necessary to define the minimum information that must be reported, in order to ensure the interpretability of the experimental results generated using microarrays as well as their potential independent verification." The February 2000 commentary in *Nature* had put it well: "With gene expression, context is everything: without it, the information is meaningless."

The MIAME proposal—not so much a standard as "a starting point for a broader community discussion"—suggested that the minimum information should include a description of the type of experiment being undertaken, details of the array used, the samples that were analyzed, what procedures were employed for the hybridization, the measurements—the main data, and what adjustments were made to compensate for various technical factors.

MIAME, which was devised by the Microarray Gene Expression Database group (MGED), "a grass-roots movement to develop standards for microarray data," was an important first move in establishing standards. It provided only half of the solution, though. As the MIAME group emphasized: "It should be noted that MIAME does not specify the format in which the information should be provided, but only its content." MIAME suggested a minimum list of things that needed to be included in microarray gene expression experiments, but said nothing about the exact form these should take.

Another paper, which appeared in August 2002, noted: "It is not enough to specify that certain data and accessory information be provided. It is essential, if MIAME is to be useful, that a standard transmission format exists for the data." The paper—written by many of those who had also contributed to MIAME—proposed something called Microarray Gene Expression Markup Language (MAGE-ML). A markup language is a way of adding structure to a simple text document. Perhaps the most famous is Hypertext Markup Language—HTML—the format in which Web pages are written. By adding special tags to text, it is possible to mark certain portions to be shown as headings, in italic type, etc., when displayed in a Web browser.

In the same way, the microarray gene expression markup language defined a set of tags that could be used to encode the MIAME data. A document written in MAGE-ML would contain both the data and the tags that made clear what those data meant. Although such a document could be read by a human, it was designed principally for computers: if MIAME data were encoded in MAGE-ML, they could be transferred easily between computers. For example, data from the Stanford Microarray Database, which will support MIAME, can be transferred across to the EBI's own ArrayExpress database, which is based on MIAME, automatically, using MAGE-ML as the means of transfer.

MAGE-ML is the result of combining two earlier markup languages, GEML (Gene Expression Markup Language) and MAML (Microarray Markup Language). GEML was created by Rosetta Inpharmatics, and MAML by the Microarray Gene Express Database group (MGED). This indicates one of the strengths of MAGE-ML, the fact that it is a collaboration between the commercial and academic worlds. Indeed, Affymetrix has already implemented MAGE-compliant software, while the U.S. National Cancer Institute uses MAGE for its database.

The movement to make MIAME the standard received an even bigger boost shortly after MAGE was published. In an editorial headed "Microarray standards at last," *Nature* wrote, with evident relief: "Harried editors can rejoice that, at last, the community is taming the unruly beast that is microarray information. Therefore, all submissions to *Nature* and the *Nature* family of journals received on or after December 1 [2002] containing new microarray experiments must include the mailing of five compact disks to the editor. These disks should include necessary information compliant with the MIAME standard. . . . Data integral to the paper's conclusions should be submitted to the ArrayExpress or GEO databases."

Nature's move had been prompted by an open letter to scientific journals proposing MIAME as the official community standard. The journal's main rival responded more cautiously: "*Science* supports the evolving standardization of microarray data, one view of which is presented in this letter. We urge our authors to follow the criteria set forth here, although it is not a requirement for publication, and to let us know your experiences and reactions."

Science may have had its doubts, but many others did not. Foremost among these were the researchers behind what has emerged as the biggest gene expression project, the International Genomics Consortium (IGC), launched in February 2001, and based in Phoenix, Arizona. Although it describes itself rather vaguely as "established to expand upon the discoveries of Human Genome Project and other systematic sequencing efforts, by combining world-class genomic research, bioinformatics, and diagnostic technologies in the fight against cancer and other complex genetic diseases" its initial plans are both concrete and ambitious.

As its Web site explained: "The centerpiece of IGC's activities will be [the Expression Project for Oncology"—the study and treatment of cancer—"or expO. The goal of expO is to collaboratively obtain and directly perform gene expression analyses on a highly-annotated set of normal and tumor samples." This is the diagnosis by database idea writ large; as such, gene expression standards are key. "This public database, called expOdb, will be of significant value, since it has the potential to accelerate oncology research efforts by virtue of implementing common standards throughout the data generation and data handling pipeline." These standards are MIAME.

"With respect to expOdb, the implementation of standards will finally establish the lingua franca long overdue in the area of gene expression analysis, with academic and corporate partners adopting a standard way of representing the results of a given hybridization experiment." IGC is likely to achieve this, because of the scale of its activities: the current goal of the expO project is to create a database of gene expression profiles of 2,500 human tumor specimens and 500 normal samples, over a three-year period.

"ExpOdb data is considered to be pre-competitive, with no intellectual property restrictions placed on findings generated by the analysis of that data." As its name suggests, the International Genomics Consortium is a kind of hybrid between the international Human Genome Project and The SNP Consortium, in both practice and principle. Although freely available, the data will only be useful to those who adopt the same standards. IGC's large gene expression database will represent an irresistible incentive for any company or research organization to fall into line and adopt MIAME, too.

The International Genomics Consortium project forms an apt culmination to what might be called the first era of functional genomics—that of truly pioneering but rather piecemeal research. The IGC's championing of MIAME will help lay a solid foundation for the next phase, when the power of gene expression is amplified enormously through the aggregation of data from many experiments carried out by different groups.

It is apt, too, that the IGC project picks up on the thread that runs through much of the functional genomics research during the half-decade since *Science* had declared in 1996 that the world was "Entering the postgenome era," and concentrates its first efforts on studying gene expression in cancer. As a result, the IGC will not only build on that pioneering work, but will help take it from the research laboratories into the clinical world where it can benefit millions of people. In doing so, it will confirm gene expression studies as perhaps the most important practical technique to emerge from the genomics revolution so far, a technique that is a key bridge between the digital world of DNA and analogue world of biology and medicine.

Notes

Interviews included in this chapter were conducted by the author in June 2003 with the following individual: P. Brown.

1. p. 213 *If the model organism projects are to be maximally* A.C. Spradling, et al., "Gene disruptions using P transposable elements: an integral component of the *Drosophila* genome project," *Proc. Natl. Acad. Sci. USA.* 92 (1995): 10824–10830.

2. p. 214 *an efficient experimental approach,* V. Smith, et al., "Genetic footprinting: a genomic strategy for determining a gene's function given its sequence," *Proc. Natl. Acad. Sci. USA.* 92 (1995): 6479–6483.

3. p. 214 *We anticipate that simply extending the methods* V. Smith, et al., "Functional analysis of the genes of yeast chromosome V by genetic footprinting," *Science* 274 (1996): 2069–2074.

4. p. 215 *The idea of using ordered arrays of DNAs to perform* M.B. Eisen and P.O. Brown, "DNA arrays for analysis of gene expression." Online at *http://cmgm.stanford.edu/pbrown/pdf/Eisen_MB_Methods_Enzymol_1999.pdf.*

5. p. 216 *First, large-scale sequencing projects have* M.B. Eisen and P.O. Brown, "DNA arrays for analysis of gene expression." Online at *http://cmgm.stanford.edu/pbrown/pdf/Eisen_MB_Methods_Enzymol_1999.pdf.*

6. p. 217 *Fortunately,* differences *in gene expression between samples* M.B. Eisen and P.O. Brown, "DNA arrays for analysis of gene expression." Online at *http://cmgm.stanford.edu/pbrown/pdf/Eisen_MB_Methods_Enzymol_1999.pdf.*

7. p. 217 *As some teams are gearing up for the final push* R. Nowak, "Entering the postgenome era," *Science* 270 (1995): 368–371.

8. p. 217 *in a matter of weeks information that might* R. Nowak, "Entering the postgenome era," *Science* 270 (1995): 368–371.

9. p. 219 *Adaptation of this technique to an automated* V.E. Velculescu, et al., "Serial analysis of gene expression," *Science* 270 (1995): 484–487.

10. p. 219 *conveying the identity of each expressed gene* V.E. Velculescu, et al., "Characterization of the yeast transcriptome," *Cell* 88 (1997): 243–251.

11. p. 219 *Unlike the genome, which is essentially a static* V.E. Velculescu, et al., "Characterization of the yeast transcriptome," *Cell* 88 (1997): 243–251.

12. p. 220 *We used DNA microarrays to characterize the changes* J.L. DeRisi, et al., "Exploring the metabolic and genetic control of gene expression on a genomic scale," *Science* 278 (1997): 680–686.

13. p. 220 *several distinct temporal patterns of expression* J.L. DeRisi, et al., "Exploring the metabolic and genetic control of gene expression on a genomic scale," *Science* 278 (1997): 680–686.

14. p. 220 *Even conceptually simple experiments,* J.L. DeRisi, et al., "Exploring the metabolic and genetic control of gene expression on a genomic scale," *Science* 278 (1997): 680–686.

15. p. 221 *To facilitate visualization and interpretation* S. Chu, et al., "The transcriptional program of sporulation in budding yeast," *Science* 282 (1998): 699–705.

16. p. 221 *Relationships among objects (genes) are represented* M.B. Eisen, et al., "Cluster analysis and display of genome-wide expression patterns," *Proc. Natl. Acad. Sci. USA.* 95 (1998): 14863–14868.

17. p. 222 *the particular clustering algorithm we used is not the only,* M.B. Eisen, et al., "Cluster analysis and display of genome-wide expression patterns," *Proc. Natl. Acad. Sci. USA.* 95 (1998): 14863–14868.

18. p. 222 *As with all exploratory data analysis tools,* P. Tamayo, et al., "Interpreting patterns of gene expression with self-organizing maps: methods and applications to hematopoietic differentiation," *Proc. Natl. Acad. Sci. USA.* 96 (1999): 2907–2912.

19. p. 222 *The study was supported in part* Whitehead Institute press release, March 12, 1999.

20. p. 223 *certain licensing rights* Affymetrix press release, April 29, 1997.

21. p. 223 *Whitehead participants in the program* Affymetrix press release, April 29, 1997.

22. p. 223 *The revolution in microelectronics has been* S.P.A. Fodor, et al., "Light-directed, spatially addressable parallel chemical synthesis," *Science* 251 (1991): 767–773.

23. p. 224 *Affymax N.V., a company set up in 1988* "Affymax, corporate backgrounder." Online at *http://www.affymax.com/about/ affymax_corpbkgrndr_v2.pdf.*

24. p. 224 *the methods described here are* M. Chee, et al., "Accessing genetic information with high-density DNA arrays," *Science* 274 (1996): 610–614.

25. p. 224 *a paper was published on a refinement* G. McGall, et al., "Light-directed synthesis of high-density oligonucleotide arrays using semiconductor photoresists," *Proc. Natl. Acad. Sci. USA.* 93 (1996): 13555–13560.

26. p. 224 *Scientists are becoming increasingly enthralled* Editorial, "To affinity . . . and beyond!" *Nature Genet* 14 (1996): 367–370.

27. p. 225 *something of a panegyric* Editorial, "The yeast genome yields its secrets," *Nature Biotechnology* 15 (1997): 1317.

28. p. 225 *Back in 1994, Dari Shalon,* Incyte press release, December 23, 1997.

29. p. 225 *Synteni's main product was GEM* Incyte press release, December 23, 1997.

30. p. 225 *Incyte acquired Synteni and its patents for $80 million.* E. Marshall, "Companies battle over technology that's free on the Web," *Science* 286 (1999): 446.

31. p. 225 *The combined technology platforms* Incyte press release, December 23, 1997.

32. p. 225 *Affymetrix filed a patent infringement suit* Affymetrix press release, January 6, 1998.

33. p. 225 *In April 1998, just a few months after* E. Marshall, "Companies battle over technology that's free on the Web," *Science* 286 (1999): 446.

34. p. 225 *16 people each paid $1,955 for this expertise;* E. Marshall, "Do-it-yourself gene watching," *Science* 286 (1999): 444–447.

35. p. 225 *Affymetrix sells a variety of standard kits*   E. Marshall, "Do-it-yourself gene watching," *Science* 286 (1999): 444–447.

36. p. 226 *Affymetrix first disclosed the problem in a 7 March*   Marshall, E., "Affymetrix settles suit, fixes mouse chips," *Science* 291 (2001): 2535.

37. p. 226 *Incyte Genomics . . . and Affymetrix . . . today announced*   Incyte press release, December 21, 2001.

38. p. 227 *This award shall be presented to individuals*   "The Takeda Awards," originally online at *http://www.takeda-foundation.jp/en/award/takeda/about. html.* Available from *http://www.archive.org.*

39. p. 227 *disclosed the know-how, tools, and designs*   "Takeda Award 2002 Achievement Facts Sheet," originally online at *http://www.takeda-foundation.jp/ en/award/takeda/2002/fact/02.html.* Available from *http://www.archive.org.*

40. p. 227 *The two gene-expression techniques*   R. Nowak, "Entering the postgenome era," *Science* 270 (1995): 368–371.

41. p. 227 *The biology of tumors, including morphology*   M.E. Garber, et al., "Diversity of gene expression in adenocarcinoma of the lung," *Proc. Natl. Acad. Sci. USA.* 98 (2001): 13784–13789.

42. p. 228 *These transcripts represented about 49,000 genes*   L. Zhang, et al., "Gene expression profiles in normal and cancer cells," *Science* 276 (1997): 1268–1272.

43. p. 228 *The number of review articles on gene expression*   D.E. Bassett, "Gene expression informatics—it's all in your mine," *Nature Genet.* 21 (1 Suppl) (1999): 51–55.

44. p. 228 *Recent work . . . demonstrated that genes*   U. Alon, et al., "Broad patterns of gene expression revealed by clustering analysis of tumor and normal colon tissues probed by oligonucleotide arrays," *Proc. Natl. Acad. Sci. USA.* 96 (1999): 6745–6750.

45. p. 229 *chemotherapy or hormonal therapy*   L.J. van't Veer, et al., "Gene expression profiling predicts clinical outcome of breast cancer," *Nature* 415 (2002): 530–536.

46. p. 230 *40% of patients respond well to current therapy*   A.A. Alizadeh, et al., "Distinct types of diffuse large B-cell lymphoma identified by gene expression profiling," *Nature* 403 (2000): 503–511.

47. p. 230 *strongly implies at least two distinct diseases*   A.A. Alizadeh, et al., "Distinct types of diffuse large B-cell lymphoma identified by gene expression profiling," *Nature* 403 (2000): 503–511.

48. p. 230 *The study of gene expression in primary human*   C.M. Perou, et al., "Distinctive gene expression patterns in human mammary epithelial cells and breast cancers," *Proc. Natl. Acad. Sci. USA.* 96 (1999): 9212–9217.

49. p. 230 *second leading cause of cancer-related*   D.A. Porter, et al., "A SAGE (Serial Analysis of Gene Expression) view of breast tumor progression," *Cancer Research* 61 (2001): 5697–5702.

50. p. 230 *in 2002, Merck revealed it would be*   M. Herper, "Genomics revolution actually happens," *Forbes.com*, December 17, 2002.

51. p. 231 *two distinct groups of tumors* L.J. van't Veer, et al., "Gene expression profiling predicts clinical outcome of breast cancer," *Nature* 415 (2002): 530–536.

52. p 231 *We created a gene expression database* S. Ramaswamy, et al., "Multiclass cancer diagnosis using tumor gene expression signatures," *Proc. Natl. Acad. Sci. USA.* 98 (2001): 15149–15154.

53. p. 232 *As large-scale gene expression data accumulates,* O. Ermolaeva, et al., "Data management and analysis for gene expression arrays," *Nature Genet* 20 (1998): 19–23.

54. p. 232 *Our primary goal in creating the Gene Expression Omnibus* R. Edgar, et al., "Gene Expression Omnibus: NCBI gene expression and hybridization array data repository," *Nucl. Acids Res.* 30 (2002): 207–210.

55. p. 233 *It is time to create a public repository for microarray* A. Brazma, et al., "One-stop shop for microarray data," *Nature* 403 (2000): 699–700.

56. p. 233 *Progress towards such standards* A. Brazma, et al., "One-stop shop for microarray data," *Nature* 403 (2000): 699–700.

57. p. 233 *We believe that it is necessary to define the minimum* A. Brazma, et al., "Minimum information about a microarray experiment (MIAME)—towards standards for microarray data," *Nature Genet* 29 (2001): 365–372.

58. p. 233 *With gene expression, context is everything:* A. Brazma, et al., "One-stop shop for microarray data," *Nature* 403 (2000): 699–700.

59. p. 233 *a starting point for a broader community discussion* A. Brazma, et al., "Minimum information about a microarray experiment (MIAME)—towards standards for microarray data," *Nature Genet* 29 (2001): 365–372.

60. p. 233 *a grass-roots movement to develop* A. Brazma, et al., "Minimum information about a microarray experiment (MIAME)—towards standards for microarray data," *Nature Genet* 29 (2001): 365–372.

61. p. 233 *It should be noted that MIAME* A. Brazma, et al., "Minimum information about a microarray experiment (MIAME)—towards standards for microarray data," *Nature Genet* 29 (2001): 365–372.

62. p. 233 *It is not enough to specify that certain data* P.T. Spellman, et al., "Design and implementation of microarray gene expression markup language (MAGE-ML)," *Genome Biology* 3 (9): research 0046.1-0046.9 (2002).

63. p. 234 *Affymetrix has already implemented MAGE-compliant* P.T. Spellman, et al., "Design and implementation of microarray gene expression markup language (MAGE-ML)," *Genome Biology* 3 (9): research 0046.1-0046.9 (2002).

64. p. 234 *Harried editors can rejoice that,* Editorial, *Nature* 419 (2002): 323.

65. p. 234 Science *supports the evolving standardization* Editor's note, *Science* 298 (2002): 539.

66. p. 234 *established to expand upon the discoveries of Human Genome* International Genomics Consortium. Online at *http://www.intgen.org/index.html.*

67. p. 235 *The centerpiece of IGC's activities will be* "expO," originally online at *http://www.intgen.org/IGCexpo.html.* Available from *http://www.archive.org.*

68. p. 235 *This public database, called expOdb,* "expO," originally online at *http://www.intgen.org/IGCexpo.html.* Available from *http://www.archive.org.*

69. p. 235 *These standards are MIAME.* R.S. Tuma, "Microarray analysis on massive scale," *BioIT World,* July 2002.

70. p. 235 *With respect to expOdb,* "expO," originally online at *http://www.intgen.org/IGCexpo.html.* Available from *http://www.archive.org.*

71. p. 235 *ExpO data is considered to be* "Expression Projects." Online at *http://www.intgen.org/expression_projects.html.*

The Common Fold

Gene expression studies provide valuable information about which genes are switched on in which circumstances, offering useful clues about what is happening within a tissue. They say nothing, though, about how variation in gene expression leads to the observed phenotypes—illnesses, for example. For that, it is necessary to pass from the realm of genomes to the result of their expression: proteins. As Chapter 1 described, these biological chemicals can be thought of a microscopic machines. This is not merely a metaphor: just as the genome can often be regarded as pure digital information, so the key property of proteins turn out to be that most analogue of qualities, shape. It is how proteins fold up their long chains of amino acids that largely determines their function and how they interact with other molecules.

This applies not only to the structural proteins that make up important parts of the cell, but also signaling proteins that carry messages, enzymes that are used as tools to break up other molecules, and the huge array of biological defense mechanisms. Protein shape can even be the cause of illness: it is believed that the new variant Creutzfeldt-Jakob disease—"mad cow" disease—is caused by a normal cellular protein misfolding within the brain.

Against this background, understanding how purely digital information determines the physical shape of proteins—a field generally known as structural genomics—emerges as a key challenge. This might appear a hopeless task. Although the DNA sequence determines completely the sequence of amino acids that go to make up a protein, there is no reason at first sight why these long chains should always fold up in the same way. It might depend on the initial conditions, for example, or simply be random.

Fortunately, this seems not to be the case. As Charles Anfisen explained in a lecture he gave on the occasion of winning the 1972 Nobel prize in chemistry, "The native conformation [of the protein] is determined by the totality of interatomic interactions"—the complex interplay of how the thousands of atoms that make up the constituent amino acids attract and repel each other—"and hence by the amino acid sequence," because the sequence specifies uniquely what those atoms are. This came to be known as the "Thermodynamic Hypothesis," since it was based on the idea that it was general principles underlying all physics—thermodynamics—that determined protein structure, not particular, contingent ones that varied from situation to situation.

Anfisen concluded his lecture on an upbeat note: "Empirical considerations of the large amount of data now available on correlations between sequence and three-dimensional structure . . . are beginning to make more realistic the idea of the *a priori* prediction of protein conformation. It is certain that major advances in the understanding of cellular organization, and of the causes and control of abnormalities in such organization, will occur when we can predict, in advance, the three-dimensional phenotypic consequences of a genetic message."

Despite this optimism, little progress towards this goal was made for the next twenty years. The main progress came from the observation that two proteins with a high degree of sequence similarity generally have the same kind of three-dimensional shape. Given Anfisen's thermodynamic hypothesis, this is not too surprising: if the sequences are similar, so are the atoms and hence the interatomic interactions, which means that the final structure, too, would be broadly the same. In fact, it turns out that even sequences that are fairly dissimilar but which nonetheless derive from a common ancestor—homologous ones, in other words—often have highly similar structures.

Again, it is not hard to see why. Since structure determines a protein's function, major changes in shape are likely to make the protein machine unusable for its original purpose. Natural selection ensures that protein shape is highly conserved. This is not true, however, of the underlying protein sequences: provided the changes in the sequence do not affect the final shape, there may be no other evolutionary pressure to constrain them. Over millions or billions of years, the protein sequence—determined by the underlying digital DNA sequence—might change greatly, but in such a way as to preserve the analogue characteristics of the protein machine that results. However, spotting these homologies is difficult, which places an even greater onus on bioinformatic tools. To derive the full benefit of a computational approach, however, requires a list of proteins whose structures have been determined and which can be used to shed light on similar and homologous protein sequences.

For many years, the principal way of establishing protein structures was X-ray crystallography—the technique that had provided key information to Watson and Crick when they were seeking a structure for DNA. The approach consists of firing a very high frequency beam of light—X-rays— towards a carefully crystallized sample of the protein under investigation. By definition, crystals possess a highly regular internal structure: essentially, the molecules line up to produce a repeated three-dimensional pattern of atoms. By measuring the angle at which X-rays emerge from the crystal after bouncing off the pattern it is possible to calculate the distance and angle between the constituent parts of the protein. The fact that proteins can be crystallized is in itself a confirmation of Anfisen's thermodynamic hypothesis: a regular structure can only be produced if the shapes of the proteins are the same; were proteins able to take up many different physical forms, there could be no pattern.

The equivalent of GenBank for protein structure is the Protein Data Bank (PDB), which holds the basic coordinates—the positions in space—of the protein's constituent parts. Set up in 1971 at Brookhaven National Laboratories, PDB soon became as indispensable in the world of protein research as GenBank was for DNA. By the early 1990s, journals were requiring PDB accession codes before accepting papers for publication, just as they demanded GenBank details. Unlike GenBank, though, the rate of acquisition of protein structures grew slowly. In 1972, there was just one protein structure; ten years later, there were 197; in 1992, there were 1,006. Only in the following decade was there something of an acceleration: by 1997, there were 6,833, and in 2002, there were 19,623.

This increasingly rapid flow of protein structures was due to improvements in X-ray crystallography and the addition of an alternative approach based on nuclear magnetic resonance (NMR)—the technique also used in medicine to produce images of internal organs non-invasively. NMR works by measuring the signals emitted by atoms when they respond to a pulse of radio waves in the presence of a very strong magnetic field. As with X-ray crystallography, through complex computational analysis it is possible to deduce the arrangement of the protein's atoms.

Despite these advances, just how much work remains to be done is revealed by comparing the size of PDB's structural database with the protein sequence databases. The earliest, the Protein Information Resource (PIR) at Georgetown University, in Washington, DC, grew out of Margaret Dayhoff's *Atlas of Protein Sequence and Structure*, published from 1965 to 1978. PIR was set up in 1984, shortly after Dayhoff's untimely death in 1983. In 1988, PIR-International was established, bringing in the Munich Information Center for Protein Sequences and the Japan International Protein Information

Database to create a worldwide network of databases similar to the GenBank-EMBL-DDBJ consortium for DNA.

In its first year (1984), PIR held 2,676 protein sequences—ten times the number of structures in PDB; by 1992, this had swelled to 47,234, forty times the number of protein coordinate sets. At the end of 2001, PDB had started to catch up: PIR stood at 274,514, only 16 times PDB's holdings. Nonetheless, the "sequence-structure" gap—the disparity between known sequences and elucidated structures—remained vast.

PIR was not the only major protein sequence bank set up in the 1980s. In Europe, SWISS-PROT was founded in 1986 by Amos Bairoch, who was first at the Department of Medical Biochemistry of the University of Geneva and then at the Swiss Institute of Bioinformatics. Since 1987 it has been maintained as a collaboration between the latter organization and the European Molecular Biology Laboratory (EMBL). EMBL's work is carried out by its daughter unit, the European Bioinformatics Institute at Hinxton, next to the Wellcome Trust Sanger Institute, under Rolf Apweiler.

SWISS-PROT is notable for the high quality of its annotation—the extra information added—which is done purely manually, thanks to its team of curators. This laudable obsession with quality created something of a problem, however, as Bairoch and Apweiler explained in 2000: "Due to the increased data flow from genome projects to the [DNA] sequence databases we face a number of challenges to our way of database annotation. Maintaining the high quality of sequence and annotation in SWISS-PROT requires careful sequence analysis and detailed annotation of every entry. This is the rate-limiting step in the production of SWISS-PROT. On one hand we do not wish to relax the high editorial standards of SWISS-PROT and it is clear that there is a limit to how much we can accelerate the annotation procedures. On the other hand, it is also vital that we make new sequences available as quickly as possible. To address this concern, we introduced in 1996 TrEMBL (Translation of EMBL nucleotide sequence database). TrEMBL consists of computer-annotated entries derived from the translation of all coding sequences (CDSs) in the EMBL database, except for CDSs already included in SWISS-PROT."

That is, the predicted genes within the GenBank/EMBL DNA database are converted into the corresponding proteins by translating the three-nucleotide codons into the appropriate amino acid. These putative proteins are then stored separately until the day when they can be checked by human curators and then moved across into the main SWISS-PROT database.

However good they may be individually, separate databases are always less useful than a single unified point of reference. The announcement on 23 October 2002 that the U.S. National Institutes of Health would be funding a $15 million project to combine PIR, SWISS-PROT, and TrEMBL to form a single database to be known as the Unified Protein Databases (UniProt) was an indication of how important a centralized protein sequence resource had become. It was also a clear sign that in the wake of the nearly-complete human genome, the focus was now shifting increasingly towards the implications of its expression as proteins.

An NIH press release gave some details of how UniProt would work in practice: "The new UniProt will consist of two parts: the SWISS-PROT section, which will contain fully annotated entries, and the TrEMBL section, which will contain those computer-annotated records that are waiting hands-on analysis. The PIR group will no longer maintain its database, but will assist in elevating the annotation of TrEMBL records to the SWISS-PROT standard. All existing PIR entries will be integrated into UniProt. Currently, SWISS-PROT holds entries on 114,000 proteins, TrEMBL, 700,000, and PIR, 283,000. By the end of the grant's three-year span, EBI scientists estimate that the total number of proteins in the UniProt database should reach well above the 2 million mark."

Clearly, the challenge of establishing the structure of two million proteins was huge, and during the 1990s, a number of techniques were developed to address the central problem: how to detect structural similarities between proteins when the sequence identity—the percentage of amino acids in common—drops below 25 percent, into what is sometimes called the "twilight zone." Here, evolutionary divergences are such that the protein sequences may not appear related as judged by standard tools, but the resulting structures nonetheless show considerable similarity.

One approach that has proved fruitful is the use of protein signature databases. The idea is to generalize traditional homology searches to allow even faint signs of an ancient common ancestor to be detected. Instead of seeking a match between the protein under investigation and some other protein whose structure is already known, matches are sought between characterizations of key aspects of the new protein and a similar characterization of a group of related proteins that are homologous—what are called protein families. In a sense, the signature represents the essence of that protein family considered from a certain viewpoint, and searching against signatures attempts to determine to which family a new protein belongs, rather than to which protein it is most similar. The advantage is clear: signatures represent a kind of average over the whole family, rather than a specific example. Since members of a given family will all have a similar structure, matching against a signature automatically provides a likely structure, too.

The success of this approach can be seen from the InterPro database, created in 1999, which pulls together the results of classifying proteins according to various signatures to produce a unified collection. At the beginning of 2003, InterPro contained 4,280 protein families, and the combined signatures covered more than 74 percent of the 800,000 proteins in SWISS-PROT and TrEMBL.

Where the constituent parts of the InterPro resource seek to find elements within the protein sequences to help place new sequences in families, other databases attempt to classify the known shapes of proteins. One of the most popular of these is SCOP, which stands for "Structural Classification of Proteins." According to the paper that introduced it, "This database provides a detailed and comprehensive description of the structural and evolutionary relationships of proteins whose three-dimensional structures have been determined."

E ven before SCOP, protein structures had been classified in a hierarchy that provides a useful way of thinking about them. The primary structure is the linear sequence of amino acids, taking no account of the three-dimensional shape they determine. At a level above this, there are secondary structures that form the basic building blocks used to create the protein shape itself. Two of these secondary shapes are extremely common: α-helices and β-sheets.

An α-helix consists of a helix, just like DNA, but one that is single-stranded, made of amino acids and much shorter: typically, there are just a few turns. A β-sheet consists of a section of the protein sequence that bends back on itself several times to create a sheet with a series of short bars, rather like a fence of pales. The α-helices and β-sheets can combine with themselves and other secondary structures to create an extraordinarily varied set of shapes. These form the tertiary structures, called domains. Some proteins have only one domain, while others have more. In the latter case, each domain is a distinct, self-contained unit made up of amino acids, connected to the other domains to create a larger, modular protein.

Similar domains—where similarity is a slightly fluid concept—can be grouped together to form a more abstract "fold," the fundamental unit of shape for protein machines. For example, α-helices can be combined with themselves in various ways to create a range of folds based on molecular tubes. The β-sheets can be put together, back to back, to create what are called β-sandwich folds. If the β-sheets are triangular in shape, they can occur in radial groups of four, six, seven, or eight to form the aptly-named β-propeller folds.

SCOP draws on these ideas in its own classification. As the 1995 paper by SCOP's creators explained: "Proteins are clustered together into families on the basis of one of two criteria that imply their having a common evolutionary origin." One is that they have at least 30 percent of their sequences in common; the other is that their functions and overall structures are very similar, even though the sequence similarities are less than this figure.

Some families can be combined to create superfamilies, an idea first introduced by Margaret Dayhoff back in the early days of protein classification.
For SCOP: "Families, whose proteins have low sequence identities but whose
structures and, in many case, functional features suggest that a common evolutionary origin is probable, are placed together in superfamilies." What
superfamilies seek to do is to move even further beyond "obvious" sequence
similarities to find proteins that in a real sense belong together. This is because their structures, or their key substructures—the active parts where the
protein machine gets to grips with other molecules—suggest that they may
have derived from a common ancestor. Even if they are not related by evolution, some of these superfamilies and families may still have the same underlying fold: it turns out that certain overall shapes are used repeatedly in
different circumstances.

When SCOP was first created, there were 3,179 entries in PDB; according to SCOP's classification, these could be grouped into 498 families and
366 superfamilies. Overall, SCOP's curators discerned just 274 basic folds
among the families and superfamilies that were known. By 2003, 17,406 PDB
entries were grouped into 1,940 families, 1,110 superfamilies and 701 folds.
The obvious question was: How many folds were there in total?

A paper from a group at the NCBI summed up the situation that was
emerging in the late 1990s: "Depending on the assumptions and methods
used, the estimates of the total number of existing protein folds produced
by different researchers varied substantially, from [approximately] 650 to
[approximately] 10,000." Things were better than they seemed, however.
"Examination of the distribution of folds by the number of protein families"
—how many families shared a common fold—"indicates that, in one sense,
the discrepancy between these estimates might be of little consequence. This
distribution contains a small number of folds with a large number of families
and an increasing number of folds that consists of a small number of families." There are a few folds that account for the vast majority of protein families, while the rest, consisting of relatively exotic folds, are very rare. As a
result, the paper continued, "It seems certain that the great majority of protein families belong to [approximately] 1,000 common folds."

Assuming this were true, a targeted program could hope to elucidate the
structure of a relatively manageable number of proteins—tens of thousands,
say—and yet, thanks to evolutionary conservatism, be able to predict through
homology the structures of practically every other protein as a result. From
the middle of the 1990s, the idea of a global "structural genomics" project,
mirroring the Human Genome Project, became increasingly widespread.

The first country to begin serious work to this end was Japan. After initial
discussions in 1995, the Protein Folds Project began in April 1997 at the
RIKEN Yokohama Institute. Nine months later, in January 1998, a meeting
took place in the United States at the Argonne National Laboratory. One of
the participants, Thomas Terwiller, later called this "the pivotal point for the

North American efforts," writing: "This meeting brought together over 80 researchers and representatives of funding agencies who thought that improvements in technology, combined with the successes of the genome sequencing projects, had set the stage for a large-scale structure determination project. . . . The Argonne meeting led to a reinforced conviction on the part of many participants that the time was indeed right for structural genomics. It set a tone of excitement and promise for the structural genomics field that has propelled it ever since." From this it is clear that Argonne occupies a similar place in the story of structural genomics as Santa Cruz does for sequencing the human genome.

A report on the Argonne meeting by Terry Gaasterland detailed some of the costs involved. "Assuming a cost of $100,000 per structure, cost estimates for the overall project range from a maximum of $10 [billion] for 100,000 protein structures . . . to $300 [million] for 3000 proteins." Naturally, the more proteins that were sequenced, the greater the number of families and new folds that would be included, and the greater the coverage of the total range of proteins found in Nature.

A follow-up meeting was held in April 24, 1998 "to discuss issues related to a genome-directed Protein Structure Initiative (PSI)," as the structural genomics project was now called in a summary of the meeting. The initial objectives of the PSI were given as "the 3-D atomic structure of at least one member from selected protein families, which is likely to represent either a new fold or a structure from an uncharacterized superfamily." The latter would allow a shape to be assigned to all proteins found to be part of that superfamily. "About 350 folds and 1,200 superfamilies have already been determined experimentally, and projections from these data suggest that there may be on the order of 1,000 folds and 3,000–5,000 superfamilies. As a minimum, to fill in the remaining vacancies in the existing table of protein folds, a PSI will need to determine at least 2,000 new protein structures. However, the practical use of such a table of motifs [folds] to predict the structures of other proteins by homology may require multiple examples from each family," which would increase proportionately the number of proteins whose structures needed to be established.

The meeting also designated one area of crucial importance: the identification of protein families and target selection within them. As the report on it noted: "The parsing of the genome into families of homologous sequences, and the subsequent selection of proteins with a high probability of having novel structural features, will define the size and scope of this project." This was discussed at a workshop held in February 1999, notable, among other things, for the neat encapsulation of the global structural genomics effort in the phrase "10,000 structures within 5 years." It also raised for the first time the issue of data sharing: "as was pointed out by several participants," the meeting report noted, "the Bermuda agreement reached by the human genome sequencing community is a possible model for international cooperation, for avoiding duplication of effort, and for open sharing of scientific information."

This was addressed directly at the First International Structural Genomics Meeting, held in April 2000 at Hinxton Hall on the Wellcome Trust Genome Campus in Cambridgeshire. By this stage, the NIH had issued a formal Request For Applications (RFA) for funding: "The purpose of this RFA is to announce support for research centers in the new and emerging field of structural genomics. These research centers are intended to serve as pilots that will lead to subsequent large-scale research networks in structural genomics and high throughput structural determination of proteins by X-ray crystallography and NMR methods." The NIH envisaged funding three to six research centers up to $3 million per year as pilot projects, very much along the lines of the early large-scale sequencing centers set up as part of the Human Genome Project. Also significant is the emphasis on high throughput: as with the HGP, the essence of the PSI was obtaining data in unprecedented quantities.

The imminent creation of pilot projects made drawing up a policy on data sharing even more urgent, and it was appropriate that this issue should be discussed in detail on the Wellcome Trust Genome Campus, since one of the main architects of the Bermuda principles, John Sulston, was based there. Part of the principles agreed upon at the Hinxton meeting was the "timely release of coordinates and associated data. Release should follow immediately upon completion of refinement." That is, once the coordinates—the positions of the atoms making up the protein—had all been established to sufficient accuracy. There is no well-defined point, though, at which those coordinates have been determined to "sufficient accuracy." Analogue quantities can always be determined to greater accuracy—there is no "right" answer. By contrast, when digital quantities are measured, the result is either correct or incorrect. To get around this problem, the Hinxton principles added: "For the time being, the decision regarding 'completion' will be made by the investigator. A longer-term goal is the automatic triggering of data release using numerical criteria," so that once a predefined level of accuracy has been attained, the results must be released.

In September 2000, the NIH announced the first awards as part of the PSI. Although the overall goal was still the same—elucidating the structure of 10,000 proteins—people had become more circumspect about the timescale, which had doubled to ten years: a five-year pilot phase followed by a second five years of full-scale production. The National Institute of General Medical Sciences (NIGMS), part of the NIH, awarded nearly $30 million to seven projects. Maintaining this funding level for the first five years would bring the total cost for this pilot phase to $150 million.

As John Norvell, director of Protein Structure Initiative, explained: "These research centers are true pilots. Each will include every experimental and computational task of structural genomics and will develop strategies for use in the subsequent large-scale research networks. By the fifth year of the award we expect each pilot to reach a production level of 100 to 200 protein structures annually, which is significantly faster than the current rate of protein structure determination."

The Second International Structural Genomics Meeting took place in Airlie, Virginia, in April 2001. One important outcome was something that came to be known as the Airlie Agreement, structural genomics' equivalent to the genomic community's Bermuda Principles on data sharing. The meeting report explained that the Airlie Agreement "provides for open sharing of scientific data and technological expertise. The agreed conditions for the sharing of data reflect the balance between two different goals—timely release of all structural genomics data to the public and considerations for intellectual property regulations that vary significantly in different countries. For projects with public funding, all data on biomolecular shapes are to be made available to the public in all countries soon after their determination." Unfortunately, a technical task forced charged with devising "numerical criteria" to define when a structure was determined had to admit defeat for the moment.

Another result of the conference was the creation of a committee to establish the International Structural Genomics Organization (ISGO). Alongside the U.S. PSI there are several other major structural genomics projects, including the Japanese RIKEN Structural Genomics Initiative, the Protein Structure Factory in Berlin, Germany, and a pan-European project called SPINE—Structural Proteomics in Europe. A year after the first PSI grants were made, the NIGMS added two more research groups, bringing the annual funding to more than $40 million.

Against this background of growing international cooperation and increased funding, structural genomics seemed to be thriving. But a news story that appeared in *Science* in November 2002 contradicted this cozy view. Under the headline "Tapping DNA for structures produces a trickle," the article began: "The two dozen labs that signed up for a venture called 'structural genomics' several years ago had hoped to be pumping out a stream of results right about now. Their goal, set in 2000, was to follow the lead of the Human Genome Project, ramp up quickly, and have each lab solve hundreds of new protein structures per year. It was a bold idea, but no one knew whether it would be possible to automate the research to this degree. So when research teams met to compare notes here last month"—at the first International Conference on Structural Genomics, organized by ISGO in Berlin, Germany—"they were disappointed to learn that everyone was having plumbing troubles. Their pipelines have sprung leaks, and instead of delivering a flood of results, so far they're delivering just a trickle."

Then follows a rather sorrow litany of low rates of success: at one lab, out of 18,000 targets only 200 structures were elucidated; at another, just 23 proteins were solved out of the initial 1,870 targets. The head of the PSI, John Norvell, was quoted as saying that these numbers "are only the initial look;"

the Human Genome Project also had similarly disappointing figures in the beginning. Indeed, this is why pilot projects are run: to find out just what the difficulties are, and to develop ways of getting around them for the second, production phase.

This certainly seemed to be the view of the NIGMS, judging by a report that the PSI's principal investigators and advisory committee members made just a few weeks after the October 2002 ISGO meeting in Berlin. As the report explained: "The principal investigators reviewed their progress to date, discussed the specific problems and bottlenecks, and discussed lessons from the pilot initiative that can assist in the design of the second, or production, phase." The report then went on to emphasize just how well things were going: "Perhaps the most striking feature of the meeting was the high praise that was expressed by every member of the advisory committee for the progress that has been made." It even spoke of "dramatic improvements in technology"—just what the pilot projects were meant to achieve.

The apparent dissonance between the *Science* reporter's impressions and the PSI report may be explained by one area that the latter singled out as needing more work. "Individuals close to the PSI are uniformly impressed by the rapid progress that is being made. However, this progress may not be apparent to other structural biologists or to members of the bioscience community in general."

The parallels between the PSI and the Human Genome Project—some intentional, others more a product of circumstances—are striking. In one respect, though, the PSI is quite different: there is no Celera to act as a gadfly to the public project. This is not simply because there is only one Craig Venter. In a sense, Kári Stefánsson has played a Venter-like role in the world of discovering genes for common diseases; his company deCODE has been engaged in a race against various companies and public research groups.

There is a reason why competition is inevitable for the realms of genomics and common disease gene discovery: both are well-defined problems and both have digital solutions and a clear end. In the case of structural genomics, which is about shapes—analogue information—races have far less point. There are so many important proteins, with so many variants, and the rate of elucidating their structure is so slow, that there is no immediate danger of running out of them. Whatever the reason, structural genomics has not seen the kind of frenzied competition that has marked so much of the traditional genomics world, and there is even real collaboration.

An attempt in 2000 by the Wellcome Trust to create a formal partnership between the public and private sectors finally came to fruition in April 2003.

The Structural Genomics Consortium (SGC), partly modeled on the highly-successful SNP Consortium, is a joint project between the Wellcome Trust, GlaxoSmithKline, and four of Canada's leading research agencies. The three-year initiative's goal is "to encourage the development of new and improved drugs and other healthcare products," and it hopes to achieve this by deter-mining the structure of 350 human proteins associated with cancer, neuro-logical health, and malaria at a cost of £40 million ($60 million). Needless to say, given the participation of the Wellcome Trust, all structures will be released freely into the public domain.

By the time the SGC was formed, the U.S. Protein Structure Initiative already offered an interesting example of how companies and research groups can work together. One of the PSI's original pilot groups, the New York Structural Genomics Research Consortium, made up of five institutions in the New York City area, declared its aim to "streamline every step of structural genomics," according to the September 2000 press release announcing the first seven PSI awards. In the process, the consortium hoped to elucidate several hundred protein structures from humans and a variety of model organisms.

Originally, the lead investigator was Stephen Burley of The Rockefeller University. In January 2002, he left Rockefeller and became chief scientific officer at the start-up Structural GenomiX (SGX), founded in 1999. Structural GenomiX was created with the aim of industrializing the process of solving protein structures using X-ray crystallography; its approach draws heavily on robotics and powerful computers. In July 2000, the president of Structural GenomiX, Tim Harris, told *The New York Times* that he expected to spend $100 million to $500 million to determine 5,000 protein shapes in five years. He also likened his company to Celera, and in one respect this was demon-strably true. In September 2001, SGX announced that it was buying "200 Tru64 UNIX-based AlphaServer DS10L systems, two AlphaServer GS80 systems in a TruCluster, one AlphaServer ES40 system, and a 140-processor Linux-based Compaq ProLiant server cluster"—firepower that even Craig Venter might have envied.

Despite its ambitious business plans, Structural GenomiX seemed happy enough to work with the New York research consortium. In February 2002, the NIGMS announced that the latter had "merged its efforts" with Struc-tural GenomiX, explaining that "researchers at Rockefeller University are selecting the target proteins, and researchers at SGX will perform most of the production and crystallization of the selected proteins. This relationship brings significant commercial resources to the overall effort."

It also brought funds to Structural GenomiX. On 14 November 2002, the company announced "the transfer of a National Institutes of Health (NIH) Center Grant in the sum of $18.1 million", adding "the NIH Grant, believed to be one of the largest protein structure research grants to date, transfers leadership of the New York Structural Genomics Research Consortium . . . from The Rockefeller University to SGX under the direction of Dr. Stephen K. Burley." Not that SGX gets all of this money: "In the first year, SGX will retain approximately 30 percent of the grant funding," the rest going to collaborators.

Providing what is in effect contract X-ray crystallography is a sensible approach for both parties. SGX derives revenues from its top-notch but costly equipment, while the public research laboratories benefit from high-throughput, industrial-scale X-ray crystallography without needing to build the facilities themselves. Indeed, the partnership might prove a useful example for traditional genome research now that the scientific interest lies in analyzing sequences, not obtaining them.

This kind of work formed the heart of Structural GenomiX' original plans. For example, in January 2001, the company described itself as "a pioneer in high throughput protein structure determination." These structures, it explained, "will be available to strategic partners across the biopharmaceutical, agricultural, and chemical industries." By December 2001, however, just before Burley moved across from Rockefeller, SGX had broadened its activities to become "a drug discovery company," albeit one "utilizing a genomics-driven, high-throughput structure-based platform to increase the efficiency and effectiveness of the drug discovery process."

One of Structural GenomiX' competitors, Syrrx, which also employs a highly-automated approach to X-ray crystallography, has made a similar transition. In 2000, for example, it described how its technical strengths would "position the Company and the field of structural genomics as an essential part of drug discovery in the pharmaceutical industry." In November 2001, though, it appointed a Vice President of Drug Discovery with the goal of establishing Syrrx as "a premier drug discovery company."

In principle, both SGX and Syrrx are well-placed to come up with new drugs. Their ability to determine molecular structures means that they can adopt a rational drug design approach, finding chemicals that fit the shapes of proteins involved in illness and diseases directly. Like the public PSI, however, both Structural GenomiX and Syrrx are finding it no mean task to industrialize the elucidation of protein structure. According to the same *Science* story that was skeptical of the PSI's progress, in November 2002, Syrrx had "delivered a total of 80 structures since the company formed in 1999," while SGX has "banked more than 100 structures." Although, as *Science* continued, "taken together, that's about the same number produced by the nearly 30 publicly financed programs worldwide and roughly 10 times the number produced by a typical major pharmaceutical firm in a year"—an impressive achievement, then—it makes SGX's original plans to elucidate the structure of 5,000 proteins in five years look difficult, to say the least. Now that Structural GenomiX and Syrrx are in the business of drug development, perhaps what matters is quality—solving the right protein structure—rather than sheer quantity.

The Protein Structure Initiative, however, is predicated on quantity: it needs as many solved proteins as possible if homology is to be broadly applicable. It may be that the PSI pilot projects will bear fruit and come up with new ways of solving problems—by extending the applicability of NMR techniques, for example—or, at least, of improving the throughput of conventional X-ray crystallography to produce those 10,000 new structures in ten years. But rather than waiting for breakthroughs in what are essentially analogue approaches—blasting X-rays at crystals that have to be slowly and laboriously grown, or setting protein solutions in massive magnetic fields—some researchers are exploring a totally digital approach.

The idea goes back to Anfisen's Thermodynamic Hypothesis. It suggests that the final folded form of a protein is determined purely by the interactions between the constituent atoms; thus one way of ascertaining this shape is to model these interactions using a computer. By running the model long enough and allowing the atoms to interact in a way that approximates the behavior of real atoms in a protein, it is theoretically possible to calculate the final form of the protein. This calculation is based on the assumption that the most stable state is the one with the lowest energy. This is like letting a ball roll down a slope: any slight perturbation from an intermediate resting place—a small hollow halfway down the slope—would cause it to roll further until it finally reached the bottom of the slope. There, no matter how much the ball is disturbed, it cannot fall any further. Modeling a protein as it folds is a matter of exploring its energy landscape (the slope) until a configuration with the minimum energy has been located.

There is a problem with this approach, however, that follows from what is known as Levinthal's Paradox. Cyrus Levinthal was a pioneer in the application of computers to biochemistry; he first started modeling proteins in 1965. A few years later he gave a lecture in Illinois in which he noted that even allowing for the various structural restrictions imposed by the laws of physics and chemistry, a typical protein would have so many theoretical configurations that searching through them for the most stable state would take far longer than the age of the universe. The fact that proteins typically fold in a few seconds means that there are other factors.

In a paper written in 1968, Levinthal suggested a resolution of this paradox through the idea of a pathway for folding: "a well-defined sequence of events which follow one another so as to carry the protein from the unfolded random coil to a uniquely folded metastable state"—a hollow on the slope. He added: "If the final folded state turned out to be one of the lowest configurational energy"—the one at the bottom of the slope—"it would be a consequence of biological evolution not of physical chemistry." That is, Nature would have selected those proteins that folded relatively quickly to a stable form: proteins that folded slowly, or not at all, would be selected against, since cells using them would be less efficient than those based solely on completely stable proteins that folded quickly.

In his lecture, Levinthal offered a specific idea about how such pathways might be created. "We feel that protein folding is speeded and guided by the rapid formation of local interactions which then determine the further folding . . . This suggests local amino acid sequences which form stable interactions and serve as nucleation points in the folding process." The idea here is that the protein may not fold along its entire length at the same time: instead, local "nucleation points"—centers of folding—form more quickly. Typically, these are secondary structures like α-helices and β-sheets. Once formed, they would stay folded, and make the folding of the rest of the protein far quicker since there were fewer alternatives to explore. It was the local interactions that determined the pathways for folding.

Even though these secondary structures were believed to form much faster than the overall protein folding time, detailed modeling of them lay beyond the reach of researchers for many years until sufficient computational power became available. The breakthrough paper that marked the start of a new era of direct modeling of protein folding appeared in *Science* in October 1998. The authors, Yong Duan and Peter Kollman, managed to cram a fairly comprehensive description of their work into one rather overextended, buzzword-filled sentence: "By using a Cray T3C, a massively parallel supercomputer consisting of hundreds of central processing units (CPUs) connected by low-latency, high-speed, and high-availability networks, with an efficiently parallelized program that scales well to the 256-CPU level for small protein-solvent systems and is six times faster than a typical current state-of-the-art program, we have conducted a 1 [microsecond] simulation . . . on the villin headpiece subdomain, a 36-residue peptide . . . starting from a fully unfolded extended state, including [approximately] 3000 water molecules."

Translated into English, this means that they used a computer with 256 processors, rather than the single chip found in most PCs, with very fast networks connecting them ("low-latency"). Latency is a problem, because the advantage of using several high-speed processors can easily be lost if data take too long to move between them. Similarly, simply running a standard program on a supercomputer with multiple processors would produce little benefit; instead, a special "parallelized" version needs to be produced that apportions tasks between the processors in a way that allows computation to proceed in many simultaneous streams.

With its 36 residues (amino acids), the villin headpiece subdomain is "one of the smallest proteins that can fold autonomously," as the paper explains. NMR studies had already solved its structure, which consists of three short helices joined together. The estimated folding time of the protein was between 10 and 100 microseconds (millionths of a second), which made it one of the fastest-folding proteins. It also meant that the Duan and Kollman's 1 microsecond simulation explored only the first one to ten percent of the total folding time.

An article on the Web site of the Pittsburgh Supercomputing Center, where the work was carried out, commented: "Simulating a millionth of a second of protein movement may sound less than impressive, until you realize that the longest prior simulations of similar proteins extended only 10 to 20 nanoseconds (billionths of a second). The limitation holding back this critical work has been the tremendous computational demand of the simulations, which must account for interactions between each atom in a protein and all the other atoms and surrounding water molecules," since proteins are generally dissolved in water in the cell. "To capture protein movement at a useful level of detail, the full set of these interactions must be recalculated every femtosecond (a millionth of a nanosecond) of protein time."

Since the computation involved some 12,000 atoms, including those of the surrounding water molecules, it is no wonder, then, that the first 200 nanoseconds of folding took 40 days of dedicated computing using all 256 processors of the Cray supercomputer. Employing an even more powerful machine that was four times faster, the next 800 nanoseconds—to complete the first microsecond, a thousand nanoseconds—took another two months.

The results were quite dramatic. "A burst of folding in the first 20 nanoseconds quickly collapses the unfolded structure, suggesting that initiation of folding for a small protein can occur within the first 100 nanoseconds," according to the Pittsburgh Web page. Duan and Kollman explained in their *Science* paper that this initial phase is characterized by a steady growth of helical structures, but that the overall shape moved between compact and more unfolded forms This seems to support Levinthal's idea of local nucleation points—the helices in this case, which appeared well before the protein had settled down in a fully-folded shape.

After all this activity, things changed. "The next 800 nanoseconds reveal an intriguing 'quiet period' in the folding," the Pittsburgh Web page explained. "From about 250 nanoseconds until 400 nanoseconds the fluctuating movement back and forth . . . virtually ceases. 'For this period in the later part of the trajectory,' says Kollman, 'everything becomes quiet. And that's where the structure gets closest to the native state. It's quite happy there for awhile, then it eventually drifts off again for the rest of the period out to a microsecond'."

The quiet period did not represent the protein in its final folded state, but what the *Science* paper called a "marginally stable non-native state"—one that is able to exist for just a short time, like the pauses in hillside hollows on the way down to the bottom, which represents the native state. Duan and Kollman pointed out that such non-native states are difficult to observe experimentally, simply because they are not fully stable. "Computer simulation can play an important role in identifying these structures," they wrote, "because of its extremely high time resolution and detailed atomic level representation." In effect, computers provide the ultimate microscope that can watch proteins fold atom by atom in a series of "snapshots," taken every million billionth of a second, allowing the elusive non-native states to be caught along the way.

Even though their simulation of protein folding was unable to model the pathway through to the final configuration, Duan and Kollman's work was nonetheless a key moment. An accompanying article in *Science* was called "A glimpse of the Holy Grail?," and noted that "the prediction of the native conformation of a protein of known amino acid sequence is one of the great open questions in molecular biology and one of the most demanding challenges in the new field of bioinformatics." Kollman himself is quoted in the Pittsburgh Supercomputing Center feature as saying: "Being able to visualize the folding process of even a small protein in a realistic environment has been a goal of many researchers. We believe our work marks the beginning of a new era of the active participation of full-scale simulations in helping to understand the mechanism of protein folding."

Kollman's view was amply confirmed just over a year later, when IBM announced in December 1999 that it would be building the world's most powerful computer with the express purpose of working towards that "goal of many researchers," as Kollman had termed it: being able to study the elaborate dance of a folding protein in a realistic environment all the way to its conclusion.

As the press release accompanying the announcement explained, "The new computer—nicknamed 'Blue Gene' by IBM researchers—will be capable of more than one quadrillion [mathematical] operations per second (one petaflop)"—a million billion calculations every second. "This level of performance will make Blue Gene . . . about 2 million times more powerful than today's top desktop PCs. . . . IBM Research believes a radical new approach to computer design and architecture will allow Blue Gene to achieve petaflop-scale performance in about five years." To put things in context, it added: "The two fastest computers in the world today are part of the ASCI program run by the U.S. Department of Energy, and which were recently tested at about 2 teraflops—two trillion [mathematical] operations per second each." Celera's recently-built supercomputer clocked in a little behind these leaders, at 1.3 teraflops.

"Blue Gene will consist of more than one million processors, each capable of one billion operations per second (1 gigaflop). Thirty-two of these ultra-fast processors will be placed on a single chip (32 gigaflops). A compact two-foot by two-foot board containing 64 of these chips will be capable of 2 teraflops, making it as powerful as the 8000-square foot ASCI computers." In other words, if successful, IBM would pack into a single circuit board more computing punch than Celera's Compaq system, which cost $80 million before the discount. "Eight of these boards will be placed in 6-foot-high racks (16 teraflops), and the final machine (less than 2000 sq. ft.) will consist of 64 racks linked together to achieve the one petaflop performance." The total cost for this lean "Blue Gene" machine, IBM estimated, would be $100 million.

An article in IBM's house journal for technology filled in some of the details. "The current expectation is that it will be sufficient to use classical techniques, such as molecular dynamics (MD), to model proteins in the Blue Gene project." Molecular dynamics was the method adopted by Kollman and Duan. As the IBM paper explained: "The MD approach is to compute all the forces on all the atoms of the computer model of the protein and solvent [the water molecules], then use that force to compute the new positions of all the atoms a very short time later. By doing this repeatedly, a *trajectory* of the atoms of the system can be traced out, producing atomic coordinates as a function of time." If the calculation starts from the known positions of the unfolded protein and the computation is run long enough, these atomic coordinates should eventually assume the final positions found in the folded protein.

The "very short time later" mentioned is extremely short: approximately one femtosecond—a millionth of a billionth of a second. "This small time-step size is required to accurately describe the fastest vibrations of the protein and solvent system," the journal explained. If comparatively long time scales were adopted—say, billionths of a second, the computation would be unable to capture the very fine detail of the atoms' movements.

"The magnitude of the computational cost can be seen when one notes that folding times of approximately [100 microseconds]," which was also the estimated folding time for the protein studied by Duan and Kollman, "are observed in some fast-folding systems, requiring the computation of approximately [100 billion] MD time steps." An accompanying table then spelled out the implications of this number. Assuming there were around 32,000 atoms in a typical protein plus the surrounding water, there would be a billion (32,000×32,000) force interactions that had to be calculated for every one of the 100 billion time steps. Each force calculation required around 1,000 computing instructions. This meant that the total number of computing instructions to calculate the folding of an average-sized but reasonably speedy protein would be 100,000 billion billion (100,000,000,000,000,000,000,000). If Blue Gene achieved its petaflop—1 million billion operations per second—the calculation would take 100,000,000 seconds: slightly more than three years of non-stop, top-speed computation.

As the paper pointed out, a petaflop system built using conventional components would consume hundreds of megawatts (millions of watts) of electrical power. Three years of this kind of electricity consumption might prove expensive even for IBM. Along with space considerations—the hypothetical "traditional" petaflop machine would require "many acres of machine room floor," according to IBM—the need to reduce power consumption dramatically was another reason for adopting a radically new, more compact design. The IBM paper estimated that Blue Gene, when running at full tilt, should consume under two megawatts.

In fact, IBM had no intention of building Blue Gene, starting it, and leaving it to hum away for three years. "It is very important to dispel the notion that the Blue Gene resource will be applied to study a single folding event of a single protein," the IBM journal emphasized. "For physically meaningful studies of protein folding, it will be necessary to simulate a large number of trajectories in order to reach conclusions supported by reasonable statistics." Finding out the time it takes for one run of a computational model to fold a protein says very little, since it is not clear to what extent the result is representative of the range of possibilities. Running it several times—IBM estimated that from 10 to 100 would be required—with different starting conditions would provide important information about the geography of the energy landscape, for example. However, the computational power of the machine is fixed: to be able to run 100 trajectories in three years would mean either that the proteins were appreciably smaller, or that only part of the trajectory were traversed. In other words, even with the huge power of Blue Gene, it still may not be possible to watch an average protein reach its final structure.

Of course, for IBM, this is not really a problem. Its business is selling computers, not modeling proteins. The whole reason it is building Blue Gene is to learn how to make even more powerful supercomputers, ultimately with a view to selling something at least loosely based on them. This was made clear when IBM announced in November 2001 that in partnership with the Lawrence Livermore National Labs it would be producing a system called Blue Gene/L, due out in 2005. Described as "marking a major expansion of the Blue Gene project," Blue Gene/L would actually be less powerful, at 200 teraflops, though this was still greater than the total computing power of the top 500 supercomputers in the world at the time of the announcement. Why IBM regarded a machine with only a fifth of the capability of the original petaflop Blue Gene as an "expansion" was explained by a comment from a senior IBM manager included in the accompanying press release: "Our initial exploration made us realize we can expand our Blue Gene project to deliver more commercially viable architectures for a broad customer set, and still accomplish our original goal of protein science simulations."

What is interesting is how one of the most extreme scientific challenges will feed back into mainstream computing and result in "more commercially viable architectures"—supercomputers with hitherto unparalleled power but for an affordable price. A year after it announced Blue Gene/L, IBM gave some details of the operating system for the Blue Gene family. Appropriately, perhaps, given the supercomputer architecture's origins in the world of bioinformatics, the chosen operating system is GNU/Linux, by now more or less the *de facto* standard for the field.

Even though IBM's Blue Gene project may well give rise to a lucrative new line of top-end machines for the company, it is hard to see the idea being pushed much beyond its current design. Already, the idea of wiring up one million processors seems at the very limit of what is possible. Improvements will no doubt be made, but probably not enough to provide the same kind of advance beyond Blue Gene as that represents beyond conventional supercomputers. However, there may be another way of reaching the next level in computing power.

In December 2000, an article appeared in *Science* under the headline "Screen savers of the world unite!" It began: "Recently, a new computing paradigm has emerged: a worldwide distributed computing environment consisting of thousands or even millions of heterogeneous processors, frequently volunteered by private citizens across the globe, linked by the Internet. This large number of processors dwarfs even the largest modern supercomputers." Moreover, "the world's supply of CPU [central processing unit] time is very large, growing rapidly, and essentially untapped." As a result, in theory at least, such distributed computing might provide power not only beyond that of Blue Gene, but one that could scale to ever-higher levels as more users join the Internet with more powerful computers.

There is a problem, though, as the article explained: "Duan and Kollman have demonstrated that traditional parallel molecular dynamics simulations can break the microsecond barrier, provided that one uses many tightly connected processors"—those linked by low-latency networks—"running on an expensive supercomputer for many months. This style of calculation requires, however, that the processors frequently communicate information and is thus poorly suited for worldwide distributed computing, where computer communication is thousands of times slower than the interprocessor communication in today's supercomputers." Fortunately, the authors of the *Science* piece, Michael Shirts and Vijay Pande, had a solution. They published it in the journal *Biopolymers*, in a special memorial issue dedicated to Peter Kollman, who had died of cancer in May 2001. The clever trick they employed depended upon the nature of the energy landscape that proteins "rolled down" as they folded.

Pande and his team noted in their paper that the progress from unfolded to folded state is not a steady, gradual progress. As Duan and Kollman had glimpsed in their truncated computation, there are often relatively extended periods where the protein is in a "marginally stable" state, waiting for random thermal fluctuations to push it over the local obstacles so that it can move further down the energy landscape.

Since the folding process can be regarded as a series of these marginally stable states followed by transitions, it is possible to split the task of calculating the progressive folding in the following way. The same simulation is run independently on all of the systems taking part in the distributed computing. They all begin with the same atomic positions, but with slightly different starting conditions (in terms of how the atoms are moving, for example). Once one of the participant computers has calculated a path that gets the protein over a local bump and further down the hill to the next intermediate resting place, it passes this information back to the central computer coordinating the distributed computation. The latter then instructs all of the other systems to stop, discard their own calculations, and start from the new position on the hill as determined by the first computer's solution. In this way, once a marginally stable state is attained, the calculation recommences on all the participating machines until one of them calculates a path that gets the protein over the next local bump.

This approach is not purely theoretical. As Pande and colleagues reported in another paper, in October 2000 they launched the Folding@home project, which invited Internet users to donate spare processing time on their PC. Computing power was only used when the user's machine went into a quiescent mode, signaled by the appearance of a special Folding@home screensaver. In the 12 months after the launch, over 40,000 participants had contributed 10,000 CPU-years—the equivalent of running a single computer for 10,000 years. Pande and his coworkers studied a range of proteins, including the villin headpiece modeled by Duan and Kollman. In general, there was "a striking agreement between predicted and experimental rates" of folding, they commented.

The distributed approach, drawing on donated computing power, offers an attractive alternative to the massive investment required to create something like Blue Gene. At the end of 2003, there were more than half a million CPUs (processors) contributing to Pande's project—a number likely to rise yet further thanks to the support from the top Web search engine Google, which allows users of its toolbar to download and run the Folding@home client with a single click. Unfortunately, like IBM's Blue Gene approach— though for quite different reasons—the distributed computing platform does not scale indefinitely when applied to protein folding, as Pande and his colleagues noted.

Despite these limitations, the Blue Gene and Folding@home projects stand as monuments to the vision and ingenuity of scientists in the face of the apparently insurmountable difficulty of modeling protein folding with computers. In a deeper sense, they also make manifest the chasm separating the complex analogue reality of a folded protein and the almost trivial digital DNA sequence that codes for it.

NOTES

1. p. 241   *it is believed that the new variant*   S. Prusiner, "Prion disease and the BSE crisis," *Science* 278 (1997): 245–251.

2. p. 242   *The native conformation [of the protein] is determined*   C.B. Anfinsen, "Principles that govern the folding of protein chains," *Science* 181 (1973): 223–230.

3. p. 243 *grew out of Margaret Dayhoff's* Atlas of Protein Sequence and Structure, "PIB Mission and History." Online at *http://pir.georgetown.edu/pirwww/aboutpir/history.html*.

4. p. 244 *SWISS-PROT was founded in 1986 by Amos Bairoch,* EBI press release, October 23, 2002.

5. p. 244 *Due to the increased data flow from* A. Bairoch and R. Apweiler, "The SWISS-PROT protein sequence database and its supplement TrEMBL in 2000," *Nucleic Acids Research* 28 (2000): 45–48.

6. p. 245 *The new UniProt will consist of two parts:* NIH press release, October 23, 2002.

7. p. 245 *At the beginning of 2003, InterPro contained* N.J. Mulder, et al., "The InterPro database, 2003 brings increased coverage and new features," *Nucleic Acids Research* 31 (2003): 315–318.

8. p. 246 *This database provides a detailed and comprehensive* A.G. Murzin, et al., "SCOP: a structural classification of proteins database for the investigation of sequences and structures," *J. Mol. Biol.* 247 (1995): 536–540.

9. p. 246 *Proteins are clustered together into families* A.G. Murzin, et al., "SCOP: a structural classification of proteins database for the investigation of sequences and structure," *J. Mol. Biol.* 247 (1995): 536–540.

10. p. 247 *Families, whose proteins have low sequence identities* A.G. Murzin, et al., "SCOP: a structural classification of proteins database for the investigation of sequences and structures," *J. Mol. Biol.* 247 (1995): 536–540.

11. p. 247 *according to SCOP's classification,* A.G. Murzin, et al., "SCOP: a structural classification of proteins database for the investigation of sequences and structures," *J. Mol. Biol.* 247 (1995): 536–540.

12. p. 247 *Depending on the assumptions and methods used,* E.V. Koonin, et al., "The structure of the protein universe and genome evolution," *Nature* 420 (2002) 218–223.

13. p. 247 *Examination of the distribution of folds by the number* E.V. Koonin, et al., "The structure of the protein universe and genome evolution," *Nature* 420 (2002): 218–223.

14. p. 247 *After initial discussions in 1995,* S. Yokoyama, et al., "Structural genomics projects in Japan," *Nature Structural Biology*, structural genomics supplement (November 2000): 943–945.

15. p. 247 *the pivotal point for the North American efforts,* T.C. Terwilliger, "Structural genomics in North America," *Nature Structural Biology*, structural genomics supplement (November 2000): 935–939.

16. p. 248 *This meeting brought together over 80 researchers* T.C. Terwilliger, "Structural genomics in North America," *Nature Structural Biology*, structural genomics supplement (November 2000): 935–939.

17. p. 248 *Assuming a cost of $100,000 per structure,* T. Gaasterland, "Feasibility of structural genomics and impact on computational biology: post-workshop review," January 26, 1998.

18. p. 248 *to discuss issues related to a genome-directed* P. Bash, and E. Lattman, Protein Structure Initiative meeting summary 4–24–98. Online at *http://www.nigms.nih.gov/news/reports/protein_structure.html.*

19. p. 248 *the 3-D atomic structure of at least one member* P. Bash, and E. Lattman, Protein Structure Initiative meeting summary 4–24–98. Online at *http://www.nigms.nih.gov/news/reports/protein_structure.html.*

20. p. 248 *About 350 folds and 1,200 superfamilies* P. Bash, and E. Lattman, Protein Structure Initiative meeting summary 4–24–98. Online at *http://www.nigms.nih.gov/news/reports/protein_structure.html.*

21. p. 248 *10,000 structures within 5 years.* Structural Genomics Targets Workshop report. Online at *http://www.nigms.nih.gov/news/meetings/structural_genomics_targets.html.*

22. p. 248 *as was pointed out by several* Structural Genomics Targets Workshop report. Online at *http://www.nigms.nih.gov/news/meetings/structural_genomics_targets.html.*

23. p. 249 *The purpose of this RFA is to announce support* "Pilot projects for the Protein Structure Initiative (Structural Genomics)." Online at *http://grants1.nih.gov/grants/guide/rfa-files/RFA-GM-99-009.html.*

24. p. 249 *timely release of coordinates and associated data.* First international structural genomics meeting, April 4–6, 2000. Online at *http://www.nigms.nih.gov/news/meetings/hinxton.html.*

25. p. 249 *These research centers are true pilots.* NIGMS press release, September 26, 2000. Online at *http://www.nigms.nih.gov/news/releases/SGpilots.html.*

26. p. 250 *provides for open sharing of scientific data* Second international structural genomics meeting, April 4–6, 2001. Online at *http://www.nigms.nih.gov/news/meetings/airlie.html.*

27. p. 250 *The two dozen labs that signed up for a venture* R.F. Service, "Tapping DNA for structures produces a trickle," *Science* 298 (2002): 948–950.

28. p. 251 *The principal investigators reviewed their progress* "Report to National Advisory General Medical Sciences Council, November 14–15, 2002." Online at *http://www.nigms.nih.gov/news/reports/psi_advisory02.html.*

29. p. 251 *Individuals close to the PSI are uniformly* "Report to National Advisory General Medical Sciences Council, November 14–15, 2002." Online at *http://www.nigms.nih.gov/news/reports/psi_advisory02.html.*

30. p. 252 *to encourage the development of new and improved drugs* Wellcome Trust press release, April 3, 2003.

31. p. 252 *In January 2002, he left Rockefeller and became* E. Marshall, "Rockefeller's star lured to San Diego company," *Science* 294 (2001): 2083–2084.

32. p. 252 *he expected to spend $100 million to $500 million* A. Pollack, "The next chapter in the book of life: structural genomics," *The New York Times,* July 4, 2000.

33. p. 252 *200 Tru64 UNIX-based AlphaServer DS10L systems,* Structural GenomiX press release, September 20, 2001.

34. p. 252 *merged its efforts* "NIGMS report on protein production workshop, March 7–8, 2002." Online at *http://www.nigms.nih.gov/news/reports/ protein_production.html.*

35. p. 252 *the transfer of a National Institutes of Health* Structural GenomiX press release, November 14, 2002.

36. p. 253 *a pioneer in high throughput protein structure determination.* Structural GenomiX press release, January 24, 2001.

37. p. 253 *a drug discovery company,* Structural GenomiX press release, December 18, 2001.

38. p. 253 *position the Company and the field of structural* Syrrx Web site, October 18, 2000.

39. p. 253 *a premier drug discovery company.* Syrrx press release, November 5, 2001.

40. p. 253 *delivered a total of 80 structures* R.F. Service, "Big biology without the big commotion," *Science* 298 (2002): 950.

41. p. 253 *banked more than 100 structures.* R.F. Service, "Big biology without the big commotion," *Science* 298 (2002): 950.

42. p. 254 *he first started modeling proteins* C. Levinthal, online at *http://www.umass.edu/molvis/francoeur/levinthal/Levinthaltext.html.*

43. p. 254 *he noted that even allowing for the various structural* C. Levinthal, "How to fold graciously," *University of Illinois Bulletin* 67 (41) (1969) 22–24. Online at *http://brian.ch.cam.ac.uk/~mark/levinthal/levinthal.html.*

44. p. 254 *a well-defined sequence of events* C. Levinthal, "Are there pathways for protein folding?" *Extrait du Journal de Chimie Physique* 65 (1968): 44–45.

45. p. 255 *We feel that protein folding is speeded* C. Levinthal, "How to fold graciously," *University of Illinois Bulletin* 67 (41) (1969): 22–24. Online at *http://brian.ch.cam.ac.uk/~mark/levinthal/levinthal.html.*

46. p. 255 *By using a Cray T3C, a massively parallel supercomputer* Y. Duan, and P.A. Kollman, "Pathways to a protein folding intermediate observed in a 1-microsecond simulation in aqueous solution," *Science* 282 (1998): 740–744.

47. p. 255 *Simulating a millionth of a second of protein movement* M. Schneider, "Watching a protein fold." Pittsburgh Supercomputing Center. Online at *http://www.psc.edu/science/Kollman98/kollman98.html.*

48. p. 256 *the first 200 nanoseconds of folding* M. Schneider, "Watching a protein fold." Pittsburgh Supercomputing Center. Online at *http://www.psc.edu /science/Kollman98/kollman98.html.*

49. p. 256 *The next 800 nanoseconds reveal an intriguing* M. Schneider, "Watching a protein fold." Pittsburgh Supercomputing Center. Online at *http://www.psc.edu/science/Kollman98/kollman98.html.*

50. p. 256 *marginally stable non-native state* Y. Duan, and P.A. Kollman, "Pathways to a protein folding intermediate observed in a 1-microsecond simulation in aqueous solution," *Science* 282 (1998): 740–744.

51. p. 256 *Computer simulation can play* Y. Duan, and P.A. Kollman, "Pathways to a protein folding intermediate observed in a 1-microsecond simulation in aqueous solution," *Science* 282 (1998): 740–744.

52. p. 257 *the prediction of the native conformation of a protein* H.J.C. Berendsen, "A glimpse of the Holy Grail?" *Science* 282 (1998): 642–643.

53. p. 257 *The new computer—nicknamed "Blue Gene" by IBM researchers* IBM press release, December 6, 1999.

54. p. 257 *Blue Gene will consist of more than one million* IBM press release, December 6, 1999.

55. p. 258 *The current expectation is that it will be sufficient* F. Allen, et al., "Blue Gene: a vision for protein science using a petaflop supercomputer," *IBM Systems Journal* 40 (2): 310–327.

56. p. 258 *The magnitude of the computational* F. Allen, et al., "Blue Gene: a vision for protein science using a petaflop supercomputer," *IBM Systems Journal* 40 (2): 310–327.

57. p. 258 *It is very important to dispel the notion* F. Allen, et al., "Blue Gene: a vision for protein science using a petaflop supercomputer," *IBM Systems Journal* 40 (2): 310–327.

58. p. 259 *marking a major expansion of the Blue Gene project,* IBM press release, November 9, 2001.

59. p. 259 *Our initial exploration made us realize* IBM press release, November 9, 2001.

60. p. 259 *the chosen operating system is GNU/Linux,* M. Kanellos, "It's Linux for IBM supercomputer project," *CNET News.com*, October 24, 2002.

61. p. 260 *Recently, a new computing paradigm has emerged:* M. Shirts, and V.S. Pande, "Screen savers of the world unite!" *Science* 290 (2000): 1903–1904.

62. p. 261 *a striking agreement between predicted and experimental rates* V.S. Pande, et al., "Atomistic protein folding simulations on the hundreds of microsecond timescale using worldwide distributed computing," 2002. Online at *http://folding.stanford.edu/papers.html*.

CHAPTER 12

The Promise of Proteomics

The relatively slow start to the Protein Structure Initiative and the immense challenges facing purely computational approaches indicate just how hard it is to move from the world of genomics to that of proteins. An alternative approach looks at things the other way around, proceeding from the proteins first and integrating genomic knowledge afterwards.

The study of the total protein complement in organisms is known as proteomics, which is derived from a term coined in mid-1994, by Marc Wilkins, an Australian postgraduate student. As he worked on a paper he found himself writing repeatedly "all proteins expressed by a genome, cell or tissue." As he later said: "This was cumbersome, inelegant and made for a lot of extra typing." He looked for a word that could express the idea succinctly, and after rejecting "proteinome" and "protome," plumped for "proteome." The rapid uptake of the word after his use of it at a scientific gathering in Italy suggests that he made a good choice. If the word is relatively new, though, the idea goes much further back, to the beginning of the 1980s.

In January 1981, a report appeared in *Science* written by Nicholas Wade. Wade later became a science correspondent at *The New York Times* and broke many of the top genomic stories—notably those involving Celera. Under the title "The complete index to man," Wade made a significant connection between two emerging fields: "A total analysis of the human genome, as well as an index of every protein produced by the various types of cell in the human body, are goals that through new techniques and advances in computing power have begun to appear almost feasible." Two things are of note here. First, that what later came to be called proteomics started around the same time as genomics, and second, that both depended on computers.

Wade then went on to describe two pioneers who had already embarked on the ambitious proteomics project, which he suggested was likely to be further along than that for genomics. "Its originators are two scientists at the Argonne National Laboratory, Norman G. Anderson and his son Leigh Anderson. Over the last few years they have laid much of the technical groundwork for cataloging the 50,000 or so different protein products that constitute the working parts of the human cells." Today, the view is that there are more like 500,000 working parts—an even more challenging prospect.

"The Andersons' plan is simple in concept," Wade wrote, "technically arduous in design. Their intent is to identify each human protein by the coordinates of the position it takes up in a standard mapping system. The mapping system is a specialized version of the technique known as two-dimensional gel electrophoresis." As its name suggests, two-dimensional (2-D) gel electrophoresis involves the same kind of approach employed in sequencing genomes —the use of gels and electric fields to separate mixtures—but applies the technique simultaneously in two directions at right angles to each other. "The proteins extracted from a particular human tissue are separated in one dimension according to their electric charge, and in the second dimension by their molecular weight. The result is a complex map, often of more than 1000 separable spots," each of which represents a different protein.

The Andersons aimed to use computers to turn these into maps of the proteome, with each protein specified by its two-dimensional coordinates on the gel. "With a 13-person team and a budget of around $1 million from Argonne," Wade explained, "the Andersons are now able to run about 10,000 gels a year. Progress has also been made on writing computer programs whereby each spot on a two-dimensional gel map can be identified and measured. . . . The grand scheme calls not just for assignment of map coordinates to each protein spot but also for study of other properties. The Andersons have plans for measuring the quantity of each protein produced and identifying each spot. . . . Once the index is compiled, it would be made available on a computer tape or otherwise as a standard biological reference work."

The Andersons are quoted as saying, "List-based biology, which this project makes possible . . . will be a science in itself." The same could be said of the human genome project, which got going more quickly than that which explored the proteome. Another similarity between the two was the criticism leveled by the scientific establishment at the list-based, industrial approach—one that the Andersons estimated would cost around $350 million over five years. "Not everyone is enthusiastic about the project," Wade wrote. "For one thing Apollo style programs"—a reference to the Apollo moon landings—"have not been particularly successful in the biological sciences. For another, biologists might be expected to oppose any such program if it seems likely to be supported out of the part of the federal budget already earmarked for biological research"—a major concern during early discussions of the Human Genome Project, too. "Then there are doubts as to whether the two-dimensional gel technique can be standardized faster than biological variability can move to defeat it."

It was the last point, along with a failure to win the kind of funds required, that stymied this first industrial biology project. The essentially analogue nature of proteins and 2-D gels meant that the pattern of spots produced varied each time they were run. Although repositories of 2-D gels exist—for example, SWISS-2DPAGE held alongside the SWISS-PROT protein database—they never took off in the way that GenBank did.

Another problem was that the quantity of protein contained in each spot was relatively small. There was no general technique for amplifying proteins in the same way that PCR was able to produce perfect copies of DNA sequences. And even when the initial sample was abundant, it was not possible simply to increase the amount to be separated—the "loading"—since this generally resulted in smeared and merged spots. Small quantities meant that it was hard to analyze the protein at each coordinate using the standard sequencing technique: Edman degradation. This involved repeatedly chopping off an amino acid from one end of the protein and analyzing it to build up the sequence a residue at a time.

An important breakthrough was reported in a 1991 paper written by Sam Hanash and a team at University of Michigan Medical School and Michigan State University. By changing the nature of the gel, it was possible to load far more of the sample under investigation. This, in turn, meant that each spot contained more of the separated proteins. The paper described how Hanash and his team were able to determine the identity of fourteen particularly dark spots, including one spot where the Edman degradation technique could not be applied for reasons to do with the detailed chemistry of the protein. The alternative approach employed in this case was mass spectrometry, which has become the key high-throughput technology for proteomics analysis, the protein equivalent of genomics' automated sequencers.

The principal variety, devised by Michael Karas and Franz Hillenkamp, rejoices in the name of matrix-assisted laser desorption/ionisation time-of-flight mass spectrometry—which, understandably, is abbreviated to MALDI-TOF mass spectrometry. The matrix is a special material that efficiently absorbs a very short burst of high energy provided by a laser. By combining a chemical such as a protein with the matrix, some of the energy absorbed by the matrix is transferred to the chemical, causing it to vaporize (the "desorption"). At the same time, both the matrix and the chemical's molecules are ionized—that is, given a small electric charge. Applying electrostatic or magnetic fields exerts a force on the charged particles, which are accelerated to a common kinetic energy through a vacuum tube.

At the other end of the tube is a detector which records when the charged particles arrive. Some simple mathematics shows that if the kinetic energy of the particles is the same, the time of flight—the "TOF" in MALDI-TOF—is determined by the ratio of a molecule's mass to its charge (m/z). That is, for a given charge, lighter ions travel faster, and heavier ones more slowly. The resulting output from the MALDI-TOF mass spectrometer is a series of peaks in the ion flux—the flow—that represent the arrival of clumps of charged particles with particular values of m/z. Despite the very short times of flight involved, the mass accuracy of MALDI-TOF systems is surprisingly high—fractions of a percent are often claimed. As well as this accuracy, the big advantage of MALDI-TOF is that the desorption process does not cause damage to the biomolecule under study, a crucial requirement for proteomics.

The key ideas for applying MALDI-TOF mass spectrometry to proteins were set out in a paper that appeared in June 1993. The modified 2-D gel electrophoresis approach devised by Hanash and his coworkers was used to separate the proteins into separate spots that generally represent single proteins. Each spot was excised—physically cut out—and digested with an enzyme called trypsin. Conceptually, enzyme digestion of proteins is very similar to the use of restriction enzymes for digesting genomes: a particular enzyme cuts proteins at a specific amino acid, just as a restriction enzyme cuts the genome at specific DNA sequences. The result of the trypsin digestion of the unknown protein is a mixture of peptide fragments—partial sequences of amino acids that are found in the protein.

It is these peptides that are analyzed using the MALDI-TOF system. Once the mass spectrometer has been calibrated using a molecule of known mass, the mass of the peptide fragments can be read off from peaks in the ion flux output (assuming the charges are the same for each). The result—a peptide mass fingerprint—is a pattern that is usually unique to the protein that gave rise to them.

The authors of the 1993 paper explain how this peptide mass fingerprint can be used to determine the protein whose 2-D gel spot was analyzed, using a program called Fragfit. "The program scans the [protein] database, generates sequence fragments based on the specified protease"—the digestion enzyme such as trypsin—"and computes the molecular masses of the fragments." That is, Fragfit took all the proteins that were in the databases and calculated where they would be cut for the given digestion enzyme. This produced a set of peptides for each of the known proteins, whose masses could then be calculated and compared against the experimental result from the MALDI-TOF measurements. Remarkably, the researchers found, "only three to five fragments. . . . are needed to correctly identify a protein." The approach is even able to pick out proteins when two spots overlap completely, so great is the discriminatory power of the peptide mass fingerprint approach. It is worth noting, however, that it requires both the existence of sequence databases that can be used for comparison purposes and bioinformatics to carry out the searches.

Mass spectrometry soon caught the attention of the scientific mainstream. In October 1995, *Science* ran a news story entitled "From genome to proteome: looking at a cell's proteins." Discussing the growing interest in proteins alongside genes, the writer pointed out that "a gene sequence does not completely describe a protein's structure: After synthesis, proteins usually undergo 'posttranslational modifications', such as addition of phosphate groups or removal of amino acids from the ends, and these changes can alter their activities. . . . But until recently, the advantages of focusing on proteins were overwhelmed by the difficulties. That is now changing fast, with the advent of powerful new methods of mass spectrometry that vastly simplify protein analysis, even on very small samples, and enable researchers to match them to their corresponding genes in the rapidly filling sequence databases."

The story went on: "It took several more years [after mass spectrometry (MS) was developed] to bring the MS tools to the present stage, where they can begin tackling large-scale work. The crucial step—identifying proteins automatically and unambiguously—was taken by Matthias Mann at the European Molecular Biology Laboratory in Heidelberg, Germany, and independently by Ruedi Aebersold and John Yates at the University of Washington, Seattle. Success was mostly a matter of getting more precise molecular weight measurements and developing more powerful database scanning software, says Mann," emphasizing again the central role of databases and computers in protein detection.

A year later, Mann and colleagues published a paper showing how powerful combining genomics with proteomics could be. It was called "Linking genome and proteome by mass spectrometry: large-scale identification of yeast proteins from two dimensional gels," and used MALDI-TOF techniques to generate peptide mass fingerprints for proteins extracted from yeast, whose genome had been published a few months before, in October 1996. As Mann and his fellow authors wrote: "In the largest individual protein identification project to date, a total of 150 gel spots . . . were successfully analyzed, greatly enlarging a yeast two-dimensional gel data base. . . . This study establishes that mass spectrometry provides the required throughput, the certainty of identification, and the general applicability to serve as the method of choice to connect genome and proteome."

Although the "method of choice," there was still something missing. As Mann later wrote in a piece for *Nature Biotechnology*: "Despite the revolutionary impact of the mass spectrometric identification methods, proteins cannot be quantified by mass spectrometric analysis because peptide signals in the mass spectrometer are extremely variable." His analysis accompanied a paper from a team led by Ruedi Aebersold that added precisely this capability by using a technique employing isotope-coded affinity tags, or ICATs, that conceptually had something in common with Patrick Brown's cDNA arrays.

For mRNA, the use of two fluorescent markers allowed the relative gene expression in two different samples to be compared by measuring the ratio of the strength of the red and green signals at each spot. For proteins, two kinds of chemical tags were attached to the protein samples whose relative abundance was under investigation. The difference lay in the nature of eight hydrogen atoms found on the tag. For one sample, the hydrogen atoms were the normal kind, which have one proton in the nucleus, the central part of the atom. For the other, a heavier isotope of hydrogen was used, generally deuterium. Chemically, deuterium is identical to hydrogen, but it contains an extra neutron in its nucleus. This meant that the tagged protein in one sample was heavier than the other by exactly eight neutrons. Not much perhaps—around 0.00000000000000000000001 grams—but enough to show up when a mixture of the two samples was analyzed using mass spectrometry. The result was a series of double spikes in the flux readings, separated by exactly eight neutrons' mass. By taking the ratio of the height of the two peaks, it was possible to obtain the relative abundance of the two proteins, just as Brown had done with fluorescent intensities from his cDNA arrays.

Alongside these increasingly powerful experimental techniques, theoretical studies of the relationships between genome and proteome were also progressing. For example, in 1999, the same year that the ICAT method was described, several papers were published that used bioinformatics to predict functional links between proteins on the basis of genomes, in ways that moved beyond simply looking for homologies.

Reflecting the increasing maturity of the proteomics world, the penultimate issue of *Nature* before the year 2000 contained a six-page news briefing entirely devoted to the subject, as well as its main editorial. In a distant echo of *Science*'s "Genome delight" in 1992, *Nature*'s editorial was entitled "The promise of proteomics." It noted that "proteomics, if defined as the study of many proteins simultaneously in order to understand the function of one restricted state of a cell, remains in its infancy," and offered some sage observations: "The number of genes in an individual human, as in any organism, is static and fixed. Given the much larger set of proteins produced by that organism at one time or another throughout its life, the goal of identifying the whole of the human proteome is a far bigger and more complex challenge. Indeed, there is no such thing as 'the' human proteome—it will differ significantly not only between individuals (much more than their genomes), but also within one individual before and after, say, a millennium party."

The editorial also sounded a note of warning to researchers: "Cataloguing hundreds of proteins in a life-threatening parasite or an organelle, while technically impressive, is no more than frustratingly tantalizing if some understanding of their activities is not also developed. As submitted papers in proteomics grow in number, *Nature* intends to play its part by insisting on conceptual insights from among the great quantities of information that such work will certainly deliver."

As if mindful of *Nature*'s stern words, the proteomics papers that appeared in the early months of 2000 steered well clear of "cataloguing hundreds of proteins." Instead, catching up with their bioinformatics colleagues, experimental researchers turned their attention to exploring how proteins worked together as part of the cell's molecular machinery. Two studies of protein-protein interactions in yeast using the same technique were published in February 2000: one by a group in Japan, the other in the United States. As a news story accompanying the second group's work in *Nature* explained: "Yeast geneticists have a clever way of seeing whether two proteins can physically associate. They attach each of them to separate fragments of a third protein, called a transcriptional activator, which has the ability to switch on genes. If the two proteins interact, then the two fragments of the activator are reunited and a [reporter] gene is switched on that produces an easily monitored colour change in the yeast cells. Because it is two hybrid proteins that are actually interacting, this method is called the two-hybrid system." One protein is called the bait, the other the prey.

The bait and prey hybrids are produced by co-opting the cell's own machinery to carry out the delicate engineering. Extra DNA encoding either the bait or prey protein fragment is placed immediately next to a copy of the gene sequence for one particular yeast protein, and the combination introduced into a plasmid—a small, circular piece of bacterial DNA. The plasmid is inserted into the yeast cell, and when its DNA is transcribed and then translated into the corresponding protein, the DNA for the bait/prey fragment is also expressed to produce one part of the transcriptional activator. The overall result is a kind of tandem molecule consisting of a yeast protein attached to one part of the transcriptional activator, which can then be used in the experiment.

As the Japanese group wrote: "Organisms with completely sequenced genomes are quite suitable for such studies, because all of the proteins can be predicted and used for the comprehensive examination of protein-protein interactions" by inserting their respective gene sequences into plasmids to create baits and preys. Since there are around 6,000 such proteins in yeast, this means that 6,000 baits and 6,000 preys needed to be produced to test the 36 million possible interactions. These interactions were explored by mating the two sexes of yeast (called "a" and "α"), one with the bait, the other with the prey, and seeing which combinations switched on the reporter gene.

The experimental approach of Takashi Ito and his colleague was to pool protein variants, 96 bait and 96 prey at a time. Different groups of bait and prey were mixed together, and those that interacted, as indicated by the bait and prey coming together to activate the reporter gene, were grown for a week or two, and separated. After the plasmids were extracted and sequenced, the results were compared to the main databases using BLAST in order to determine which particular genes were present in the plasmids—and thus which proteins had interacted. Some 430 different pool matings were performed, which led to 3,962,880 protein-protein combinations. Although a mere ten percent of the total permutations possible, this is an extraordinary number, and is a further indication of the new scale of genomics-based biology.

In the United States, Peter Uetz and his fellow researchers used a similar pooling technique for part of their experiment, but also created an array of hybrid proteins—384 of them on 16 small plates—for the bait. A smaller set of 192 hybrid proteins were used as the prey. This meant that only 384×192 = 73,728 possible interactions were tested with arrays. However, it allowed the protein pairs to be identified more surely—since no other steps were required—and hence enabled the two methods to be compared.

The Japanese group found 183 independent reactions, while Uetz and collaborators found 692 from the pooled library and 281 from the arrays. As Uetz wrote: "Although the library approach permits a much higher throughput, the array screens generate more candidate interactors." Both teams used their results to provide some of those conceptual insights that *Nature* was demanding. For example, by linking together all the proteins that interacted in a single graphical representation it was possible to create a kind of map showing biochemical pathways within the cell.

A couple of years after these papers appeared, in January 2002, two studies were published in the same issue of *Nature* that added an extra dimension to such protein networks. Both reported on work to elucidate hundreds of protein complexes in yeast: groups of proteins that fit together physically in order to create much of the key biological machinery in a cell. Where the two-hybrid approach can only discover binary relationships—those that involve two proteins—studying protein complexes allows more of the richness in protein interactions to be captured.

The basic technique was similar to that employed for the two-hybrid experiments: DNA code containing a chemical tag joined to a bait protein was introduced into the yeast genome—directly this time, rather than via a plasmid. When the bait protein was expressed in the cell, so was the attached tag. The latter could be used to fish out the bait protein, often pulling with it other proteins attached to it. The additional proteins could then be identified using standard mass spectrometry methods, and an even more detailed map of interactions between proteins drawn up.

Two things are striking about these papers, published in the January 10, 2002 edition of *Nature*. First, proteomics had come a long way from its origins studying spots on 2-D gels: the protein complexes are situated right at the heart of cell biology. The other notable feature is that both of these studies were produced largely by researchers at proteomics companies—

Cellzome, in Heidelberg, Germany, and the Canadian MDS Proteomics—rather than in academic institutions.

The trailblazer in the area of commercial proteomics was once again the Anderson father-and-son team. When it became clear that public funding for their protein project would not be forthcoming, they set up their own company in 1985 to do it privately. Their proprietary proteomics platform came to be called ProGEx, "the culmination of 16 years of research and development that helped catalyze the entire proteomics revolution," as the later owner of that technology, Large Scale Biology Corporation (LSBC), put it. Based on 2-D gels and mass spectrometry, ProGEx was capable of analyzing one million proteins a week according to the company.

The result of these industrial proteomics capabilities was the long-awaited completion of the first version of its proprietary proteome database, the Human Protein Index, in December 2001. As the LSBC annual report for 2000 explained: "It includes information about approximately 115,000 proteins that represent all of the major tissues in the body. Based on results of protein characterization obtained in our high-throughput mass spectrometry facility, we estimate that the HPI currently covers the protein products of 18,000 human genes." The same report described one of the key elements of the company's strategy: to "become the definitive source of information about human proteins," close to the Celera's early statements that it intended "to become the definitive source of genomic and related medical information." The similarities do not end there.

First there was a shift towards drugs. In the annual report for 2001, the company's stated goal was "to develop therapeutic products using our proprietary technology and expertise in proteins." This time it was a foreshadowing of Celera, whose new mission of "the discovery and development of new therapeutic drugs" came slightly later. Then, during a major reorganization announced on June 4, 2002, the management of Large Scale Biology Corporation made various changes "to protect the timeframe and resources required to commercialize successfully its product pipeline and platform technologies." The chairman and CEO of the company characterized these actions as "critical, unavoidable and painful, all at the same time." One of the most painful was that as part of the reorganization, both Andersons resigned from the company that had been built around their life-work—just as Venter had done a few months before.

Another pioneer in the field of proteomics is Oxford GlycoSciences (OGS), founded in 1988 by Oxford University to identify and analyze a particular class of modified proteins called glycoproteins. The company first started positioning itself in the proteomics market in March 1996, when it launched its ProteoGraph "for 'genome-scale' sequence analysis of proteins," and followed this up a year later with a "proteome partnership" with Oxford University. In May 1999, OGS announced "a new dedicated Proteome data manufacturing facility" that would allow high throughput analysis of human proteins based on 2-D gels and mass spectrometry. As a result, in June 2001, it revealed that it was "building a Protein Atlas of the Human Genome that will, for the first time, use sequence information obtained directly from naturally occurring human proteins to identify unambiguously all protein-coding genes in the human genome." This was a novel reversal of the approach generally employed, whereby bioinformatics was used to locate likely genes in the recently-completed draft human genome, after which the proteins they coded for could be calculated.

The Protein Atlas would be made available on a subscription basis by Confirmant, a joint venture between OGS and the UK communications company Marconi, announced at the same time as the Atlas. According to Confirmant, apparently undaunted by Celera's experiences as an information company, its plan "is to become a leading provider of bio-information." A longer-term aim is "to be at the forefront of the development of on-line, real-time diagnostics, made available to physicians and healthcare facilities on a pay-per-use/subscription fee basis, and providing accurate, patient-specific and cost-effective disease diagnosis and therapy."

Against this background of activity, Celera Genomics emerged as something of a latecomer to the corporate field. The first hint that it might be moving into proteomics came in a *Nature* story published in February 2000: "Celera Genomics . . . is now said to be contemplating an industrial-scale Human Proteome Project, this time well ahead of any comparable public venture. The goal would be to identify the properties and functions of every protein expressed in an organism." In March 2000, *Science* provided more details of Celera's plans. There are some classic Venter quotations: "We're going to dominate in our own way. We're going to have the biggest facility and the biggest database," respectively capable of identifying up to one million proteins a day and storing 500 terabytes (500 thousand billion bytes) of data, according to *Science*. Even allowing for the handy $944 million that Celera had recently raised in a stock offering, Venter's goals were characteristically ambitious: "We'll be working through every tissue, organ, cell," he told the journal.

At least Venter hoped to get a little expert help, as both *Nature* and *Science* reported. "Celera is in advanced discussions with Denis Hochstrasser," *Nature* wrote, "one of the founders of GeneBio—the commercial arm of the Swiss Institute of Bioinformatics, which is among the world's leading protein research centres—and an authority on two-dimensional polyacrylamide gel electrophoresis (2D-PAGE) technology. The goal is to combine new technologies with the workhorse 2-D electrophoretic gel technique to develop an industrial-scale attack on the proteome."

The sticking point in the negotiations between Celera and Hochstrasser was a familiar one: "Reaching a deal now seems to hang on the question of data access," *Nature* explained. "Amos Bairoch, a co-founder of GeneBio, says that joining up with a private company will result in restrictions on data being placed in the public domain. He would prefer the Swiss groups to collaborate with a publicly funded international human proteome project, with all data being put rapidly into the public domain."

This never happened, but neither did the collaboration with Celera. Instead, Hochstrasser and Bairoch, along with several other luminaries of the protein world, formed a new company, called GeneProt, in March 2000, on a scale that was not dissimilar to Celera. For example, in October 2000 GeneProt announced that it would be spending $70 million with Compaq—Celera's original IT supplier—for a supercomputer employing 1,420 of Compaq's Alpha processors, each capable of more than a billion sequence comparisons per hour. The press release noted that the company hoped to have its first "Proteomics factory" operational by the end of March 2001, and another "factory" in the United States, established in the second half of 2001.

Also in October 2000, even before these were up and running, GeneProt signed a valuable deal with the pharmaceutical company Novartis, headquartered in Basel, Switzerland. In return for an equity investment of $43 million from Novartis, the press release explained, "GeneProt will analyze the protein profile (proteome) of three human diseased tissues or body fluids and their healthy counterparts"—the idea being that a comparison of the two would allow key changes in the proteomes for these tissues to be established and drug candidates discovered. The Novartis money doubtless came in useful for the purchase of the Compaq supercomputer, as well as the 51 MALDI-TOF machines, announced in December 2000, each of which could cost over $150,000, according to *Science*.

GeneProt proudly proclaimed the opening of the "world's first large-scale proteomic discovery and production facility" on April 26, 2001. In addition to its 51 mass spectrometers, it also boasted what GeneProt now billed as the "world's most powerful commercial supercomputer." Unfortunately, some of the company's thunder had been stolen by an announcement three weeks earlier, which, at the time, was hailed by many as the most significant proteomics project so far, a defining moment comparable to Celera's shock move three years earlier.

One factor that doubtless contributed to the impact was the hypnotic combination of big names involved: Myriad Genetics, founded by the Nobel Prize-winner Walter Gilbert as one of the first genomics companies; Oracle, which produces the leading enterprise database software package; and Hitachi, a giant Japanese electronics company with a turnover of $75 billion. Together, they launched Myriad Proteomics, "a landmark alliance to map the human proteome in less than three years," as the press release trumpeted. More specifically, the collaboration, valued at $185 million, would "analyze all proteins and their interactions within cells of the body. The alliance partners expect to collect this information in a proprietary database of all human protein interactions, all bio-chemical pathways and a comprehensive catalog of purified proteins by 2004."

Details were given of exactly how the new company hoped to achieve this ambitious plan. "Myriad will apply two complementary proteomic technolo-gies. The company will use its proprietary ProNet protein interaction tech-nology, which is an industrialized high-throughput version of the yeast two-hybrid system," similar to that employed by Ito and Uetz in their papers of February 2000. The other element was "ProSpec, a proprietary mass spec-trometric technology for the identification of protein complexes." The press release claimed that an important advantage of ProSpec was that it "is ideally suited to identify proteins in complexes even if those proteins undergo sec-ondary changes after they are expressed in the cell."

These post-translational modifications consist of various kinds of changes applied to a basic protein structure defined by the underlying digital gene sequence. Their impact on the proteome can be enormous: as one review noted, "for some proteins, in excess of 1,000 variants . . . have been described." However inconvenient it may be for experimentalists, this added layer of com-plexity helps explain the enormous discrepancy between the observed number of genes in the human genome—around 30,000—and the estimated number of proteins in the proteome—probably ten times as many, if not more.

The press release emphasized that Myriad Proteomics would "identify all human protein interactions and biochemical pathways," and "generate the full complement of expressed human proteins in a purified form." According to Oracle, as far as the total amount of data generated was concerned, "Myriad Proteomics plans on ending its first year in the five to six terabyte range"—five to six million million bytes—"possibly increasing volume as much as ten-fold each year." This data flood was partly a result of the large number of expected proteins, but was also due to the fact that there were many aspects to capture. By contrast, the human genome, for all its great size, was essentially a very long string composed from four letters that could fit on a CD-ROM.

Other researchers in the field were quick to cast doubts on the feasibility of such a gigantic scheme. Speaking to *The New York Times*, the head of Hybrigenics, a French company also mapping protein interactions, said: "There's no way they can come close to it," and added: "anybody who knows what he's talking about would not mention something like that." In fact, the same news story reported a more realistic goal for Myriad Proteomics. According to *The New York Times*, company executives said that "they are not trying to find every protein in every type of cell"—despite the fact that the press release gave precisely this impression. Instead, "the venture will con-centrate mainly on protein interactions and will look only at 10 or 12 major cell types out of the hundreds that exist in the body." This was still a major project, but manageable. The company claimed that by studying even this more limited set of interactions, "it will be possible to determine all the metabolic pathways"—how biological chemicals are processed—"in the body, which would be of interest to drug companies seeking to understand the causes of disease." These drug companies would be the principal market for Myriad Proteomics' database when completed.

Even so, some people were still unimpressed with the Myriad Proteomics project. One with a surprising viewpoint was Craig Venter. The same story in *The New York Times* quoted him as saying, "We don't think there's much value in a general survey of proteins"—a rather different position from that laid out in *Science* a year earlier, when he spoke of "working through every tissue, organ, cell." Talking to *The Wall Street Journal*, Venter was even more to the point: "There ain't no such thing as a proteome," he said. Although this may have been strictly speaking true, his comment probably had as much to do with the fact that Celera was beginning its painful transition to a drug company, and would not, therefore, be embarking on its own "general survey of proteins" as originally planned.

Somehow *The San Francisco Chronicle* managed to avoid quoting Venter in its story about Myriad Proteomics, but did have some interesting practical details about the project. "Sudhir Sahasrabudhe, Myriad's executive vice president for research, said it will cost more than $500 million to complete the protein map, which means the subsidiary [of Myriad Genetics] will seek Wall Street financing at some point," it wrote. As a result, "to justify that financing, Sahasrabudhe said Myriad Proteomics will end up filing tens of thousands of patents on protein interactions that cause disease or promote healing."

A few months later, one of Myriad Proteomics' main rivals, Oxford Glyco-Sciences, fired off its own protein patent salvo when it announced that it had filed for 4,000 of them. As *Science* pointed out on the day of the announcement, even though genomic companies like Incyte and Human Genome Sciences (HGS) had applied for patents on thousands of genes and associated proteins, it might still be possible to patent other proteins that were missed by their approach—for example, those produced by post-translational modifications. But the overall result, *Science* noted, would be "a confusing landscape of competing gene and protein patent claims, perhaps setting the scene for legal battles for control over the future of genetic medicine."

The story in *The San Francisco Chronicle* also reported that "unlike the public Human Genome Project, Myriad will not make its protein map public. Sahasrabudhe said some thought has been given to giving academic researchers a peek at the data, but free access will take a back seat to selling the information to drug companies." It was an all too familiar combination—patents and proprietary databases—that threatened to lock out academic researchers from the key information in a hot field. This time there was no public consortium—no Human Proteome Project—to save the day. However, there was HUPO: the Human Proteome Organisation.

It was not entirely coincidental that a group of leading researchers decided to announce the formation of HUPO a week before the simultaneous publication of the first human genome papers in *Nature* and *Science* in February 2001. As Sam Hanash, the first president of HUPO, explains to me: "The proteomics community has been getting together on a regular basis and the notion of an international proteomic organization was previously tossed around on numerous occasions. The sequencing of the genome . . . had a big positive impact on proteomics, in the sense that people felt that our time has come. Quickly after that HUPO came into existence."

Despite providing the spur to HUPO's formation, it was not the Human Genome Project that acted as a model. Instead, as its name proclaimed, HUPO intended to play the same role in proteomics as HUGO—the Human Genome Organisation—did for genomics. HUGO was set up in 1989, and has as its principal mission "to promote international discussion and collaboration on scientific issues and topics crucial to the progress of the world-wide human genome initiative in order that the analysis of the human genome can be achieved as rapidly and effectively as possible." Some of its most important contributions have been to the debate about patents on DNA sequences, particularly on the issue of patenting ESTs and SNPs.

In a similar vein, when HUPO was announced on February 8, 2001, the accompanying press release stated that the reason for its creation was "to assist in increasing awareness of [proteomics] across society, particularly with regard to the Human Proteome Project and to engender a broader understanding of the importance of proteomics and the opportunities it offers in the diagnosis, prognosis and therapy of disease." Although a Human Proteome Project was seen as the next logical step after the Human Genome Project, a large-scale protein project had already been suggested well before the HGP even started. Norman Anderson, the pioneer in this field, later wrote about his own efforts to create a similar public program in the United States. "In 1980, under the auspices of Senator Cranston, an attempt was made to launch the Human Protein Index Project (HPI) as a serious national objective. Nearly all supporters of the project lost in the election of that year. In 1983 some of the proponents of the HPI proposed that a dual effort involving the complete sequencing of the human genome and a parallel protein project be launched. Of these two, the Human Genome Project was the first to succeed, in part because the basic technology was widely available."

However, unlike the Human Protein Index, which eventually appeared as a proprietary product, the Human Proteome Project showed no signs of materializing. Another editorial in *Nature* a couple of months after the launch of HUPO offered some reasons why that was. Under the headline "The proteome isn't genome II," the writer commented: "HUPO will struggle to emulate its predecessor [HUGO] . . . because human proteomics is not a single project with one endpoint that lends itself to HUGO-style coordination. Traditionally, a proteome has been defined as the complete set of proteins that is produced by the genome during the lifetime of the organism. That is a lot of proteins—as many as half a million. And in biological terms, what really matters are the snapshots of proteins produced at a particular time, under particular conditions, by particular types of cells. Defined in this way, the human proteome is almost infinitely dynamic." In a word, the proteome was analogue, unlike the digital and hence finite genome. As such, it was impossible to capture through a single, coordinated project, however massive.

In June 2001, HUPO appointed Hanash as its inaugural president; until then, a "global advisory council" had been in place. "I think it was simply a question of arranging election in a formal fashion," he explains. "We should not minimize the difficulties and the logistics involved in starting something on an international level." Described as a "pioneer in cancer proteomics," Hanash said at the time of his elevation, with a certain understatement: "There is a need to develop a real focus for HUPO that does not compete with other ongoing activities but that synergizes other efforts in proteomics."

At least HUPO started with some advantages, as one of its early press releases explained: "Unlike HUGO at its inception, the HUPO council is not faced with the daunting task of capital raising so that work might commence on the Human Proteome Project. . . . Collectively, organizations represented by members of the HUPO council already have in excess of one billion dollars to start studies on the Human Proteome." HUPO's main task lay elsewhere: "Rather, much of its initial role will no doubt be linked to defining the exact nature of the task at hand."

A HUPO workshop held in October 2001 in Virginia, called "Defining the proteome agenda," went some way to doing that. It noted that "proteomics is in an exponential growth phase," mostly due to the fact that "the major undertaking of sequencing the human and other important genomes has largely been accomplished, which has opened the door for proteomics by providing a sequence-based framework for mining the human genome."

Echoing the editorial in *Nature*, participants emphasized the magnitude of the task facing them: "It is obvious that whereas the genome sequence is fairly one-dimensional and finite, the proteome is multi-dimensional, with quasi infinite dimensions stemming from the large number of cell lineages and sub-types and additionally, from the various body fluids, each with its own proteome. Moreover the proteome is dynamic and constantly changing in response to various environmental factors and other signals, thus giving rise to near-infinite dimensions of states. It was pointed out that the absence of a simple focal goal analogous to the sequencing of the human genome, and the complexity and diversity of both the technologies and the resultant proteome data, make the initiation of a single large international human proteome project much more difficult compared to the human genome project. Additionally, the need for sophisticated tools for proteome data integration is much greater than for genomic data. Consequently many participants felt that it was unrealistic to initiate a human proteome project that would exhaustively tackle all aspects of the human proteome. Instead, it would be more appropriate to begin a planning and discussion phase to identify appropriate short-term milestones and measures of success, as we prioritize the stages of the unfolding human proteome project. It was noted that the decision to launch the human genome project was made after no less than two years of discussion, which was followed by three years of pilot effort."

Three key areas were singled out at the meeting: expression proteomics, functional proteomics, and the development of a proteome knowledge base. Expression proteomics involves "the identification and quantitative analysis of all proteins encoded in the human genome and assessment of their cellular localization and their post-translational modifications." Functional proteomics revolves mostly around protein interactions, and the pathways they formed. Finally, it was recognized that "a critical issue pertaining to proteome mining efforts has to do with organizing proteome related data into a knowledge base." Indeed, "several participants [in the HUPO workshop] felt that a protein encyclopedia may well be our best shot at a unified human proteome project." As ever, the question of how to store and present information was central. Hanash comments: "The data has to come out in the public domain with as much curation as possible."

In its final recommendations, the meeting report said: "There was consensus that a proteome project should be developed that combines the elements of expression proteomics, functional proteomics and a proteome knowledge base. Technology development should be an integral component of the project. There should be open access to the data resulting from the project at a pre-competitive level with data accessible to all users"—the last of these a nod to HUGO's championing of a similar open access for genomic data.

A few months later, HUPO announced its first initiatives, which aimed to implement these recommendations. Although HUPO had been founded to increase awareness about proteomics research, it gradually became more involved in organizing projects itself. Hanash explains why: "There is a clear need for an organized effort in proteomics on an international level. The traditional funding agencies have not done so and we felt that it was an activity that HUPO should engage in."

In April 2002, *Science* gave some details its plans: "The list is a mix of technology, tools, and research. For example, HUPO's bioinformatics plan would develop community-wide standards for presenting mass spectrometry and protein-protein interaction data." Both of these were sorely needed: one of the huge strengths of digital genomic data is that they are instantly compatible—just strings of four letters. In the analogue world of proteins, things are not so simple: flux readings from mass spectrometers are not readily comparable, and protein-protein interactions need all kinds of additional annotations to make them suitable for aggregation. This project was later baptized the Proteomics Standards Initiative, and one of its broader aims is to persuade journals to require submission of the results of mass spectrometry and protein-protein interactions to public databases in standard formats, as a condition of acceptance—just as is starting to happen in the world of gene expression thanks to MIAME.

The *Science* article continued: "HUPO also wants to identify thousands of new proteins present in small amounts in blood"—later dubbed the HUPO Plasma Proteome Project (PPP)—"which would be very valuable to companies developing diagnostic tests. All the data would be freely available through public databases." Diagnostic tests promise to be one of the most important applications of proteomics. As two leading researchers said in 2003: "We expect that precise clinical diagnosis based on highly discriminating patterns of proteins in easily accessible samples, particularly body fluids, may be the area in which proteomics will make its first significant contribution."

Diagnostics is an area where proteomics offers many advantages over genomics or functional genomics. The chief scientific officer of Oxford GlycoSciences, Raj Parekh explained to *Science* in March 2000, "the genome tells you what could theoretically happen." Its digital code stores all the subroutines that are available to the cell, even though only a proportion of them will be used in a given tissue at a given time. "Messenger RNA"—the transcription of the genetic information—"tells you what might happen," he continued; things are only approximate, since the messenger RNA contains no information about crucially important post-translational modifications. These were only revealed in proteins. As Parekh put it: "The proteome tells you what is happening." The theory underlying protein-based diagnostics is that altered medical conditions produce different proteomic profiles—the particular complement of proteins in a tissue. By measuring a patient's protein profile, the medical state can be read off. An important paper that appeared in February 2002 showed how this approach might work in practice.

A group of researchers, which included Emanuel Petricoin and Lance Liotta—coauthors with Sam Hanash of the first HUPO workshop report—examined the protein expression patterns of patients with and without ovarian cancer. As they wrote: "Protein profiling might reflect the pathological state of organs and aid in the early detection of cancer." Early diagnosis was a key consideration: "Ovarian cancer presents at a late clinical stage in more than 80% of patients, and is associated with a 5-year survival of 35% in this population. By contrast, the 5-year survival for patients with stage I [early] ovarian cancer exceeds 90%, and most patients are cured of their disease by surgery alone," without the need for chemotherapy. "Therefore," they continued, "increasing the number of women diagnosed with stage I disease should have a direct effect on the mortality and economics of this cancer without the need to change surgical or chemotherapeutic approaches." Establishing characteristic protein profiles for ovarian cancer would be an effective way of doing this.

"These profiles can contain thousands of data points, necessitating sophisticated analytical tools. Bioinformatics has been used to study physiological outcomes and cluster gene microarrays, but to uncover changes in complex mass spectrum patterns of serum proteins"—those found in the clear liquid left after blood clots—"higher order analysis is required." The problem was to reduce the huge number of peaks among the 15,200 readings obtained by mass spectrometry to a usable set of markers. Each of these peaks represented a particular protein present in the serum as well as its relative abundance.

A set of all the peaks from four patients (two healthy and two already diagnosed with cancer) were used to "train" the analysis software. Standard techniques were applied to pull out from all of the peaks a manageably small set that provided good discrimination between the healthy and diseased samples. For ovarian cancer, it turned out that the optimum was to use the measurements of the protein abundance at five points, corresponding to five key proteins. It was not necessary to determine exactly which these were, since it was only the pattern that mattered. A new patient's serum profile was measured at these five points and compared with the two reference sets to establish which it most resembled.

The success of this approach—according to the paper, 63 out of 66 control samples were accurately classified as non-cancer, while all those patients known to have ovarian cancer were correctly diagnosed—bodes well for the use of protein profiles. Researchers have now started applying it to other diseases. The fact that protein profiles could in principle be applied to illnesses affecting any organ, and were noninvasive, was also a major boon. Other advantages are that diagnosis requires only a very small sample of blood—a finger prick—and that the results are available within 30 minutes.

The ovarian cancer study used a modified form of MALDI-TOF to analyze the serum proteins. Called SELDI-TOF (for "surface-enhanced laser desorption and ionization time-of-flight"), it differs from traditional MALDI-TOF by preselecting the proteins to be analyzed. This is achieved by preparing a surface that binds to only a subset of proteins found in the serum. The system is manufactured by Ciphergen, which sells it as a small array of treated spots. The sample is added to a spot, one of eight on each array, where some of the proteins bind to the surface. The other proteins are washed off, and the array is placed in a specially designed MALDI-TOF unit. Although the latter is relatively compact—about the size of a small filing cabinet—it is not something that a general physician is likely to use. If protein profiles are to become an everyday clinical tool, a doctor needs a way to measure them in the surgery, using a simple and relatively cheap technology to obtain a result immediately, rather than sending them away to a laboratory.

The most promising technology for realizing this vision is the protein chip—a device that allows hundreds or even thousands of proteins to be measured at once from a sample without the need for complex and expensive MALDI-TOF devices. Instead, the idea is to produce the protein equivalents of the gene expression arrays that have already proved so powerful; the result can be read off by a simple scanning device.

Two researchers at Harvard University, Gavin MacBeath and Stuart Schreiber, adapted for proteins the cDNA microarray developed by Patrick Brown's laboratory. Writing about their work in *Science*, in September 2000, they said: "One of the primary objectives in pursuing this approach was to make the technology easily accessible and compatible with standard instrumentation," rather than starting from scratch. This was a clearly a sensible and efficient approach, since it allowed other laboratories that had already produced cDNA microarrays to move into protein chips by building on their work.

MacBeath and Schreiber described how they placed 1,600 spots of protein per square centimeter on a chemically treated microscope slide. The treatment was necessary to ensure that the proteins were immobilized on the slide surface, but in a way that they preserved their folded shape. In fact, the approach of MacBeath and Schreiber had the advantage that the proteins "can attach to the slide in variety of orientations, permitting different sides of the protein to interact with other proteins or small molecules in solution." This was important since there is always the danger that the attachment process might diminish the ability of the protein to interact—for example, by orienting the part with the key shape towards the microscope slide.

A few months later, a team led by Brown applied his microarray technology to proteins. A key difference from the work of MacBeath and Schreiber was the use of matching kinds of proteins called antibodies and antigens. Antibodies are special proteins within the body that recognize other proteins, called antigens. Typically the antigen will be a characteristic property of some infectious agent—a virus or bacterium, for example. The body uses antibodies to recognize these antigens and to mark them for destruction by other proteins. The key thing about antibodies is their specificity: this makes them perfect for protein arrays, since there is less danger that they will bind to the wrong protein, leading to false positives—an incorrect signal that the corresponding antigen is present.

"We characterized the performance of the protein microarrays with approximately 115 antibody/antigen pairs," Brown and his colleagues wrote, "using both printed arrays of antibodies to detect antigens and printed arrays of antigens to detect antibodies." Although 115 may not sound like much, it represented a considerable advance over anything that had been done previously. Moreover, the work also broke new ground by looking at the sensitivity and reproducibility of the approach: "To assess the applicability of this method to real-world samples, we examined protein microarray detection in various concentration ranges and background conditions." This was an important factor, since protein concentrations can vary enormously in cells, unlike the more circumscribed variation of cDNA levels. The results were mixed. Only 50 percent of the antigens and 20 percent of the antibodies provided accurate measurements of their corresponding proteins below certain concentrations.

Nonetheless, it was an important first step in what was likely to be a long journey. Writing later that year about research on protein chips, *Science* noted: "Complex diagnostic arrays . . . could be years away. As Brown and others have found, working with antibodies is tough." Antibodies are large compared to the molecules used for cDNA expression arrays. "Separate [antibody] probes therefore must be placed farther apart, limiting the number that can fit into an array. And even though antibodies harbor small active sites that are more specific in their binding than those of many other proteins, they contain large protein-based supporting structures that can cross-react with proteins other than those to which they are designed to bind, confounding results." The primary difficulty, though, is finding the right antibody. The *Science* article quoted Brown as saying: "to measure a protein is a new problem every time"—a product of the analogue nature of proteins, which are essentially all different, unlike cDNAs, which are in some sense all the same: pure digital information.

The central role that antibodies play in proteomics is reflected by the fact that one of the other early HUPO initiatives is the creation of a collection of antibodies for primary proteins made by the 30,000 human genes. Such a resource will be invaluable for researchers who want to apply Brown's methods without having to go through the pain of finding the right antibodies first. Most protein chip companies have also adopted an antibody-based approach, with all the challenges that this implies. One exception is SomaLogic, founded by Larry Gold, a professor since 1970 at the University of Boulder at Colorado, to where the bioinformatics pioneer Stan Ulam retired after leaving Los Alamos.

SomaLogic dispenses with antibodies and uses aptamers instead. Aptamers are short sequences of nucleotides, typically RNA—the single-stranded cousin of DNA that performs many important roles in the cell. Although RNA is very close to DNA, its single-stranded nature means that it can fold up rather like a protein. Because aptamers have 3-D physical shapes as well as linear information, they can carry out the same role as antibodies, such as binding to a unique, specific protein. As Gold said at the beginning of 2003: "Whatever you can do with an antibody you can do with an aptamer." However, since an aptamer is made out of nucleic acids, standard cDNA techniques can be used to fix it to a chip. At a stroke this solves one of the big problems with proteins: finding a way to fix them to the chip without changing their properties.

The main challenge of using aptamers is creating the right one for a given protein. In a 1990 paper published in *Science*, however, Gold and his colleague Craig Tuerk came up with a brilliant solution to the problem. They called it

SELEX (a mercifully short version of the more daunting "systematic evolution of ligands by exponential enrichment"). Instead of trying to engineer an aptamer that fits a particular protein, the trick is to create a pool of thousands of RNAs, with random variation in parts of their sequence. This is then subjected to selection for binding to the protein in question: only those aptamers that show some tendency to fit the protein are kept. These RNA sequences are amplified and varied to produce a new pool that is subjected to the same selection, and the cycle is repeated. The end result is an aptamer targeted very precisely to the protein used for selection—just like an antibody, but without the associated problems—that can be used as part of a protein array. SomaLogic is still in the early stages of commercializing its SELEX technology, which has now developed into a variant called PhotoSELEX that strengthens the bonding between the aptamer and the protein; it also increases the initial pool to a million billion different molecules.

When or even whether protein chips will become routine parts of medical practice, and using which technology, is still not clear. In addition to diagnostic uses, though, there are others that researchers can apply immediately in their exploration of the proteome. The kind of thing that was possible now, rather than at some distant future date, was shown by a paper in *Science* at the end of 2001. A team from Michael Snyder's laboratory at Yale created an array the size of a standard microscope slide that contained some 5,800 different yeast proteins in duplicate. This made it possible to explore protein-protein interactions across almost the entire yeast proteome in a single experiment. High-throughput tools like these will be indispensable for the next, and perhaps most challenging, stage in understanding how the digital genome drives the analogue cell: systems biology.

NOTES

Interviews included in this chapter were conducted by the author in June 2003 with the following individual: S. Hanash.

1. p. 267 *a term coined in mid-1994, by Marc Wilkins,* J. Cohen, "The proteomics payoff," *Technology Review* (October 2001).

2. p. 267 *This was cumbersome, inelegant* J. Cohen, "The proteomics payoff," *Technology Review* (October 2001).

3. p. 267 *after rejecting "proteinome" and "protome,"* J. Cohen, "The proteomics payoff," *Technology Review* (October 2001).

4. p. 267 *The rapid uptake of the word* J. Cohen, "The proteomics payoff," *Technology Review* (October 2001).

5. p. 267 *A total analysis of the human genome,* N. Wade, "The complete index to man," *Science* 211 (1981): 33–35.

6. p. 268 *The proteins extracted from a particular human tissue* N. Wade, "The complete index to man," *Science* 211 (1981): 33–35.

7. p. 268 *List-based biology, which this project* N. Wade, "The complete index to man," *Science* 211 (1981): 33–35.

8. p. 270 *The program scans the [protein] database,* W.J. Henzel, et al., "Identifying proteins from two-dimensional gels by molecular mass searching of peptide fragments in protein sequence databases," *Proc. Natl. Acad. Sci. USA.* 90 (1993): 5011–5015.

9. p. 271 *a gene sequence does not completely describe* P. Kahn, "From genome to proteome: looking at a cell's proteins," *Science* 270 (1995): 369–370.

10. p. 271 *In the largest individual protein identification project* A. Shevchenko, et al., "Linking genome and proteome by mass spectrometry: large-scale identification of yeast proteins from two dimensional gels," *Proc. Natl. Acad. Sci. USA.* 93 (1996): 14440–14445.

11. p. 271 *Despite the revolutionary impact of the mass* M. Mann, "Quantitative proteomics?" *Nature Biotechnology* 17 (1999): 954–955.

12. p. 272 *proteomics, if defined as the study of many proteins* Editorial, "The promise of proteomics," *Nature* 402 (1999): 703.

13. p. 273 *Yeast geneticists have a clever way of seeing* S. Oliver, "Guilt-by-association goes global," *Nature* 403 (2000): 601–603.

14. p. 273 *Organisms with completely sequenced genomes* T. Ito, et al., "Toward a protein-protein interaction map of the budding yeast: a comprehensive system to examine two-hybrid interactions in all possible combinations between the yeast proteins," *Proc. Natl. Acad. Sci. USA.* 97 (2000): 1143–1147.

15. p. 274 *Although the library approach permits a much higher throughput,* P. Uetz, et al., "A comprehensive analysis of protein-protein interactions in *Saccharomyces cerevisae,*" *Nature* 403 (2000): 623–627.

16. p. 275 *they set up their own company in 1985 to do it privately.* M. Herper, "Proteins are back to confuse investors," *Forbes.com,* June 19, 2001.

17. p. 275 *the culmination of 16 years of research and development* Large Scale Biology Corporation Web site. Online at *http://www.lsbc.com/wt/tert.php?page_name=progex.*

18. p. 275 *the Human Protein Index, in December 2001.* "Large Scale Biology Corporation," Annual report 2000.

19. p. 275 *to protect the timeframe and resources* Large Scale Biology Corporation press release, June 4, 2002.

20. p. 275 *critical, unavoidable and painful,* Large Scale Biology Corporation press release, June 4, 2002.

21. p. 276 *for 'genome-scale' sequence analysis of proteins,* Oxford GlycoSciences press release, March 11, 1996.

22. p. 276 *proteome partnership* Oxford GlycoSciences press release, April 29, 1997.

23. p. 276 *a new dedicated Proteome data manufacturing facility* Oxford Glyco-Sciences press release, May 4, 1999

24. p. 276 *building a Protein Atlas of the Human Genome* Oxford GlycoSciences press release, June 15, 2001.

25. p. 276 *is to become a leading provider of bio-information.*   "Confirmant business model." Online at *http://www.confirmant.com/abt2.html.*

26. p. 276 *to be at the forefront of the development*   "Confirmant business model." Online at *http://www.confirmant.com/abt2.html.*

27. p. 276 *Celera Genomics . . . is now said to be*   D. Butler, "Celera in talks to launch private sector human proteome project," *Nature* 403 (2000): 815–816.

28. p. 276 *We're going to dominate in our own way.*   R.F. Service, "Can Celera do it again?" *Science* 287 (2000): 2136–2138.

29. p. 276 *We'll be working through every tissue,*   R.F. Service, "Can Celera do it again?" *Science* 287 (2000): 2136–2138.

30. p. 276 *Celera is in advanced discussions with Denis Hochstrasser,*   D. Butler, "Celera in talks to launch private sector human proteome project," *Nature* 403 (2000): 815–816.

31. p. 277 *for a supercomputer employing 1,420*   GeneProt press release, April 26, 2001.

32. p. 277 *the company hoped to have its first "Proteomics factory"*   GeneProt press release, October 2, 2000.

33. p. 277 *GeneProt will analyze the protein profile (proteome)*   GeneProt press release, October 17, 2000.

34. p. 277 *51 MALDI-TOF machines, announced in December 2000,*   GeneProt press release, December 12, 2000.

35. p. 277 *each of which could cost over $150,000,*   R.F. Service, "A proteomics upstart tries to outrun the competition," *Science* 294 (2001): 2079–2080.

36. p. 277 *world's most powerful commercial supercomputer.*   GeneProt press release, April 26, 2001.

37. p. 277 *a landmark alliance to map the human proteome*   Myriad Proteomics press release, April 4, 2001.

38. p. 277 *analyze all proteins and their interactions*   Myriad Proteomics press release, April 4, 2001.

39. p. 278 *Myriad will apply two complementary proteomic*   Myriad Proteomics press release, April 4, 2001.

40. p. 278 *for some proteins, in excess of 1,000 variants*   S.D. Patterson and R.H. Aebersold, "Proteomics: the first decade and beyond," *Nature Genetics supplement* 33 (2003): 311–323.

41. p. 278 *identify all human protein interactions*   Myriad Proteomics press release, April 4, 2001.

42. p. 278 *Myriad Proteomics plans on ending its first year*   "Oracle customer profile: Myriad Proteomics." Online at *http://www.oracle.com/customers/profiles/PROFILE7830.HTML.*

43. p. 278 *There's no way they can come close to it,*   A. Pollack, "3 companies will try to identify all human proteins," *The New York Times,* April 5, 2001.

44. p. 279 *There ain't no such thing as a proteome,*   D.P. Hamilton and A. Regalado, "In hot pursuit of the proteome," *The Wall Street Journal,* April 4, 2001.

45. p. 279 *Sudhir Sahasrabudhe, Myriad's executive vice president* T. Abate, "Oracle helps to fund protein map," *The San Francisco Chronicle*, April 5, 2001.

46. p. 279 *to justify that financing, Sahasrabudhe said* T. Abate, "Oracle helps to fund protein map," *The San Francisco Chronicle*, April 5, 2001.

47 p. 279 *when it announced that it had filed for 4,000 of them.* Oxford Glyco–Sciences press release, December 7, 2001.

48. p. 279 *a confusing landscape of competing gene and protein patent* R.F. Service, "Gene and protein patents get ready to go head to head." *Science* 294 (2001): 2082–2083.

49. p. 279 *unlike the public Human Genome Project,* T. Abate, "Oracle helps to fund protein map," *The San Francisco Chronicle*, April 5, 2001.

50. p. 280 *to promote international discussion and collaboration* "HUGO's Mission," online at *http://www.hugo-international.org/hugo/HUGO-mission-statement.htm.*

51. p. 280 *to assist in increasing awareness of [proteomics]* HUPO press release, February 8, 2001.

52. p. 280 *In 1980, under the auspices of Senator Cranston,* N.G. Anderson, "The history of proteomics." Originally online at *http://www.healthtech.com/2001/hpr/.* Available from *http://www.archive.org/.*

53. p. 280 *HUPO will struggle to emulate its predecessor* Editorial, "The proteome isn't genome II," *Nature* 410 (2001): 725.

54. p. 281 *pioneer in cancer proteomics,* HUPO press release, June 25, 2001. Online at *http://www.grg.org/HUPO.htm.*

55. p. 281 *There is a need to develop a real focus for HUPO* HUPO press release, June 25, 2001. Online at *http://www.grg.org/HUPO.htm.*

56. p. 281 *Unlike HUGO at its inception,* HUPO press release, June 25, 2001. Online at *http://www.grg.org/HUPO.htm.*

57. p. 281 *proteomics is in an exponential growth phase,* HUPO workshop meeting report. Online at *http://www.hupo.org/documents/reports_show.htm?code=reports&num=27.*

58. p. 281 *It is obvious that whereas the genome* HUPO workshop meeting report. Online at *http://www.hupo.org/documents/reports_show.htm?code=reports&num=27.*

59. p. 282 *the identification and quantitative analysis of all proteins* HUPO workshop meeting report. Online at *http://www.hupo.org/documents/reports_show.htm?code=reports&num=27.*

60. p. 282 *a critical issue pertaining to proteome mining* HUPO workshop meeting report. Online at *http://www.hupo.org/documents/reports_show.htm?code=reports&num=27.*

61. p. 282 *The list is a mix of technology, tools, and research.* J. Kaiser, "Public-private group maps out initiatives," *Science* 296 (2002): 827.

62. p. 283 *HUPO also wants to identify* J. Kaiser, "Public-private group maps out initiatives," *Science* 296 (2002): 827.

63. p. 283 *We expect that precise clinical diagnosis*   S.D. Patterson and R.H. Aebersold, "Proteomics: the first decade and beyond," *Nature Genetics supplement* 33 (2003): 311–323.

64. p. 283 *the genome tells you what could theoretically*   R.F. Service, "Can Celera do it again?" *Science* 287 (2000): 2136–2138.

65. p. 283 *Protein profiling might reflect the pathological state of organs*   E.F. Petricoin, et al., "Use of proteomic patterns in serum to identify ovarian cancer," *Lancet* 359 (2002): 572–577.

66. p. 285 *One of the primary objectives in pursuing this approach*   G. MacBeath and S. L. Schreiber, "Printing proteins as microarrays for high-throughput function determination," *Science* 289 (2000): 1760–1763.

67. p. 285 *can attach to the slide in variety of orientations,*   G. MacBeath and S.L. Schreiber, "Printing proteins as microarrays for high-throughput function determination," *Science* 289 (2000): 1760–1763.

68. p. 285 *We characterized the performance*   B.B. Haab, et al., "Protein microarrays for highly parallel detection and quantitation of specific proteins and antibodies in complex solutions," *Genome Biology* 2(2): research0004.1–0004.13

69. p. 286 *Complex diagnostic arrays . . . could be years away.*   R.F. Service, "Searching for recipes for protein chips," *Science* 294 (2001): 2080–2082.

70. p. 286 *Separate [antibody] probes*   R.F. Service, "Searching for recipes for protein chips," *Science* 294 (2001): 2080–2082.

71. p. 286 *to measure a protein is a new problem every time*   R.F. Service, "Searching for recipes for protein chips," *Science* 294 (2001): 2080–2082.

72. p. 286 *one of the other early HUPO*   J. Kaiser, "Public-private group maps out initiatives," *Science* 296 (2002): 827.

73. p. 286 *Whatever you can do with an antibody*   A. Pollack, "3-D RNA folds and molds like a key for a specialized work," *The New York Times*, January 21, 2003.

CHAPTER 13

Sum of the Parts

Progress in mapping the "interactome"—all the protein-protein interactions—in yeast and elsewhere brought with it a problem: how to store and disseminate the knowledge gained from the process. Building on the success of GenBank and its ilk, the obvious solution would be to enter the interactions in a database, and a number of these have been created—for example, DIP (the Database of Interacting Proteins) and BIND (the Biomolecular Interaction Network Database). However, as a review pointed out in 2001, "In contrast to the protein sequence databases for which a simple structure can be defined, the diverse nature of protein interactions has hindered representation." Part of the problem is that by definition, protein interactions do not occur in isolation, and capturing that in a standard way is not easy. Moreover, the authors noted, "one computationally difficult problem is the integration of data produced in various laboratories into interaction databases."

Beyond these practical problems lay a deeper issue pinpointed in an editorial that appeared in *Nature Biotechnology* in March 2003. "Sydney Brenner has commented that 'the more you annotate the genome, the more you make it opaque'." Constantly building databases of facts about genes, the proteins they code for, and the latter's interactions gives nothing but a heap of data. Ultimately it becomes self-defeating: the more you have, the less you understand. "The time is coming," the editorialist continued, "when proteomics research will have to move away from merely collating lists of proteins and mapping interactions to a more integrated approach in which proteomic data sets are interpreted in the context of many other types of biological data. . . . we will also need to embrace systems biology approaches that detect feedback loops and connections between pathways that have eluded decades of bio-chemical and genetic analysis carried out on an isolated, reductionist level."

Systems biology is both the logical outgrowth of genome sequencing, transcriptomics and proteomics, and their culmination, for it seeks to take the data they generate and integrate them into a single, unified picture. As the *Nature Biotechnology* editorial indicated, systems biology stands in contrast to the traditional reductionist approach that tries to understand isolated elements of the genome or cell without taking cognizance of the fact that they exist in wider contexts. A basic tenet is that the whole is greater than the sum of the parts, and that the currently separate genomic disciplines can be fully understood only when they are put together to form a coherent picture that relates and reflects knowledge at all levels simultaneously.

An important element of this bigger picture is the *pathway*, which represents the sequential and logical course of chemical reactions within a cell. Typically, pathways take the form of pairs of proteins linked by enzymes—a special kind of protein that speeds up a chemical reaction without being altered itself. Two of the most famous pathway diagrams are the Boehringer Mannheim Pathways Wallcharts. As their home page notes: "These wall-charts, as edited by retired Boehringer Mannheim researcher Dr. Gerhard Michal, have a long tradition of prominence on the walls of life science lab-oratories." The Boehringer Mannheim Pathways Wallcharts take the form of complicated biological circuit diagrams indicating how chemicals are related and changed within the cell by chemical processes. Although there is a digi-tized version available online, complete with keyword searches, the pathways are inherently hand-crafted, and represent the collective knowledge built up and published over the years by thousands of researchers.

Such a pathway, however useful it may be, is not systems biology, which requires a much more integrated approach linking genes with proteins and their interactions. A first step in this direction is provided by the WIT—short for the gnomic "What Is There"—database. As a paper by the creators of the WIT system explained: "Using the WIT genome analysis system, a major part of the central metabolism of an organism"—the way in which chemicals such as nutrients are processed by cells—"can be reconstructed entirely *in silico*."

The analysis consists of taking the genome of an organism and finding potential genes within it using bioinformatics. These regions are then com-pared by the FASTA program against a database of known genes from other organisms that have been assigned metabolic functions. That is, they play some role in the processing of chemicals within a cell. From the hits of this search, it is possible to assign likely functions to the coding regions of the genome under investigation. These can then be assembled into pathways that can accommodate the proteins and their assigned functions by choosing templates from another database, put together by hand, called the Metabolic Pathway Collection. What is interesting here is that just as novel proteins are assigned a function by comparing them to other, known proteins, so the metabolic pathway of a genome can be drawn up by comparing the interacting proteins with those of a pathway that has already been studied.

A similar approach is adopted by the BioCyc Knowledge Library, a database of metabolic pathways. At its heart lie two manually-curated databases, EcoCyc and MetaCyc. EcoCyc was created by Peter Karp, working at SRI International, an independent research outfit founded in 1946 as the Stanford Research Institute. Karp later wrote: "The EcoCyc project began in 1992 with the goals of integrating within a single DB [database] the then incomplete genome map of *E. coli*, with detailed descriptions of the enzymes and pathways of *E. coli* metabolism." Where EcoCyc concentrates on *E. coli*, MetaCyc contains pathways from over 150 organisms. A program called PathoLogic can use EcoCyc and MetaCyc to predict further metabolic pathways. The BioCyc site explains: "The input required by PathoLogic is an annotated genome for the organism, such as in the form of a Genbank entry. The output produced by PathoLogic is a new pathway/genome database for the organism." There are over a dozen of these genome-derived pathway databases, including HumanCyc, "the first available curated database of human metabolic pathways," according to SRI, released in 2003.

The other major pathway database is KEGG: the Kyoto Encyclopedia of Genes and Genomes. Created in 1995 by Minoru Kanehisa, who had worked on GenBank at Los Alamos, it consists of a wide range of integrated databases, including pathways, genes, and proteins. As a paper by Kanehisa and his colleagues points out, KEGG is unusual in that it "computerizes such data and knowledge not as text information to be read by humans but as graph information to be manipulated by machines," where a graph is a set of points and lines joining them. The reason KEGG adopts this somewhat abstract approach is that it addresses one of the fundamental problems with pathways: how to cast them in a form that can be searched and manipulated by computers in a way analogous to that employed with such success for DNA sequences.

Pathway databases such as WIT, BioCyc, and KEGG concentrate on metabolic pathways, which have been more intensively studied and are better characterized than other kinds—for example, signaling pathways, which convey information around the cell. With typical boldness, Sydney Brenner decided that it would be in precisely this area that the Molecular Sciences Institute (MSI), a not-for-profit research organization he founded in 1996, would be working.

The MSI's Web site explains: "We believe that the key challenge for biological sciences ... will be to accumulate, organize, and rigorously analyze and evaluate the complex data that will result from the current genome sequencing endeavors. To meet this challenge, we will develop technologies to accumulate higher-value types of data than those coming from conventional genomics; generate intellectual, mathematical, and computational frameworks to aid our thinking about complex biological processes; and synthesize data and frameworks to allow us to make testable predictions about the behaviors of living systems. The goal of the Institute is to weave the scientific disciplines of physics, engineering, computer science, and mathematics as integral components with biology, genetics and chemistry in this new 'Post-Genomic' biological paradigm." Specifically, "the flagship activity . . . is the Alpha Project. The focus . . . is to examine extra- to intra-cellular information flow and processing (how cells receive, amplify, and integrate signals from a variety of stimuli)" for a key signaling pathway in yeast.

Brenner's five-year project is characteristically ambitious, as is one conceived by Alfred Gilman, a fellow Nobel laureate. Gilman shared with Martin Rodbell the 1994 Nobel Prize in physiology or medicine for their work on the role played by a special class of molecules called G-proteins in passing signals into and out of cells. As the press release accompanying the announcement explained: "It has been known for some time that cells communicate with each other by means of hormones and other signal substances, which are released from glands, nerves and other tissues. It is only recently that we have begun to understand how the cell handles this information from the outside and converts it into relevant action—i.e. how signals are transduced in cells. . . . Gilman and Rodbell found that G-proteins act as signal transducers"—mediating between outside and inside the cell—"which transmit and modulate signals in cells. They receive multiple signals from the exterior, integrate them and thus control fundamental life processes in the cells."

Gilman's background helps to explain *Nature's* news story in November 1999 that he was "seeking funds for a multi-laboratory, multidisciplinary initiative to map how molecules in a cell interact with each other in response to internal and external signals." As he told the journal: "The research community is doing a good job of describing signaling molecules and seeing how they interact, but we now need to put [the data] together in a large collaboration so that we can address the big question of how they all work together as a system." The money came through in the form of a "Glue Grant" from the National Institute of General Medical Sciences (NIGMS), part of the U.S. National Institutes of Health, in September 2000. The press release announcing the money explained the name: "In an effort to 'glue' together large groups of scientists pursuing some of the biggest unsolved problems in biomedicine today, the National Institute of General Medical Sciences has provided $5 million for the first of five years to a consortium of basic scientists called the Alliance for Cellular Signaling (AfCS). NIGMS anticipates spending a projected total of $25 million on the project over the course of five years."

Because the Alliance would initially consist of some 50 scientists spread around 20 different academic institutions throughout the United States, coordination was an important issue. "The communications 'glue' for the consortium," the press release noted, "will be a sophisticated virtual conferencing system that can be operated using 'Internet2,' a new university-based version of the Internet." Just as the basic Internet was of fundamental importance for the success of the Human Genome Project—which would have been unthinkable without it—so more advanced Net technologies that will allow video conferencing and rapid data sharing are being built into the Alliance's plans from the start. A later article describing the Alliance put it this way: "The AfCS does not function without the Internet."

Gilman and his team seem to have learned another key lesson from the enormous achievements of the HGP: "Alliance scientists working in the specially designed core laboratories have pledged to forgo two of the most coveted products of the biomedical science endeavor: intellectual property rights and first rights in peer-reviewed journals, the respected anthology of scientific progress. Instead, all of the data produced in the core laboratories will be deposited immediately into the publicly accessible database"—the Bermuda Principles, applied now to the world of signaling.

In December 2002, *Nature* announced that in conjunction with the Alliance it was launching the Signaling Gateway, "an online resource that will combine news and reviews with scientific databases." The gateway pages provided more details: "At the heart of this collaboration is the Molecule Pages, a relational database of all significant published qualitative and quantitative information on signaling proteins. Although the emphasis is on mouse, a wide range of orthologs"—proteins in other species derived from a common ancestor—"will be covered. This database will also allow entirely new insights to be gleaned through intelligent data mining: the Molecule Pages database was developed with the specific aim of allowing interactions, and indeed whole pathways, to be modelled. Our goal is to filter the data to present only validated information. Thus, invited experts will enter much of the data and every Molecule Page will be comprehensively reviewed by *Nature*. We regard a Molecule Page as a new fully-fledged form of publication."

The last point was important. Since Molecule Pages would require both expertise and effort yet brought no financial remuneration, there needed to be some other incentive for scientists to spend time compiling and revising them. The common currency in these circumstances is peer esteem. As *Nature* reported: "Gilman says it is essential that the effort be recognized by faculty committees and granting bodies, in much the same way that they consider the value of authoring a widely cited review article." Once again, the new kinds of knowledge being generated as a result of genomics—in this case, pathway information about proteins—meant that leading journals like *Nature* acknowledged they needed to take on new roles to accommodate this "new fully-fledged form of publication" as the Signaling Gateway put it.

Two technologies that are likely to play an important part in the AfCS project are gene expression profiles and protein-protein interactions. A paper that appeared just a few weeks before the Signaling Gateway announcement in *Nature* gave a hint of some of the computational techniques that can be brought to bear on this kind of experimental data in order to tease out the pathways that give rise to them. The group of researchers, all at Harvard Medical School, asked: "How can one bridge the gap from [gene expression] transcript abundances and protein-protein interaction data to pathway models? Clustering expression data into groups of genes that share profiles is a proven method for grouping functionally related genes"—a technique known as "guilt by association"—"but does not order pathway components according to physical or regulatory relationships." Clustering genes—for example, using Eisen's hierarchical approach—according to their expression profiles indicates which genes have most in common in terms of when or how they are expressed; it says nothing about the causal relationships—which gene affects which other. It was precisely this area that the Harvard group aimed to address, combining protein interactions with the gene expression data to create signal transduction pathways.

These networks transmit information from the cell's membrane down to the nucleus, where various genes are activated by DNA-binding proteins in response to the external stimulus. The protein-protein interactions can be combined quite readily into complex, interconnected networks, but they include many possible routes through this map, only some of which correspond to signaling pathways actually encountered in cells. "Our program, NetSearch," the Harvard group explained, "draws all possible linear paths of a specified length through the interaction map starting at any membrane protein and ending on any DNA-binding protein." NetSearch imposes a number of constraints on the paths through the protein network: they must begin at the membrane (where the external signal originates) and finish at a protein that interacts with the DNA in the nucleus (where the effect of the signal is manifest). Moreover, it only looks for pathways of a specified length.

For paths of up to length eight, searching through the network created from the published literature on yeast's protein-protein interactions produced 4.4 million candidate pathways that began at a membrane protein and ended on a protein that binds to DNA. Since all of these were consistent with the protein interactions, by themselves they provided very little useful information. The Harvard team then went on to whittle down this number using the gene expression profiles. "Microarray expression data is . . . used to rank all paths according to the degree of similarity in the expression profiles of pathway members." The idea is that proteins that form part of an actual rather than possible pathway must exist simultaneously for the latter to function, so the expression profiles of their corresponding genes will in general be coordinated. "Linear pathways that have common starting points and end-points and the highest ranks"—as measured by the similarity of the gene expression profiles—"are then combined into the final model of the branched networks." Various starting and finishing proteins were used to produce particular kinds of signaling networks, many of whose details were already known. The results were encouraging: the predicted pathways were generally highly consistent with the known roles of the proteins included.

Gene expression profiles were used by the Harvard group as a way of establishing which proteins are expressed together and were therefore likely to form part of the same signaling pathway. There is another kind of linkage, however, that is even more deeply connected with expression profiles: the regulatory networks formed by genes and the proteins that control them, generally known as *transcription factors*. These proteins bind to special sequences of the genome, called regulatory binding sites, near the gene whose expression they modify. Since transcription factors are proteins, they are produced by genes, which are themselves regulated by transcription factors.

Given the central importance of transcription factors for gene expression—and thus proteins, their interactions, and the pathways they form—it is perhaps not surprising that a database devoted to them was created as far back as 1988. Called TRANSFAC, it consists of data on eukaryotic transcription factors, their target genes, and the regulatory binding sites. Yet it was not until 2000 that analysis of regulatory networks really took off, thanks to a key experimental breakthrough.

In principle, gene expression profiles can be used to explore the effect of knocking out particular genes. If a gene coding for a key regulator is disabled, the effects on the overall gene expression are likely to be dramatic, since the absence of that transcription factor may be felt at several locations along the genome. A paper published in *Science* in December 2000 involving researchers from Stanford University (as well as The Institute of Genomic Research's head, Claire Fraser) reported on this kind of traditional approach. The team produced a mutant strain of the bacterium *Caulobacter crescentus*—which had been sequenced by TIGR—that was defective in a key regulator called *CtrA*. The use of cDNA arrays showed that as a result of this missing transcription factor, 84 other genes had decreased expression levels, while 60 genes showed increases.

Although this implied a clear correlation between the regulator and these genes, it did not reveal the explicit relationship. It might be, for example, that a gene's expression went down because the loss of *CtrA* shut off another gene producing a transcription factor for the first gene. As the authors of the paper put it: "We found that the master regulator *CtrA* directly or indirectly controls at least 26 percent of cell cycle-regulated genes." What was needed was a way of observing precisely to which sites the various transcription factors bound, and hence which genes they controlled directly.

One approach was published precisely one week later, in another *Science* paper, from a group at the Whitehead Institute, led by Richard Young. For once, Eric Lander did not form part of the team, but the Whitehead publicity machine was in play as usual. As the press release accompanying the *Science* article explained: "Researchers at the Whitehead Institute have invented a powerful new microarray technique that can decipher the function of master switches in a cell by identifying the circuit, or the set of genes, they control across the entire genome. The researchers show that the technique can correctly identify the circuits controlled by two known master switches in yeast. In addition, the technique allows researchers to unravel in a week what takes years to achieve by conventional methods."

The breakthrough was conceptually simple, but ingenious in execution. In order to establish exactly which genes a given transcription factor acted on, it was fixed, chemically, to its binding sites around the genome. The DNA—of yeast in the Whitehead team's experiment—was then broken into small fragments using high-frequency sound waves. Some of these fragments contained the binding site, to which was still attached the transcription factor. Antibodies specific to that protein were used to pick out those fragments. The protein was then removed, leaving the short DNA sequences that contained the binding site. These were amplified and labeled with the usual fluorescent dye. A reference sample was produced in the same way, except that no particular protein was fished out using an antibody. This meant that it consisted of a mixture of all of the different binding sites. This mixture was amplified and labeled with another colored dye.

The two labeled samples were then added together and hybridized to a single cDNA array. This was slightly different from the usual arrays that Brown and his team had pioneered. Where the latter had consisted of all of yeast's genes as single-stranded DNA, for the Whitehead experiment the array was spotted with all the DNA sequences between the genes. This was where the binding sites lay, and so the relative intensity of the two fluorescent dyes indicated which intergenic regions had been bound to by a particular protein—often more than one site was involved. Searching the complete yeast genome for the sequences of these intergenic regions allowed the nearest gene to be located, which was therefore the one regulated by the particular transcription factor that had been fished out by the corresponding antibody.

By a quirk of fate, the Whitehead's frequent rival, the group at Stanford led by Patrick Brown, had devised exactly the same technique contemporaneously. Their paper was published in *Nature* a month after the Whitehead one in *Science*. Frustratingly, perhaps, for Brown and his colleagues, they had submitted their paper first, on August 30, 2000, but it had only been accepted on December 1. The Whitehead group had submitted their paper on the

September 18, but had been accepted on November 16. On this occasion, *Science* seems to have bested *Nature*.

The *Science* paper also had the better closing summary: "Expression analysis with DNA microarrays allows investigators to identify changes in mRNA levels in living cells, but the inability to distinguish direct from indirect effects limits the interpretation of the data in terms of the genes that are controlled by specific regulatory factors. Genome-wide location analysis"—of the kind devised by both the Whitehead and Stanford teams—"provides information on the binding sites at which proteins reside through the genome under various conditions in vivo [in living cells], and will prove to be a powerful tool for further discovery of global regulatory networks."

The Whitehead team, led once more by Richard Young, followed up this technical advance with an impressive practical application of it. The particular object of study was the cell cycle of yeast. As Young and his team pointed out: "A fundamental question associated with any biological phenomenon is 'how are the regulators regulated?' Most of the key cell cycle regulators . . . are themselves expressed in a cell-cycle dependent fashion, so it is important to understand how their expression is regulated." The Whitehead team were proposing to study how the various transcription factors regulated each other during the different phases of the yeast cell's development.

Applying the technique developed by the Stanford and Whitehead teams to nine transcription factors that had been identified in earlier work as involved in cell cycle changes, it was possible to elucidate the underlying pattern of this intertwined regulatory network. The result was something of a surprise: "Cell cycle transcriptional regulators that function during one stage of the cell cycle regulate the transcriptional regulators that function during the next stage, and this serial regulation of transcriptional regulators forms a complete regulatory circuit," Young and his coauthors wrote. "Thus, the transcriptional regulatory network that controls the cell cycle is itself a cycle of regulators regulating regulators." Despite the rather confusing formulation, the idea is straightforward enough. For each phase of the cell, various transcription factors are active, attaching to binding sites for various genes. Some of these genes produce more transcription factors for the next phase of the cycle: these attach to the binding sites for genes that are involved in this next phase, including some for transcription factors for the succeeding phase, and so on.

Young and his colleagues concluded their paper meditating on this point. "Understanding how biological processes are regulated on a genomic scale," they wrote, "is a fundamental problem for the coming decades. Maps of metabolic pathways have been key to studying basic biology, uncovering disease mechanisms, and discovering new drugs over the last century. Maps of genome regulatory networks will almost certainly play an equally important role in future biological discovery." Creating that map for yeast was the obvious next move for the Whitehead team, and the results of their efforts were revealed in a paper in *Science* that followed a year later, in October 2002. The overall effect of the three publications is a kind of intellectual crescendo: a series of results, each of which built upon and extended those of its predecessors—science at its best.

Young's group studied the 141 transcription factors that were known for yeast. Of these, 106 proved amenable to the genome-wide location analysis approach developed previously: for various reasons it was not possible to obtain results for the others. Nearly 4,000 reactions between these regulators and corresponding binding sites on the yeast genome were observed, involving about 2,300 genes, or 37 percent of the yeast genome. Particularly striking was the diversity of the relationship between the transcription factor and a gene's promoter region, where the binding sites are located. For example, more than a third of the promoter regions found were bound by two or more regulators. Roughly 100 regions had four regulators, while some had more than 10. Similarly, the number of promoter regions that a particular transcription factor could bind to also varied widely. One super-factor bound to no less than 181 different promoter regions, so expressing this particular protein would have massive ripple effects.

The Whitehead group used this information about which transcription factors bound to which genes to examine regulatory structures—what they called network motifs. For example, the auto regulation motif consisted of a transcription factor that binds to the promoter region of its own gene. This creates a feedback loop: if the factor causes the gene expression to increase, more of the protein is produced which increases the gene expression yet further (positive feedback). Using these network motifs, Young and David Gifford, the bioinformatics expert on the team, pieced together the overall gene regulatory network, drawing on gene expression data to provide clues about the way in which the transcription factors worked together, just as the Harvard group had done.

The Whitehead press release that accompanied the publication of the paper underlined an important aspect of this work. Previously, around 300 researcher-years were needed to find just some of the binding sites of a single transcription factor; the approach adopted by Young, and his team cut that down to a researcher-week—tens of thousands of times faster. "Without this increase in productivity," he said, "we just wouldn't be able to create a comprehensive view of how the genes in the cell are controlled." The press release also revealed that Young's group had already moved on to the next level, studying the regulatory network for the human genome, drawing on the finished sequence data as it became available. This was an ambitious undertaking, since there are around 1,700 transcription factors involved, against the 140 found in yeast. Like the earlier investigations, this work tackled how genes within the cell are regulated: it did not address directly how that regulatory network is integrated with the extensive metabolic or signaling pathways formed by the other genes' proteins. A full understanding of the cell at a molecular level will require a systems biology approach that combines these different kinds of pathway together, melding genome with transcriptome and proteome.

It would be hard to think of an individual better qualified to attempt this grand unification of biology than Leroy Hood. He began talking about systems biology back in the late 1980s. "It was a real voice in the wilderness," he tells me, "because there weren't all the things that we have today that make it possible to really do it effectively." His early scientific career, discussed in Chapter 3, can be seen in retrospect as a carefully-planned series of steps to create the high-throughput tools he would need for an integrated systems biology approach. As well as the tools, Hood says that three other things "really made systems biology a reality." The first, naturally, was the availability of the full genomes of key organisms. The second, more surprisingly, perhaps, was the Internet: "It gave us a tool for dealing with all this information, making it available to everybody," Hood explains, "and that was really key—its role can't be underestimated." The last was the idea that "biology is an informational science."

As all the pieces began to fall into place, Hood set about creating an academic environment where he could begin to implement his plans for systems biology. In 1992, after more than a decade and a half as professor of biology at Caltech, Hood moved to the University of Washington School of Medicine to set up a new department. Its title—"Department of molecular biotechnology"—was indicative of the new world Hood's work inhabited, as was the main source of funding: Microsoft's Bill Gates. During his earlier work at Caltech, Hood brought into his lab computer scientists, chemists, and engineers—as well as biologists—to address the challenges he encountered as he worked on his DNA sequencer. One benefit to flow from this experience was to make him realize "the critical importance of cross-disciplinary biology to the future of systems biology," he says. Now, in his new department, it became one of the guiding principles. The approach seemed to work, as he later noted: "By 1995 or so, we had filled all the space we had been allocated. The department was enormously successful. We had terrific people. We had great funding."

To capitalize on this success, Hood's group needed more space. "In 1996, I went to the President of the University of Washington . . . with a proposal to raise money for a new building to house our rapidly growing (and space-limited) department with the intent of creating a new thrust in systems biology. I was told that there were ten approved buildings in front of mine and that the process could take ten years." Hood was hardly someone prepared to wait ten years. So despite the "terrific people" and "great funding," and after "much agonizing," he resigned from his post at the University of Washington in December 1999 to start again with his own Institute of Systems Biology (ISB), an independent organization. As *Nature* explained: "An initial $5 million came from an anonymous donor, and in July the drugs giant Merck & Co.

provided a matching sum." Other companies made donations in kind: "The agribiotech firm Monsanto, for instance, has let Hood keep the 30 automated DNA sequencers he used when leading the team that in April completed a draft of the rice genome." Hood soon put these and other tools to good use, and barely a year after founding ISB had produced his first systems biology paper, which was published in *Science* in May 2001.

The opening paragraph offers as good an introduction to the rationale behind systems biology as could be desired: "For organisms with fully sequenced genomes, DNA arrays are an extremely powerful technology for measuring the mRNA expression responses of practically every gene. Technologies for globally and quantitatively measuring protein expression are also becoming feasible and developments such as the two-hybrid system are enabling construction of a map of interactions among proteins. Although such large-scale data have proven invaluable for distinguishing cell types and biological states"—for example, different kinds of tumors—"new approaches are needed which, by integrating these diverse data types and assimilating them into biological models, can predict cellular behaviors that can be tested experimentally." Hood and his team then went on to propose such a strategy, based on the idea of pathways.

There were four basic steps. First, define all of the genes in the genome, and the subset of genes, proteins, and other small molecules involved in the pathway of interest. Second, perturb each element of the pathway through a series of manipulations; these might be genetic—for example, deleting genes—or environmental (changing the growth conditions or temperature). For each perturbation, it was necessary to detect and quantify the corresponding response of the cell in terms of changes to its mRNA and protein profiles. For the latter, the use of the ICAT (isotope-coded affinity tags) technology, developed by Ruedi Aebersold, cofounder of the ISB, and one of the coauthors of the *Science* systems biology paper, was crucial.

The third step was to compare the observed responses to the perturbations with the current, pathway-specific model, and with all the other known protein-protein and protein-DNA interactions. Even though the focus was on a particular pathway, it was important to ensure that the model included links out to the wider pathways and that the model was consistent with existing data about transcription factors and their binding sites, for example. The final step was to formulate new hypotheses to explain observations not predicted by the model, and then to repeat the whole process using additional experiments suggested by these hypotheses.

As this makes clear, at the heart of the systems biology technique lies the idea of making perturbations. But as Hood points out, "The big insight wasn't the perturbations themselves, because if you think about hypothesis-driven biology"—the traditional kind—"it's been doing that for 30 years," by taking a system, making changes and comparing the results with those predicted by theory. "I think the new insight was you could do the perturbations and not measure one or two genes, or one or two proteins, but you could measure tens of thousands of behaviors. It was that global analysis after perturbation that really is the essence of systems biology." This new scale is also the essence of genomics. The key technical advances in the field—automated DNA sequencing, high-density gene expression arrays, mass spectrometry, pooled two-hybrid studies, protein chips—were all ones of throughput. They provided ways of gathering vastly more information, not new kinds of information. And they all depended on bioinformatics to sift through these data mountains.

To test this global approach for pathways, Hood and his team chose one that was well-characterized: the galactose utilization (GAL) metabolic pathway in yeast, which breaks down a sugar, galactose. Hood's work explored the way in which chemicals such as the sugars galactose and glucose controlled metabolism through nine GAL genes producing proteins that played key roles in the GAL pathway. This indicates the difference from Young's work on regulatory networks, which concentrated on the interwoven relationships between the transcription factors and the genes they regulated. The GAL gene pathway was perturbed genetically by deleting the genes involved one at a time, and environmentally by growing each of these variants in the presence or absence of galactose. Standard cDNA microarray techniques were used to study the effects of these changes throughout the yeast genome, as revealed by changes in mRNA transcription levels. The end result was that the changes in mRNA expression predicted by the initial model were in "good agreement" with the observations, Hood and his team wrote. Nonetheless, "a number of observations were not predicted by the model . . . in many cases, these suggest new regulatory phenomena that may be tested by hypothesis-driven approaches." As Hood says, "The big question was, could we use systems approaches to discover completely new things? The resounding answer was, we could."

Although an indubitable success, the first systems biology paper has a certain exploratory feel as Hood and his collaborators try out their approaches for a fairly straightforward and well-understood system. The next paper, published less than a year later, is already considerably more ambitious, and attempts to delineate part of the genomic regulatory network during development, making it similar to Young's work at the Whitehead Institute.

Whereas the first paper chose a familiar model organism, the second opts for an unusual one: the sea urchin. As Hood and colleagues had explained in a review of systems biology written in 2001: "The sea urchin is a powerful model for studying . . . regulation because its development is relatively simple (the embryo has only 12 different cell types); enormous numbers of eggs can be obtained in a single summer (30 billion); the eggs can be fertilized synchronously [in step with each other] and development stopped at any stage; and many transcription factors can be readily isolated and characterized." Another big bonus was that one particular gene involved in development, *endo16*, had already been studied extensively, using techniques that were very

similar to those employed by Hood. The *endo16* gene has 34 binding sites—
known as *cis-regulatory* elements—spread alongside it across a promoter region
about 2,300 bases long, together with 13 transcription factors that bind to
them. Work by Chiou-Hwa Yuh, Hamid Bolouri, and Eric Davidson discovered that the binding sites fall into seven distinct regions of DNA.

The DNA sequence of the first of these in particular possesses remarkable
properties, specifying "what is essentially a hard-wired, analog computational
device," as the authors of the original *endo16* paper put it, one built using
binding sites to create a logic unit. "The requirement for this logic device is
that there are many different inputs to the regulatory system"—in the form
of various combinations of transcription factors binding to their particular
regions —"that must be sorted appropriately. It is to us a remarkable thought
that every developmentally active gene in the organism may be equipped with
devices of this nature."

Through an explicit reconstruction of the set of logical rules governing the
transcription of the *endo16* gene, Davidson and his team had shown that
the regulation is completely specified by the pattern of binding sites and
their associated transcription factors. Since the latter are either attached or
detached, each binding site is like a switch with two states, on or off, according to whether the transcription factor is attached or not. If each binding site
has just two states, this means that the overall effect of all the sites together
is a complex logical switch with several digital inputs (the presence or absence
of transcriptional factors) and a single digital output—whether the *endo16*
gene is transcribed or not. As Hood emphasized in an article called "The digital code of DNA," published in *Nature* in 2003: "The regulatory networks
are uniquely specified by their DNA-binding sites and, accordingly, are basically digital in nature."

Hood's ambitious plan was to build on the *endo16* work and to extend it to
include many more genes and their cis-regulatory elements, in a collaboration with Yuh, Bolouri, Davidson, and others. As they wrote in the second
Science systems biology paper: "A complete cis-regulatory network model
would portray both the overall intergenic architecture"—the binding sites
located between the genes—"of the network and the information processing
functions of each node"—how the binding sites worked together to create
more of those analogue computational devices—"at the level of detail achieved
for the *endo16* cis-regulatory system. . . . The primary necessity is to discover
the logic map of the intergenic regulatory interactions, and to represent this
map as a first-stage regulatory model."

The paper reported on their work in drawing up that map using the same
systems biology approach employed for the GAL metabolic pathway. The
authors noted that the number of genes involved in their study was around
50—"only a tiny fraction of the total being expressed in the embryo, which is
estimated at about 8500." Despite this, the work involved was considerably
greater than that for yeast, and required new tools, notably in the bioinfor-

matics sphere. The work on *endo16* had shown that it was vital to have detailed knowledge about the intergenic cis-regulatory elements. As Hood and his team noted, though, "the task of finding these elements on the scale of the [gene regulation] network required an approach different from the traditional methods, which boil down to searching experimentally over all the genomic DNA surrounding a gene of interest. . . . To solve this problem, we turned to computational interspecific sequence analysis"—comparative genomics.

Bacterial artificial chromosome clones (BACs) containing all the genes of interest in a more or less central position (so that there was the intergenic DNA on both sides) were created for two sea urchin species: the main one under study (*Strongylocentrotus purpuratus*) and another (called *Lytechinus variegatus*). The last common ancestor of these species lived about 50 million years ago, so their genomes were at just the right degree of evolutionary divergence: close enough that important stretches like cis-regulatory sequences would be conserved, but distant enough that other, nonfunctional DNA would have changed to some extent. This meant that a computational comparison of the intergenic DNA for the two species—using a program aptly called FamilyRelations—allowed short patches of conserved sequence to be located, and with them, the cis-regulatory elements.

The fruit of all the perturbations, bioinformatics, and modeling was a network representing the way in which the regulatory elements are connected during the different developmental phases of the sea urchin. The result was a diagram of eerie beauty—and daunting complexity, even though it showed the interactions of just "a tiny fraction" of the total involved in the developmental process. It is undoubtedly an extraordinary achievement and a fitting culmination of Hood's decades of work across the entire spectrum of genomics. Within its success, however, lies also the seed of something strangely close to defeat. As Hood's approach is applied to more genes, to produce an even more intertwined network, there will clearly come a point when the resulting complexity exceeds the ability of the human mind to comprehend it in its totality.

Peter Karp, the creator of the EcoCyc pathway database, had already foreseen this situation back in 2001. Writing in *Science*, he commented: "The *E. coli* metabolic network . . . involves 791 chemical compounds organized into 744 enzyme-catalyzed biochemical reactions. On average, each compound is involved in 2.1 reactions. I posit that the majority of scientists cannot grasp every intricate detail of this complex network." In addition, he posed a question: "What happens when a scientific theory is too large to be grasped by a single mind?" Karp's suggestion is to use Artificial Intelligence, specifically the subfield of knowledge representation, which is concerned with "devising symbolic encodings of complex collections of information in a manner that supports inference (reasoning) processes across that information." Assuming that it might be possible to apply this technique to the kind of knowledge that Hood and others are generating, it raises questions: even if such symbolic encodings, stored in computers, are useful, do they represent an understanding of the cellular processes they describe? Or are scientists doomed to become so dependent on computer-aided exploration that they simply give up all hope of attaining any kind of detailed, global knowledge?

If it is, in fact, impossible to know exactly in this deep sense how a cell works, an alternative approach is to develop computer-based simulations of biological processes. Assuming these become more accurate in terms of their outputs, the fact that their underlying equations may not represent how a cell "really" works would be a moot point if that reality can, in any case, only be grasped through the medium of computer-based databases. Philosophical issues aside, genome-based computational modeling is becoming an increasingly important way of approaching systems biology.

Some tools, like the freely available Gepasi (GEneral PAthway SImulator), convert metabolic pathways into mathematical equations that represent the details of the chemical reactions that drive them, and then solve these using standard computational techniques. Alongside Gepasi, which is currently evolving into a new package called Copasi (COmplex PAthway SImulator), there are several others based on pathways, including Jarnac, "an interactive metabolic systems language," DBSolve, "a mathematical simulation workbench," and Cellerator, which is designed to generate computational models of signaling pathways. One of the most fruitful areas for applying computational modeling, however, has been that of regulatory networks. One reason for this was noted in a paper published in *Science* in 1995 by Harley McAdams and Lucy Shapiro. "As network size increases, intuitive analysis of feedback effects"—produced by transcription factors regulating genes that produce transcription factors—"is increasingly difficult and error prone." The work of teams at the Whitehead Institute under Young and at the ISB under Hood had made explicit just how complex those feedback effects can be. As McAdams and Shapiro pointed out, though: "Electrical engineers routinely analyze circuits with thousands of interconnected complex components," with all kinds of feedback. This held out the hope that engineering techniques for studying circuits could be applied to modeling regulatory networks.

Interestingly, Hood believes that the way to deal with a regulatory network that would otherwise be too complex to grasp will be to "divide it into subcircuits that in some cases behave exactly as electrical engineering control circuits." Young's group had already started to do this in their October 2002 *Science* paper through the identification of what they called network motifs. And since, as Hood says, "The ultimate objective [of systems biology] would be mathematical formulation," modeling techniques developed by electrical engineers for circuits might form the basis of just such a formulation.

"Electrical circuits are typically described by circuit diagrams and characterized by simulation models," McAdams and Shapiro wrote in *Science*. "The simulation provides a calculating tool for predicting time behavior of the interconnected system. The circuit diagram shows the overall organization of the circuit and the detailed interconnectivity between components." This approach is clearly closely related to the work of Young and Hood, but with the difference that the application of tools from the discipline of electrical engineering allows such circuits to be modeled quantitatively—predicting measurable levels of proteins—as well as qualitatively—how those levels are interrelated.

To test the idea of using circuit simulations for gene networks, McAdams and Shapiro applied the idea to a well-explored subsystem, the regulatory network used by a virus, bacteriophage lambda, to choose between two very different courses of action, called *lysis* and *lysogeny*. After the virus has infected an *E. coli* bacterium, it can either produce more copies of itself, which are spread into the surrounding environment by bursting open the host cell (lysis), or the genome of the virus can be incorporated into the genome of the bacterium, to lie dormant before being released later (lysogeny). The virus chooses which of these two courses to take based on the physical state inside the bacterium, using what is called the lambda decision circuit.

The paper noted that there is an important factor to be considered in circuit simulations. "Electrical switching circuits are frequently characterized as networks of idealized switching devices; that is, devices with instantaneous transitions between states at precise times. However, practical electrical devices exhibit finite transition times and transient responses"—they do not switch instantly or "cleanly" from one state to another. The same is true of most biological networks: "Biochemical mechanisms . . . that determine the dynamic balance between protein production and decay, and thus determine signal levels, are important parameters in genetic circuit logic. Time delay mechanisms, especially transcription delays"—the time it takes for a gene to be turned into its corresponding mRNA—"and signal accumulation delays" —while the level of protein builds up to an effective concentration—" are central to the correct function of the circuits." Summing up their work, McAdams and Shapiro wrote: "We conclude from experience with the [lambda] decision circuit that construction of a simulation model of a genetic circuit that is hypothesized to explain experimental observation provides a powerful test of the hypothesis. The simulation forces identification of connectivity and explicit accounting for timing and sequencing of events."

One of the most important aspects of this work was its emphasis on making modeling realistic through the inclusion of timing delays. A 1997 paper from McAdams, this time with Adam Arkin, extended this approach by considering this factor in greater detail: "In biochemical regulatory networks, the time intervals between successive events are determined by inevitable delays while signal molecule concentrations either accumulate or decline"— that is, a transcription factor needs to reach a critical concentration in the cell before it alters the expression of a gene. The paper explored what determined the time required for protein concentration to grow to the critical level.

The earlier paper by McAdams and Shapiro incorporated timing delays into the modeling of regulatory networks, but had assumed that the change in protein levels occurred smoothly. In fact, McAdams and Arkin noted, the situation was probably more complex: "It has been proposed that the pattern of protein concentration growth is stochastic"—arising from random processes— "exhibiting short bursts of variable numbers of proteins at varying time intervals." This stochastic behavior is a result of the low concentration of transcription factors regulating gene expression in many cells. As a result, the production of the corresponding mRNA—and hence protein—is "lumpy" rather than smooth. If the lumps are big enough, they might trigger other reactions in the regulatory network that would not be produced by a steady flow.

To explore this effect, McAdams and Arkin drew on earlier work by Gillespie, who had devised a way of computing systems where some elements were stochastic rather than smooth. This was essentially the Monte Carlo technique that Stan Ulam had hit upon while playing solitaire. In Ulam's case, he applied it to deal with the stochastic nature of thermonuclear reactions within the hydrogen bomb when he was working at Los Alamos, rather than to gene expression, but there is a certain poetic justice that it should finally turn up in this field, too, given his early work in bioinformatics. The McAdams-Arkin paper concluded: "In summary, there is compelling evidence from many directions that outcomes of regulated events in both prokaryotic and eukaryotic organisms are not deterministic."

In their next paper, published in the journal *Genetics* in 1998, McAdams and Arkin, together with John Ross, applied their new stochastic gene expression techniques to the lambda decision circuit that McAdams and Shapiro had modeled in 1995. "The random developmental path choice between lysogenic or lytic path in individual cells was shown to result from the inevitable fluctuations in the temporal pattern of protein concentration growth" due to the inherently lumpy nature of gene expression. According to this analysis, the lambda decision circuit turned out to be a proverbial throw of the protein dice. More generally, the authors noted, this also meant that a collection of genomically identical cells, kept together in the same, unvarying environment, will eventually diverge in terms of their physical characteristics purely as a result of the tiny variations caused by the lumpy production of proteins within them.

This obviously had interesting implications for the whole issue of genetic determinism, which assumes that the same genome will always generate the same characteristics. At the end of their *Genetics* paper, Arkin, Ross, and McAdams asked: "If random processes of gene expression tend to make the pattern of protein production inherently erratic, how do cells achieve the regulatory determinism necessary for most functions?" After all, reliable, deterministic responses are clearly necessary for a broad range of circumstances, otherwise cells cannot grow and react appropriately to external stimuli. "One possibility is that the overall regulatory architecture can suppress deleterious effects of molecular-level reaction fluctuations," they suggested. Even though there are local manifestations of non-deterministic behavior, overall, things act in a deterministic fashion where it is needed. "Another possibility is that the stochastic pattern of signal protein production may only cause uncertainty in timing of regulatory events, not uncertainty in outcome. Within broad limits the duration of many cellular functions may be less important to proper cellular function than the proper sequencing of events." Again, even though there are random variations in exactly when certain events occur within the cell, provided they do occur eventually, the cell can wait before it proceeds.

Whether either or both of these go some way to explaining how non-deterministic effects are dealt with inside the cell, this work suggests that any systems biology approach that aims for a realistic level of simulation will need to consider the possible effects of stochastic gene expression. One person who agrees is Leroy Hood. "Stochastic processes certainly become important as you get down to low numbers of molecules," he says. "I'm more and more convinced that there's really important biology that does occur down at the level of messages that are expressed at just one or two or three or four copies in the cell," and that systems biology will need to take account of this.

Alongside these kind of detailed but partial models of gene regulatory networks, there are general software environments designed to allow the salient features of entire regulatory, metabolic, and signaling pathways to be captured and modeled in an integrated fashion. One of the first comprehensive attempts to provide this was E-CELL, which came from a team of bioinformatics researchers led by Masaru Tomita. As Tomita wrote in 2001: "To conquer and directly challenge the task of whole-cell modeling, the E-CELL Project was initiated in 1996 at the Shonan-Fujisawa Campus of Keio University (Fujisawa, Japan), following the publication of the entire genome sequence of *Mycoplasma genitalium*" by The Institute for Genomic Research (TIGR).

Tomita explained the reason for their choice: "*M. genitalium* has the smallest genome (580kb) and smallest number of genes ([approximately] 480) of all living organisms currently known . . . The size of its genome is one order of magnitude less than that of *Escherichia coli*"—which is about 5 Mb in size—"and thus is an ideal candidate for whole-cell modeling." Thanks to work at

TIGR, it was known that many of the 480 genes were not necessary for survival. "Therefore, in collaboration with TIGR, a minimal set of genes . . . were selected and the first hypothetical 'virtual cell' with the 127 genes was constructed." This self-surviving cell (SSC) model had 105 genes coding proteins, and 22 coding RNA that performed key roles in the cell. The cell was "run" by 495 rules, which typically specified a reaction in a metabolic pathway, but also included interactions between proteins, and stochastic ones between proteins and DNA—the binding of transcriptional factors, for example. Much of the information required for building pathways came from EcoCyc and KEGG: "Both of these knowledgebases provide links between information on genes, enzymes and metabolic pathways which proved essential in our effort to construct a model cell," Tomita and colleagues wrote in 1999.

Each reaction rule defined how the quantities of the substances involved changed after the time step—generally one thousandth of a second. Using the initial levels of proteins, the rules were applied and the new levels calculated. These were then used for the next round of calculation, and so on. The overall behavior of the cell could be monitored visually through various graphical interfaces. Similarly, the expression of all the genes could be monitored in the "Genemap Window." Moreover, each gene could be knocked out—made inoperative—simply by clicking on its icon in the Genemap Window. It is therefore possible to conduct real-time knock-out experiments to explore the effects of gene deletions. Clicking on the icon reactivates the gene.

Although E-CELL used *M. genitalium* as a test case, the software can be adapted to any set of genes, proteins, and pathways. Tomita and his team decided to try modeling a real cell, rather than a hypothetical one like the SSC. This would allow the simulation results to be compared directly against the experimentally measured values. "Human erythrocytes"—red blood cells—"were chosen for the model," Tomita wrote in 2001, "because intracellular metabolism is limited in human erythrocytes and because they do not replicate, transcribe or translate genes." These processes, then, could be omitted from the model. "Also, there are already several studies on the modeling of erythrocytes. It is possible to compare computer models with real red blood cells because a considerable amount of experimental data about red blood cells has accumulated." The result of running the E-CELL erythrocyte simulation was that, after tuning some of the model's values, it settled down to a state that was comparable with experimental data.

According to Tomita, "One of the major problems in constructing large-scale cell models is lack of quantitative data. Most of the biological knowledge available is qualitative (such as functions of genes, pathway maps, which proteins interact with what)." Since Tomita was having problems finding the right kind of data, he took Hood's route of creating his own research laboratory to provide it. "For this new type of simulation-orientated biology, we set up the Institute for Advanced Biosciences (IAB) of Keio University. The institute consists of three centers for metabolome research, bioinformatics, and genome engineering, respectively." "Metabolome" is the name given to all the molecules—not just the proteins—involved in metabolic processes within a given cell. As Hood had done, Tomita assembled a very broad-based team with a wide range of skills: enzyme engineering, analytical chemistry, genetic engineering, computer sciences, and mathematics.

Remarkably, the aims of Tomita's IAB go even further than those of Hood's ISB: "The ultimate goal of this international research institute is to construct a whole-cell model *in silico* based on a large amount of data generated by high-throughput metabolome analyses, and then to design a novel genome based on the computer simulation and create real cells with the novel genome by means of genome engineering"—an unprecedented way of checking the validity of such a model.

If Tomita is unusual in his desire to turn his digital silicon cell into analogue reality, he is certainly not alone in his efforts to create a realistic, whole-cell simulation. For example, the U.S. Department of Energy (DOE) has major plans as part of what it calls its Genomes to Life program, begun in 1999 as the follow-up to its participation in the Human Genome Project. "DOE's Genomes to Life program will make important contributions in the quest to venture beyond characterizing such individual life components as genes and other DNA sequences toward a more comprehensive, integrated view of biology at a whole-systems level." One component is the Microbial Cell Project, launched in June 2001 and folded into the Genomes to Life project in 2002: "The aim is nothing less than to model not only the physical distribution (over time and under different physical circumstances) of all the gene products but to incorporate into this model the spectrum of gene regulatory, gene-protein and protein-protein interactions."

The Silicon Cell Consortium in Amsterdam, Holland, has a similar hope. "The long-term goal of the Silicon Cell (*SiC*) Consortium is the computation of Life at the cellular level on the basis of the complete genomic, transcriptomic, proteomic, metabolomic, and [other] information that will become available in the forthcoming years. Completing this ambition will take more than a decade." Initially, the project will concentrate on two model organisms: *E. coli* and yeast.

The Canadian Project CyberCell is focusing its attention on the first of these. "The objective of Project CyberCell is to develop an accurate simulation of a living cell within the virtual environment of a computer, one that can be manipulated at different levels of molecular resolution, and that can respond, adapt and evolve to exploit this virtual environment. Project CyberCell has selected the bacterium *E. coli* as its model. As the project evolves, this model has the potential to generate concepts and technology for extending cellular simulation to more complicated cell types and eventually multi-cellular organisms."

Although Project CyberCell began as a purely Canadian endeavor, it has now become part of something much larger, which traces its origins back to the same part of the world. The International *E. coli* Alliance (IECA) was founded on August 4, 2002, in Edmonton, Canada. It has as its mission "to consolidate the global efforts to understand a living bacterial cell" by creating a "complex computer model, integrating all of the dynamic molecular interactions required for the life of a simple, self-replicating cell": *E. coli*. The Steering Committee includes E-CELL's Tomita, whose Institute of Advanced Biosciences is also working on an "electronic *E. coli*." *Science* reported that the "mammoth international modeling effort . . . is expected to occupy hundreds of scientists for 10 years at a cost of at least $100 million."

The creation of an international virtual *E. coli* project signals something of a coming-of-age for computer modeling of cells. It also exposes a key issue that needs to be addressed, however. The only way that a global project on this scale can succeed is if the simulation is modular, with elements parceled out to different groups according to their expertise. This implies standards for exchanging data between the various parts of the model.

Important work in this regard has already been achieved with the Systems Biology Workbench (SBW), an open source application integration environment that essentially allows users of one modeling tool to call up another from within the first environment, passing data between them without needing to worry about how this is achieved. Researchers backing SBW include those behind E-CELL, Gepasi, Jarnac, DBSolve, and others. An important part of SBW is a standard way of describing computer models of cells called Systems Biology Markup Language (SBML), a structured format like MAGE-ML, which allows models to be passed between compliant programs.

One reason why SBML is particularly important relates to the perennially thorny question of publishing results. Just as the sequencing community needed to devise a way for the genomic data that lay behind papers to be accessible to other scientists—not least to allow results to be checked—so the wing of the systems biology community that employs computational simulations requires an equivalent way of making the models that buttress published results available. Assuming the authors are willing to make details of their models public, SBML allows other researchers to import that data into different simulation software, provided it supports SBML. If they are not, then their results are essentially unverifiable, and probably of little value.

One of the main architects of the Systems Biology Workbench and its attendant SBML is Hiroaki Kitano, director of the Sony Computer Science Laboratories, in Tokyo. He has proposed what he calls the Human Systeome Project, with the defined goal "to complete a detailed and comprehensive simulation model of the human cell at an estimated error margin of 20 percent by the year 2020, and to finish identifying the system profile"—the key values that define the model—"for all genetic variations, drug responses, and environmental stimuli by 2030."

The mention of genetic variations and drug responses is significant. If something like the Human Systeome Project could craft a virtual cell, with genomic information linked directly to proteomics and metabolomics, it would be possible to create models for any combination of genetic variation. Even single-letter changes in the digital code can have profound consequences for the overall dynamics of the cell, as genomic changes ripple through affected proteins and the pathways they delineate. Working from the personalized virtual cell that would result, doctors could not only explore the detailed consequences of particular genotypes, but also observe safely, *in silico*, particular responses to carefully tailored combinations and concentrations of drugs.

In this sense, systems biology may not only unify genomics, proteomics, and the rest, but deliver on their promise—hitherto unfulfilled—of exact diagnosis and personalized therapy. As Hood says, once systems can be modeled in all their complexity, "you can do two things you could never do with systems before. One is you could predict the behavior of the system given virtually any perturbation." That is, one could take a standard model and feed in the genotype of the patient, plus current values for gene expression and protein profiles measured as part of a regular medical check-up. If the model were good enough, one could run it into the future to calculate the likelihood of various medical conditions developing in the coming years—allowing the prediction in detail of future illnesses before they happen.

"The second thing [you can do] is you can redesign the system to have completely new emergent properties," Hood explains. One could use the model to tweak aspects of the system implicated in any future illnesses, with a view to eliminating their appearance; for example, different combinations of drugs could be administered virtually to explore how effective they are in correcting protein profiles that are outside the norm. "It's this latter trait"— the ability to carry out "what if?" modeling of a person's health—"that is really the key to preventive medicine which comes out of systems biology," Hood says. Perhaps the human systeome will provide the necessary global level of detail to turn this dream into a reality, or it may be that researchers will need to move up yet another level, modeling not cells but entire bodies— what has already been dubbed the "physiome."

In either case, the simulation, if successful, is likely to be far beyond human capabilities to grasp it in its entirety. The end result will be ironic and yet oddly fitting. Ironic in that the final outcome of this quest to analyze and to understand will be something that cannot be understood, only used as the most complex black box every created. But oddly fitting, too, in that life, the mysterious result of DNA, should be transmuted by the power of systems biology into the equally inscrutable output of another digital code.

NOTES

The author conducted interviews included in this chapter in May 2003 with the following individual: L. Hood.

1. p 293   *In contrast to the protein sequence databases*   I. Xenarios, and D. Eisenberg, "Protein interaction databases," *Current Opinion in Biotechnology* 12 (2001): 334–339.

2. p 293   *one computationally difficult problem*   I. Xenarios, and D. Eisenberg, "Protein interaction databases," *Current Opinion in Biotechnology* 12 (2001): 334–339.

3. p 293   *Sydney Brenner has commented that*   Editorial, *Nature Biotechnology* 21 (2003): 213.

4. p 294   *These wallcharts, as edited by*   "Biochemical pathways." Online at *http://biochem.boehringer-mannheim.com/publications/metamap.htm*.

5. p 294   *Using the WIT genome analysis system,*   R. Overbeek, et al., "WIT: integrated system for high-throughput genome sequence analysis and metabolic reconstruction," *Nucleic Acids Research* 28, (2000): 123–125.

6. p 295   *The EcoCyc project began in 1992*   P.D. Karp, "Pathway databases: a case study in computational symbolic theories," *Science* 293 (2001): 2040–2044.

7. p 295   *The input required by PathoLogic*   "BioCyc Introduction." Online at *http://biocyc.org/intro.shtml*.

8. p 295   *the first available curated database of human metabolic*   SRI International press release, February 10, 2003.

9. p 295   *computerizes such data and knowledge*   M. Kanehisa, et al., "The KEGG databases at GenomeNet," *Nucleic Acids Research* 30 (2002): 42–46.

10. p 295   *We believe that the key challenge*   "About The Molecular Sciences Institute." Online at *http://www.molsci.org/msiDescription.html*.

11. p 296   *the flagship activity . . . is the Alpha Project.*   "The Molecular Sciences Institute." Online at *http://www.molsci.org/Dispatch?action-NavbarWidget:-project=1&NavbarWidget:-project=alpha*.

12. p 296   *It has been known for some time that cells*   The Nobel Assembly press release, October 10, 1994.

13. p 296   *seeking funds for a multi-laboratory,*   A. Abbott, "Alliance of US labs plans to build map of cell signalling pathways," *Nature* 402 (1999): 219–220.

14. p 296   *In an effort to 'glue' together large groups*   NIH press release, September 5, 2000.

15. p 297   *The AfCS does not function without*   Alliance for Cellular Signaling, "Overview of the Alliance for Cellular Signaling," *Nature* 420 (2002): 703–706.

16. p 297   *Alliance scientists working in the specially*   NIH press release, September 5, 2000.

17. p 297   *an online resource that will combine news*   A. Abbott, "Into unknown territory," *Nature* 420 (2002): 600–601.

18. p 297 *At the heart of this collaboration* "AfCS-Nature Signaling Gateway—about us," online at *http://www.signaling-gateway.org/aboutus/index.html.*

19. p. 297 *Gilman says it is essential that the effort* A. Abbott, "Into unknown territory," *Nature* 420 (2002): 600–601.

20. p. 298 *How can one bridge the gap from* M. Steffen, et al., "Automated modelling of signal transduction networks," *BMC Bioinformatics* 3 (2002): 34.

21. p. 298 *Microarray expression data* M. Steffen, et al., "Automated modelling of signal transduction networks," *BMC Bioinformatics* 3 (2002): 34.

22. p. 299 *We found that the master regulator* CtrA M.T. Laub, et al., "Global analysis of the genetic network controlling a bacterial cell cycle," *Science* 290 (2000): 2144–2148.

23. p. 300 *Researchers at the Whitehead Institute* Whitehead Institute press release, December 21, 2000.

24. p. 301 *Expression analysis with DNA microarrays* B. Ren, et al., "Genome-wide location and function of DNA binding proteins," *Science* 290 (2000): 2306–2309.

25. p. 301 *A fundamental question associated with* I. Simon, et al., "Serial regulation of transcriptional regulators in the yeast cell cycle," *Cell* 106 (2001): 697–708.

26. p. 301 *the results of their efforts were revealed in a paper* T.I. Lee, et al., "Transcriptional regulatory networks in *Saccharomyces cerevisae*," *Science* 298 (2002): 799–804.

27. p. 302 *around 300 researcher-years were needed* Whitehead Institute press release, October 24, 2002

28. p. 302 *Without this increase in productivity,* Whitehead Institute press release, October 24, 2002.

29. p. 303 *By 1995 or so, we had filled all the space* R. Zacks, "Under biology's hood," *Technology Review,* September 2001.

30. p. 303 *In 1996, I went to the President of the University of Washington* L. Hood, "My life and adventures integrating biology and technology. A commemorative lecture for the 2002 Kyoto prize in advanced technologies." Online at *http://www.systemsbiology.org/extra/2002Kyoto.pdf.*

31. p. 303 *much agonizing,* L. Hood, "My life and adventures integrating biology and technology. A commemorative lecture for the 2002 Kyoto prize in advanced technologies." Online at *http://www.systemsbiology.org/extra/2002Kyoto.pdf.*

32. p. 303 *An initial $5 million came from an anonymous* P. Smaglik, "For my next trick . . ." *Nature* 407 (2000): 828–829.

33. p. 304 *The agribiotech firm Monsanto,* P. Smaglik, "For my next trick . . ." *Nature* 407 (2000): 828–829.

34. p. 304 *For organisms with fully sequenced genomes,* T. Ideker, et al., "Integrated genomic and proteomic analyses of a systematically perturbed metabolic network," *Science* 292 (2001): 929–934.

35. p. 305 *The sea urchin is a powerful model*   T. Ideker, et al., "A new approach to decoding life: systems biology," *Annual Review of Genomics and Human Genetics* 2 (2001): 343–372.

36. p. 306 *The endo16 gene had 34 binding sites*   T. Ideker, et al., "A new approach to decoding life: systems biology," *Annual Review of Genomics and Human Genetics* 2 (2001): 343–372.

37. p. 306 *what is essentially a hard-wired,*   C-H Yuh, et al., "Genomic cis-regulatory logic: experimental and computational analysis of a sea urchin gene," *Science* 279 (1998): 1896–1902.

38. p. 306 *the regulatory networks are uniquely specified*   L. Hood and D. Galas, "The digital code of DNA," *Nature* 421 (2003): 444–448.

39. p. 306 *A complete cis-regulatory network model*   E. Davidson, et al., "A genomic regulatory network for development," *Science* 295 (2002): 1669–1678.

40. p. 306 *only a tiny fraction of the total*   E. Davidson, et al., "A genomic regulatory network for development," *Science* 295 (2002): 1669–1678.

41. p. 307 *the task of finding these elements*   E. Davidson, et al., "A genomic regulatory network for development," *Science* 295 (2002): 1669–1678.

42. p. 307 *The* E. coli *metabolic network*   P.D. Karp, "Pathway databases: a case study in computational symbolic theory," *Science* 293 (2001): 2040–2044.

43. p. 308 *an interactive metabolic systems language,*   "Jarnac Metabolic Simulation Package." Online at *http://www.cds.caltech.edu/~hsauro/Jarnac.htm*.

44. p. 308 *a mathematical simulation workbench,*   I. Goryanin, et al., "Mathematical simulation and analysis of cellular metabolism and regulation," *Bioinformatics* 15 (1999): 749–758.

45. p. 308 *As network size increases, intuitive analysis*   H.H. McAdams and L. Shapiro, "Circuit simulation of genetic networks," *Science* 269 (1995): 650–656.

46. p. 309 *Electrical circuits are typically described*   H.H. McAdams and L. Shapiro, "Circuit simulation of genetic networks," *Science* 269 (1995): 650–656.

47. p. 310 *In biochemical regulatory networks,*   H.H. McAdams and A. Arkin, "Stochastic mechanisms in gene expression," *Proc. Natl. Acad. Sci. USA* 94 (1997): 814–819.

48. p. 310 *The random developmental path choice*   A. Arkin, et al., "Stochastic kinetic analysis of developmental pathway bifurcation in phage λ-infected *Escherichia coli* cells," *Genetics* 149 (1998): 1633–1648.

49. p. 311 *To conquer and directly challenge*   M. Tomita, "Whole-cell simulation: a grand challenge of the 21st century," *TRENDS in Biotechnology* 19 (6) (2001): 205–210.

50. p. 311 *M. genitalium has the smallest genome*   Tomita, M., "Whole-cell simulation: a grand challenge of the 21st century," *TRENDS in Biotechnology* 19 6 (2001): 205–210.

51. p. 312 *Both of these knowledgebases provide*   M. Tomita, et al., "E-CELL: software environment for whole-cell simulation," *Bioinformatics* 15 (1999): 72–84.

52. p. 312 *Human erythrocytes . . . were chosen for the model,* M. Tomita, "Whole-cell simulation: a grand challenge of the 21st century," *TRENDS in Biotechnology* 19 (6) (2001): 205–210.

53. p. 312 *One of the major problems in constructing* M. Tomita, "Whole-cell simulation: a grand challenge of the 21st century," *TRENDS in Biotechnology* 19 (6) (2001): 205–210.

54. p. 312 *For this new type of simulation-orientated* M. Tomita, "Whole-cell simulation: a grand challenge of the 21st century," *TRENDS in Biotechnology* 19 (6) (2001): 205–210.

55. p. 313 *Tomita assembled a very broad-based team* R. Triendl, "Computerized role models," *Naturejobs* (June 27, 2002): 7.

56. p. 313 *The ultimate goal of this* M. Tomita, "Whole-cell simulation: a grand challenge of the 21st century," *TRENDS in Biotechnology* 19 (6) (2001): 205–210.

57. p. 313 *DOE's Genomes to Life program* "Genomes to Life: Program overview." Online at *http://www.doegenomestolife.org/program/index.html.*

58. p. 313 *Microbial Cell Project, launched in June 2001* "Microbial Cell Project Links." Online at *http://microbialcellproject.org/funding/.*

59. p. 313 *The aim is nothing less than to model* "Microbial Cell Project." Online at *http://www.microbialcellproject.org/MCPbrochure8.pdf.*

60. p. 313 *The long-term goal of the* "The Silicon Cell—computing the living cell." Online at *http://www.bio.vu.nl/hwconf/Silicon/index.html.*

61. p. 313 *The objective of Project CyberCell is to develop* "Project CyberCell." Online at *http://129.128.166.250/main.html.*

62. p. 314 *to consolidate the global efforts to understand* "Back to the basics . . . of life." Online at *http://ecmc2.sdsc.edu/project.html.*

63. p. 314 *mammoth international modeling effort* C. Holden, "Alliance launched to model E. coli," *Science* 297 (2002): 1459–1460.

64. p. 314 *to complete a detailed and comprehensive simulation* H. Kitano, "Systems Biology: toward system-level understanding of biological systems." Online at *http://www.sbw-sbml.org/general/papers/foundations/kitano.pdf.*

CHAPTER 14

Genomic Prescriptions

Whatever the area of genomics—whether basic sequencing or the most complex systems biology—the underlying justification is that it will contribute to a deeper understanding of human biology, more accurate diagnosis of disease, and ultimately better prevention and treatment. Reflecting this fact, most papers in genomics, however distant they might seem from clinical application, conclude with an almost obligatory invocation of their medical potential. What can be regarded as the first publication of the high-throughput, digital genomics era, Venter's 1995 report in *Science* on the sequencing of *Haemophilus influenzae*, was no exception: "The success of the whole genome shotgun sequencing offers the potential to accelerate research in a number of areas. . . . Knowledge of the complete genomes of pathogenic organisms"—those causing disease, like *H. influenzae*—"could lead to new vaccines."

The epochal nature of the TIGR paper was clear as soon as it was published. In 1997, one of the Wellcome Trust's senior scientists said: "It is incredible to realize that two years ago, everyone was very skeptical that Craig Venter could do what he did. The world of microbial genomics"—where *microbe* refers to any organism too small to be visible to the naked eye, and includes viruses, bacteria, and others—"was changed overnight." As well as demonstrating that the whole-genome shotgun method could provide unparalleled insights into pathogenic bacteria, the 1995 paper from Venter and his team was important because it took sequencing to the next level.

Until that time, the pathogens whose genomes had been sequenced were viruses. Unlike *H. influenzae*, viruses are not independent organisms, but subvert their hosts for certain vital functions like reproduction. This means that their genomes are simpler and smaller; they were tractable with the manual sequencing techniques that were available before the development of high-throughput approaches. For example, the very first genome to be sequenced, that of the bacteriophage phi-X174 virus, has just 5,386 DNA letters. It was completed in 1978 by Fred Sanger and his team. Even the genome of the vaccinia virus, responsible for smallpox and thus one of the deadliest human pathogens, is less than 200,000 base pairs long.

The 1995 paper on *H. influenzae*, whose genome has over 1.8 million DNA letters, broke the symbolic one million base pairs barrier, and in doing so finally brought all disease-causing bacteria within reach. The new whole-genome shotgun method was particularly suitable for these because, as Venter and his team pointed out, "this approach eliminates the need for initial mapping efforts and is therefore applicable to the vast array of microbial species for which genome maps are unavailable." In the decade following the *Science* paper, the sequence of every major pathogen afflicting mankind was elucidated. Taken together with the complete human genome, this achievement offers those in medicine the hope of entering into a new age of full, integrated digital knowledge after centuries of a partial, analogue kind.

Naturally, Venter's own research outfit, The Institute for Genomic Research (TIGR), led the way. In August 1997, his team published a major paper on the sequence of the gastric pathogen *Helicobacter pylori* in *Nature*, finding 1.6 Mb (megabases) and 1,600 predicted genes. As the introduction pointed out: "For most of this century the cause of peptic ulcer disease was thought to be stress-related. . . . The discovery that *Helicobacter pylori* was associated with gastric inflammation and peptic ulcer disease was initially met with scepticism. However, this discovery . . . has revolutionized our view of the gastric environment, the diseases associated with it, and the appropriate treatment regimens. . . . *H. pylori* is probably the most common chronic bacterial infection of humans, present in almost half of the world population." The medical importance of sequencing the genome of a pathogen infecting several billion people could hardly be in doubt.

The paper is notable as a demonstration of how fast genomics was moving. Whereas the original *H. influenzae* paper had included several pages simply listing the proteins that had been identified in the sequence, the one on *H. pylori* integrated many of these into a detailed metabolic pathway. Peter Karp, who created the EcoCyc pathway database, was included as a coauthor. This was not the first time such a pathway diagram had appeared: an earlier paper from German researchers reporting on the sequencing of the pathogen *Mycoplasma pneumoniae*, a cause of atypical pneumonia, had pioneered the idea.

TIGR's next paper, detailing the sequence of *Treponema pallidum*, which causes venereal syphilis, also included a metabolic pathway diagram. This was something of an achievement, because as Venter and his team explained: "Despite its importance as an infectious agent, relatively little is known about *T. pallidum* in comparison with other bacterial pathogens." As a result, "existing diagnostic tests for syphilis are suboptimal, and no vaccine against *T. pal-*

lidum is available." The availability of the 1.1 Mb genome and its 1,041 predicted genes would provide invaluable help for researchers in both areas.

The next two pathogen genomes came from other research groups. *Chlamydia trachomatis*, responsible for the eye disease trachoma, as well as genital tract infections, was tackled by a group at Stanford University under Ronald Davis, and a related paper appeared in *Science* in October 1998. More significant in many ways was the sequence of *Rickettsia prowazekii*, the agent of louseborne typhus, which is estimated to have infected 20–30 million people in the wake of the First World War. Aside from the medical value of the sequence, 1.1 Mb long and with 834 genes, which appeared in *Nature* a month later, it provided insight into one of the most remarkable events in the evolution of life: the origin of mitochondria.

Today, mitochondria are small structures that act as the power sources within eukaryotic cells. It is here that nutrients are "burned" to produce water, carbon dioxide, and energy. Mitochondria contain their own DNA, and it is believed that they arose through the symbiotic combination of a simpler eukaryote and a bacterium, a coming-together of two organisms in a mutually beneficial partnership. Gradually the bacterium's genome lost genes that were unnecessary in this new environment, until it was reduced to a basic function of generating energy. The sequence of *Rickettsia prowazekii* was found to be more closely related to mitochondria than that for any other bacterium so far sequenced, adding support to the symbiosis theory.

Alongside groups producing key but sporadic papers like that of the *Rickettsia* pathogen, TIGR soon had a major rival capable of matching it in sustained pathogen sequencing: the Sanger Centre in Cambridge. The stimulus for this sudden interest was Venter's pioneering *H. influenzae* paper, while the $25 million funding came from the Wellcome Trust. For its first project, the Pathogen Genome Sequencing Unit tackled one of the most serious diseases: tuberculosis. Sometimes called the White Plague, it has one of the biggest pathogenic genomes (4.4 Mb.) TIGR's *H. pylori* might infect more people in the world, but as the Sanger paper, published in *Nature* in June 1998, pointed out: "The tubercle bacillus [*Mycobacterium tuberculosis*] continues to claim more lives than any other single infectious agent."

Important results have already flowed from this work, thanks to the application of comparative genomics. Alongside the human variety of tuberculosis, the Sanger team sequenced the bovine form, *Mycobacterium bovis*. There were two reasons for this work: first, to aid the fight against the increasing problem of tuberculosis in animals. As a press release accompanying the sequencing of the bovine form explained, tuberculosis "has achieved the dubious distinction of overtaking man as the main threat to the survival of the black and white rhinoceros. It is spreading rapidly through the game reserves of southern Africa where it affects a wide range of species including buffalo, lions, cheetah and baboons. It is a worldwide problem that affects natural populations, domesticated breeds and industry."

Second, the work was carried out in the hope of elucidating how human tuberculosis arose. The original theory was that the bovine form had crossed the species barrier to humans at the time of the domestication of cattle: 10,000 to 15,000 years ago. Comparing the two genomes revealed that this was unlikely. Since the bovine sequence is shorter than that of the human variety, and has lost stretches still retained by the human form, it is more probable that man gave tuberculosis to cattle or that the two organisms evolved separately from a common ancestor. As a result, the Sanger press release pointed out that, "this work on the post-genomic applications of the genome sequence . . . calls for a rethink on our previous understanding of the dynamics between human and animal disease."

TIGR responded to the Sanger triumph with its own bacterial block-buster, published in August 2000. The pathogen in question is *Vibrio cholerae*, which causes cholera, a disease responsible for a number of pandemics in the last two hundred years. (A pandemic is similar to an epidemic, but involves many more countries, and often the entire world.) TIGR's paper in *Nature* explains: "When untreated, cholera is a disease of extraordinarily rapid onset and potentially high lethality." The project prompted a series of characteristic comments from Venter about the resistance of traditional molecular biologists to genome-based science and how "almost every preconceived notion that scientists have had about every genome from any species was shown to be wrong" once the sequence was in hand. "Some [scientists] argued that sequencing *Vibrio cholerae* was a total waste of time and money," he recalled, "because . . . [they were sure that] there was one large chromosome which mostly resembled *E. coli*. Therefore, scientists in the cholera field said, we would learn nothing from sequencing the cholera genome. But we sequenced the *Vibrio cholerae* genome anyway. The National Institute of Allergy and Infectious Diseases actually funded it. They decided that the whole genome shotgun technology worked well with pathogens."

"It turned out that the cholera genome, instead of having one chromosome, had two. One chromosome closely resembles *E. coli*, but the other chromosome looks nothing whatsoever like *E. coli*. It probably carries most of the genes responsible for cholera not only being an infectious agent but also being able to go into a dormant state and hide in the ocean. It is typical of preconceived notions that they have been shown to be wrong by using a technique that is not based on preconceived notions of the genome." Just to ram home how mistaken these scientists had been, the title chosen by Venter for the *Nature* article was "DNA sequence of both chromosomes of the cholera pathogen *Vibrio cholerae*." Certainly, the second chromosome is by no means negligible: it has just over a million bases, compared to nearly three million in the larger one.

The leader of the team behind the cholera paper was Claire Fraser, Venter's wife and long-time research collaborator. Fraser took over the running of The Institute for Genomic Research when Venter left to found Celera in 1998. TIGR has flourished under her leadership: in 1998 there were 170 staff; by 2002 there were 325. The annual budget—most of which came from grants from the NIH, the U.S. Department of Energy, and the National Science Foundation, showed a similar growth: from $24 million a year in 1998 to around $50 million four years later. Fraser consolidated TIGR as one of the top two microbial sequencing centers, alongside the Sanger Centre. If Fraser was the undisputed princess of pathogens, it was equally clear that the prince was Bart Barrell, head of the Sanger group, a former assistant to Fred Sanger himself, and coauthor of the phi-X174 virus paper. After Barrell's group had sequenced *Mycobacterium tuberculosis*, it tackled an equally fearsome close relative, *Mycobacterium leprae*, the pathogen responsible for leprosy.

Comparing the two provided some interesting insights. The leprosy genome was smaller than that for tuberculosis—3.3 Mb versus 4.4 Mb—and the number of active genes far fewer. The leprosy bacillus seems to have lost more than half of the 4,000 genes with which it started. *Mycobacterium tuberculosis* retains these. The February 2001 paper in *Nature* explained that this was a result of genes becoming inactivated once their functions were no longer required in their particular ecological niche—humans, in this case. This reduced gene set might also explain the leprosy pathogen's very slow rate of growth and its inability to grow in an artificial medium in the laboratory. Fortunately for researchers, but perhaps not for the animal concerned, large quantities were eventually produced using the nine-banded armadillo as a host.

In October of the same year, the Sanger team published another genome fraught with historical baggage: that of the bacterium *Yersinia pestis*, better known as the plague. The accompanying press release from the Sanger Centre contains a number of fascinating facts: that the plague—or "Black Death" as it was known in medieval times—wiped out one third of the European population during the 14th century, and that the total deaths attributable to it throughout history amount to around 200 million people. The release also reveals that one of the last known casualties of the disease in the UK was a Mrs. Bugg, and that the sample of the bacteria used for the study came from a vet in Colorado, USA. He died in 1992 after a plague-infested cat sneezed on him as he was trying to rescue it from underneath a house.

The sequencing of its 4.6 Mb genome provided some important hints about what turned *Yersinia pestis* from a relatively mild stomach bug into such a devastating killer around 1,500 years ago. The key event seems to have been adapting to transmission by a blood-feeding insect—rat fleas in this case. This dual lifestyle—spending some of its time in rats and some of its time in humans—may have allowed the *Yersinia pestis* genome to acquire DNA from other pathogens, thus creating its deadly capabilities.

The Sanger Centre also offered a comment from one of the team that sequenced the plague pathogen: "The benefits of making this kind of information publicly available greatly outweigh the risk of someone getting it and using it for nefarious purposes." This is the old argument about how soon DNA sequences should be made public, but with an added twist. In the case of pathogens—especially deadly ones like the plague—some would argue that the sequence information should never be released, since it might be misused for biological weapons. However, this overlooks the fact that the core knowledge—how to sequence DNA—is so widespread that people intent on creating such a device and with enough resources could simply carry out the sequencing themselves. Moreover, the digital nature of sequences—the fact that they are all essentially the same—means that it will steadily and inevitably become easier for anyone to sequence anything as the underlying technology progresses and becomes cheaper. It is not hard to conceive a situation in which machines will be available that can automatically sequence organisms without calling for any technical skills on the part of the user—just like most advanced technologies once they mature.

A similar argument has been raging for many years within the computer community: should security flaws in software be disclosed immediately or hidden for as long as possible? If they are disclosed, people can help come up with fixes for them; however, these flaws might also be exploited. If, on the other hand, the weaknesses are withheld, they might be discovered anyway by those who are looking to exploit them, but there is less likely to be any fix. The situation for pathogens is vastly more serious, but the issues are largely the same.

In any case, the genomic community had already voted with its sequencers: over the period of less than five years, all of the most dangerous bacterial pathogens—the plague, typhus, tuberculosis, meningitis, cholera and typhoid fever (published by Barrell's group just a few weeks after the plague genome)—had been sequenced and entered into GenBank, where they joined the equally deadly viral diseases that had been elucidated earlier. Even if the world decided to withdraw sequences judged potentially dangerous, it would be too late: the genomic genie is out of the bottle.

One major disease is missing from the list of pathogens above: malaria. It is not caused by a bacterium, but by a eukaryotic parasite; of the four species that cause the disease, the most serious is *Plasmodium falciparum*. Its life cycle is even more complex than that of the plague pathogen, involving two hosts and many different forms, each adapted to the very different environments they inhabit in turn: red blood cells and the liver in humans, and the gut and salivary glands of the mosquito. Despite the fact that there are around 300–500 million cases of malaria each year, and nearly 3 million deaths—many of which are children under five years of age—relatively little progress has been made against the disease. Mosquito eradication campaigns, however, have been quite successful in the past. In part, this failure seems due to the complexity of the parasite's life cycle; it can also be attributed to the lack of a coordinated international effort to tackle the disease.

The Multilateral Initiative on Malaria (MIM) had been set up in January 1997, but six months later *Nature* reported that "several delegates [at a subsequent international conference] reminded the meeting that MIM's efforts would come to nothing unless it focused on the fundamental issue of boosting the paltry funds now available for malaria research." Fortunately, a month later, the same journal could report "Britain's Wellcome Trust last week gave a much-needed boost to malaria research with a decision to invest £8 million [$12 million] in an international effort to sequence the genome of *Plasmodium falciparum*." The story explained that the Wellcome decision was as a direct result of the new pathogen sequencing projects then underway: "The experience has convinced the trust that genome research is the most 'cost-effective' means to support research in infectious diseases," according to *Nature*.

Alongside its work on the tuberculosis pathogen, the Sanger Pathogen Genome Sequencing Unit had chosen to make chromosome 3 of the malarial parasite its other pilot project. The *Plasmodium falciparum* genome is unusual because of the very high percentage of the chemical letters A and T: for a number of practical reasons this meant that established sequencing techniques could not be applied unmodified. In particular, even though each of the fourteen chromosomes was relatively short—the total length of the genome was later established as 23 Mb—assembling the shotgun fragments was much harder, since it was more difficult to work out from the sequence alone which pieces were overlapping. Before the Sanger team's initial malaria paper appeared in *Nature* in August 1999, another group had published the results of their own pilot project in this area. "The complete sequencing of chromosome 2," they wrote, "has shown that the sequencing of the A+T-rich *P. falciparum* genome is technically possible." The team came from TIGR, and was led by Craig Venter and the malaria expert Stephen Hoffman.

The initial work on the *Plasmodium falciparum* genome reflected the friendly rivalry between the two principal pathogen sequencing centers in the world—TIGR and the Sanger Centre. Similarly, the larger malaria project, which also included sequencing the principal vector (carrier) of the parasite, the mosquito *Anopheles gambiae*, turned into a kind of symbolic reconciliation of not just the public and private sequencing centers, but of *Nature* and *Science*, too. Where the journals had been engaged in rather unseemly competitive jostling over publishing the draft human genome in February 2001, in October 2002 they joined together to present a coordinated publication of work on the malarial parasite and its vector.

Nature devoted most of its October 3, 2002 issue to the genome of *Plasmodium falciparum*, which had been sequenced by the Sanger Centre (nine chromosomes) and TIGR (four chromosomes), together with a Stanford University group under Ronald Davis, which sequenced one chromosome. The main paper describing the overall results read like a Who's Who of pathogen genomics; it included Craig Venter, Claire Fraser, and Bart Barrell among the principal authors.

The accompanying papers in *Nature* revealed how far things had progressed since the publication of the draft human genome 18 months before. For example, there was a paper that examined the genome of another malarial parasite, *Plasmodium yoelii yoelii*, which infects rats. As with other comparative genome projects, a relatively light whole-genome shotgun coverage was employed to obtain the chief features of the sequence quickly. Proteomics was well to the fore, too. Two papers looked at how the complement of proteins changes during the various transformations of the malaria parasite in the four stages of its life cycle. Understanding which proteins are expressed when and where provides valuable leads in the hunt for drugs effective against the disease.

Science's issue explored the other side of the problem: the mosquito vector of malaria, *Anopheles gambiae*. Emphasizing the theme of harmony, the editorial in *Science* noted: "The bulk of the sequencing work for *A. gambiae* was completed in a public-private partnership, that, although not the first of its kind, is another shining example of the possibilities of such programs." The private component was principally Celera, while publicly funded institutions included TIGR, EBI, and the French Genoscope. The main paper reporting on the work to sequence *Anopheles gambiae* began with a flourish: "The mosquito is both an elegant, exquisitely adapted organism and a scourge of humanity." Like *Nature*, the *Science* issue included a major study in comparative genomics, pairing the 278 Mb *Anopheles gambiae* with the 180 Mb fruit fly—two species that diverged around 250 million years ago. The journal also carried a number of articles examining the options for controlling malaria; one suggestion, for example, was to use genetically modified mosquitoes that are resistant to the parasite.

This raises the question of whether high-tech approaches to eradicating malaria—however innovative and ingenious they might be—are really the most effective way of dealing with the disease. Indeed, some would go so far as to say that the entire genomics approach is misguided. In 2000, *Science* ran two articles expressing different viewpoints on the issue. One, written by Stephen Hoffman, who led the team behind the main *Anopheles gambiae* paper in *Science*, was strongly in favor of taking the genomics route.

"Knowing the sequence of the *Plasmodium falciparum* genome and the genomes of other parasites that cause malaria," he wrote, "as well as the specifics of gene and protein expression at different stages in the life cycle and under pressure from different drugs, will increase our chances of developing new and better drugs, and vaccines. Having genomic information for *A. gam-*

biae, the major vector in Africa, will make possible new approaches to development of insecticides. Investment in *Plasmodium* and *Anopheles* genomics will facilitate development of new ways to prevent development of infectious sporozoites"—the parasite form injected by the insect's bite—"in *Anopheles* mosquitoes and for reducing contact between infectious mosquitoes and humans. Finally, knowledge of the human genome offers unprecedented potential for understanding who is and is not susceptible to dying from malaria, and who might benefit most from a particular type of vaccine."

These views were not shared by Chris Curtis, however, at the London School of Hygiene & Tropical Medicine. In the other *Science* viewpoint, he wrote: "A frank appraisal of the probable outcome of most molecular/genomics research supposedly aimed at reducing the death toll from malaria shows little likelihood that it could pass the 'so what? test'," he wrote dismissively. "In this context, it is important to distinguish research that might help to explain retrospectively some biological facts, from research that could actually help to guide disease controllers, especially those working in countries with annual health budgets of less than $10 per person." In particular, he doubted whether any of the likely insights derived from the genomes would benefit the people who most needed them: "It would be nice to think that knowing the gene sequences of *Anopheles* and *Plasmodium* species will lead to discovery of targets against which new insecticides or antimalarial drugs can be produced. However, I suspect that any such discoveries would be patented and only developed at prices unaffordable to governments or villagers in tropical countries."

In fact, the previous year German researchers had used the preliminary *Plasmodium falciparum* sequences for chromosomes 13 and 14 available from the Sanger Centre and TIGR to investigate a particular biochemical pathway in the *Plasmodium* parasite. They showed how it could be blocked using a drug, fosmidomycin, that had been developed some time ago for quite different purposes in humans. As their paper in *Science* concluded: "The efficacy of these drugs"—fosmidomycin and a derivative—"against multi-drug resistant parasites and their low manufacturing costs and high stability make them very attractive as a potential new class of antimalarial drugs." The results of the first human trials, in Gabon, Africa, were encouraging: "Our findings indicate that fosmidomycin is an effective, new antimalarial compound," researchers wrote in December 2002.

D rugs—especially low-cost ones—that attack the malarial parasite are clearly valuable for the millions of people who are already infected. One danger is that selection pressures will eventually cause a new variety of *Plasmodium falciparum* to evolve that is resistant to this particular form of chemical attack. Ultimately, a better long-term solution might be to prevent people from getting malaria in the first place by boosting their immune defenses through a vaccine. Traditional vaccines were pioneered by the English doctor Edward Jenner at the end of the eighteenth century. He infected an eight-year-old boy with cowpox, a mild variant of the deadly smallpox; smallpox was at that time the leading cause of adult death. Two months later, Jenner intentionally infected the boy with smallpox itself. Happily, the boy was completely resistant. As we now know, his immune system had been primed by the cowpox and was therefore able to recognize and defeat the more severe smallpox virus.

Until recently, there were four kinds of vaccines: those that use live, but attenuated (weakened) agents—like cowpox to protect against smallpox; killed whole organisms; parts of pathogenic organisms; and genetically engineered vaccines. All of these depend on proteins that are characteristic of the pathogen to prime the immune system for when it encounters the real thing. In 1990, though, a different approach based on using DNA sequences was discovered.

These have come to be known as DNA vaccines, a name that has an interesting origin, as a 1997 American Academy of Microbiology report on the area explained:

> The World Health Organization, among the first to realize that something new was happening in vaccinology, convened a meeting in May of 1994 to hear its pioneers present their results. On the second day of the meeting, a vote was taken on a name for the new technique from a list of candidates: genetic immunization, polynucleotide vaccines, gene vaccines, and nucleic acid vaccines. Voters split; however, the majority chose nucleic acid vaccines, with subterms DNA vaccines or RNA vaccines. The rationale for choosing the name nucleic acid vaccines focused on public perception. To gain wide acceptance, the new technology's name needed to convey its purpose as a protective vaccine without suggesting that it modified the genetic information of the recipient.

It seems that exponents of DNA vaccines were keen to draw a distinction between the new approach and gene therapy, which did involve modifying the underlying DNA of the patient. Ironically, DNA vaccines actually grew out of a failed attempt to achieve precisely this kind of modification. As a 1993 news story in *Science* accompanying the publication of the first DNA vaccine paper explained, researchers "were attempting to engineer live mice to make new proteins by chemically coercing their muscle cells into taking up DNA." That is, they were trying to carry out a chemical-based gene therapy that would cause a sequence coding for a particular protein to be taken up by the mouse muscle and then expressed.

Fortunately, the researchers followed an important standard scientific practice: "As a control, they left out the chemical." To check whether it was the chemical that produced any observed effects, they tried injecting just the DNA directly into the muscle, confident that nothing would happen. But "confoundingly, the animals' muscle cells took up the DNA and produced even higher levels of the protein" than the main experimental approach. *Science* continued: "According to the gospel of biotechnology, that just wasn't supposed to happen: elaborate genetic engineering tricks are needed to slip foreign DNA into cells. But here it appeared to sail right in and start producing proteins. If the finding were true, it could have enormous implications for the development of vaccines, which rely on foreign proteins to prime the immune system to recognize and attack invading pathogens."

The initial work was carried out by scientists at a small company called Vical. After showing its early results to the pharmaceutical giant Merck, Vical entered into a research collaboration and licensing agreement with the drugmaker in May 1991. Merck was granted a worldwide exclusive license for DNA vaccines against seven major human infectious diseases, including influenza, AIDS, hepatitis B and C, and tuberculosis. It was the first of these that formed the subject of the joint Vical/Merck paper published in *Science* in March 1993. DNA from an influenza virus was inserted into a plasmid—a small, circular piece of bacterial DNA—that was then injected into the muscles of mice. As *Science* explained: "Not only did the vaccine work, but the Merck/Vical team has evidence suggesting it may be able to outwit the influenza virus's notorious ability to mutate its way around the immune system—and therefore vaccines. What [team leader] Liu and her colleagues found is that immunized mice remained healthy even though the virus used to challenge them"—that is, infect them after the DNA vaccination—"surfaced 34 years after the strain of virus coded for by the naked DNA," making the two viruses highly diverse in many of their details.

The promise of "naked DNA" vaccines naturally prompted a flurry of research that attempted to apply the approach to other diseases. Two important areas of early research were AIDS and malaria, both of which lacked effective vaccines. For example, in October 1994, Stephen Hoffman published a paper reporting on the injection into mice of a plasmid containing the gene for a *Plasmodium yoelii yoelii* protein, and how it primed the animal's immune system against the malarial parasite. Four years later, Hoffman published a paper that showed how the efficacy of a DNA vaccine in mice could be boosted by using it together with a recombinant virus—one made by adding to the cowpox virus the same sequence used for the DNA vaccine inserted into the plasmid. A similar result was obtained by Adrian Hill in Oxford. Working with mice, Hill found that "priming with a DNA vaccine and boosting with a recombinant replication-defective vaccinia strain"—that is, a specially engineered variety of the cowpox virus that was unable to reproduce itself—"led to unprecedented complete protective efficacy in a murine [mouse] malarial model." Work has begun on using human trials "involving small numbers of volunteers, both in Oxford UK and in The Gambia, West Africa with very encouraging results." Vaccines are either injected directly into muscles or attached to tiny gold beads that are fired into the skin.

Coming up with a DNA vaccine for malaria would represent an enormous breakthrough. It would also be important as a solution that was particularly suitable for developing nations. As the 1997 American Academy of Microbiology report noted: "In contrast to many conventional vaccines . . . DNA vaccines remain stable at both high (below boiling) and low temperatures. DNA vaccines can be stored either dry or in an aqueous solution [dissolved in water]. The good stability of DNA vaccines should facilitate distribution and administration and eliminate the need for 'the cold chain'—the series of refrigerators required to maintain the viability of a vaccine during its distribution. Currently, maintaining the cold chain represents 80 percent of the cost of vaccinating individuals in developing nations."

DNA vaccines are also much easier to make than conventional vaccines because they are digital, and thus essentially the same in terms of their production. Ordinary vaccines, by contrast, are analogue—proteins that generally require unique processes to manufacture them. This is not only more expensive, but may require specialized equipment. As the American Academy of Microbiology report explained: "All DNA vaccines can be produced using similar fermentation, purification, and validation techniques." Once production facilities for one DNA vaccine have been created, in principle they can be used to produce any other DNA vaccine simply by changing the sequence that is inserted into the plasmid.

This is likely to prove an increasing advantage as further DNA vaccines are developed. Already, the list of DNA vaccines under development is wide ranging. Researchers at The Ohio State University have succeeded in immunizing mice against anthrax by injecting them with plasmids containing DNA from the pathogen. In 2000, a team from the NIH Vaccine Research Center and the Centers for Disease Control and Prevention reported in *Nature* that a plasmid-based DNA vaccine to prevent infection by another dreaded pathogen, the Ebola virus, worked in monkeys. More surprising, perhaps, is the possibility that DNA vaccines might be effective against illnesses like Alzheimer's. In 2001, the NIH made a $1.1 million grant to the University of South Florida to build on earlier work that showed how a conventional protein-based vaccine could prevent memory loss in mice that mimicked humans with Alzheimer's disease; part of the grant was specifically to enable researchers to develop a DNA vaccine version.

It was the very first DNA vaccine paper, published back in 1993, that noted an even more exciting possibility: "this approach to vaccination should be applicable to tumors as well as to infectious agents." If a suitable protein can be found in a cancer, it might be possible to use the corresponding sequence to create a DNA vaccine that would prime the immune system against the protein and hence the developing tumor. A cancer vaccine: it seems almost too good to be true—and perhaps it is. The company that stumbled across the DNA vaccine idea in the first place, Vical—which later adopted as its slogan "the naked DNA company"—has been pursuing the idea of a vaccine against metastatic melanoma, a particularly serious form of skin cancer. Its DNA vaccine Allovectin-7 had shown great promise, but in September 2002 the company announced that it was discontinuing its low-dose trial because a review of the preliminary results of some of the final-stage tests "indicated that the study would not meet statistical significance of its primary endpoints"—which roughly means that the results were not good enough to justify proceeding. However, Vical said that it would continue with its high-dose trial.

The company could also draw some comfort from a grant that it and Ohio State University had won a few months earlier to carry out preclinical research to develop DNA vaccines against anthrax, and a U.S. government contract to manufacture an experimental Ebola vaccine based on the work reported in *Nature* two years earlier. In the press release announcing the latter, the company explained the advantages of its approach for dangerous pathogens like anthrax and Ebola: "Vical's technology . . . is particularly well-suited to highly virulent bioterrorism targets because it allows development of a vaccine without handling the pathogen itself." Instead, fragments of its DNA are used. "This approach may have significant safety and manufacturing advantages over traditional vaccines that use live, weakened, or dead pathogens to produce an immune response."

Whether or not DNA vaccines emerge as an effective way to treat cancer, advanced genomics and bioinformatics are already providing invaluable new information about the genetic basis of the most common cancer, and suggesting new ways of preventing, detecting and treating them.

The links between cancer studies and genomics are long-standing. The Human Genome Project owed its existence in part to the fight against cancer. The Nobel laureate Renato Dulbecco had written an opinion piece for *Science* in 1986 entitled "A turning point in cancer research: sequencing the human genome," in which he advocated an international project to sequence the entire human genome as the best way to advance cancer research. As Robert Cook-Deegan wrote in his definitive history of the genesis and early years of the Human Genome Project: "For most biologists, Dulbecco's *Science* article was their first encounter with the idea of sequencing the human genome, and it provoked discussions in the laboratories of universities and research centers throughout the world." In doing so, it helped prepare the way for the subsequent developments.

History aside, there is an even more profound reason why cancer and the genomics are so intimately bound up with each other: in a sense, cancer is the quintessential disease of the genome. As a group of leading cancer researchers wrote in an analysis piece published in *Nature* in 2001: "All cancers are caused by abnormalities in DNA sequence." These abnormalities can be provoked by carcinogens like those found in cigarette smoke, or they may be the result of mistakes when a cell's DNA is copied. Cancers arise when changes mount up to confer an advantage on the abnormal cell—making it grow faster than those surrounding it. What is advantageous for the cell, however, can be disastrous for the organism, as nearby and distant tissues are invaded by the proliferating tumor, driven by its faulty DNA program. Sadly, this sequence of events is all too common: "Cancer is the most common genetic disease: one in three people in the western world develop cancer, and one in five die from it," the researchers wrote in *Nature*.

Several of the authors of the *Nature* article formed part of a group working on the Cancer Genome Project, billed as "the world's largest cancer genome study" when it was announced in October 2001 as part of the five-year, £300 million ($450 million) plan for Wellcome Trust's newly renamed Sanger Institute. The head of the project is Mike Stratton, who was also leader of the team that identified the *BRCA2* gene. As he explained at the time of the project's announcement: "Our goal is to identify large numbers of new genes that are mutated in cancer and to measure the frequency of mutations in every major cancer. There are more than 100 different types of cancer, but we need to understand what makes them all different. This information will then be used to develop new, more specific drugs for improved treatment. The scale of the Cancer Genome Project is without match anywhere in the world." This scale is a consequence of the bold approach employed, which depends critically on the availability of the complete human genome. Essentially, the aim is to examine every human gene for cancer-related mutations in a range of tumors by comparing DNA from tumor tissue with the corresponding sequences in the reference human genome. Clearly, searching through the 30,000 or so genes for multiple samples is a massive task, but by good fortune, the approach turned up significant results from just the first 20 genes examined.

One of the genes was *BRAF* (pronounced "B-RAF"), which codes for a protein that plays a key role in a signaling pathway controlling cell growth and division. A preliminary analysis of 15 cancer cell collections (mostly from breast and lung cancers) showed that in three cases there were single nucleotide substitutions—a one-letter change in the DNA coding for the *BRAF* protein. Three single-letter changes on their own were suggestive but hardly conclusive—they might be common SNPs without any practical significance. So the Cancer Genome Project team investigated another 530 cancer cell samples from a wide range of different tumors. This revealed that *BRAF* mutations were significantly more common for melanomas (cancer of the skin). An analysis piece that accompanied the *BRAF* paper in *Nature* described the 59 percent rate of *BRAF* mutations found in the melanomas as "staggering." Searches in another 378 tumors found two regions in the *BRAF* gene that turned up frequently in melanomas, and highlighted one mutation in the DNA sequence as particularly likely to occur.

The single letter change of T (thymine) to an A (adenine) at position 1796 in the DNA sequence for the *BRAF* gene accounted for 35 of the 38 mutations in melanomas. Further research provided a plausible explanation of why something as apparently trivial as a single letter change might lead to something as devastating as cancer. The altered DNA letter causes a corresponding change in the *BRAF* protein that effectively jams the signaling pathway controlling cell growth in the "on" position. As a result, the cell is able to grow abnormally. The *Nature* paper pointed out: "The high frequency of *BRAF* mutations in melanoma and the relative lack of effective therapies for advanced stages of this disease suggest that inhibition of BRAF activity may be an important new strategy in the treatment of metastatic melanoma"—skin cancer that has spread to other sites. "The identification of *BRAF* as a commonly mutated target in human cancer at such an early stage of our genome-wide screen suggests that systematic searches through cancer cell genomes for somatic mutations"—those in ordinary cells—"ultimately will provide a much more complete picture of the number and patterns of mutations underlying human oncogenesis"—the development and growth of tumors.

The *BRAF* discovery was a triumph, even though it had undoubtedly been a piece of good fortune that such a promising result had been obtained so quickly; the news piece accompanying the report in *Nature* was titled "Lucky draw in the gene raffle." In many ways, though, the Cancer Genome Project represents the application of what might be called traditional genomic approaches, albeit on a massive, almost industrial scale. Parallel to this important work, there are several exciting new areas of research that suggest that the processes affecting not just cancer, but the expression of the entire genome, are more complex than was originally thought. In particular, it seems that there are factors that would escape even meticulous searches such as those undertaken by the Cancer Genome Project.

As the *BRAF* gene shows, cancers can arise when the normal regulatory machinery of the cell goes awry. Another way for this to occur is for key genes, known as tumor suppressor genes, to be inactivated. These are genes that are normally turned on when tumors occur; they can set off various kinds of molecular events to halt or kill the cancerous growth. If tumor suppressor genes are unable to produce their respective proteins, a vital element of the body's defenses is lost. A series of papers in the late 1990s revealed a novel way in which tumor suppressor genes might be inactivated that did not involve changes in the genes of the kind encountered in *BRAF*. More remarkably, the entire DNA sequence of As, Cs, Gs, and Ts for the surrounding regions also remained invariant. This meant, for example, that the inactivation could not be due to a simple change in the binding site for a transcription factor that would normally switch the gene on. This apparent paradox was resolved by the observation that certain regions next to genes—those called "upstream"—did change, but in a subtle way not involving any alteration to the basic DNA code.

One of the important indicators of the likely presence of a gene among the billions of chemical letters found in genomes is the presence of what is known as a CpG island: these are regions that have a relatively high number of the chemical pair C and G (the 'p' refers to the phosphate group that joins them). The C (cytosine) letter has the property that it can add an extra group of atoms, (one carbon and three hydrogen) in a process known as methylation—"methyl" is the name given to the CH_3 group. Research has shown that aberrant methylation of CpG islands can cause the gene that is "downstream" of the CpG island to be inactivated. If this gene is a tumor suppressor, it means that abnormal methylation could potentially cause a cascade of molecular events that culminates in the proliferation of a cancer.

The way in which adding a methyl group to the cytosine causes the downstream gene to be inactivated has an intriguing parallel in computing. When programmers are writing code, they may want to enter comments that will not be processed by the computer as it runs the program. In some languages, this can be achieved simply by prefixing the lines of a comment with a special symbol—generally #—which signals that what follows is not to be executed as computer code. In the same way, when testing software, it is often convenient to inactivate particular parts of the program. This is frequently achieved by turning what is otherwise functional code into a comment, for example, by prefixing the line of code with a #. The added methyl group CH_3 functions like the attached # sign: both cause the code that comes after them—whether DNA code or computer code—to be ignored.

A paper published in 2000 explored more thoroughly the idea that methylation was linked with cancer. The large team—23 researchers from across the U.S.—carried out a major analysis of methylation in nearly 100 human tumors. As they explained, previous investigations of aberrant CpG-island methylation in human cancer had concentrated on a few genes of interest, and examined less than 15 out of the estimated 45,000 CpG islands in the genome. The current study reported on an analysis of 1,184 randomly selected CpG islands in 98 human tumors.

The effort was repaid: "We estimate that an average of 600 CpG islands . . . of the 45,000 in the genome were aberrantly methylated in the tumours," the researchers wrote.

As well as establishing that aberrant methylation of CpG islands was common in tumors, the team also made an important discovery concerning the way that methylation varied in different tumors: "We identified patterns of CpG-methylation that were shared within each tumour type . . . Thus, the methylation of particular subsets of CpG islands may have consequences for specific tumour types." It seemed that each kind of tumor had its own signature in terms of methylation; if such patterns could be reliably established, they would offer yet another way—along with gene expression and protein profiles—of discriminating among tumors using bioinformatics, in this case purely on the basis of their methylation patterns.

A paper published two years later by a German group built on this work to create special microarrays for measuring methylation in tissues. As models for its approach, the paper cited recently published advances in cDNA arrays: the work at the Whitehead Institute that had succeeded in distinguishing two forms of leukemia (ALL and AML), and the paper from Brown's group revealing two distinct kinds of lymphoma. The German researchers noted: "As for mRNA expression profiles, genome-wide methylation patterns represent a molecular fingerprint of cancer tissues and therefore tumour class prediction and discovery should be feasible using methylation profiles," similar to the ones gleaned from gene expression.

Most of the authors of the 2002 paper were employed by the company Epigenomics, based in Berlin, Germany. Along with the Sanger Centre, Epigenomics was one of the prime movers behind the Human Epigenome Consortium, set up in December 1999 "to undertake the twin Herculean tasks of compiling methylation patterns for every tissue and raising an undetermined wad of cash to get going," as *Science* put it. Some of that "wad of cash" came from the European Commission, which announced in September 2000 that it would be giving €1.2 million ($1.2 million) for a pilot project.

The head of the Sanger side, Stephan Beck, explained: "As part of the human Epigenome pilot study, we have been determining the methylation patterns of genes within the Major Histocompatibility complex (MHC), a region on . . . chromosome 6 that is essential to immunity and is associated with more diseases than any other region in the human genome. Differentially methylated CpGs . . . have been catalogued as methylation variable positions (MVPs). MVPs can be epigenotyped for disease association in a similar way as single nucleotide polymorphisms (SNPs)." Just as the particular pattern of SNPs that are found in an individual's genome form the genotype, so the specific pattern of methylation makes up the epigenotype. The full-scale Human Epigenome Project was launched in October 2003.

A further indication of the growing importance of methylation patterns for genomics and medicine came in March 2003, when Roche announced a collaboration with Epigenomics "to develop a range of molecular diagnostic and pharmacogenomic cancer products based on Epigenomics' DNA-methylation technologies . . . Under the terms of the agreement, Roche will make an upfront payment of €4 million [$4 million] and in addition provide [research and development] funding, milestone payments and royalties on product sales. Both partners estimate that if all products are successfully launched, the total value of the agreement could exceed €100 million (about $100 million)." Although this was a big "if," the deal was clearly comparable to other trailblazing agreements made between genomic start-ups and major pharmaceutical companies, such as Human Genome Science's $125 million deal with SmithKline Beecham and deCODE's, also with Roche, which was potentially worth $200 million.

Cancer is not the only area where methylation may prove important—and even lucrative—for companies. Just as the methyl group can be added to cytosine, C, in animal and plants, so it can be attached to another letter—A, or adenine—in bacteria, with often similarly dramatic results. A paper published in *Science* in 1999 described a specially-created mutant of the bacterium *Salmonella typhimurium*, a leading cause of human gastroenteritis, and an organism that was used as a mouse model of human typhoid fever. The mutant form lacked the ability to produce DNA adenine methylase (DAM), a protein involved in methylating adenine. Remarkably, these variants turned out to be avirulent—unable to cause the usual disease—and yet still able to function as live vaccines for typhoid fever in mice. When given to a mouse, they stimulated production of antibodies that would protect against the full pathogen, even though not causing any ill effects themselves. Indeed, immunized mice were able to withstand around 10,000 times a dose that was normally fatal for them. This is a perfect combination for a vaccine: able to prime the immune system fully and yet posing no threat itself.

Such a vaccine for humans is sorely needed against *Salmonella typhimurium*, since antibiotics are fast losing their efficacy against it. A World Health Organization report had warned in 1997: "Over the years, antibiotic resistant strains have developed that are difficult to control and there is a body of evidence in the scientific literature suggesting the possibility that some of these strains may have emerged due to use of antibiotics in intensive animal husbandry. . . . The incidence of bacterial resistance has increased at an alarming pace in recent years and is expected to continue rising at a similar or even greater rate in the future as antimicrobial agents or antibiotics lose their effectiveness." Vaccines using DAM-deficient mutants might well be the answer—and not just for *Salmonella typhimurium*. The *Science* paper pointed out: "DNA adenine methylases are potentially excellent targets for both vaccines and antimicrobials. They are highly conserved"—the amino acid sequences of the proteins are very similar—"in many pathogenic bacteria that cause significant morbidity and mortality," including cholera, typhus, the plague, syphilis, pathogenic *E. coli*, and *H. influenzae*. Later work showed that mice immunized with a DAM-deficient mutant of *Yersinia pseudotuberculosis*, which normally causes blood poisoning in mice, were highly protected against the virulent form. This offers hope that the technique might work for the human equivalent, *Yersinia pestis*—the plague.

It is remarkable how an apparently obscure area of genomics—the methylation of DNA nucleotides—has turned out to be a possible source not only of much-needed vaccines against drug-resistant pathogens, but also of novel tests for diagnosing and classifying cancers. In this respect, it is perhaps a preview of a field that promises to become one of the most interesting in the wake of the Human Genome Project: *epigenetics*, generally defined as the study of changes in gene expression that can be inherited but occur without a direct change in the DNA sequence.

One reason why epigenetics may prove so important is that it could help resolve some of the remaining mysteries of DNA. For example, given that practically every cell in the human body has exactly the same DNA that derives from the original DNA program in the fertilized egg, how is it possible for different cell types—muscles, skin, nerves—to arise and then reproduce unchanged for decades? How does the cell mark the switch? Another conundrum that seems to fly in the face of traditional genomics is the fact that it is possible for genes in a developing embryo to "remember" whether they came from the mother or the father—even though at the level of DNA letters there is no obvious difference. This phenomenon, called "imprinting," is most noticeable in the crosses of some animals. For example, when a horse is crossed with a donkey, different results are obtained according to whether a jack (male donkey) mates with a mare (female horse)—resulting in the familiar mule—or a stallion (male horse) with a jenny (female donkey). In this case the offspring is visibly different from a mule and is known as a hinny.

Methylation, described earlier, is one example of an epigenetic phenomenon. Abnormal methylation patterns may explain why few cloned mammal embryos survive to birth or live long after being born: genetic errors at the level of the sequence are ruled out because, if they survive, cloned animals can reproduce sexually, yielding normal offspring. Similarly, the observed differences between twins with identical genomes might also be due to subtle epigenetic divergences that have so far escaped detection.

Another kind of epigenetics involves the way in which DNA is packed physically into the nucleus. The immense sequence of each chromosome is wrapped around bead-like collections of proteins called histones, to form the nucleosome. Each of the histone proteins has a short tail made up of amino acids. Just as DNA letters can add the methyl group, there is increasing evidence that the amino acids in the histone tails can add a variety of groups to create what has been called a nucleosome or histone code. According to proponents of the theory, it is the particular combinations of chemical groups that help determine whether one cell type will change into another, or simply reproduce itself, for example. "We envision that this 'nucleosome code' . . . permits the assembly of different epigenetic states, leading to distinct 'readouts' of the genetic information, such as gene activation versus gene silencing"— whether particular genes are expressed or not—"or, more globally, cell proliferation versus cell differentiation." The histone code might operate as a kind of marker system, flagging to the cell's machinery which sections of the genome should be expressed according to the circumstances. It may even represent a completely new level of complexity in gene expression. In addition, it seems likely that some diseases involve changes to the histone code at various sites.

While details of the histone code remain sketchy, and its clinical applications far off, a third epigenetic effect is now relatively well understood and is already showing promise in a wide variety of medical situations. The story begins back in 1990, when a group of biologists at the DNA Plant Technology Corporation in California published a paper detailing their efforts to produce a deeper-hued petunia by introducing an extra gene that coded for a key protein in the production of plant color. Instead of the deeper hues, they found that 42 percent of the plants with the extra gene turned white: the two copies of the genes seemed to be switching each other off in some way. Closer examination showed that the mRNA levels for the gene were reduced fiftyfold. The team, led by Richard Jorgensen, termed this "co-suppression."

Although confirmed by other plant researchers, and for the fungus *Neurospora crassa*, where the effect was called "quelling," the result remained something of a curiosity until 1998, when Andrew Fire and Craig Mello reported on work they and fellow researchers had carried out on the nematode worm. At first sight it had nothing to do with the earlier results: Fire and his colleagues were exploring the phenomenon of RNA interference, the use of specially-constructed RNA to manipulate gene expression by interfering with the mRNA. It was believed that this arose from the hybridization—the fusing together—of the mRNA with its complement, called antisense RNA, to prevent the former from being translated by the ribosomes into the corresponding protein.

For example, assume that the mRNA were represented by the (unrealistically short) sequence ACGGUGUUAC (since RNA uses the four chemical letters A, C, G, and U instead of A, C, G, and T). The antisense RNA would be UGCCACAAUG, which, it was supposed, would hybridize with the normal (sense) mRNA to produce the double-stranded (ds) RNA

ACGGUGUUAC
UGCCACAAUG

and so block the production of the protein encoded by the mRNA, leading to reduced gene expression.

However, as Fire and his colleagues noted in their paper, which appeared in *Nature* in February 1998: "Despite the usefulness of RNA interference in *C. elegans*, two features of the process have been difficult to explain. First, sense and antisense RNA preparations are each sufficient to cause interference." If the hybridization model were correct, it might have been expected that only antisense RNA would work. "Second, interference effects can persist well into the next generation"—in other words, it was epigenetic.

To explore this intriguing phenomenon further, Fire and his colleagues injected single-stranded RNAs—both sense and antisense, separately—into nematodes. Just as the Vical researchers had done for their work with naked DNA, Fire and his team also included a control experiment to provide a check on background effects. This consisted of injecting sense and antisense RNA together. As they wrote in *Nature*: "To our surprise, we found that double-stranded RNA"—formed by the hybridization of the sense and antisense strands of RNA injected together—"was substantially more effective at producing interference than was either strand individually."

Only a few molecules of injected double-stranded RNA were required for each cell, which meant that there was likely to be some kind of amplification process involved, since otherwise such a small number of molecules would be unable to affect the much larger production of mRNA. This might also explain the puzzling earlier results: the reason that both sense and antisense RNA seemed to work was probably due to their contamination with tiny quantities of double-stranded RNA, the true cause of the interference. Even though the quantities were minimal, and thus easily overlooked, they were enough to trigger the extremely sensitive RNA silencing process that Fire and Mello had discovered. Clearly something new and important was going on here. The mechanism that was gradually elucidated over the next few years proved to have profound implications for a wide range of work, including clinical applications.

Central to the RNAi (RNA interference) process is a family of enzymes—proteins—found across a wide range of species, called Dicer. As its name suggests, Dicer's job is to cut things up—in this case, double-stranded RNA. The results are what are known as short interfering RNAs—siRNAs. Although these are very small—just over 20 nucleotides long—compared to the DNA coding sequences for genes or their mRNA transcripts, they are highly targeted. These double-stranded siRNAs then bind to a group of proteins that form what is known as the RNAi silencing complex—a molecular machine that is able to destroy RNA—where they lose the sense strand. The remaining anti-sense strand functions as a kind of template that only matches the single-stranded RNA that has the complementary sequence. If the silencing complex with a particular antisense template comes across the matching single-stranded RNA, it binds to it and breaks it down.

In the experiment of Fire and Mello, the dsRNA that they injected into the nematode worm corresponded to a 742-nucleotide segment of a particular gene, called *unc-22*. The Dicer enzyme cut this up into double-stranded siRNAs, which then bound to the RNAi silencing complex, and lost one strand to leave the template exposed. When the silencing complex met an mRNA transcript from the *unc-22* gene, the template matched part of it, and so the silencing complex removed the mRNA. No mRNA meant no gene expression, as the *Nature* paper reported. The amplification effect might be explained in part by the fact that a single, long dsRNA can give rise to many siRNAs, since these are much shorter. Each of these can in turn target and destroy the corresponding long mRNA sequence. Other processes may also be involved.

As well as the *how*, the *why* of RNA interference also gradually became clearer. Remarkably, it seems that the mechanism represents the genome's immune system. For example, when certain viruses invade a cell, they copy themselves by passing through a double-stranded RNA form—the trigger required for RNA interference. As a result, corresponding siRNAs would be generated and the RNAi silencing complex primed to detect and destroy precisely the sequence found in the viral RNA, thus eliminating it.

Alongside the theoretical interest of what is clearly an ancient defense mechanism, much of the excitement over RNAi derives from that fact that it provides an extremely powerful experimental technique for exploring gene function. In theory, it allows any gene to be switched off at any point in an organism's life cycle. This was demonstrated by a paper published in *Nature* in 2003, which studied the effect of systematically inactivating 86 percent of the 19,427 predicted genes in the nematode genome one at a time in order to deduce their likely roles in the organism.

Traditionally, the way genes have been investigated is to produce a mutant permanently lacking that gene and to observe the differences compared with normal varieties. For an organism like the nematode worm, however, the work involved in producing 20,000 mutants—the estimated number of genes—was considerable. Moreover, those mutants lacking a vital gene would die at an early stage of development, rendering them useless for later experiments. RNAi offered a promising alternative, since normal worms could be used, and throughout their life cycle. In fact, things were even easier thanks to the remarkable fact that gene silencing also occurs when a worm simply grazes on a lawn of *E. coli* bacteria—its favorite food—that have been genetically modified to express the corresponding dsRNA.

Producing gene knock-outs for more complex animals is even harder than for nematodes—and ethically impossible for humans—so the development of RNAi methods for mammals was even more of a breakthrough. The pace of development in the RNAi world can be judged from the fact that the effect was first described in mammals in May 2001, and yet less than two years later, Cancer Research UK, the leading British cancer charity, was already applying it to humans on a massive scale, as part of what it called a "groundbreaking initiative on RNA interference." The press release explained: "Scientists will build on the huge success of the Human Genome Project, inactivating almost 10,000 genes, one at a time, in order to find out precisely what they do and how they might contribute to cancer's development. Their ultimate aim will be to identify the cluster of genes which constitute the essence of cancer—likely to be ideal targets for new anti-cancer drugs."

In addition to the "classic" RNAi approach—switching normal genes off one at time—the Cancer Research UK scientists would also be approaching the problem from another angle, trying to block abnormal genes: "Researchers will also bombard cancer cells with 30,000 pieces of interference RNA in order to answer one of the ultimate questions in cancer biology—what is the genetic essence of a malignant cell? They will screen the treated cells for the handful which have reverted to type and become normal again. The set of genes switched off by RNA interference in these cells may represent the most crucial group of cancer genes in the human genome and are likely to be extremely good targets for future anti-cancer drugs."

The potential of RNAi does not end there. Since RNAi seems to have originated in part as an ancient immune system against viruses that threatened cells hundreds of millions of years ago, one hope might be that it could be co-opted to attack other, more recent kinds. An early paper exploring this idea in mice showed that RNAi could reduce the gene expression of a protein found in the virus causing human hepatitis C. The same month, July 2002, two papers reported on success in inhibiting infection by the AIDS virus HIV-1, while another detailed how siRNA could protect human cells against infection by the virus that causes polio.

RNAi might also help in the fight against cancers that are caused by viral infections. In September 2002, researchers at the University of York announced that using it they had succeeded in turning off two key genes in the human papilloma virus, which causes the majority of cases of cervical cancer. The silencing of one viral gene caused the growth of the tumor cells to slow; when the other gene was silenced, all the cancer cells died. Unlike many current forms of cancer treatment, the disappearance of the tumor took place without any adverse affects on normal cells—something that one of the researchers behind the work, Jo Milner, called "absolutely remarkable."

Milner also noted: "These cancer cells were not engineered in the laboratory. They were derived from a human tumour many years ago. Despite growing as cancer cells for years (due to the viral infection) our work demonstrates that the cells' normal control systems have remained intact. As soon as we silenced the viral genes, the infected cancer cells 'committed suicide'," a process known as apoptosis. Even though the cells were not "engineered in the laboratory," the experiment was conducted there: one caveat for all of this work is that turning experimental results, however promising, into clinical therapies remains a major task.

One of the principal challenges in producing a clinical solution is how to get the siRNA into human cells—especially ones that are difficult to access, like those in the brain. Simply injecting them would not achieve this, so a team led by Beverly Davidson at the University of Iowa borrowed a technique that has been widely used in gene therapy. An adenovirus—which typically causes respiratory infections, and is very adept at insinuating its DNA into human cells—was genetically modified to express a preconstructed siRNA once inside the host cell. Unlike gene therapy—which started from the reasonable idea of trying to correct the bugs in the DNA program directly, but which has failed to live up to the great hopes many had when it was first carried out in the early 1990s—this approach does not change the cell's DNA. This is important, because earlier successes in gene therapy have more recently turned to tragedy when the inserted gene ended up causing cancer. Instead of correcting bugs in the code, it disrupted other sections of the program with serious results. RNAi, on the other hand, leaves the faulty DNA untouched. It achieves its effects by jamming the genomic signal afterwards, when it is on its way to a ribosome, and before it results in the production of the erroneous protein.

Davidson's work in 2002 showed not only that this virus-mediated strategy worked in mice, but also that it could be applied to a major class of neurodegenerative diseases involving genes that result in defective proteins—the best known of which is Huntington's disease. Nancy Wexler, one of the lead researchers who in 1993 had located the gene responsible for Huntington's, said: "When I first heard of this work, it just took my breath away."

R NA's role in gene silencing would be important enough, particularly because of its clinical potential, but it assumes an even greater significance in the context of other recent results. The first clue that RNA was much more than a simple intermediary between genes and proteins came in 1993, when researchers led by Victor Ambros found that a gene called *lin-4* of the nematode worm encoded for a very small RNA—just 22 nucleotides long. Unusually, this RNA was not converted into a protein, but acted directly on mRNA to block its translation into a protein. This remained something of an oddity—rather like co-suppression in plants—until a few years afterwards, when another RNA was found in the nematode, *let-7*, that also produced no protein but regulated another mRNA by binding to it. Significantly, it, too, was extremely small—21 nucleotides long—and both of the affected proteins were involved with developmental timing, regulating when and how the worm grew.

The second gene had been discovered by a group led by Gary Ruvkun, and less than a year later, he and his team published a paper in *Nature* that transformed the significance of the earlier discoveries. An extensive series of database searches using BLAST detected genes homologous to *let-7* across a huge swathe of the animal kingdom, including just about every higher model organism—from the nematode worm, fruit fly, sea urchin, and sea squirt to the zebrafish, frog, mouse, and humans. Moreover, these genes were frequently involved in major developmental transitions. This was a remarkable finding, because it suggested that some of the most fundamental and profound changes in all higher animals were determined not by proteins—hitherto believed to be the principal way of regulating gene expression—but by short pieces of RNA. Ruvkun and his team also recognized that their results, involving what they dubbed "small temporal RNAs" (stRNAs), were suggestive of something else: "The 21-[nucleotide] length of the *let*-7 RNA is highly conserved"—it was mostly the same across a very wide range of species—"indicating that this size is central to its function. It may be significant that this length is similar to the 21-25 [nucleotide] RNAs observed during RNA interference (RNAi)-directed downregulation of target messenger RNAs."

A paper published in *Science* the following year confirmed the connection. As the authors put it: "The RNA interference and stRNA pathways intersect. Both pathways require the RNA-processing enzyme Dicer to produce the active small-RNA component that represses gene expression." The increasingly complex picture that emerged encouraged researchers to look for more small RNA. In the past, the focus had been on much longer RNA sequences: if smaller molecules were detected, they were generally regarded as by-products or even as experimental errors. Once researchers started looking, they began to find what were called microRNAs (miRNAs) or non-coding RNAs (ncRNAs) in increasing numbers—one 2001 issue of *Science* reported on over 100 of them.

Reflecting on this growing collection of RNAs, Gary Ruvkun wrote in a review of the area: "The number of genes in the tiny RNA world may turn out to be very large, numbering in the hundreds or even thousands in each genome." He then offered a striking metaphor: "Tiny RNA genes may be the biological equivalent of dark matter"—the hidden material believed to permeate the universe, and which is needed to explain many otherwise anomalous observations—"All around us but almost escaping detection, until first revealed by *C. elegans* genetics." At the end of 2002, this "dark matter" emerged in a blaze of publicity when *Science* magazine chose the rapid succession of discoveries about RNA's "astonishing feats" as the winner of its "Breakthrough of the Year" award. Tiny RNA, it seemed, had hit the big time.

If its importance is no longer in doubt, the underlying mechanism coordinating possibly thousands of RNA genes still remains a mystery. One elegant theory, however, not only provides a framework for RNA, but also offers an explanation for the single most puzzling result to come out of genomics. The title of Australian researcher John Mattick's 2001 paper presents his idea in a nutshell: "Non-coding RNAs: the architects of eukaryotic complexity." He wrote: "The genome sequencing projects have revealed an unexpected problem in our understanding of the molecular basis of developmental complexity in the higher organisms: complex organisms have lower numbers of protein coding genes than anticipated." For decades, scientists had quoted a figure of 100,000 genes in the human genome, only to find less than a third of that number when the draft sequence was analyzed. This raised the immediate question: where does the observed complexity come from, if the basic building blocks are largely the same for all higher animals?

For Mattick, the answer lay in the regulation of the gene expression—how and when the building blocks are deployed. Guided by striking discoveries like the highly-conserved small temporal RNAs that are able to bring about profound organism-wide effects, he suggested that directing this choreography were the non-coding RNAs, which emerged, therefore, as "the architects of eukaryotic complexity."

As Mattick pointed out in his paper, these non-coding RNAs "represent the vast majority of genomic output in higher organisms." In humans, fully 98 percent of all transcriptional output is RNA that does not code for proteins. "The failure to recognize the possible significance of these RNAs," Mattick said, "is based on the central dogma, as determined from bacterial molecular genetics, that genes are synonymous with proteins, and that RNAs are just temporary reflections of this information." Boldly, Mattick proposed that it was time to move beyond such neat but erroneous simplicities.

If his view is right, it might solve another long-standing mystery: why in eukaryotes genes are broken up into stretches of DNA called exons, which code for distinct parts of the protein, separated by other regions known as introns, which do not. The traditional view is that this modular approach permits the exons, and hence the domains they code for, to be put together in different ways, allowing several proteins to be derived from one gene. This may well be one reason, but Mattick noted that it is not necessarily the prime one. He pointed out, for example, that there is a good correlation between how many introns there are on average and developmental complexity. Introns and other non-coding RNAs show interesting patterns of conservation across large evolutionary distances, which indicates that they contain important structures that Nature has chosen to reuse across species.

Summarizing, Mattick wrote: "These observations suggest that a complex network of RNA signaling with a sophisticated infrastructure operates in higher eukaryotes, which enables direct gene-gene communication"—without the need for intermediary transcription factors acting on binding sites, that is—"and the integration and regulation of gene activity at many different levels. . . . This is reminiscent of network control in other information processing systems, such as computers and the brain." He added, in conclusion: "Understanding the biology of higher organisms will not simply require understanding of the proteome, which is the focus of so much research at present, but also the identification of all non-coding RNAs"—sometimes called the RNome—"their expression patterns, processing, and signaling pathways." In other words, the current fields of functional genomics and systems biology will need to be reinvented—or at least revisited—taking non-coding RNA into account. No less a person than Leroy Hood agrees: "You've got no choice but to do it," he says. More profoundly, the nature of the genome will need to be reevaluated too: "Far from being evolutionary junk," Mattick wrote, "introns and other non-coding RNAs form the primary control architecture that underpins eukaryotic differentiation and development"—they mold life itself.

Another pioneer of the RNA frontier, Sean Eddy, offered a historical parallel—and a prescription. "The current situation in RNA is reminiscent of the early days in protein sequence analysis. Not too long ago, the protein sequence database was published on paper"—Margaret Dayhoff's *Atlas*—"and algorithms for rigorous sequence comparison were well known to the cognoscenti but were too impractical and expensive to run on the computers of the time. Then the sequence database expanded rapidly, and fast, practical, heuristic tools like BLAST and FASTA appeared forthwith." The way forward is clear. "If we are indeed at the forefront of a significant expansion of known ncRNA [non-coding RNA] gene sequences, it is time for RNA computational biologists to step up and apply our known body of theory to the development of practical analysis programs and well-organized databases." What is needed now is a BLAST and a GenBank for the world of RNA, Eddy suggested, a new generation of bioinformatics.

During the first 50 years of DNA studies, research concentrated on elucidating the sequences of genes as well as the structure and properties of their physical correlates, the proteins. This was decoding the *what* of genomics. The apotheosis of this first era was the official completion of the Human Genome Project on April 14, 2003, and its subsequent annotation. The next 50 years will see the focus shift to the next level, to decoding the *how* of genomics. If Mattick is right, at the center of it all will be the elusive RNA, at once information and structure, hovering between the two worlds of digital and analogue, uniting them.

NOTES

The author conducted interviews included in this chapter in May 2003 with the following individual: L. Hood.

1. p. 321 *The success of the whole genome shotgun* R.D. Fleischmann, et al., "Whole-genome random sequencing and assembly of *Haemophilus influenzae* Rd," *Science* 269 (1995): 496–512.

2. p. 321 *It is incredible to realize that two years* N. Wade, "Thinking small paying off big in gene quest," *The New York Times*, February 3, 1997.

3. p. 322 *It was completed in 1978 by Fred Sanger* F. Sanger, "The early days of DNA sequences," *Nature Medicine* 7 (2001): 267–268.

4. p. 322 *this approach eliminates the need for initial* R.D. Fleischmann, et al., "Whole-genome random sequencing and assembly of *Haemophilus influenzae* Rd," *Science* 269 (1995): 496–512.

5. p. 322 *For most of this century the cause of peptic ulcer disease* J.F Tomb, et al., "The complete genome sequence of the gastric pathogen *Helicobacter pylori*," *Nature* 388 (1997): 539–347.

6. p. 322 *Despite its importance as an infectious agent,* C.M. Fraser, et al., "Complete genome sequence of *Treponema pallidum*, the syphilis spirochete," *Science* 281 (1998): 375–388.

7. p. 323 *the $25 million funding came from the Wellcome* N. Wade, "Thinking small paying off big in gene quest," *The New York Times*, February 3, 1997.

8. p. 323 *The tubercle bacillus . . . continues to claim* S.T. Cole., et al., "Deciphering the biology of *Mycobacterium tuberculosis* from the complete genome sequence," *Nature* 393 (1998): 537–544.

9. p. 323 *has achieved the dubious distinction of overtaking* The Sanger Institute press release, March 1, 2002.

10. p. 324 *this work on the post-genomic applications* The Sanger Institute press release, March 1, 2002.

11. p. 324 *When untreated, cholera is a disease of extraordinarily* J.F. Heidelberg, et al., "DNA sequence of both chromosomes of the cholera pathogen *Vibrio cholerae*," *Nature* 406 (2000): 477–483.

12. p. 324 *almost every preconceived notion that* J.C. Venter, "Whole genome shotgun sequencing." Talk at Conference of the Max Planck Society, Ringberg Castle, October 4–7, 2000. Online at *http://www.mpiwg-berlin.mpg.de/ringberg/Talks/venter/venter.html.*

13. p. 324 *Some [scientists] argued that sequencing* J.C. Venter, "Whole genome shotgun sequencing." Talk at Conference of the Max Planck Society, Ringberg Castle, October 4–7, 2000. Online at *http://www.mpiwg-berlin.mpg.de/ringberg/Talks/venter/venter.html.*

14. p. 324 *It turned out that the cholera genome,* J.C. Venter, "Whole genome shotgun sequencing." Talk at Conference of the Max Planck Society, Ringberg Castle, October 4–7, 2000. Online at *http://www.mpiwg-berlin.mpg.de/ringberg/Talks/venter/venter.html.*

15. p. 325 *in 1998 there were 170 staff;* P. Raeburn, "A genome project against disease," *Business Week*, June 24, 2002.

16. p. 325 *The accompanying press release from the Sanger Centre* The Sanger Centre press release, October 4, 2001.

17. p. 326 *The benefits of making this kind of information* The Sanger Centre press release, October 4, 2001.

18. p. 327 *around 300–500 million cases of malaria* M.J. Gardner, et al., "Genome sequence of the human malaria parasite *Plasmodium falciparum*," *Nature* 419 (2002): 498–511.

19. p. 327 *several delegates [at a subsequent international conference] reminded the meeting* D. Butler, "Malaria meeting charts rocky path ahead," *Nature* 388 (1997): 219.

20. p. 327 *Britain's Wellcome Trust last week gave* D. Butler, "Funding assured for international malaria sequencing project," *Nature* 388 (1997): 701.

21. p. 327 *The experience has convinced the trust* D. Butler, "Funding assured for international malaria sequencing project," *Nature* 388 (1997): 701.

22. p. 327 *The complete sequencing of chromosome 2* M.J. Gardner, et al., "Chromosome 2 sequence of the human malaria parasite *Plasmodium falciparum*," *Science* 282 (1998): 1126–1132.

23. p. 328 *The bulk of the sequencing work for* K.S. Aultman, et al., "*Anopheles gambiae* genome: completing the malaria triad," *Science* 298 (2002): 13.

24. p. 328 *The mosquito is both an elegant, exquisitely* R.A. Holt, et al., "The genome sequence of the malaria mosquito *Anopheles gambiae*," *Science* 298 (2002): 129–149.

25. p. 328 *Knowing the sequence of the* Plasmodium falciparum S.L. Hoffman, "Research (genomics) is crucial to attacking malaria," *Science* 290 (2000): 1509.

26. p. 329 *A frank appraisal of the probable outcome* C.F. Curtis, "The case for deemphasizing genomics in malaria control," *Science* 290 (2000): 1508.

27. p. 329 *The efficacy of these drugs* H. Jomaa, et al., "Inhibitors of the nonmevalonate pathway of isoprenoid biosynthesis as antimalarial drugs," *Science* 285 (1999): 1573–1576.

28. p. 329 *Our findings indicate that fosmidomycin is an effective,* M.A. Missinou, et al., "Fosmidomycin for malaria," *Lancet* 360 (2002) 1941–1942.

29. p. 330 *Traditional vaccines were pioneered by* For an excellent introduction to both traditional and DNA vaccines, see: "The scientific future of DNA for immunization," American Academy of Microbiology. Online at *http://www.asm.org/Academy/index.asp?bid=2183.*

30. p. 330 *The World Health Organization, among the first* "The scientific future of DNA for immunization, American Academy of Microbiology." Online at *http://www.asm.org/Academy/index.asp?bid=2183.*

31. p. 330 *were attempting to engineer live mice* J. Cohen, "Naked DNA points way to vaccines," *Science* 259 (1993): 1691–1692.

32. p. 330 *As a control, they left* J. Cohen, "Naked DNA points way to vaccines," *Science* 259 (1993): 1691–1692.

33. p. 331 *confoundingly, the animals' muscle cells* J. Cohen, "Naked DNA points way to vaccines," *Science* 259 (1993): 1691–1692.

34. p. 331 *Vical entered into a research collaboration* "Vical Products: Partnership Programs," online at *http://www.vical.com/products/partnership.htm.*

35. p. 331 *Not only did the vaccine work, but the Merck/Vical* J. Cohen, "Naked DNA points way to vaccines," *Science* 259 (1993): 1691–1692.

36. p. 331 *priming with a DNA vaccine and boosting* "Howard Hughes Medical Institute," Adrian Hill. Online at *http://www.hhmi.org/grants/awards/indiv/scholars/hill.html.*

37. p. 331 *involving small numbers of volunteers, both* "Malaria Vaccine Trials, Clinical trials." Online at *http://www.malaria-vaccines.org.uk/5.shtml.*

38. p. 332 *All DNA vaccines can be produced* "The scientific future of DNA for immunization," American Academy of Microbiology. Online at *http://www.asm.org/Academy/index.asp?bid=2183*

39. p. 332 *Researchers at the Ohio State University* New DNA-based vaccine approach protects mice against anthrax., Ohio State University release. Online at *http://www.osu.edu/units/research/archive/anthrax.htm.*

40. p. 332 *reported in* Nature *that a plasmid-based* N.J. Sullivan, et al., "Development of a preventive vaccine for Ebola virus infection in primates," *Nature* 408 (2000): 605–609.

41. p. 332 *In 2001, the NIH made a $1.1 million grant* "NIH adds $1.1 million to USF Alzheimer's vaccine research," University of South Florida press release, October 23, 2001.

42. p. 332 *this approach to vaccination should be* J.B., Ulmer, et al., "Heterologous protection against influenza by injection of DNA encoding a viral protein," *Science* 259 (1993): 1745–1749.

43. p. 333 *indicated that the study would not meet* Vical press release, September 18, 2002.

44. p. 333 *it and Ohio State University had won* Vical press release, July 3, 2002.

45. p. 333 *a U.S. government contract to manufacture* Vical press release, July 16, 2002.

46. p. 333 *Vical's technology . . . is particularly well-suited* Vical press release, July 16, 2002.

47. p. 333 *This approach may have significant safety* Vical press release, July 16, 2002.

48. p. 333 *For most biologists, Dulbecco's* Science *article* R. Cook-Deegan, "*The Gene Wars*" (New York/London: Norton, 1995), 107.

49. p. 333 *All cancers are caused by abnormalities* A.P. Futreal, et al., "Cancer and genomics," *Nature* 409 (2001): 850–852.

50. p. 334 *Cancer is the most common genetic disease:* A.P. Futreal, et al., "Cancer and genomics," *Nature* 409 (2001): 850–852.

51. p. 334 *the world's largest cancer genome study* Sanger Institute press release, October 15, 2001.

52. p. 334 *Our goal is to identify large numbers* Sanger Institute press release, October 15, 2001.

53. p. 334 *"staggering."* P.M. Pollock and P.S. Meltzer, "Lucky draw in the gene raffle," *Nature* 417 (2002): 906–907.

54. p. 335 *The high frequency of* BRAF *mutations* H. Davies, et al., "Mutations of the BRAF gene in human cancer," *Nature* 417 (2002): 949–954.

55. p. 336 *We estimate that an average of 600* CpG *islands* J.F. Costello, et al., "Aberrant CpG-island methylation has non-random and tumour-type-specific patterns," *Nature Gen.* 25 (2000): 132–138.

56. p. 337 *As for mRNA expression profiles, genome-wide* P. Adorján, et al., "Tumour class prediction and discovery by microarray-based DNA methylation analysis," *Nucleic Acids Research* 30, (2002): e21.

57. p. 337 *to undertake the twin Herculean tasks* M. Hagmann, "Mapping a subtext in our genetic book," *Science* 288 (2000): 945–947.

58. p. 337 *which announced in September 2000* European Commission press release, September 21, 2000.

59. p. 337 *As part of the human Epigenome pilot study,* "Epigenetic variation and disease project." Online at *http://www.sanger.ac.uk/careers/phd/ abstracts/beck.shtml.*

60. p. 337 *to develop a range of molecular diagnostic* Roche press release, March 18, 2003.

61. p. 338 *Over the years, antibiotic resistant strains* "WHO information fact sheet No 139." Online at *http://www.who.int/inf-fs/en/fact139.html.*

62. p. 338 *DNA adenine methylases are potentially excellent* D.M. Heithoff, et al., "An essential role for DNA adenine methylation in bacterial virulence," *Science* 284 (1999): 967–970.

63. p. 339 *Abnormal methylation patterns may explain why few cloned* R. Jaenisch and A. Bird, "Epigenetic regulation of gene expression: how the genome integrates intrinsic and environmental signals," *Nature Gen.* 33 (2003): Suppl:245–254.

64. p. 339 *the observed differences between twins* C. Dennis, "Altered states." *Nature* 421 (2003): 686–688.

65. p. 339 *We envision that this 'nucleosome code'* T. Jenuwein and C.D. Allis, "Translating the histone code," *Science* 293 (2001): 1074–1080.

66. p. 340 *detailing their efforts to produce a deeper-hued* C. Napoli, et al., "Introduction of chimeric chalcone synthase gene into petunia results in reversible co-suppression of homologous genes *in trans.*" *Plant Cell* 2 (1990): 279–289.

67. p. 340 *Despite the usefulness of RNA interference* A. Fire, et al., "Potent and specific genetic interference by double-stranded RNA in *Caenorhabditis elegans,*" *Nature* 391 (1998): 806–811.

68. p. 342 *inactivating 86 percent of the 19,427 predicted genes* R.S. Kamath, et al., Systematic functional analysis of the *Caenorhabditis elegans* genome using RNAi, *Nature* 412 (2003): 231–237.

69. p. 342 *groundbreaking initiative on RNA interference.* Cancer Research UK press release, February 4, 2003.

70. p. 342 *Scientists will build on the huge success* Cancer Research UK press release, February 4, 2003.

71. p. 343 *Researchers will also bombard cancer cells* Cancer Research UK press release, February 4, 2003.

72. p. 343 *absolutely remarkable.* University of York press release, September 5, 2002.

73. p. 343 *These cancer cells were not engineered* University of York press release, September 5, 2002.

74. p. 344 *When I first heard of this work,* B. Homes, "Gene therapy may switch off Huntington's." *New Scientist,* March 3, 2003. Online at *http://www.newscientist.com/news/news.jsp?id=ns99993493.*

75. p. 345 *The 21-[nucleotide] length of the let-7 RNA is highly conserved* A.E. Pasquinelli, et al., "Conservation of the sequence and temporal expres-

sion of *let*-7 heterochronic regulatory RNA," *Nature* 408 (2000): 86–89.

76. p. 345 *The RNA interference and stRNA pathways* G. Hutvágner, et al., "A cellular function for the RNA-interference enzyme Dicer in the maturation of the *let*-7 small temporal RNA," *Science* 293 (2001): 834–838.

77. p. 345 *one 2001 issue of* Science *reported on* G. Ruvkun, "Glimpses of a tiny RNA world," *Science* 294 (2001): 797–799.

78. p. 345 *The number of genes in the tiny RNA world* G. Ruvkun, "Glimpses of a tiny RNA world." *Science* 294 (2001): 797–799.

79. p. 345 *astonishing feats* "Small RNAs make big splash," *Science* 298 (2002): 2296–2297.

80. p. 345 *The genome sequencing projects have revealed* J.S. Mattick, "Non-coding RNAs: the architects of eukaryotic complexity," *EMBO reports* 2 (2001): 986–991.

81. p. 346 *fully 98 percent of all transcriptional output* J.S. Mattick, "Non-coding RNAs: the architects of eukaryotic complexity," *EMBO reports* 2 (2001): 986–991.

82. p. 347 *Far from being evolutionary junk,* J.S. Mattick, "Non-coding RNAs: the architects of eukaryotic complexity," *EMBO reports* 2 (2001): 986–991.

83. p. 347 *The current situation in RNA* S.R. Eddy, "Computational genomics of noncoding RNA genes," *Cell* 109 (2002): 137–140.

84. p. 347 *If we are indeed at the forefront* S.R. Eddy, "Computational genomics of noncoding RNA genes," *Cell* 109 (2002): 137–140.

Further Reading

Chapter 1

The story of how the double helix structure was discovered is told in *The Double Helix* (Penguin, London 1997) by James Watson, one of the most famous and entertaining of scientific memoirs. The definitive history of early molecular biology is *The Eighth Day of Creation* (Cold Spring Harbor Laboratory Press, New York 1996) by Horace Freeland Judson. An excellent general introduction to the world of genes is *Genome* (Fourth Estate, London 2000) by Matt Ridley.

More technical books are *Genomes 2* (BIOS Scientific Publishers, Oxford 2002) by T.A. Brown, and *Human Molecular Genetics 2* (BIOS Scientific Publishers, Oxford 1999) by Tom Strachan and Andrew P. Read. These and an early edition of the classic text on cell biology, *Molecular Biology of the Cell* (Garland Science Publishing, New York 2002) by Bruce Alberts and others are freely available from http://www.ncbi.nlm.nih.gov/entrez/query.fcgi?db=Books. Also online, and a good place to begin exploring, are Kimball's Biology Pages (at http://biology-pages.info/), which offer a search engine, index, and a rich set of internal hyperlinks.

Chapter 2

A good starting point for the early history of bioinformatics is Robert Cook-Deegan's *The Gene Wars* 283–298 (Norton, New York/London, 1995). An excellent introduction to most aspects of bioinformatics can be found online at http://www.ebi.ac.uk/2can/home.html.

Information about Margaret Dayhoff is taken from the memorial Web site at http://www.dayhoff.cc, set up by her husband. As well as a biography there is also a listing of her publications.

Chapter 3

The best history of the Human Genome Project, especially the often byzantine politics that led up to it and proceeded through its early days, is *The Gene Wars* (Norton, New York/London, 1995) by Robert Cook-Deegan. Well worth reading for its fascinating personal perspective on the project is Sir John Sulston's autobiography, *The Common Thread* (Bantam Press London/New York 2002), coauthored with Georgina Ferry. The nematode worm and its dedicated scientific community are explored in Andrew Brown's *In the Beginning Was the Worm* (Simon & Schuster/Columbia University Press, London/New York).

Chapter 4

More about Craig Venter and the growing competition between the public and private genome projects can be found in Kevin Davies' *Cracking the Genome* (Simon & Schuster, New York, 2000)/*The Sequence* (Weidenfeld and Nicolson, London, 2001), which benefits from the author's firsthand knowledge of the people and the events.

Chapter 5

The coverage of *The New York Times* (at http://www.nytimes.com/library/national/science/genome-text-index.html), mostly by Nicholas Wade, provides interesting contemporary views on the founding of Celera and its effect on the Human Genome Project.

Chapter 6

The New York Times archive (at http://www.nytimes.com/library/national/science/genome-index.html) brings together the newspaper's coverage of the final stages of the human genome projects leading up to the publication of the draft sequence.

The public consortium's human genome paper is available from *Nature's* Genome Gateway (at http://www.nature.com/genomics/human/), while Celera's *Science* paper can be found at http://www.sciencemag.org/content/vol291/issue5507/. Both of these sites contain a wealth of material relating to genomics that is freely available and well worth exploring.

Chapter 7

For more on open source software, GNU/Linux and their broader implications, see the present author's book *Rebel Code: Linux and the Open Source Revolution*, Perseus Books/Penguin Books, Cambridge/London, 2001.

Glossary

10X   Shotgun coverage: every base is sequenced 10 times on average

2-D gel electrophoresis   Separating proteins using electric fields applied in two dimensions

ABI   Applied Biosystems Incorporated

ABI   Association of British Insurers

AceDB   A *Caenorhabditis elegans* database

adenine   DNA base, represented by A

AI   Artificial intelligence

Airlie Agreement   Structural genomics community rules on data sharing

algorithm   Mathematical method or technique

ALL   Acute lymphoblastic leukemia—cancer of blood-forming tissues

allele   One possible variant of a given gene

alpha helix   Single-stranded helix made up of amino acids; very common in proteins

amino acid   One of 20 basic units that make up proteins

AML   Acute myeloid leukemia—cancer of blood-forming tissues

analogue   Smoothly varying

annotation Extra information added to sequences—for example, location of genes

Anopheles gambiae One of the vectors of the malarial parasite

antibiotic Substance used to combat and kill bacteria

antibody Protein that binds to a specific antigen, generally to help destroy it

antigen A substance that stimulates the production of an antibody

apoptosis Programmed cell death

aptamer Single-stranded nucleotide chain

Arabidopsis thaliana Thale cress; small plant used as model organism

ARPANET U.S. computer network, precursor of Internet

ArrayExpress Main European gene expression database

assembly Putting together short stretches of DNA to form larger sequence

association study Comparison of affected and unaffected groups

autosome Other than X or Y chromosomes

avirulent Unable to cause disease

BAC Bacterial artificial chromosome; also short for "BAC clone"

bacterial artificial chromosome *E. coli* DNA containing foreign sequence to be amplified

bacteriophage A virus that infects bacteria

bacterium Microscopic, single-celled organism with no nucleus

bactig Contig obtained from BAC clones

bait One of two protein fragments in two-hybrid system

base Main element of nucleotide; a measure of sequence length

base pair One base from each helix strand in DNA; a measure of sequence length

Beowulf Open source clustering software

Bermuda Principles Data release policy for Human Genome Project, agreed in 1996

beta sheet Amino acid sequence folded back on itself; very common in proteins

BGI Beijing Genomics Institute

binary   Number system based on two digits

binding site   DNA sequence where transcription factor attaches

biobank   Large-scale, often nationwide, stores of genomic information

bioinformatics   The marriage of molecular biology and computing

Bionet   Early online U.S. bioinformatics resource

bit   Binary digit—either a 1 or 0

BLAST   Basic Local Alignment Search Tool—key sequence search program

browser   Software for using the World Wide Web

byte   Eight bits

C. elegans   *Caenorhabditis elegans*

Caenorhabditis elegans   Nematode worm

catabolism   Chemical breakdown of substances

cDNA   Complementary DNA, derived from mRNA

CDS   Coding sequences; regions in genome coding for proteins

cell   Smallest functioning unit of life

cell lineage   The succession of dividing cells leading to a given cell type

chemotherapy   The treatment of cancer using drugs

chromosome   The packaged and folded form of DNA in nucleus

Ciona intestinalis   Sea squirt

clone   Copy of physical DNA segment

cluster   Linked, local group of computers running together

codon   Group of three nucleotides specifying an amino acid or the protein end

comparative genomics   Study of genomes by comparing sequences from different organisms

compartmentalized shotgun   Shotgun sequencing applied to sections of the genome

complementary   Sequence with each letter replaced by its complement $(A \leftrightarrow T, C \leftrightarrow G)$

consensus   Idealized sequence made up of most common variants at each base

contig   Unbroken sequence formed from assembly of shotgun fragments

control   Data used to calibrate or check the main work

CpG island   Regions of genome with many alternating C and G bases

CPU   Central processing unit, the main chip in a computer

CSA   Compartmentalized shotgun assembly—assembling in pieces

cSNP   SNP in protein-coding region of genome

cytosine   DNA base, represented by C

Dario rero   Zebrafish

database   Structured, computerized store of data

dbSNP   Main SNP database at GenBank

DDBJ   National Japanese DNA sequence database

denatured   Converted from double strands to single strands

deoxyribonucleic acid   Full name of DNA, two helices made up of nucleotides

deoxyribose   The sugar component of DNA

diauxic shift   Shift from fermentation to respiration in yeast

dideoxy method   Sanger's technique for sequencing DNA

digital   Changing by discrete jumps

DNA   Deoxyribonucleic acid

DNA chip   Dense array of oligonucleotides

DNA microarray   High-density collection of cDNA samples, usually on microscope slide

DNA vaccine   Vaccine based on naked DNA

DOE   U.S. Department of Energy

domain   Self-contained protein structure

dominant   Trait that is manifest regardless of other paired allele

Drosophila melanogaster   Fruit fly, one of the earliest organisms used for genetics research

ds   Double-stranded

E. coli   *Escherichia coli*

EBI   European Bioinformatics Institute

electrophoresis   Separation of molecules by electric field

ELSI   Ethical, Legal and Social Implications; HGP program

EMBL   European Molecular Biology Laboratory

ENCODE   ENCyclopedia Of DNA Elements

Entrez   Integrated DNA, protein, and bibliographic databases

enzyme   Protein that speeds up chemical reaction without being altered

epigenetics   Inheritable changes in gene expression without changes in DNA bases

epigenotype   Pattern of methylation across genome

erythrocyte   Red blood cell

Escherichia coli   Bacterium widely used for research

EST   Expressed Sequence Tag

eukaryote   An organism with a nucleus containing chromosomes

expO   Expression Project for Oncology

Expressed Sequence Tag   Partial sequence of cDNA derived from mRNA

FAQ   Frequently asked questions

FASTA   Program for searching for sequence similarities, published in 1988

FASTP   Program for searching for sequence similarities, published in 1985

femtosecond   Millionth of a billionth of a second

fluorescence   Visible glow produced by radiation of another frequency

flux   Flow of ionized peptide fragments in MALDI-TOF mass spectrometer

fold   Fundamental unit of shape for proteins

founder effect   Descending from a small population

free software   Doubly-free programs: they cost nothing, and can be used in any way

Fugu rubripes   Pufferfish

functional genomics   Study of the function of genes

GAIC   UK Genetics and Insurance Committee

gametes Special cells whose fusion produces offspring

Gb Gigabase—one billion bases

Gbyte Gigabyte—one billion bytes; alternatively 1,073,741,824 bytes

gel Gelatinous material, used for separating charged materials

gel electrophoresis Separating DNA or proteins by using electric fields across a gel

GEML Gene Expression Markup Language

GenBank National U.S. DNA sequence database

gene Section of genome that is transcribed into RNA

gene expression Transcription of DNA into RNA and then (generally) into proteins

GeneChip Affymetrix' DNA chip

genetic map Maps showing the relative position of genes along chromosomes

genetics Study of genes, originally without reference to the DNA sequence

genome The complete DNA sequence of an organism

genome browser Software for viewing the genome and related information

genomics The study of genomes

genotype The particular set of SNPs in a genome; to establish some of these

GEO Gene Expression Omnibus, U.S. gene expression database

germ cell Reproductive cell, producing egg or sperm

gigabase One billion bases

gigabyte One billion bytes; alternatively 1,073,741,824 bytes

Globus Open source grid software

GNU/Linux Open source operating system

grids Linked, separated group of computers running together

guanine DNA base, represented by G

guilt by association Assumption that genes expressed together are functionally related

H. influenzae *Haemophilus influenzae*

haemochromatosis   Inherited disease characterised by excessive iron in the body

Haemophilus influenzae   First bacterium to be sequenced

haplotype   Blocks of DNA passed down from generation to generation

HapMap   Project to determine the haplotype blocks in the human genome

heredity   Genetic transmission of traits

heuristic   A rule of thumb that works well enough

HGP   Human Genome Project

HGS   Human Genome Sciences

Hidden Markov Model   Probabilistic mathematical technique

hierarchical shotgun   Shotgun sequencing applied on a clone-by-clone basis

histone   Protein making up structures around which DNA is wrapped

histone code   Effects of extra chemical groups added to histones

HMM   Hidden Markov Model

homology   When two or more sequences derive from a common ancestor

hormone   A protein messenger that modifies a biological process

HUGO   Human Genome Organisation

HUPO   Human Proteome Organisation

hybridization   Binding together of complementary DNA or RNA strands

hypothesis   A tentative explanation for observations

IBEA   Institute for Biological Energy Alternatives

ICAT   Isotope-coded affinity tags

icon   Graphical element of computer interface

IGC   International Genomics Consortium, functional genomics project

IHSD   deCODE's Icelandic Health Sector Database

in silico   In a computer (literally, in silicon)

in vitro   In a test tube (literally, in glass)

in vivo   In living animals (literally, in a living thing)

interactome   The collection of all protein-protein interactions in a cell

ISGO   International Structural Genomics Organization

IT   Information technology

JGI   Joint Genome Institute, Department of Energy

junk DNA   Early name for DNA that does not code for genes or control sequences

Kb   Kilobase—one thousand bases

LD   Linkage disequilibrium

leukemia   Cancer of blood-forming tissues

lineage   Successive stages of cells in developing organism

linkage analysis   Locating disease genes by studying affected families

linkage disequilibrium   Correlations among neighboring alleles

locus   Section of genome sequence

lymphatic system   Parts of the body that produce and store lymphocytes

lymphocyte   A type of white blood cell, part of immune system

lymphoma   Cancer of the lymphatic system

lysis   Rupture of bacterium by virus

lysogeny   Insertion of viral genome into bacterial genome

MAGE-ML   Microarray Gene Expression Markup Language

MALDI-TOF   Matrix-assisted laser desorption/ionization time-of-flight

mapping   Establishing the rough location on the genome

marker   Recognisable feature of DNA sequence

markup language   Way of embedding structure in a text file

mass spectrometry   Technique for measuring molecular mass

Mb   Megabase, one million bases, one million base pairs

Mbp   Megabase pair, one million base pairs, one million bases

Mbyte   Roughly one million bytes; exactly 1,048,576 bytes

MD   Molecular dynamics

megabase   One million bases

megabyte   One million bytes; alternatively 1,048,576 bytes

meiosis   Cell production with mixing of paired chromosomes

Mendelian   Following Mendel's laws of inheritance, as found by crossing plants

messenger RNA   RNA intermediary between genes and proteins

metabolic pathway   Series of chemical reactions involved in metabolism

metabolism   Transformation of substances within cell

metabolome   Complete set of all substances involved in metabolism

methyl   Chemical group consisting of carbon and three hydrogen atoms

methylation   Addition of methyl group

methylation variable position   Presence or absence of methyl group at particular DNA position

metric   Generalized kind of distance

MGED   Microarray Gene Expression Database

MHz   Million Hertz per second/million cycles per second

MIAME   Minimum information about a microarray experiment

microarray   High-density collection of cDNA samples, usually on microscope slide

microbe   Microscopic organism

micron   Millionth of a meter

microsatellite   Genetic marker with variable number of short repeats

microsecond   Millionth of a second

miRNA   MicroRNA

mitochondrion   Main source of energy in eukaryotes

mitosis   Cell duplication without mixing of paired chromosomes

model organisms   Well-studied organisms representative of various kinds of life

molecular dynamics   Modeling of molecules using atom-by-atom calculation of forces

molecule   The smallest unit of any substance, made up of linked atoms

MOLGEN   Early set of bioinformatics programs

monogenic, monogenetic   One gene

Monte Carlo   Modeling based on repeated simulations using random inputs

Mosaic   Most popular early Web browser that integrated graphics

Mouse Sequencing Consortium   Joint public and private group sequencing mouse genome

MRC   UK Medical Research Council, one of the main grant-giving bodies

mRNA   Messenger RNA

MSC   Mouse Sequencing Consortium

murine   Pertaining to the mouse

mutant   Organism that possesses a mutation

mutation   A change in DNA

MVP   Methylation variable position

Mycoplasma genitalium   Bacterium with smallest known genome

nanosecond   Billionth of a second

NCBI   U.S. National Center for Biotechnology Information

ncRNA   Non-coding RNA, not translated into protein

NHGRI   U.S. National Human Genome Research Institute

NIGMS   U.S. National Institute of General Medical Sciences

NIH   U.S. National Institutes of Health

NLM   U.S. National Library of Medicine

NMR   Nuclear magnetic resonance

non-genic   Outside the genes

non-Mendelian   Not following Mendel's laws of inheritance

NSF   U.S. National Science Foundation

nuclear magnetic resonance   Method for determining 3-dimensional shape of proteins

nucleosome   Group of histone proteins wrapped around by DNA

nucleotide   Made up of base, the sugar deoxyribose, and a phosphate group

nucleus   Enclosed region of cell containing chromosomes

oligonucleotides   Short stretches of single-stranded DNA

oncogene   A gene that can lead to the development of cancer

oncology   Study and treatment of cancer

open source Doubly-free software: costs nothing, and can be used in any way

organelle Structures within the cell with specialized functions

orthologue Gene or protein related by evolution from common ancestor

ovum Egg; female gamete

paralogue Gene or protein related by gene duplication within genome

parasite An organism that lives off its host without benefitting it

pathogen An organism causing disease

pathway Sequential chemical reactions

PCR Polymerase chain reaction

PDB Protein Data Bank

peptide A chain of two or more amino acids

peptide mass fingerprint Set of peaks from mass spectrometry

petaflop One quadrillion (million billion) computing operations per second

pharmacogenetics Older name for pharmacogenomics

pharmacogenomics Customized medicine based on a patient's genome

phenotype Observable characteristic

phosphate A chemical combination of the elements phosphorus and oxygen

Phrap Phil's revised assembly program, used for assembling sequences

Phred Phil's read editor, used for editing sequences

physical map Overlapping set of clones with markers that covers the genome

physiome All information contained in a multicellular organism

PIR Protein Information Resource

plasmid Additional, circular DNA sequence found in bacteria

Plasmodium falciparum Main eukaryotic parasite responsible for malaria

PLoS *Public Library of Science*

PNAS *Proceedings of the National Academy of Sciences*

polymerase chain reaction Technique for copying DNA billions of times perfectly

post-translational   Occurring after mRNA is converted to protein

prey   One of two protein fragments in two-hybrid system

primer   One of two short DNA sequences used to initiate PCR

prokaryote   Single-celled organism lacking nucleus or other internal organelles

promoter region   DNA sequence where several transcription factors attach

protein   Folded linear chain of amino acids

protein chip   High-density collection of proteins fixed to common base

protein family   Group of proteins that are homologous—derive from a common ancestor

protein signature   One characteristic feature of protein family

Protein Structure Initiative   U.S. structural genomics project

proteome   Total protein complement in an organism at a given time

proteomics   Study of the proteome

PSI   Protein Structure Initiative

PSI   Proteomics Standards Initiative

PTO   U.S. Patent and Trademark Office

quaternary   Number system based on four digits

RAM   Random access memory: temporary computer store for programs, data

receptor   Protein on cell's surface that can bind to certain chemicals

recessive   Trait that is manifest only if paired alleles are identical

recombinant   Combining DNA from different sources, genetically engineered

recombination   Swapping of DNA sections between matching pairs of chromosomes

regimen   Plan of medication

regulatory network   Ensemble of proteins and their genes that affect gene expression

relational database   Database in the form of tables, allowing different views of data

residue   Amino acid

restriction enzyme   Bacterial protein that cuts DNA at specific sequences

RFLP   Restriction fragment length polymorphism

ribonucleic acid   Full name of RNA, single strand made up of nucleotides

ribosome   Molecular machine that builds proteins based on RNA sequences

RNA   Ribonucleic acid; single strand of nucleotides

RNome   All non-coding RNAs

SAGE   Serial Analysis of Gene Expression

Sanger method   Frederick Sanger's technique for sequencing DNA

SBML   Systems Biology Markup Language

SBW   Systems Biology Workbench

SEQ   Early interactive bioinformatics software

sequence   An ordered series of nucleotides or amino acids

sequencer   Automated machine for obtaining DNA sequences

serum   The clear liquid left after blood clots

SGC   Structural Genomics Consortium

shotgun sequencing   Breaking up DNA to be sequenced into smaller pieces, then assembling

signalling pathway   Linked series of proteins that can pass on information

single nucleotide polymorphism   Positions in sequence where two alternative bases occur quite often

siRNA   Short interfering RNA

SNP   Single nucleotide polymorphism

SOM   Self-organizing map

somatic   Pertaining to ordinary cells rather than germ cells

spermatozoon   Male gamete

ss   Single-stranded

stochastic   Determined by chance

stRNA   Small temporal RNA

Strongylocentrotus purpuratus   Sea urchin

structural genomics   Determining protein structures, especially from DNA sequences

STS   Sequence-tagged site; short DNA sequence used for mapping

SUMEX-AIM   Stanford University Medical Experimental computer for AI in Medicine

superfamily   Collection of protein families with common evolutionary origin

SWISS-PROT   European protein sequence database, hand-annotated

synteny   Stretches of extensive sequence similarity in two species

systems biology   Integration of all types of genomic knowledge to produce unified model

Systems Biology Workbench   Open source application environment for modeling

systeome   All information contained in a cell

TCAG   TIGR Center for the Advancement of Genomics

terabyte   One trillion bytes, one thousand billion bytes

teraflop   One trillion computing operations per second

Tetrahymena thermophila   Single-celled organism

Tetraodon nigroviridis   Fish

The SNP Consortium   Group of public and private organisations creating dense map of SNPs

thymine   DNA base, represented by T

TIGR   The Institute for Genomic Research

trace   Readout from sequencing machine, generally around 500 bases long

trait   Observable characteristic of a gene

transcription   Process of converting DNA into equivalent RNA sequence

transcription factor   Protein that controls a gene's expression

transcriptome   All the mRNAs in a given tissue at a given time

transduction   Conversion of a signal from one form into another

translation   Process of converting mRNA into equivalent protein

TrEMBL   European protein sequence database, computer-annotated

TSC The SNP Consortium

tumor suppressor gene Gene whose protein can block tumor growth

twilight zone Where sequence identity between proteins drops below 25 percent

two-hybrid system Used to detect protein-protein interactions in yeast

UniProt Unified Protein Databases, main protein sequence database

uracil Base in RNA replacing thymine in DNA; represented by U

vaccine A substance that immunizes against a specific disease

vector Carrier (of a disease, for example)

vertebrate Animal with backbone

virus Self-replicating code (DNA or computer) that requires a host system

wet lab Traditional biology laboratory

WGA Whole-genome shotgun assembly—assembling all at once

whole-genome shotgun Shotgun sequencing applied to all the genome at once

Xenopus tropicalis Frog, used as model animal

XML Extensible Markup Language—way of creating markup languages

X-ray crystallography Method for determining 3-dimensional shape of proteins

Index